Financing Health Care in East Asia and the Pacific

Financing Health Care in East Asia and the Pacific

Best Practices and Remaining Challenges

John C. Langenbrunner
Aparnaa Somanathan

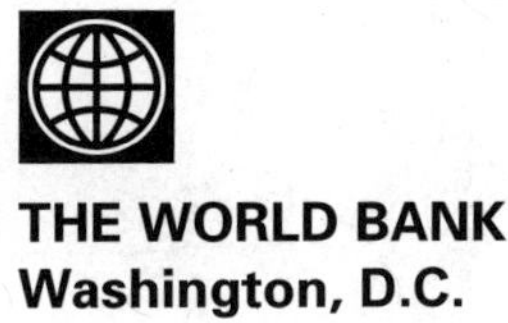

THE WORLD BANK
Washington, D.C.

1818 H Street NW
Washington DC 20433
Telephone: 202-473-1000
Internet: www.worldbank.org

1 2 3 4 14 13 12 11

ISBN: 978-0-8213-8682-8
eISBN: 978-0-8213-8736-8
DOI: 10.1596/978-0-8213-8682-8

Library of Congress Cataloging-in-Publication Data

Financing health care in East Asia and the Pacific: best practices and remaining challenges.
p.; cm. — (Directions in development)
ISBN 978-0-8213-8682-8 — ISBN 978-0-8213-8736-8
1. Medical economics—East Asia. 2. Medical care, Cost of—East Asia. I. World Bank.
II. Series: Directions in development (Washington, D.C.)
[DNLM: 1. Delivery of Health Care—economics—Far East. 2. Economics, Medical—Far East. 3. Health Care Costs—Far East. 4. Population Dynamics—Far East. W 84 JA14]
RA410.55.E18F56 2011
338.4'73621095—dc22

2010022089

Cover design: Quantum Think

Contents

Acknowledgments		*xv*
About the Book		*xvii*
Abbreviations		*xxi*
Chapter 1	**Overview**	**1**
	Key Messages	2
	Establishing the Baseline: Understanding the Current Situation	5
	Preparing for What Comes Next: The Changing Population and Emergent Disease Profile	10
	Improving the Performance of Health Care Financing	11
	Reforming Service Delivery and Organization of Care	21
	Notes	25
	Reference	25
Chapter 2	**Understanding the Macroeconomic Context and the Health Sectors in East Asia and the Pacific**	**27**
	Macroeconomic Context	27
	Effects on the Poor	29

	Health Status and Health Outcomes	34
	Demographic and Epidemiologic Trends	37
	Millennium Development Goals	44
	Health Financing Levels and Trends	44
	Linking Health Expenditures and Delivery of Services	52
	Notes	64
	References	64
Chapter 3	**Importance of Investing in Health and a Framework for Managing and Using Funds**	**67**
	Health and Its Effects on Economic Growth	67
	Health Care Financing Function and Goals	69
	References	71
Chapter 4	**Mobilization of Revenues for Health**	**73**
	Assessment of the Mix of Health Financing Revenues	73
	Analysis and Discussion	97
	Note	114
	References	114
Chapter 5	**Pooling and Management of Funds**	**117**
	Pooling: Is It Important?	117
	Pooling and Management of Funds in East Asia and the Pacific	119
	Notes	134
	References	134
Chapter 6	**Resource Allocation and Purchasing**	**137**
	A Resource Allocation and Purchasing Framework	137
	For Whom to Purchase Services: Reaching All in the Health Sector	138
	Resource Allocation, Targeting, and Decentralization	140
	What to Buy: Refining and Standardizing the Benefits Package	146
	From Whom to Buy: Contracting for Improved Cost and Quality	163

	How to Pay: Implementing New Incentive Payment Systems	170
	Demand-Side Financing (Purchasing)	188
	Notes	193
	References	194
Chapter 7	**Connecting Financing and Delivery of Services: Institutional and Organizational Characteristics in East Asian and Pacific Countries**	**199**
	Overview and Links to Health Care Financing	199
	Decentralization and Organizational Issues in the Delivery Systems	200
	Dimensions of Governance and Stewardship	219
	Medical Tourism	231
	Analysis and Discussion	235
	Note	238
	References	238
Chapter 8	**Assessing Performance in East Asia and the Pacific: Efficiency and Equity of Health Financing**	**243**
	Efficiency	243
	Equity	246
	Distribution of Public Subsidies for Health Care	256
	Note	259
	References	260
Appendix A	**National Health Account Activity in East Asia and the Pacific**	**265**
Appendix B	**Medical Tourism in East Asia and the Pacific**	**287**
Appendix C	**Health Financing in East Asia and the Pacific: Review of Project Appraisal Documents**	**305**
Index		**309**

Boxes

2.1	China's Experience with Rising Levels of Noncommunicable Diseases	45
4.1	Types of Voluntary Health Insurance	78
4.2	Effect of China's New Cooperative Medical Scheme on Out-of-Pocket Spending	92
4.3	Donor Financing in Cambodia	94
4.4	Health Shocks and Impoverishment in China	112
5.1	The Czech Republic Risk Adjustment Reforms	130
5.2	Public Financing Reforms in Chile	132
6.1	Core Policy Levers Related to the Uses of Financing	138
6.2	Provider Payment Pilots in Urban and Rural China	179
6.3	Steps for Implementing a Global Budget for Hospitals	188
7.1	Demand-Side Governance: The Affiliated Network for Social Accountability	223
8.1	The Mixed Public-Private Health System in Hong Kong SAR, China	259
A.1	Country-Level Criteria for Institutionalization of NHAs in Low- and Middle-Income Settings	285
B.1	Selected Available Treatments for Medical Tourists in the Philippines	299

Figures

1.1	Annual Economic Growth Rates in EAP countries: 2004–2015	6
2.1	Population Diversity in the Larger Countries in East Asia and the Pacific, 2007	28
2.2	Population Diversity in the Smaller Countries in East Asia and the Pacific, 2007	28
2.3	Gross Domestic Product Growth Per Capita, 2007	28
2.4	Proportion of Poor People in East Asia and the Pacific, 1990–2007	32
2.5	Rural Population as a Share of Total Population	32
2.6	Trends in Fertility Rates in East Asia and the Pacific, 1980–2005	33
2.7	Infant Mortality by Income Per Capita, 2005	34
2.8	Infant Mortality Rate Relative to Health Spending, 2005	34
2.9	Infant Mortality Relative to Income and Health Spending, 2005	35
2.10	Child Mortality by Income Per Capita, 2005	35

2.11 Child Mortality Performance Relative to Income and Total Health Spending, 2005 36
2.12 Child Mortality and Government Health Spending Relative to Income, 2005 36
2.13 Maternal Mortality versus Income Per Capita: A Global Comparison, 2005 37
2.14 Life Expectancy Relative to Income and Health Spending, 2005 38
2.15 East Asian and Pacific Population Pyramids, 2000 and 2020 38
2.16 International Comparison of DALYs and Health Spending, 2002 41
2.17 Adult Literacy Rate versus Income, 2005 41
2.18 Expected Increases in Health Expenditures from 2000 to 2020 Because of Population and Epidemiologic Dynamics 44
2.19 Nominal Elasticity of Health Spending, 1989–2004 49
2.20 GDP and Health Expenditure Per Capita, 2005 50
2.21 Total Health Spending versus Income, 2005 52
2.22 Government Health Spending versus Income, 2005 52
2.23 Global Comparison of Hospital Beds to Population and GDP 53
2.24 Global Comparisons for Physician and Health Workers to Population Trend Line, 2000–06 54
3.1 Flow of Funds and Functions for Health Financing 71
4.1 Share of Tax and Social Insurance Revenues in Total Health Expenditure in High-Income Economies Globally 75
4.2 Out-of-Pocket Payments as a Proportion of Total Health Expenditure for High-Income Economies, 2005 79
4.3 Sources of Financing for Health Care in Low- and Middle-Income Countries in East Asia and the Pacific, 2000–07 82
4.4 Share of Tax and Social Insurance Revenues in Total Health Expenditure for East Asia and the Pacific, 2005 83
4.5 Share of Tax and Social Insurance Revenues in Total Health Expenditure, LMIC Regional Averages, 2005 83
4.6 Out-of-Pocket Payments as a Proportion of Total Health Expenditure for Low- and Middle-Income Countries in East Asia and the Pacific, 2005 91

4.7	Performance Relative to Income and Health Spending, 2005	98
4.8	Variations in Infant Mortality across Countries and within Indonesia, 2006	98
4.9	Government Health Spending and Out-of-Pocket Payments in Asia, 2007	99
4.10	Tax Revenue as a Share of Gross Domestic Product, 2006	100
4.11	Informal Sector as a Share of Total Employment in East Asia and the Pacific	102
4.12	Health Expenditure as a Share of Total Government Expenditure, 2005	105
4.13	Proportion of Households Incurring Catastrophic Payments	111
5.1	Concentration of Total Health Expenditure in France, 2001	118
5.2	Expenditures by Age Group for Organisation for Economic Co-operation and Development Countries, Normalized Gross Domestic Product Per Capita, 1999	118
5.3	Effects of Risk Pooling	119
5.4	Administrative Costs as a Proportion of Expenditures in the National Health Insurance System of the Republic of Korea, 1994–2006	120
5.5	Type and Coverage of Health Insurance Systems in Indonesia, 1999	123
5.6	Per Capita Expenditures: Urban versus Rural Insurance in China, 2007	128
6.1	Uninsured Populations in East Asia and the Pacific, Selected Countries	139
6.2	Government Health Expenditure Variations by Province, China	142
6.3	Per Capita Allocations for Health under China's New Cooperative Medical Scheme, 2003	143
6.4	New Benefits Package: Kyrgyz Republic	160
6.5	Share of Government Health Spending Allocated to Prevention and Public Health	162
6.6	Developing Case-Mix Groupings	187
7.1	Decentralization and Organizational Reform	202
7.2	Governance Indicators in East Asia and the Pacific, 2007	220

7.3	CPIA Scores on Transparency, Accountability, and Corruption in East Asia and the Pacific, 2006	221
7.4	Means of Limiting Corruption in Service Delivery	222
7.5	Informal Payments among Health Services in East Asia and the Pacific	224
8.1	Pabón Lasso Diagram for East Asian and Pacific and OECD Countries	247
8.2	Progressivity of Taxes, Social Insurance Payments, and OOP Financing in East Asia and the Pacific	248
8.3	Socioeconomic Inequalities: The Share of Children Under Five Receiving Medical Treatment for Fever	250
8.4	Socioeconomic Inequalities: Prenatal Care Visits to Medically Trained Personnel	251
8.5	Socioeconomic Inequalities: Deliveries Attended by Medically Trained Personnel	252
8.6	Distribution of Public Health Services in East Asia and the Pacific	252
8.7	Distribution of Public Subsidies for Hospital and Nonhospital Care	257
8.8	Distribution of Public Subsidies for Hospital and Nonhospital Care (Kakwani Indexes)	257
B.1	Foreign Patients Treated in Thailand, 2002	294
B.2	Revenues from Domestic and Foreign Patients in Thailand, 2004	295
B.3	Number of Foreign Patients Treated in Thai Hospitals and Revenue Generated, 2002–05	295
B.4	Number of Foreign Patients in Malaysia, 2005–07	297
B.5	Share of Medical Tourists in the Philippines from Selected Regions, 2007	300

Tables

1.1	Inequities in Outcomes: Under-Five Mortality in Selected EAP Countries	9
2.1	Selected Demographic, Human Development, and Economic Indicators for East Asian and Pacific Countries, 2000–07	30
2.2	Age-Dependency Ratios in East Asia and the Pacific, 1960–2050	40
2.3	Estimated Total DALYs by Cause in East Asia and the Pacific, 2002	42

2.4	Relative Performance against Selected Millennium Development Goals	46
2.5	Main Health Financing Indicators, 2000–07	47
2.6	Total Health Expenditure as a Share of GDP, 2000–05	48
2.7	Regions of the World: Selected Economic and Development Indicators, circa 2005	51
2.8	Health System Characteristics	55
2.9	Public and Private Provision of Care, 2007 or Latest Available Year	58
3.1	Global Averages of Nominal Elasticity of Health Spending on Income, 1989–2004	68
4.1	Sources of Financing for Health in High-Income Economies in East Asia and the Pacific, 2000–07	76
4.2	Source of Financing for Health Care in Low- and Middle-Income Countries in East Asia and the Pacific, 2000–07	81
4.3	Characteristics of Sources of Financing for Social Health Insurance Systems in East Asia and the Pacific	85
4.4	Share of Smokers in the General Population and Tobacco Tax Rates in East Asia and the Pacific and the European Union	104
4.5	User Fees and Exemptions	107
5.1	Governance Factors	133
6.1	Selected Regional Indicators, Vietnam	141
6.2	Need Factors Used for Resource Allocation across Western Europe	145
6.3	Benefits Packages in East Asia and the Pacific	147
6.4	Summary of Provider Payment Systems in East Asia and the Pacific	171
6.5	Provider Payment Methods and Indicative Incentives for Provider Behavior	184
6.6	Indonesian Household and Community CCT Programs	191
7.1	China's Government and Health Administrative Structure	213
7.2	School and Health Center Absenteeism Rates in Selected Countries	225
7.3	Regulation of Providers in East Asia and the Pacific	229
8.1	Government Expenditures on Curative versus Preventive and Public Health Expenditures in East Asia and the Pacific, Various Years	245

8.2	Income-Related Inequality and Inequity in Annual Per Capita Health Care Use: Probability of Use and Volume of Use	254
A.1	Typology as Applied to East Asian and Pacific Economies	267
A.2	Detail of Health Expenditure Resource-Tracking Work in East Asia and the Pacific	268
A.3	World Bank–Supported NHA or Public Sector Accounting Activity in East Asia and the Pacific	272
A.4	Coverage of SHA Tables in the Three Regional Health Account Data Collections, 2002–05	273
A.5	Regional Health Account Data Collections: Variables of ICHA–Health Financing Agents, by Economy, 2006–07	274
A.6	Regional Health Account Data Collections: Variables of ICHA–Health Providers, by Economy, 2006–07	276
A.7	Regional Health Account Data Collections: Variables of ICHA–Health Financing Agents, by Economy, 2006–07	280
B.1	Comparison of Costs for Medical Procedures	290
B.2	Number of Hospitals Accredited by the JCI in East Asia and the Pacific, 2008	291

Acknowledgments

This book was prepared by a team led by John C. Langenbrunner (lead health economist, World Bank) and Aparnaa Somanathan (senior economist, Human Development Sector, East Asia and Pacific Region, World Bank), with contributions from primary authors and analysts Hans-Erik Edsand, Banafsheh Siadat, and Ajay Tandon. Natsuko Kiso provided invaluable support in developing and analyzing the data set for the exercise. Ryoko Tomita Wilcox provided excellent analytical and editorial support to the whole document. Anna Pigazzini ensured that the document became a book by coordinating with the Publication Unit. Chris Stewart edited the document.

The authors would like to thank Emmanuel Jimenez (sector director) and especially Fadia Saadah (health sector manager) for her leadership in initiating this work and for her overall guidance. Juan Pablo Uribe pushed us and made sure the work was finalized. The authors also would like to thank George Schieber and Adam Wagstaff, each of whom provided key technical guidance on approach and emphasis during the conceptualization and drafting stages of the book. George Schieber reviewed and commented on an earlier draft. The authors thank Samuel Lieberman and Ravi Rannon-Eliya for key inputs and perspective in the early stages of the book. Some initial drafts benefited from peer reviewers Jan Bultman and Bukhuti Shengelia. Peter Berman and George Schieber served as peer reviewers of the later draft.

The data and background information in the book draw on a series of 14 country profiles written by a team of researchers: Huong Lan Dao, Ruwanthi Elwalagedara, Deni Habiento, Alejandro N. Herrin, Rozita Halina Hussein, John C. Langenbrunner, Gabriel Leung, Jui-fen Rachel Lu, Ravi P. Rannan-Eliya, Banafsheh Siadat, Viroj Tangcharoensathien, Keith Tin, Laksono Trisantaro, Tsilaajav Tsolmongerel, Bong-Min Yang, Y. Zhan, and Y. Zhao under the leadership of the Institute for Health Policy (IHP) in Colombo, Sri Lanka. This activity was led by the IHP and John C. Langenbrunner and Banafsheh Siadat at the World Bank. The majority of the country profiles were written under contract between IHP and the Bank.

About the Book

This is an exciting time in East Asia and the Pacific region. No region would appear to be moving so rapidly. In this dynamic environment, many countries in the region have been approaching the World Bank requesting technical assistance and knowledge about health financing best practices and options. There is great interest in expanding knowledge sharing and learning from other East Asian and Pacific countries about their experiences in health financing. Moreover, some common issues appear to be emerging: universal insurance, options for financing health insurance, institutional setups of health financing options, provider payment mechanisms, equity considerations, ways to reach the poor and impoverished, and ways to meet the challenges of a changing demographic and epidemiologic profile.

Under a generous grant from the Health, Nutrition, and Population hub in the World Bank in fiscal year 2008, the region was requested to provide an overview of health financing systems in the region. This overview examined the different health financing mechanisms in terms of performance on dimensions of efficiency and equity and in terms of relative roles of government. In addition, the analysis was to identify gaps in knowledge needing to be addressed strengthen and reform existing health financing mechanisms and thereby expand health coverage and benefits.

This book's primary audience is senior officials of various government ministries (including health, economics and planning, and finance) across countries of the region. It will also be useful for World Bank staff members, the donor community, and interested researchers and policy analysts.

This volume was prepared in close collaboration with key East Asia and Pacific staff members, who contributed to the writing of some sections as well as providing documents, data, and key feedback on early outlines of the volume. The Bank team further sought the guidance of two health economists in the Bank: George Schieber and Adam Wagstaff. In these early discussions it was proposed to develop a series of profiles for 15 countries in the region. Each profile followed a template developed early in the process and reviewed internally. Many of the profiles were then developed by the Institute for Health Policy (IHP) in Colombo, Sri Lanka, using EQUITAP data and other assembled information. A number of other country profiles were developed internally by Bank team and staff members.

The country profiles were used as background pieces for this volume which subsequently attempted to synthesize data and information from the profiles and the region. The volume also reflects the systematic review, synthesis, and analysis of existing data, surveys, documents, regulatory and budget documents, peer-reviewed publications, and reviews across the sector.

The countries covered in this volume are listed in the table on the next page, with the names and the country code used throughout the volume. The table provides the level of economic development as measured by per capita income according to the World Bank's income classification. The categories are used in the volume to group countries for analytic purposes.

The volume shows that the East Asia and Pacific (EAP) region is characterized by wide variations in the types of health financing systems. There are variations in the predominant sources of financing (social insurance, general revenues, or out-of-pocket payments) as well as variations in the extent to which the systems provide financial protection. The continued high prevalence of communicable diseases as well as emerging new diseases (for example, Severe Acute Respiratory Syndrome), coupled with the rapid aging of the population in the region, places existing financing systems under increased pressure.

The need to mobilize additional financial resources for health has highlighted variations in technical and allocative efficiency, both within and between countries. Large inequalities in access to care and

East Asia and Pacific Countries

Name	Country Code	World Bank income classification for fiscal year 2008
American Samoa	ASM	Upper middle income
Cambodia	KHM	Low income
China	CHN	Lower middle income
Fiji	FJI	Lower middle income
Hong Kong SAR, China	HKG	High income
Indonesia	IDN	Lower middle income
Japan	JPN	High income
Kiribati	KIR	Lower middle income
Korea, Dem. Rep.	PRK	Low income
Korea, Rep.	KOR	High income
Lao PDR	LAO	Low income
Malaysia	MYS	Upper middle income
Marshall Islands	MHL	Lower middle income
Micronesia	FSM	Lower middle income
Mongolia	MNG	Low income
Myanmar	MMR	Low income
Northern Mariana Islands	MNP	Upper middle income
Palau	PLW	Upper middle income
Papua New Guinea	PNG	Low income
Philippines	PHL	Lower middle income
Samoa	WSM	Lower middle income
Singapore	SGP	High income
Solomon Islands	SLB	Low income
Taiwan, China	TWN	High income
Thailand	THA	Lower middle income
Timor-Leste	TMP	Low income
Tonga	TON	Lower middle income
Vanuatu	VUT	Lower middle income
Vietnam	VNM	Low income

Source: World Bank 2008c.
Note: Because of lack of data, American Samoa, the Democratic People's Republic of Korea, Myanmar, and the Northern Mariana Islands have largely been excluded. Data for these countries are provided, where available.

inadequate financial protection, particularly between those who are poor and those who are better-off, demands a closer examination of the health financing systems in the region. These issues highlight the need to understand how features of the current health financing system can be reformed and strengthened to improve outcomes, especially for the poor. Many countries in the region have introduced wide-ranging reforms in their health financing systems, but implementation of these reforms sometimes has been weak.

I hope that you will find the volume useful, whether you are working to improve the health financing system in the region, or are working in another country facing similar challenges. Every region on the globe can find the lessons and challenges useful in some way.

Cristian Baeza
Sector Director
Health, Nutrition, and Population Network
The World Bank
June 2011

Abbreviations

AIDS	acquired immune deficiency syndrome
ANSA-EAP	Affiliated Network for Social Accountability in East Asia and the Pacific
APNHAN	Asia-Pacific National Health Accounts Network
BMI	Basic Medical Insurance (China)
BoD	burden of disease
CBHI	community-based health insurance
CCT	conditional cash transfer
CEO	chief executive officer
CMS	Cooperative Medical Scheme (China)
CPIA	Country Policy and Institutional Assessment
CSMBS	Civil Servant Medical Benefit Scheme (Thailand)
CSS	Civil Servants Scheme (Lao PDR)
DALYs	disability adjusted life years
DHA	domestic health account
DHO	district health office (Lao PDR)
DoH	Department of Health (Papua New Guinea, the Philippines)
DRG	diagnosis-related group
ECPS	essential and complementary package of services (Mongolia)

EU	European Union
FFS	fee-for-service (model)
FONASA	Fondo Nacional de Salud, or National Health Fund (Chile)
GDP	gross domestic product
GGR	general government revenue
GP	general practice
HEF	health equity fund
HI	horizontal inequity
HIC	high-income country
HIV	human immunodeficiency virus
HMO	health maintenance organization
HSA	health savings account
ICHA	International Classification of Health Account
JCI	Joint Commission International
LGU	local government unit
LIC	low-income country
LMICs	low- and middle-income countries
MIC	middle-income country
MoH	Ministry of Health (various countries)
MoHRSS	Ministry of Human Resources and Social Security (China)
NCD	non communicable disease
NCMS	New Cooperative Medical Scheme (China)
NGO	nongovernmental organization
NHA	national health account
NHI	National Health Insurance (program) (Republic of Korea; Taiwan, China)
NHIP	National Health Insurance Program (the Philippines)
OECD	Organisation for Economic Co-operation and Development
OOP	out-of-pocket (payments)
PHO	provincial health office (Lao PDR)
PMTP	Philippine Medical Tourism Program
SAR	Special Administrative Region (China)
SHA	system of health accounts
SHI	social health insurance
SHIF	Social Health Insurance Fund (Lao PDR)
SSIGO	State Social Insurance General Office (Mongolia)
SWiM	Sector Wide Management (donor approach)
TB	tuberculosis
UEEMI	Urban Employee Essential Medical Insurance (China)
WHO	World Health Organization

CHAPTER 1

Overview

Health financing is all about investing in the achievement of better health for all. Investing in health and nutrition is important for individuals and governments. Recent research from the Macroeconomic Commission, recent books on health and wealth (for example, Spence and Lewis 2009), and others suggest that better health does not have to wait for an improved economy. Measures to reduce the burden of disease (BoD), to provide maternal and early child care, to allow children to have healthy childhoods, and to increase life expectancy will, in themselves, contribute to creating richer economies. Globally, countries tend to value health and spend relatively more on health (as a share of GDP) as GDP grows, and increase financial protection levels to reduce impoverishment against catastrophic costs.

Health financing links closely with health systems, which consist of *actors* performing *functions* geared toward the health system achieving *goals*. The overriding goal is better health or improved outcomes. A second basic goal is financial protection. The ability to buy food and have shelter should not be compromised by unforeseen (and largely unforeseeable) health shocks that possibly require large amounts of spending on health care. A third goal is responsiveness, or patient satisfaction. How well a health system responds to people's nonmedical expectations in areas such as treat with dignity is important. The key actors in any health system include patients and households, health care providers, health financiers and insurers, and the government. Subsidiary goals are efficiency and equity. Because demand for care is virtually unlimited, spending wisely is important—in terms of both "doing things right" (technical efficiency) and "doing the right things" (allocative efficiency). Although countries may not necessarily achieve full equity, they will strive for some acceptable level of inequality.

Within this framework of health systems, health sector financing mechanisms can generate sufficient and sustainable funds to motivate health care consumers, insurers, and providers in a manner that helps societies optimize health outcomes and financial protection for their given spending level. The success of the financing process depends on the performance of three important functions: (a) revenue collection, (b) pooling and management of resources, and (c) purchasing of services and interventions. Following an assessment of the current macroeconomic, health status, and health sector situation in the region, this volume analyzes each of those functions.

Key Messages

Key messages emerging from this book include the following:

- Sustained growth over the past decade has created fiscal space for an increase in government and insurance revenues for health. The recent economic downturn has affected economies to various degrees and presents new challenges in spending wisely. Policies that provide opportunities to the poor have produced dramatic advances in reducing poverty over the past decade; however, inequality in the region has grown.
- Current performance of the sector or of the functions of health financing is not optimal in terms of either efficiency or equity. Governments need to address the pro-rich structures of many health sectors because large income inequalities in outcomes remain and because public (government or social insurance) health spending in low-income countries (LICs) and middle-income countries (MICs) is not pro-poor.
- Rapid changes in the economic, demographic, and epidemiological profiles should be monitored in many East Asian and Pacific countries for improved planning and for integration of health financing policies with needed delivery system reforms. Patterns of economic growth, urbanization, and workforce changes will help identify optimal

approaches for raising and pooling revenues for health care. Many countries are moving to a profile dominated by an aging population and noncommunicable diseases (NCDs). These changes are likely to increase health care costs by 20 to 40 percent between 2000 and 2020 and are likely to increase the need for improved financing mechanisms in the medium to long term.

- Most countries in East Asia and the Pacific allocate relatively less from public spending for health than do countries in other regions when adjusting for per capita income and per capita GDP. Fiscal capacity and policy priorities are twin dimensions in improving levels of public funding or prepayment for health. Within this context, policy makers have several choices: general revenues, payroll contributions (as is common for social insurance funds), special assessments (such as "sin taxes" on tobacco and alcohol), and capture of efficiency gains.
  - The sustainability of general government revenue (GGR) financing depends critically on economic growth and strong administrative capacity to raise taxes.
  - The sustainability of social health insurance (SHI) financing depends on economic growth. Economic growth is essential for ensuring the sustainability of payroll taxes (contributions) as well as the existence of a large formal labor market, administrative capacity for collection, good regulatory and oversight structures, and appropriate incentive structures. The relatively low reliance on social insurance as a form of public prepayment in East Asia and the Pacific may reflect the absence of one or more of these enabling factors.
  - Policy makers can increase the use of sin taxes, which are relatively underused in the region, as a source of revenue for health.
  - Potential gains in efficiency (both technical and allocative) are apparent in almost every country in the region. Capturing gains in efficiency effectively increases levels of public funding for health.
- Pooling of prepayment funds must improve, whether funds are government revenues or insurance based, to increase equity and efficiency. Equity funds for the poor (as, in Cambodia, China, and the Lao People's Democratic Republic) should be integrated into the broader pool across groups. Segmentation in geographic-based populations and in occupation-based groups must be reduced. Models in the region for greater pooling provide best-practice case studies (for example, in China; Japan; the Republic of Korea; and Taiwan, China) from which East Asian and Pacific countries might learn.

- The tools of "strategic purchasing" must be expanded to improve equity and efficiency:
  - Extend coverage step by step by following some of the successful models in East Asia and the Pacific, such as China, the Republic of Korea, and Thailand, to better target and protect the poor.
  - Adjust allocation formulas to better achieve equity of funding relative to need or demand.
  - Review benefit packages to emphasize public goods, goods with externalities, and other interventions with proven outcomes. Catastrophic expenditures should be financed for the poor and near-poor by using a targeting mechanism. Benefit packages should be more equitable in government and insurance programs. Packages should be continuously updated to address changing disease profiles and new interventions with proven results.
  - Use contracting to include both public and private providers, and selectively contract according to relative performance measures such as quality and costs. Cambodia historically has been a regional leader in selective contracting and contract evaluation.
  - Move provider payment from inputs-based (for example, line-items) and fee-for-service (FFS) models to broader service package models that are activity based (per episode or per global budgets) and performance based. Thailand is perhaps the regional leader in moving beyond FFS payment, having a sophisticated mix of geographic caps, facility global budgets, and case-mix (often referred to as *diagnosis-related group,* or DRG) adjusters for hospital admissions.
  - Use demand-side purchasing with conditional cash transfers (CCTs) and vouchers to better target services to poor and vulnerable groups, as well as to improve the choice of services and the provider response to consumer needs.
- Decentralization has played a prominent role in East Asia and the Pacific in both financing and delivery, but with very mixed results. Elements of decentralization should be reconsidered. Although the objective was to encourage innovation and improve responsiveness to local needs, decentralization has often fractured the risk pool, created inequities across localities, and generated confusion regarding roles and responsibilities for the financing and provision of public health services (for example, in Indonesia and the Philippines). Some recentralization of financing may improve efficiency and equity in many countries.

- Autonomization of hospitals has started but needs development to address broader issues, such as residual claimant status, decision rights (including flexibility in civil service rules), community participation in governance, and retention of social responsibilities to treat the poor as well as the higher-income groups. Some countries, such as Vietnam, are allowed to charge fees for reinvestment, but this practice has hurt access and reduced financial protection for the poor. Improved autonomization also will better ensure response and impact to incentives created by the new provider payment reforms that are now emerging.
- A number of governance issues challenge health financing and sector performance, including the following:
  - Operational viability and effectiveness of health insurance organizations.
  - Informal payments by consumers and patients to providers.
  - Absenteeism of providers, including public providers doubling as private practitioners.
  - Accountability and consumer voice.
  - Regulation of the emergent medical tourism industry in the region.
  - Regulation and coordination of public with private providers across the sector as the private sector grows on the delivery side.

Establishing the Baseline: Understanding the Current Situation

East Asia and the Pacific is extremely diverse, perhaps more so than other regions of the world. It contains great variations in size and population, from small Pacific Islands with less than 100,000 inhabitants to countries such as China and Indonesia (the first and fourth most populated countries in the world). Relative to other regions of the world, East Asia and the Pacific is the most populated. It contains the world's fastest-growing economies, the second-largest number of fragile situations after Africa, and a wide spectrum of political and government organizations (from democracies to military dictatorships). Although many of these countries are highly centralized, fiscal and political decentralization is an important trend.

The region is extremely dynamic, with the developing East Asian and Pacific countries capping six years of strong economic performance in 2007 with a growth rate of 10.1 percent (see Figure 1.1). Improvements in the business environment have facilitated private sector growth. The region has demonstrated some resilience to the adverse global economic developments of 2008 to 2010. However, inequality in the region has

Figure 1.1 Annual Economic Growth Rates in EAP countries: 2004–2015

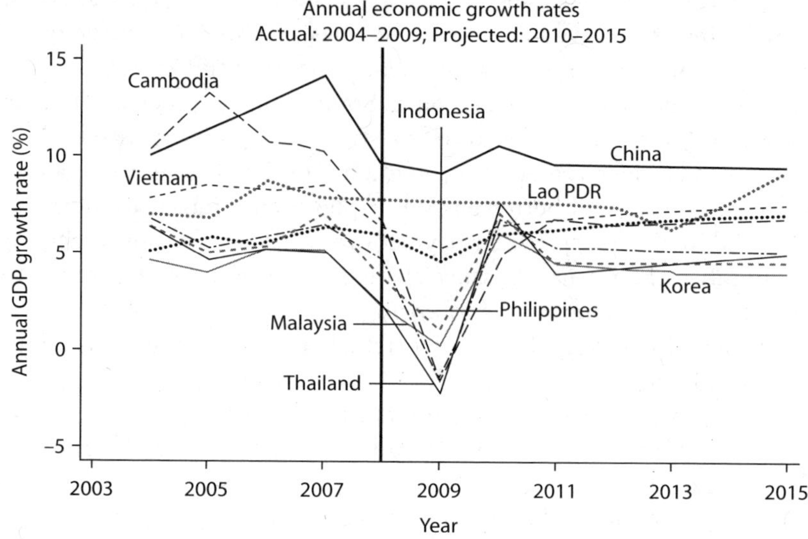

Source: IMF World Economic Outlook

grown despite sustained economic growth and despite policies that have provided opportunities to the poor and have produced dramatic advances in reducing poverty. MICs in the region and emerging MICs such as Indonesia and Vietnam have seen inequality rise dramatically in their domestic economies. But LICs such as Lao PDR have not escaped. There has been rapid urbanization, yet some of the countries remain predominantly rural. The region contains at least one fragile state (Timor-Leste) and contains many conflict-affected areas, but such conflicts have tended to be limited to relatively small geographic zones.

Health Status and Health Outcomes Relative to Health Expenditures

In recent years, the region has presented a surprising profile of relatively good health outcomes despite spending relatively little for health. However, health financing systems in the East Asia and the Pacific will need to be revamped over the short and medium term. New and more complicated disease profiles, such as NCDs, will challenge gains in health outcomes. Present spending patterns are uneven and poorly targeted. Large percentages of the population remain at financial risk.

East Asian and Pacific countries perform relatively well in regional comparisons of commonly used health and expenditure indicators. In general, countries in the region do well on health outcomes when compared with other countries of the world that have similar income levels. Outcomes on infant mortality, child mortality, and life expectancy are favorable when regressed on levels of income and levels of health spending. Countries in the region are performing relatively better on the basis of outcomes. In contrast, maternal mortality reveals a more mixed picture in East Asia and the Pacific.

At present, East Asian and Pacific countries spend less on health, both as a share of GDP and in per capita terms, relative to other countries at comparable levels of income. Levels of total and public (government) health spending are low. The lower level of health spending is reflected in the lower levels of health system inputs such as doctors, nurses, and beds per capita. Lower public spending further correlates with dismal levels of financial protection in many countries, even in some of the high-income countries (HICs).

East Asian and Pacific countries also have fewer disability-adjusted life years (DALYs) per capita than other countries with comparable income levels, which correlates with the higher literacy and education levels found in East Asia. The BoD figures for the region indicate that, for communicable diseases and maternal, perinatal, and nutritional conditions, the BoD in DALYs is greatest in China (37,084,000) because of its large population; it is also high in Indonesia (14,371,000). For NCDs, China again exhibits the highest levels (133,056,000), followed by Indonesia (29,959,000), Japan (11,206,000), and the Philippines (8,635,000).

This good performance to date of fewer DALYs per person and relatively good outcomes, coupled with relatively modest expenditures, may be hypothesized as attributable to historic levels of investments in related sectors such as education (especially that of women), clean water and sanitation, basic public health, good housing, and infrastructure. A relatively worse performance in areas such as maternal mortality, an outcome indicator perhaps more reliant on health system inputs than infant and child mortality, may reflect current lower levels of health inputs and suggest the need for greater future investments in health services and systems.

Current Patterns of Health Expenditures

Total health expenditures as a share of GDP increased modestly per year on average in countries in the region between 2000 and 2005. This increase in spending was driven largely by sustained increases in public sector spending in countries such as China, Japan, Malaysia, and Thailand. By contrast, in Cambodia, Lao PDR, and the Pacific Island countries, increased donor spending explains a large proportion of the growth in overall spending. Only in Vietnam, with the initiation of user fees, has the increase in overall health spending been driven by an increase in out-of-pocket (OOP) spending. In East Asia and the Pacific, total health spending as a share of GDP was between 3 percent and 10 percent in 2005.

Per capita health expenditures in the region tend to correlate with GDP per capita, although there are some outliers, such as Cambodia. For instance, using global comparators, per capita health spending levels in Indonesia, Malaysia, the Philippines, and Thailand are lower relative to their income levels. Cambodia and Vietnam are above the expected levels of government (public) funding for health relative to income. Both GDP per capita and health expenditure per capita are in the middle range compared to other regions. Eastern Europe and Central Asia, Latin America and the Caribbean, and the Middle East and North Africa perform better on average on both indicators; South Asia and Sub-Saharan Africa perform worse.

East Asian and Pacific countries and territories generally conform to the global pattern of reliance on OOP expenditures declining and government share of total financing increasing as national income rises. The government share of total health financing ranged from 20 percent to 30 percent in low-income East Asian and Pacific countries (such as Cambodia, Lao PDR, and Vietnam), compared to 50 percent to 60 percent in MICs (such as Malaysia and Thailand), which is consistent with global trends. Meanwhile, OOP spending finances 70 percent to 80 percent of total expenditures in most LICs in East Asia and 40 percent to 50 percent, or less, of expenditures in MICs and HICs.

Current Levels of Health Sector Performance in East Asia and the Pacific

Many countries in East Asia and the Pacific that have made significant progress toward achieving the Millennium Development Goals still have large income inequalities in outcomes (see Table 1.1 below). Underlying this problem are large inequalities in the financing and delivery of health care. Improved averages in health outcomes could very well be achieved through a pattern that benefits primarily the better-off inhabitants, while largely bypassing the poor. Given relatively low levels of health spending in the region, efficiency improvements can also be critical for generating additional public sector resources for health care.

Table 1.1 Inequities in Outcomes: Under-Five Mortality in Selected EAP Countries

Country	*Year*	*Under-Five Mortality Rate*	*Ratio Between Lowest and Highest Economic Quintiles*	*Rural-Urban Ratio*
Cambodia	2005	106	3.0	1.5
Indonesia	2007	51	2.4	1.6
Philippines	2008	37	3.4	1.7
Vietnam	2007	33	3.3	2.2

Source: Demographic and Health Surveys

Efficiency and equity are two dimensions used to assess health sector performance. *Efficiency* is typically defined as maximizing outcomes from inputs, although it has many dimensions. In East Asia and the Pacific, the evidence suggests poor allocative efficiency (for example, relatively low shares of expenditures on primary and outpatient care as well as low hospital occupancy rates) and poor technical efficiency (relatively long lengths of stay), but data and information with which to understand the problem of efficiency in greater depth are limited.

Some greater understanding of the dimension of equity in financing revenues across health sectors in the region exists. The incidence of the health care financing burden in high-income economies and territories in East Asia and the Pacific is similar to that in European countries; tax financing is the most progressive and social insurance is slightly regressive, whereas direct OOP payments are proportional (for example, in Hong Kong SAR, China) or regressive (for example, in Japan and Taiwan, China). The incidence is quite different in low- and middle-income East Asian and Pacific countries. In LICs and MICs, both tax and social insurance financing are highly progressive because their incidence is limited to skilled, professional groups and to a narrow tax base. Direct payments are also progressive in all low- and middle-income East Asian and Pacific countries, except China.

Significant evidence of pro-rich differentials in health care allocation and use in the East Asian and Pacific region exists. Public sector inpatient services are strongly pro-poor in Hong Kong SAR, China, and moderately pro-poor in Malaysia. In contrast, they are pro-rich in China; Indonesia; the Republic of Korea; Taiwan, China; Thailand; and Vietnam. Outpatient care services, particularly nonhospital outpatient care services, are moderately pro-poor or relatively proportional to income in most economies.

In LICs, inequalities in access to services are caused by deficiencies in both breadth and depth of coverage. Unemployed, agricultural, and informal sector workers either have no coverage (for example, in Indonesia and Vietnam) or have shallow coverage that entitles them to a less comprehensive benefits package (for example, in China and the Philippines). Coverage inefficiencies may be due either to poor design of the package or to affordability of coverage within a country's current fiscal space. In tax-financed systems in which universal coverage has not been achieved, the poor face significant financial barriers to access in the form of formal and informal user charges at public health facilities (for example, in Cambodia, Lao PDR, and Papua New Guinea). Targeted fee waiver or exemption schemes (for example, the health card in Indonesia) and health equity funds (HEFs) (for example, in Cambodia and Lao PDR) are established to help the poor overcome financial barriers to access. There is, however, little compelling evidence of the success of these targeting mechanisms in improving equity in access to care.

In HICs, where universal coverage has been achieved, inequalities still exist because of shallow coverage. The more catastrophic expenditures may be outside the domain of health insurance, and the benefits packages offered under different insurance schemes may vary widely. In countries where the social insurance law mandates the same benefits for all (for example, in Japan), inequities are fewer. Similarly, in high-income tax-financed countries and territories where universal coverage has been achieved (for example, in Hong Kong SAR, China, and in Malaysia), inequalities are not as widespread because restrictions on access to services are fewer.

Benefit incidence studies in Asia have typically found that public health spending in LICs and MICs is not pro-poor. Public subsidies for inpatient care are especially pro-rich, although there are some exceptions. The distribution of public subsidies is considerably more pro-poor in Hong Kong SAR, China; Malaysia; Sri Lanka; and Thailand for both hospital and nonhospital care.

What are the potential explanations for the unusually pro-poor distribution of subsidies in these economies? Although the level of national income is a critical factor in improving the distribution of public subsidies, the mix of public and private services that are offered also play a role. Targeting the poor is successful in richer countries because they can afford a system of universal public health care funded by general taxation with minimal user charges. An alternative explanation for the pro-poor distribution of public health subsidies lies in the types of private sector alternatives available to the rich. In these countries, the combination of a universal public provision, an attractive private sector alternative to the basic package, and incomes that make demand for this alternative effective leads to redistribution through public provision in precisely the way that theory predicts. This result suggests that effective targeting of public spending on health care depends not only on policies concerning the publicly run system, but also on the scale, location, and allocation of public spending.

Preparing for What Comes Next: The Changing Population and Emergent Disease Profile

Changes in the demographic and epidemiologic profile of East Asian and Pacific countries are likely to be key determinants of health care costs and financing in the medium to long term. Demographic and epidemiologic profiles and changing patterns in those profiles are important drivers in the demand for health care as well as in the patterns of health spending and financing. In East Asia and the Pacific, the total fertility rate has decreased and individuals are living longer, as exhibited by the increase of life expectancy from 67.2 years in 1990 to 70.9 years in 2006.

In the short term, there will be relatively more of both genders of working age. If workers are in fairly good health, this increase could provide a demographic dividend whereby a health workforce can support economic expansions and help improve overall productivity. However, a less than healthy workforce could put greater pressure on the health and social protection systems. Of the 22 East Asian and Pacific countries for which data were available, all except Timor-Leste exhibited a decline in the age-dependency ratio from 1960 to 2005.[1] In total, nine countries have experienced a 40 percent or greater drop in the age-dependency ratio, indicating less demand on the economically productive segments of the population.

Notably, however, over the next 50 years, the age-dependency ratios for many East Asian and Pacific countries are expected to increase dramatically from their 2005 levels. This increase will be the case for current HICs such as Japan, the Republic of Korea, and Singapore, as well as for MICs such as China. In the medium term, with an aging population, the role of NCDs in the overall disease burden profile can also be expected to increase in East Asia and the Pacific, effectively placing greater challenges on meeting growing demands for primary and secondary prevention and treatment of chronic diseases. As life expectancy increases, there can be greater demands (on average) on the health system, particularly from individuals who are in their later years of life and have increased medical needs.

The combination of the population growth, the nutritional transition, an aging population, and a shifting epidemiologic profile suggests that policy makers will need to be concerned about the overall macrolevel efficiency of heath care expenditures. Pressure on the economically productive segments of the population to provide revenues for the health sector will continue to increase. In contrast, this book estimates that demand will grow significantly by 2020 as a result of population dynamics and changes in patterns of aging alone. Overall, most countries in the region could see expenditures grow by 20 to 40 percent between 2000 and 2020.

Improving the Performance of Health Care Financing

The success of the health financing process depends on the performance of three important functions: (a) revenue collection, (b) pooling and management of resources, and (c) purchasing of services and interventions. For each of the three functions, strengths and weaknesses are assessed and opportunities for restructuring are reviewed. International best-practice models are provided as examples of what policy makers may consider for future directions. A related consideration is the governance and regulatory arrangements in place in the current financing sectors. These arrangements include the organizational characteristics of purchasers and providers, incentive regimes within organizations, and institutional characteristics that are embedded in the transactions that occur between various government organizational units and in the public and private sectors.

In each function, a number of challenges emerge from the analysis. Public and prepayment levels of funding for health are low according to international comparisons. Funds are not pooled and managed in optimal ways. The allocation of funds policies in many countries is inequitable and inefficient. Policies have discouraged access to services for the poor and vulnerable groups. Allocation and payment incentives have encouraged unnecessary services, and a less than optimal quality of services has been delivered.

Not every country faces all of these challenges, but each country will need to assess performance within and across each of these functions.

Depending on political feasibility and impact, some functions can be prioritized over others.

Sources of Revenues

Underlying the push for health financing reform in East Asia and the Pacific is a growing concern among policy makers that the current level of funds available for health expenditures is inadequate for meeting emergent health needs and achieving universal coverage. A high reliance on donor funding in LICs and on OOP sources of financing in LICs and MIC, and a perceived lack of sustainability of current sources of public financing are other factors underlying these calls for reform.

As in many Organisation for Economic Co-operation and Development (OECD) countries, in high-income East Asian and Pacific economies, public prepayment, comprising taxes and social insurance, accounts for the largest share of health financing. A large portion of prepayment revenues in social insurance systems is raised through wage-related contributions that are shared among employers and employees. Hong Kong SAR, China, is the only high-income economy in the region that collects more than half of its publicly funded prepayment through taxation rather than social insurance. Voluntary (or private) health insurance accounts for a relatively small share of overall health expenditures in high-income East Asian and Pacific economies.

Despite the significance of public prepayments in total financing, the share of OOP payments in total health expenditures is relatively high in high-income East Asian and Pacific economies compared to other OECD countries. In the Republic of Korea, for instance, copayments are 20 percent for inpatient care and 30 to 55 percent for outpatient care. In tax-financed economies such as Hong Kong SAR, China, OOP payments are predominantly used to pay for services obtained from private health care providers; in social insurance–financed countries, OOPs consist of copayments, coinsurance, and deductibles.

Public prepayments account for a higher share of health financing in middle-income East Asian and Pacific countries than in other MICs globally, thanks in part to stronger economic growth in recent years. General Government Revenue (GGR) accounts for a significant portion of public prepayment in East Asian and Pacific MICs, regardless of the country's type of health financing model or system. Most MICs in East Asia and the Pacific also have SHI (financed through payroll contributions) for civil servants and other formal sector workers. The relatively minor role played by private health insurance in East Asian and Pacific MICs, however, is still somewhat surprising, given the high OOP share of total spending, the existence of a middle class, and the viable financial market that is conducive to private health insurance growth.

The share of OOP payments in total health financing varies significantly across MICs in East Asia and the Pacific. In China, the Philippines, and Indonesia, OOP payments account for a very high share of total expenditures (49 percent, 45 percent, and 38 percent, respectively). By contrast, OOP payments account for only 15 percent or less of total spending in Fiji, Samoa, and Tonga and only 5 percent in Mongolia (although informal payments in Mongolia have not been well studied).

LICs in East Asia and the Pacific, as well as those elsewhere, have low public health spending and limited ability to mobilize domestic resources to increase the share of public prepayments for health care. On average across East Asia and the Pacific, public prepayment revenues for health account for 30 percent or less of total health expenditures; most of the remaining 70 percent is from private sources in the form of OOP payments.

Historically, GGR has financed public prepayment for health care in East Asian and Pacific LICs. Low economic growth, weak tax administration capacity, and limited potential for increasing GGR has led to the imposition of fees. In recent years, a range of social and community-based insurance schemes has been introduced, partly to diversify the revenue base for health care (for example, SHI in Vietnam) and partly to provide low-income households with a means of financial protection in the face of rising user fees (for example, HEFs in Cambodia and Lao PDR). Voluntary health insurance accounts for less than 5 percent of total health expenditures in East Asian and Pacific LICs and mainly supplements private care for middle- and upper-income groups. Donor financing accounts for a significant share of health spending in LICs. Yet complete, consistent data on donor spending are rarely available.

OOP payments are the principal means of financing health care throughout much of East Asia and the Pacific and are a significant burden on household resources in many LICs and MICs. The proportion of households incurring catastrophic payments (defined as such at 15 percent, 25 percent, and 40 percent of both food and nonfood expenditures) for health care is highest in China and Vietnam. In the absence of health insurance and other social safety nets to protect against the catastrophic costs of health care, poor households faced with health shocks are vulnerable to further poverty.

Many countries continue to assess the relative merits of various options for improving public prepayment levels. For example, Malaysia and Hong Kong SAR, China, have each considered a move to an SHI model from a GGR model. Each of the options will need to be assessed within a particular country context. The sustainability of GGR financing depends critically on economic growth and strong administrative capacity to raise taxes. In LICs, the tax and nontax resource base is low and economic growth is weak. By contrast, most MICs have the infrastructure to raise general tax revenues, but the administrative capacity to raise taxes is weak. These countries lack appropriate tax structures and incentives, including clear rules and transparency.

The sustainability of SHI financing depends on economic growth, which is essential for ensuring the sustainability of payroll taxes. A large formal labor market, administrative capacity for collection, good regulatory and oversight structures, and appropriate incentive structures are also essential. In MICs in East Asia and the Pacific, economic growth has been strong in recent years, but many of the other enabling factors are not present. LICs and MICs in East Asia and the Pacific have large rural populations and small formal labor markets. Even in the context of a limited formal labor market, weak administrative capacity and lack of good regulatory oversight and incentive structures constrain the collection of social insurance contributions. Nonenrollment for formal sector workers in insurance schemes and full or partial evasion of payments among those who are enrolled mean that the collection of social insurance contributions is no more efficient than the collection of tax revenues in most MICs (for example, in China and Vietnam). Evasion exists even in countries where enrollment is mandatory, because workers and employers can take advantage of lax enforcement and not enroll in the scheme at all (for example, in Indonesia).

Some forms of taxes, such as taxes on tobacco, cigarettes, and alcohol, represent an alternative source of revenue with a relatively untapped potential in most East Asian and Pacific countries. The tobacco tax rate is less than 50 percent of the price of cigarettes in all Asian countries except Singapore and Thailand. In the 15 countries that were members of the European Union prior to May 1, 2004,[2] taxes on the price of cigarettes average 58 percent, although the proportion of smokers in the population is quite similar.

Reducing inefficiencies in health financing and provision can also generate additional resources for health. Improved revenue-raising capacity, though important, is not sufficient for increasing allocations for health. East Asian and Pacific countries generally commit less of a percentage of overall public funding for health relative to other countries in similar income categories. Alternatively, fiscal space for health may need to be generated by improving the efficiency of sector outlays. Improvements in efficiency can increase effective fiscal space; at the same time, improved performance and the promise of success can attract additional resources from ministries of finance.

Finally, fiscal capacity and policy priorities are twin dimensions of improving levels of public prepayment for health. Regardless of which of the discussed options a country chooses, overall levels of public prepayment tend to track with a country's GDP per capita. This correlation is true both globally and in East Asia and the Pacific. At the same time, there is significant variation in public spending as a share of GDP for countries with similar GDP (for example, Cambodia has much higher levels of prepayment than Lao PDR even though both are lower-middle-income countries). This variation may be due to either variation in fiscal capacity or public sector priorities to invest in health spending as a share of the public budget. Analysts will want to disentangle these two factors to understand how much of the variation is due to fiscal context and how much is due to public policy priorities.

Pooling and Management of Funds

Pooling of funds is a major challenge in the region. Small and numerous pools exist in many countries. This fragmentation limits the potential for cross-subsidy, while perhaps unnecessarily increasing administrative costs in countries with very limited funding. Many countries in the region—Indonesia, Mongolia, the Philippines, and Vietnam—have established a national SHI program as a way to pool funds, and Cambodia is also developing the blueprint.

Fragmentation can also involve planned segmentation in any country, thereby leading to "inequity by design." Many LICs and MICs, especially in Latin America, have experienced this problem. Cambodia plans a separate administrative structure for its civil servants and formal sector workers. This approach has been administratively unsuccessful in Thailand and in other countries with fragmented insurance pools. The decision is more political than technical. The government in Thailand, for example, has not been able to address the issue with civil servants politically.

Similarly, it is important to integrate new health insurance funds for poorer groups into the broader pooling of funds. New HEFs for the poor are now well established institutionally in Lao PDR and Cambodia and could be used to make contributions to SHI for the poor. Similarly, in China, the medical assistance programs that subsidize lower-income groups with current coverage could be folded into larger social insurance pools. Perhaps China's biggest challenge will be pooling funds across geographic areas to pool urban and rural populations.

Regionally, countries could adopt various approaches, including consolidation of a multipool system and establishment of a single national pool. The Republic of Korea went from more than 380 funds to one national fund over a 12-year period in the 1990s and in the early part of the 2000s. Taiwan, China, moved from three insurance funds to a single insurance fund model as well. Japan is an interesting model from the region because it effectively has a single fund. In Japan, a single pooling fund was created in 1983 so that the multiple insurers that developed over time could share costs equally. This single pool pays for 70 percent of all costs.

Globally, there are also useful models for pooling, such as those in Europe, Canada, and Latin America, that adjust risks prospectively or retrospectively into insurance pools or adjust pools geographically by province (as, in Kazakhstan). Given that decentralization is a popular option in East Asia and the Pacific, these adjustments might be models or interim models for several countries, including China and Indonesia. However, care would need to be taken to ensure that pools would be sufficiently large to cover population risks. This factor is less of an issue in more populous countries but may be an issue in less populous countries such as Cambodia.

In East Asian and Pacific countries with multiple pools, pooling might take two tracks related to the timeframe available. In the short term, the health sector should assess disparities across risk pools and develop a risk-adjustment mechanism across payers. Some regulatory framework and stewardship capacity would be needed, but this capacity would increase equity, better spread risks, and encourage purchasers to better manage purchasing arrangements. Providing the necessary regulatory framework and stewardship capacity will be an important challenge for LICs such as Cambodia and Lao PDR.

Bureaucratically, there are also hurdles in several East Asian and Pacific countries. In many countries, such as Cambodia, China, Lao PDR, and Mongolia, different government ministries manage different funds. A decision would need to be made in each country about whether the Ministry of Social Security or the Ministry of Health (or some other ministry) would bring various funds under one umbrella.

Strategic Purchasing of Services

Many countries have adopted a general *strategic purchasing* of health services framework, which recognizes a number of components of purchasing, or *policy levers* that can be used for better allocating resources by purchasers across geographic areas or directly to providers. These components include (a) coverage and targeting of funds, (b) creation of the benefits package, (c) contracting, and (d) establishment of payment rates and the incentive framework for providers. Elements of strategic purchasing are emerging in the region, but a significant agenda that remains to capture value for money expended.

Coverage and targeting

Many governments have made great strides in extending coverage step by step. For example, China has gone from almost no coverage to almost universal coverage (more than 90 percent) for its rural population of more than 700 million citizens since the early part of the 2000s. Thailand achieved universal coverage earlier through its insurance scheme, which is based on general revenues. Nevertheless, challenges remain for achieving universal coverage in the entire region. In most countries, coverage appears to be linked to formalization of labor and payment of the payroll tax.

A second issue is that, under a current insurance or allocation system arrangement, some insured groups and some regions may not be receiving equitable funding relative to need or demand; thus, there may be a mismatch of equity of access and equity of quality of services. This disparity can be a particular issue in the region because so many countries—China, Indonesia, Malaysia, the Philippines, Thailand, and Vietnam—use some form of fiscal decentralization. In the short term, the easiest approach for countries is a move toward more population-based allocation methods.

Benefits package

Given low levels of health spending in LICs, a widely held view is that the state should first finance a small package of services for universal coverage, essentially encompassing public goods, goods with externalities, and other interventions with proven results. All other clinical care and catastrophic expenditures should be financed for the poor by using some targeting mechanism. In reality, decisions about which package of services the government should buy are made on the basis of not only economic criteria, but also social and political criteria. Although cost-effectiveness of spending is referred to frequently in policy documents in many of the LICs in the region, almost no country has a benefits package that was defined purely on this basis. Globally, tradition, corruption, and political pressures mean that increased health resources are often allocated to tertiary care centers and urban health facilities. The regional experience follows this global pattern.

For most MICs in Eastern Europe and Latin America, concerns about the design of the package relate more to the depth of coverage than to its breadth; however, the same is not true of all MICs in East Asia and the Pacific. For instance, China and the Philippines have not yet achieved high levels of coverage of publicly financed services. Underinsurance is a key issue even for countries expanding to universal coverage over time and for HICs such as the Republic of Korea.

There is a further issue of variations in packages across insurance schemes within a country. Formal sector and urban-based programs or insurance schemes tend to have richer packages relative to parallel programs (for example, those in Cambodia, China, Indonesia, Lao PDR, and Thailand). In most tax-financed systems in both Europe and Asia, the benefits package is not explicitly defined. High-income tax-financed systems in Asia (such as those in Malaysia and Hong Kong SAR, China, with systems based on the U.K. National Health Scheme) are no different. Low-income tax-financed systems in East Asia and the Pacific, such as those in the Pacific Islands, also do not explicitly define benefits.

As the BoD in East Asia and the Pacific increasingly shifts to NCDs and as the prevalence of chronic diseases increases, preventive and promotive services, as well as screening services, become important. The benefits packages need to be continually updated to address the changing disease profile and to coordinate with basic public health programs. The provision of early treatment can prevent longer-term complications and can help reduce costs overall.

Contracting

There is significant external contracting with providers across most countries in East Asia and the Pacific, and it seems to occur across all income groups. Indeed, some countries, such as Cambodia, have a rich and well-documented tradition of contracting. An important issue in contracting in many East Asian and Pacific countries is whether the payer is to contract with both the public sector and the emergent private sector. In terms of delivery of care, the private sector is growing. It remains small in some countries; however, it has experienced significant growth in Cambodia (mostly because of nongovernmental organizations), Indonesia, Mongolia, and the Philippines. Progress with contracting both public and private providers can be found in countries such as Malaysia, Mongolia, and Thailand in addition to such high-income economies as Japan, the Republic of Korea, and Taiwan, China. Contracting policies will need to level the playing field because many public facilities receive separate subsidies for salaries and capital investment.

Some countries, such as Mongolia and Thailand, also use the element of gatekeeping in contracts with primary care providers. This model can be used to better encourage the use of primary care and more cost-effective outpatient services. However, there is hardly any contract evaluation in the region, and no evidence (outside of Cambodia) of selective contracting on the basis of quality, costs, and performance. There is more often the situation of soft, relational contracts in which both parties (the purchaser and the provider) expect that a contract will be automatically extended in the ensuing years. Selective contracting is a goal for many countries in the region in the next few years.

Provider payment

A rich variety of provider payment systems is found in the East Asian and Pacific region, and many countries appear to be in transition. Currently, there is an overreliance on FFS payments. Except for HICs, countries most often use FFS in conjunction with supply-side financing using line-item budgets, as is practiced in China, Lao PDR, the Philippines, and Vietnam. This method can create a toxic mix of incentives. On the one hand, line-item budgets are often unresponsive to patient needs and demands. On the other hand, the FFS overlay can encourage unnecessary demand, often by generating new revenues for underfunded line-item budgets or by reallocating revenues across line-item budgets. Unnecessary outlays can negatively affect purchasers or can fall on consumers as OOP costs.

At the same time, many countries are now looking to move beyond FFS, especially as they grapple with increased health expenditures and as cost-containment and efficiency become areas of higher priority. New provider payment strategies or new provider payment pilots are emerging in several countries (China, Indonesia, Mongolia, and Vietnam, for example) regardless of income. Thailand is perhaps the regional leader in moving beyond FFS, with its sophisticated mix of geographic caps, facility global budgets, and case-mix (DRG) adjusters for hospital admissions.

Governments in East Asia and the Pacific that have multiple purchasers (for example, Cambodia, China, Indonesia, and Lao PDR) will also need to strongly consider new and more consistent sets of payment rules and systems across insurers. Variations across payers can distort providers' incentives and can distort practice patterns by encouraging overuse of highly paid services by some payers. Variations also can discourage access to relatively poorly paid services and discourage equitable treatment for groups under some payers relative to others. New payment systems need to restructure incentives, but establishing more uniform rules across payers will also help improve equity across groups.

Demand-side purchasing

Although a third-party such as the Ministry of Health or a health insurance organization primarily purchases services, consumers and households may buy services. Two mechanisms are typically used on behalf of the patient: CCTs and vouchers. The effectiveness of CCTs in tackling both health and educational components strongly suggests that CCTs are an adequate tool for demand financing. Various forms of CCTs have grown in popularity and are found in East Asian and Pacific countries such as Cambodia and Indonesia.

Critical factors for implementing a successful CCT program include,

- Appropriate design of the program in accordance with the specific context of each country.
- Use of an effective targeting mechanism that adequately differentiates the poor from the nonpoor.
- Efficient monitoring and enforcement of the conditions.
- Sufficient cash transfer to create a reasonable incentive for the target group to fulfill conditions.
- Transparent and efficient administrative capacity.
- Balance of demand and supply-side incentives and investments.

Vouchers serve as another optional tool for demand financing by providing assistance to economically constrained families through subsidies directed toward health and education. Voucher programs have been used in both health and education, but rigorous impact evaluations are scarce. Vouchers also require sophisticated consumers who know what to buy and where to buy, as well as requiring sophisticated risk adjusters to protect providers. Vouchers may be best used for a more basic function of providing subsidies to poor individuals, but vouchers can be applied for the achievement of more specific targets in health. However, beyond monetary means, determinants such as physical inaccessibility in the form of distance and poor transportation will also play a key role in whether higher-quality service will reach the target groups. Voucher programs have been implemented in East Asia and the Pacific in the past decade in China, Indonesia, and Vietnam.

Reforming Service Delivery and Organization of Care

Financing reforms cannot be made without physical and human capital delivery system changes. Service delivery, organization of care, and governance play critical roles in optimal performance.

Decentralization

In East Asian and Pacific countries, change in the organization of care delivery has often been bound in a concept of decentralization. Decentralization is usually discussed in terms of financing and delivery; however, decentralization through financing can lead to fragmentation and fracturing of the risk pool. At the delivery level, decentralization offers more promise as a way to provide greater satisfaction to patients and responsiveness to local care needs.

The impetus for decentralization in East Asia and the Pacific has stemmed from a variety of factors and motivations. In some instances, decentralization was not an end in itself but a means to achieving broader health sector reforms. In these settings, the objective was to decentralize authority and fiduciary responsibility to provincial (and lower-level) entities to improve efficiency and health outcomes. In other settings, decentralization was sought to bring the delivery of services closer to the people for better response to local needs. Other cases revealed political motivations for decentralization, such as the appeasement of provincial interests.

In many cases, decentralization was part of a broader public administration reform, with little scope for health. In only a few examples, such as in some of the Pacific Island countries, did the health sector take a lead role in decentralization. For many countries in the region, decentralization occurred in the context of economic and political crises, many in the aftermath of the East Asian financial crisis (1997), when per capita income, and with it public sector spending on health, declined dramatically.

Decentralization has played a prominent role in East Asia and the Pacific in both financing and delivery, but with very mixed results.

There is little or no evidence of effectiveness or improved equity in these countries. Indeed, although the objective was to encourage innovation and improve responsiveness to local needs, the impact has often been to fracture the risk pool and create inequities across localities. The appropriate roles of different levels of government have been poorly defined.

The response has, not surprisingly, been to recentralize in many cases, such as in Lao PDR, Papua New Guinea, and, more recently, China under its 2009 health care reform plan. In other cases, the push for new forms of SHI has effectively meant that at least the financing of health care must be pooled and recentralized. This discussion and dialogue is now occurring in multiple countries, including China, the Philippines, and Vietnam. In other cases, new forms of insurance, such as the HEFs in Cambodia and Lao PDR, may encourage greater pooling and centralization of financing.

Within the context of decentralization, there has also been a push for hospital, facility, and provider autonomy within East Asian and Pacific countries. Full autonomization of providers has not yet occurred in any LIC or MIC in the region. Most efforts are in the early stages of development and will require some greater focus and development in the future. At this stage, autonomization has most often been used to raise more user fees rather than to encourage better management and quality of services. Equity of user fees is often an issue in China and Vietnam; social objectives are often not explicit. Efficiency objectives are limited by the facility's ability to make its own internal decisions about cost structure as well as a general lack of accountability and risk.

The issue of autonomization, in the past analysis, suggests that strategic purchasing and, more specifically, contracting and payment reforms may not be as successful in the near future without greater autonomy at the facility level. As in some other regions of the world, such as Eastern Europe, contracting and payment reforms may not have the intended effect on behavior if the management space and flexibility are not present in the delivery sector. Thus, contracting and payment reforms will need to assess this enabling factor carefully, either before or during implementation.

Governance

There remains an important agenda in East Asia and the Pacific that is closely tied to financing policies and reform. Government is the natural lead actor for stewardship and oversight. Although some other functions can be—and in some countries are—discharged with negligible government involvement, oversight cannot be. Indeed, the more health system functions the government leaves to other actors, the greater challenge it faces vis-à-vis increased oversight. Leaving health care delivery to private nonprofit providers or to autonomous public sector hospitals means that the government workload switches from line management of treatment facilities to creating and operating an effective oversight system. Leaving SHI to an autonomous health insurance agency, as has been done in many countries, requires the government to establish clear rules explaining the degree of freedom the insuring agency has in various areas. The government must retain a voice in agency governance without interfering in the agency's day-to-day decisions.

Additional issues of health sector governance in East Asia and the Pacific are also reviewed in this book because such areas influence health service quality. The issues include (a) informal payments by consumers and patients to providers; (b) absenteeism of providers, including public providers doubling as private practitioners; (c) accountability and consumer voice; (d) regulation of the emergent medical tourism industry in the region; and (e) regulation and coordination of providers across the sector.

The frequency of informal payments within health services varies widely among countries globally and in the region. The incidence of informal payments ranges from as high as 81 percent in Vietnam, to 74 percent in China, to less than 10 percent in Thailand. Anecdotal reports of informal payments exist in other countries in the region, such as Mongolia, but those accounts are not well documented to date. Solving the problem of informal payments is not straightforward. Salary regulation may need to be combined with a variety of incentives to be effective. Incentives could include performance-based compensation for high productivity and quality care provision along, with clear rules, norms, and, most important, accountability. Cambodia and the Philippines are two examples of countries that have implemented a form of performance-based incentives to improve effectiveness and reduce corruption in the health care system.

Absenteeism is one more dimension in East Asia and the Pacific that dilutes the financing and provision of care services; the absence of doctors and health clinic workers compromises equity and reduces the effectiveness of public health spending. In many East Asian and Pacific countries (for example, in China, Lao PDR, and Vietnam), wages represent a large proportion of government expenditures. Health workers may combine public sector medical work with private sector work in which a fee is required for service. This type of medical practice could be referred to as *dual practice* and is closely related to the issues of absenteeism and informal payments.

In many East Asian and Pacific countries, the private sector plays an increasingly dominant role in health care delivery. For example, the share of beds in private hospitals in Thailand grew from 5 percent in 1970 to 14 percent in 1989. In Indonesia, 50 percent of all hospitals are run privately, and the proportion of physicians running private practices in Malaysia increased from 43 percent in 1975 to 70 percent in 1990. Low salaries in the public sector may encourage privatization and dual practice in private clinics. The proportion of the total income generated from dual practice for medical personnel and private sector activities is more than 50 percent in Thailand and up to 90 percent in Cambodia.

The lack of accountability among policy makers, poor people, and providers lays the ground for much of the inadequate health care provision and the absence of personnel in East Asian and Pacific countries, as in many other developing countries. Enhancing the individual's power to choose by enhancing competition between health services providers, could help improve overall care and reduce absenteeism because providers must improve care to attract patients. Government subsidies in the form of vouchers may be one option for providing the means for poor people to access alternative health care and to improve their choices, although vouchers have limitations as discussed earlier.

Emergence of Medical Tourism

Medical tourism combines the search for new revenues, the development of a more diverse delivery system, and the importance of coordination and governance across the health sector. As a result of the financial crisis in 1997, many private hospitals in East Asia began pursuing health revenues beyond their borders. As the success and future potential of the private sector to attract foreign patients to East Asian and Pacific countries became apparent over the past decade in countries such as Malaysia and Thailand, government participation (for example, in the Philippines) was intensified to maximize the direct gain from increased health revenues along with the benefits to the tourism sector overall.

Despite the apparent advantages of revenue generation, the new, growing market does raise issues concerning equity and the impact of less than equal access to affordable and high-quality health care for the local population. Increasing government focus on meeting private hospitals' demand may result in diminution of necessary funding and staff members for local residents. Currently, no evidence suggests that increased revenues generated by medical tourism in East Asia and the Pacific have resulted in reallocation of sufficient resources for improving coverage, access, or quality of health care for the local population. The recent economic downturn in 2008 and 2009 has seen some lessening of demand for medical tourism.

Notes

1. Timor-Leste's ratio increased from 0.79 to 0.91 over this period.
2. These countries were Austria, Belgium, Denmark, Finland, France, Germany, Greece, Ireland, Italy, Luxembourg, the Netherlands, Portugal, Spain, Sweden, and the United Kingdom.

Reference

Spence, Michael, and Maureen A. Lewis, eds. 2009. *Health and Growth.* Washington, DC: World Bank.

CHAPTER 2

Understanding the Macroeconomic Context and the Health Sectors in East Asia and the Pacific

Macroeconomic Context

East Asia and the Pacific contains great variations in size and population, from small Pacific Islands with fewer than 100,000 people to countries such as China and Indonesia, which are respectively the first- and fourth-biggest countries in the world (figures 2.1 and 2.2). Relative to other regions of the world, East Asia and the Pacific is the most populous. It contains the world's fastest-growing economies and the second-largest number of fragile states after Africa. It contains a wide spectrum of political and government organizations, from democracies to military dictatorships. Although many countries are highly centralized, fiscal and government decentralization is an important trend among many countries, including China, Indonesia, Malaysia, the Philippines, and Vietnam.

The region is extremely dynamic. In 2007, the developing countries of East Asia and the Pacific capped six years of strong economic performance. The region is demonstrating considerable resilience at present to adverse global economic developments, with strong GDP growth per capita (figure 2.3). Improvements in the business environment over recent years have facilitated private sector growth, which averaged 10.1 percent in the six years to 2007. East Asia is ranked as one of the most

Figure 2.1 Population Diversity in the Larger Countries in East Asia and the Pacific, 2007

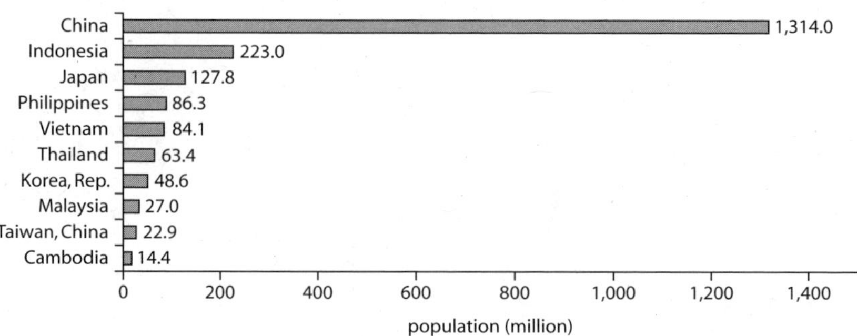

Source: World Bank's World Development Indicators database.

Figure 2.2 Population Diversity in the Smaller Countries in East Asia and the Pacific, 2007

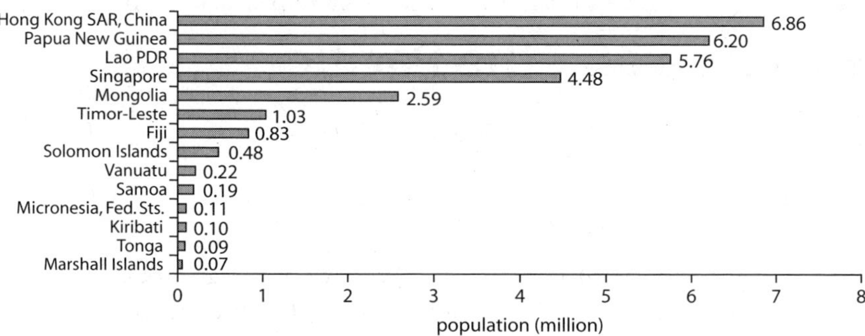

Source: World Bank's World Development Indicators database.

Figure 2.3 Gross Domestic Product Growth Per Capita, 2007

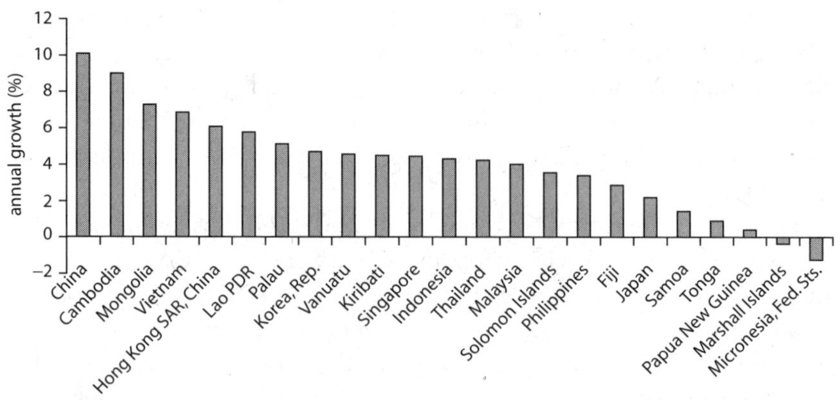

Source: World Bank's World Development Indicators database.
Note: Data for Taiwan, China, are not available.

friendly business environments in the developing world, and many rapid reformers have improved major facets of the investment climate. East Asian countries top the "Doing Business" rankings for low- and middle-income countries (LMICs) (World Bank 2009). An average of 12 positive reform changes to the business environment were enacted per year since 2003 in eight of the largest developing countries in the region, with some countries making more than three major changes per year. However, the larger economies are feeling the effects of prolonged rapid growth and the amassing of large foreign exchange reserves from brisk exports and rising capital inflows, including the risk of overheating, the formation of asset bubbles, and the emergence of financial sector and macroeconomic vulnerabilities (as occurred in the Western countries in late 2008).

The extraordinary increase in real commodity prices—particularly energy and food prices—and the recent natural disasters in China and Myanmar are new challenges. Most recently, the severe downturn in commodities will present other types of challenges, such as losses of revenues from copper mining in Mongolia. The effect of these price trends is determined by each country's dependence on trade in these commodities. Net commodity exporters (such as Malaysia, Papua New Guinea, Timor-Leste, and Vietnam) have received windfall gains, which strengthen government revenues and exports. However, rising food prices have adversely affected the urban and landless poor throughout the region. The Pacific Island economies are vulnerable to increases in the price of energy because there is little scope for diversification away from crude oil. Meanwhile, net food importers, such as Cambodia, Mongolia, and Timor-Leste, have seen adverse effects on household consumption.

A number of additional economic indicators, such as gross domestic product (GDP) per capita (in current international purchasing power parity), GDP growth per capita (annual percentage), ratio of debt to GDP, and inflation over the past decade, are presented as markers of the relative fiscal space available to finance health expenditures (table 2.1).

Effects on the Poor

Sustained growth and policies that provide opportunities to the poor have produced dramatic advances in poverty reduction. The proportion of poor people (consuming less than US$2 per day) fell to 25 percent in 2007, compared to 69 percent in 1990 and 47 percent in 2000 (figure 2.4). For the region's fast-growing countries, growth has been accompanied by exceptionally rapid urbanization. By 2025, the region's

Table 2.1 Selected Demographic, Human Development, and Economic Indicators for East Asian and Pacific Countries, 2000–07

Economy	*Total population (million)*	*Rural population share (%)*	*GDP per capita (PPP, current international $)*	*Annual GDP growth per capita (%)*	*Inflation, GDP deflator*	*Inflation, GDP deflator (annual %, 1996 = 100; average 1996–2005/06)*	*Poverty headcount ratio at US$2 a day (PPP, % of population)*	*Agriculture, value added (% of GDP)*	*Gini index*	*Primary school enrollment (% net)*	*Secondary school enrollment (% net)*	*Debt (as a % of GDP)*
Cambodia	14.4	79.7	1,618.8	9.0	122.5	—	—	30.1	41.7	89.9	23.9	33.0
China	1,314.0	58.7	4,644.0	10.1	121.5	2.1	35.0	11.7	46.9	—	—	17.9
Fiji	0.8	48.7	4,548.5	2.9	151.1	—	—	15.0	—	90.4	80.9	—
Hong Kong SAR, China	6.9	—	39,061.6	6.1	99.9	−0.3	—	—	—	—	77.9	—
Indonesia	223.0	50.8	3,454.4	4.3	180.8	17.6	42.9	12.9	39.4	94.5	57.4	35.0
Japan	127.8	34.0	31,947.2	2.2	92.7	—	—	—	—	99.8	99.9	195.4
Kiribati	0.1	51.8	3,687.9	4.5	128.2	—	—	7.1	—	—	68.3	—
Korea, Rep.	48.6	19.0	22,988.1	4.7	111.7	—	—	3.2	—	97.6	93.9	32.1
Lao PDR	5.8	79.0	1,980.1	5.8	2,105.8	—	33.0	42.0	—	83.7	34.9	77.1
Malaysia	27.0	31.8	12,536.1	4.0	207.4	2.5	7.9	8.7	46.2	99.2	72.0	—
Marshall Islands	0.1	33.1	6,429.1	−0.3	205.1	—	—	—	—	—	—	65.9
Micronesia, Fed. Sts.	0.1	77.6	5,665.1	−1.2	112.0	—	—	—	—	—	—	—

Mongolia	2.6	43.1	2,887.3	7.3	123.1	—	—	21.9	—	91.4	81.5	40.0
Palau	0.1	30.3	14,209.1	5.2	133.8	—	—	—	—	—	—	11.6
Papua New Guinea	6.2	86.5	1,817.1	0.4	414.4	—	—	41.8	—	—	—	47.5
Philippines	86.3	36.6	3,152.8	3.4	472.6	6.4	43.0	14.2	44.5	92.9	60.2	55.8
Samoa	0.2	77.4	5,148.4	1.5	144.5	—	—	12.2	—	90.4	66.0	39.4
Singapore	4.5	—	44,708.2	4.5	100.1	—	—	0.1	—	—	—	96.0
Solomon Islands	0.5	82.7	1,838.6	3.6	1,059.3	—	—	—	—	61.8	—	52.3
Taiwan, China	0.1	—	—	—	—	—	—	—	—	—	—	—
Thailand	63.4	67.4	7,598.5	4.3	193.3	—	25.0	10.7	42.0	94.2	71.0	27.4
Timor-Leste	1.0	73.1	2,140.7	−6.7	109.3	—	—	32.2	—	68.1	—	0.0
Tonga	0.1	75.7	5,405.4	0.9	146.8	—	—	28.5	—	98.4	66.4	48.0
Vanuatu	0.2	76.1	3,768.4	4.6	240.2	—	—	15.6	—	87.8	38.1	32.2
Vietnam	84.1	73.1	2,363.1	6.9	229.1	—	—	20.4	37.0	84.5	68.9	43.3

Sources: Country documents from task team leaders; World Bank's World Development Indicators database; World Bank 2006, 2008b; Wagstaff 2007. Data for debt as a share of GDP come from IMF article IV reports from 2006 to 2008.

Note: — = not available; PPP = purchasing power parity. Data reflect the latest available year (2000–07). Data are not available for American Samoa, the Democratic People's Republic of Korea, Myanmar, and the Northern Mariana Islands.

Figure 2.4 Proportion of Poor People in East Asia and the Pacific, 1990–2007

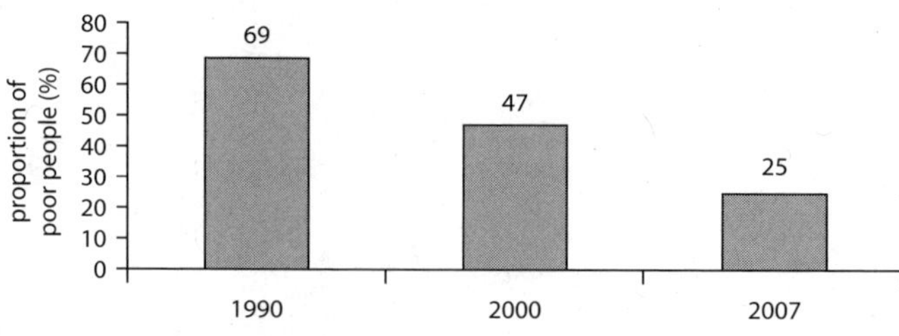

Source: World Bank 2008c.
Note: Poor people are those who consume less than US$2 per day.

Figure 2.5 Rural Population as a Share of Total Population

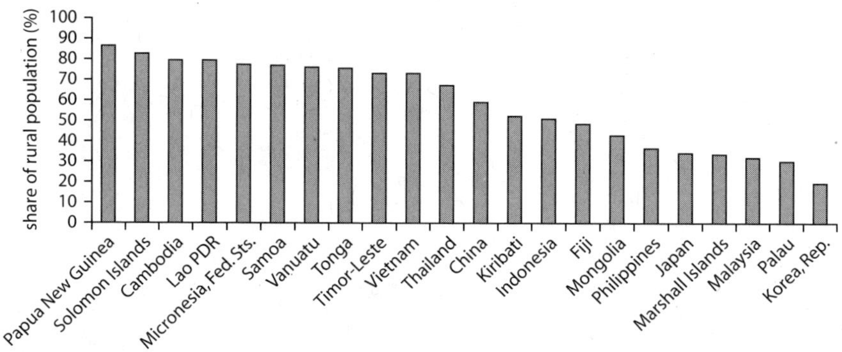

Source: World Bank's World Development Indicators database.
Note: Data for Hong Kong SAR, China; Singapore; and Taiwan, China are not available.

urban population is likely to increase by 500 million (over 68 percent), with particularly rapid growth in China, Indonesia, the Philippines, Thailand, and Vietnam. Yet some countries remain predominantly rural, including Cambodia, China, the Lao People's Democratic Republic, and Vietnam (figure 2.5).

Social conditions have changed dramatically over a single generation in these economies. In 1980, the average citizen of China and Thailand had a two-in-three chance of drawing his or her primary income from farming; by 2006, more than one-half of the population drew their income from nonfarming sources. Fertility rates are decreasing (figure 2.6). Thirty years ago, the average household in the Philippines had more than five children; today it is closer to three. In Indonesia, a child born in 1980 had a one-in-three chance of growing up illiterate, but now more than 98 percent of youth are literate, and they have a one-in-six chance

Figure 2.6 Trends in Fertility Rates in East Asia and the Pacific, 1980–2005

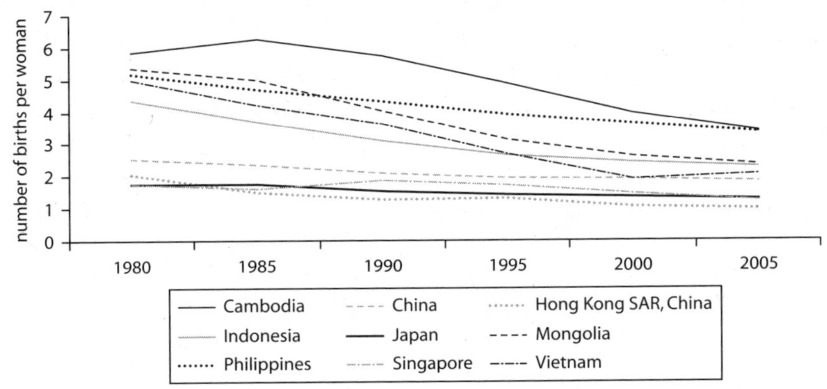

Source: World Bank's World Development Indicators database.

of completing high school. Each of these achievements is tangible and makes a difference in the region's well-being and health status overall.

Despite dramatic economic and social transformation, the region's development has come with its own internal contradictions; although poverty has declined and human development indexes have improved, inequality in the region has grown. The Theil index of inequality in per capita consumption showed an increase for the major countries of the region, taken as a whole, from 35.5 percent in 1990 to 42.6 percent in 2002. Around three-quarters of the income disparity in the region is due to inequality within countries, and only one-quarter is due to inequalities between countries. Middle-income countries (MICs) and emerging MICs such as Indonesia and Vietnam have seen inequality rise dramatically in their domestic economies, but lower-income countries such as Lao PDR have not escaped.

Gaps between urban and rural areas account for most of such inequality, but there are also regional divides. The strong relationship between such patterns of inequality and access to health, education, and the range of social services, together with concerns over the potential cost of inequality for social harmony, has brought "shared growth" onto the development agenda of most countries in the region.

The region also contains at least one fragile state[1] (Timor-Leste) and many conflict-affected areas, but such conflicts have tended to be limited to relatively small geographic zones. Fragility means not just low growth but also a failure in the normal growth process such that poverty can become a persistent condition. Weak governance, corruption, and insecurity combine in a downward spiral. Countries of former long-standing conflict such as Cambodia and Vietnam are now recovering, but Cambodia still has a relatively low income level. In many of the low-income countries (LICs), donors play a significant role in financing health care, and this dimension will be important to examine as options and solutions are developed.

Health Status and Health Outcomes

In general, the region does well on health outcomes when compared with countries of the world with similar income levels. Figures 2.7 and 2.8 show outcomes on infant mortality when regressed on levels

Figure 2.7 Infant Mortality by Income Per Capita, 2005

Source: World Bank's World Development Indicators database.
Note: Both axes are in log scale.

Figure 2.8 Infant Mortality Rate Relative to Health Spending, 2005

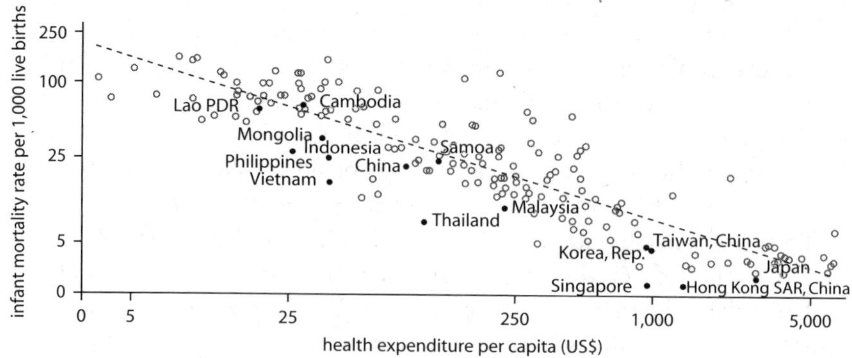

Source: World Bank's World Development Indicators database.
Note: Both axes are in log scale.

of income and levels of health spending. Figure 2.9 combines these measures to show relative performance, which is quite positive for all countries except Cambodia.

Figure 2.10 shows the mortality rate of children under five years old relative to other countries with similar levels of income. Figures 2.11 and 2.12 combine the measure of child mortality with similar income and relative spending measures to look at relative performance. On the two commonly used global indicators—infant mortality and child mortality—countries of the region are performing better in terms of outcomes.

Figure 2.9 Infant Mortality Relative to Income and Health Spending, 2005

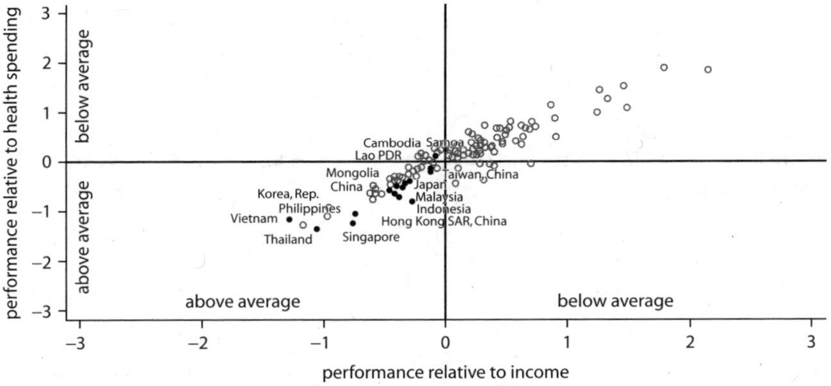

Source: World Bank's World Development Indicators database.
Note: Both axes are in log scale.

Figure 2.10 Child Mortality by Income Per Capita, 2005

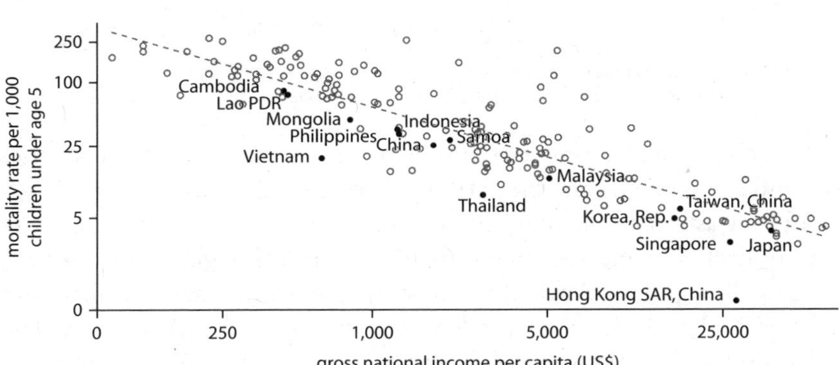

Source: World Bank's World Development Indicators database.
Note: Both axes are in log scale.

Figure 2.11 Child Mortality Performance Relative to Income and Total Health Spending, 2005

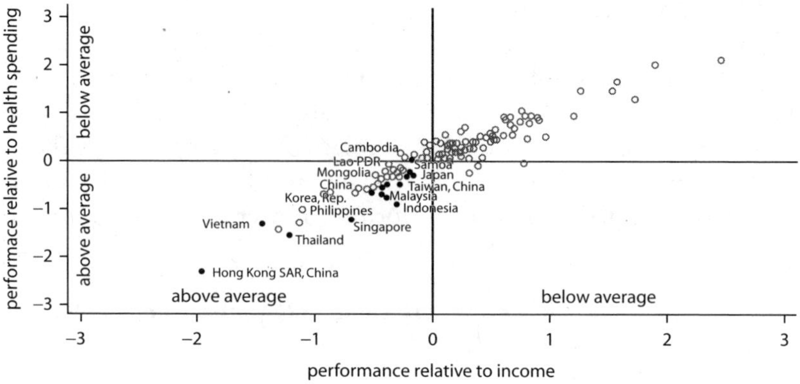

Source: World Bank's World Development Indicators database.
Note: Child mortality refers to mortality rates of infants and children under age five.

Figure 2.12 Child Mortality and Government Health Spending Relative to Income, 2005

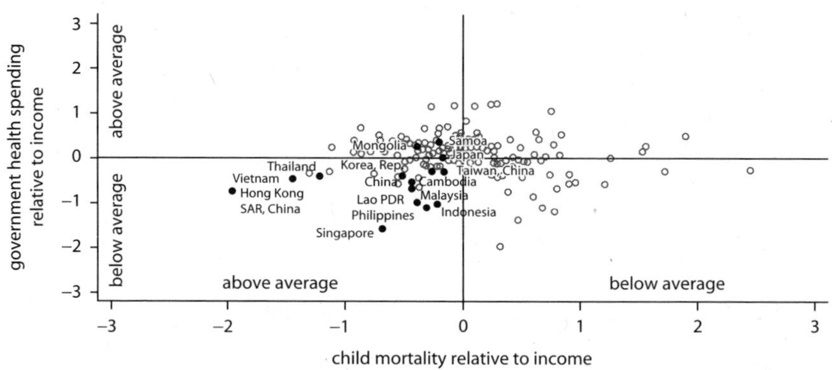

Source: World Bank's World Development Indicators database.
Note: Child mortality refers to mortality rates of infants and children under age five.

Although regional countries tend to spend less than do other countries of similar income levels, they still produce better health outcomes.

In contrast, maternal mortality rate outcomes reveal a more mixed picture in East Asia and the Pacific (figure 2.13). Although some countries, such as China, Mongolia, and Vietnam, have low maternal mortality rates relative to their income level, other countries, such as Indonesia and Lao PDR, do significantly worse. A complex array of socioeconomic, environmental, and cultural factors influence maternal mortality. These factors

Figure 2.13 Maternal Mortality versus Income Per Capita: A Global Comparison, 2005

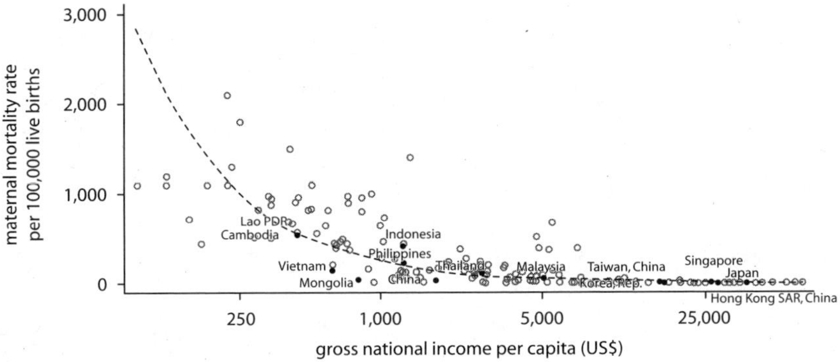

Source: World Bank's World Development Indicators database.
Note: The *x* axis is in log scale.

include low social status of women, malnutrition, and unequal access to health care resources (for example, skilled attendants) in some areas.[2]

Demographic and Epidemiologic Trends

Demographic and epidemiologic profiles and changing patterns in those profiles are important drivers in demand for health care, as are the patterns of health spending and financing.

Demographic Transition, Total Fertility Rates, and Life Expectancy

Within the East Asian and Pacific region, the total fertility rate is declining while life expectancy is rising. The total fertility rate decreased from 2.5 to 2.0 births per woman over the period from 1990 to 2006. Although families are having fewer children, individuals are living longer, as evidenced by increases in life expectancy from 67.2 years in 1990 to 70.9 years in 2006. Given its high average level of income and health spending relative to countries in other regions, East Asia and the Pacific does well in terms of life expectancy (figure 2.14).

However, as individuals live longer, there can be greater demands on average on the health system, particularly in the later years of life, when medical needs increase. The population of East Asia and the Pacific will be aging over the next 20 years, with more male and female retirees, as reflected in the population pyramid (figure 2.15). There will be relatively more working-age people of both genders, and if workers are in relatively good health, this situation could provide a "demographic

Figure 2.14 Life Expectancy Relative to Income and Health Spending, 2005

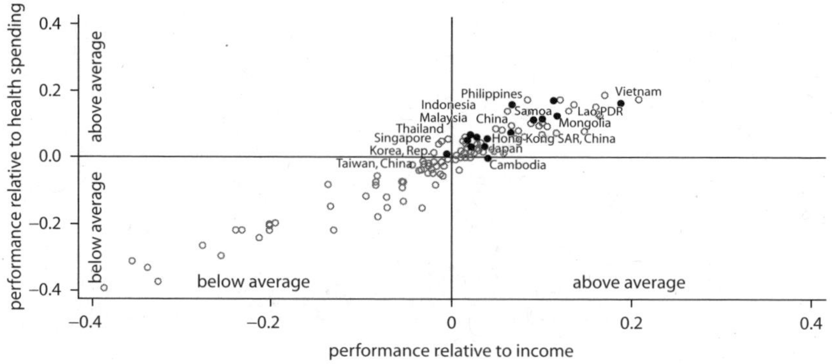

Source: World Bank's World Development Indicators database.

Figure 2.15 East Asian and Pacific Population Pyramids, 2000 and 2020

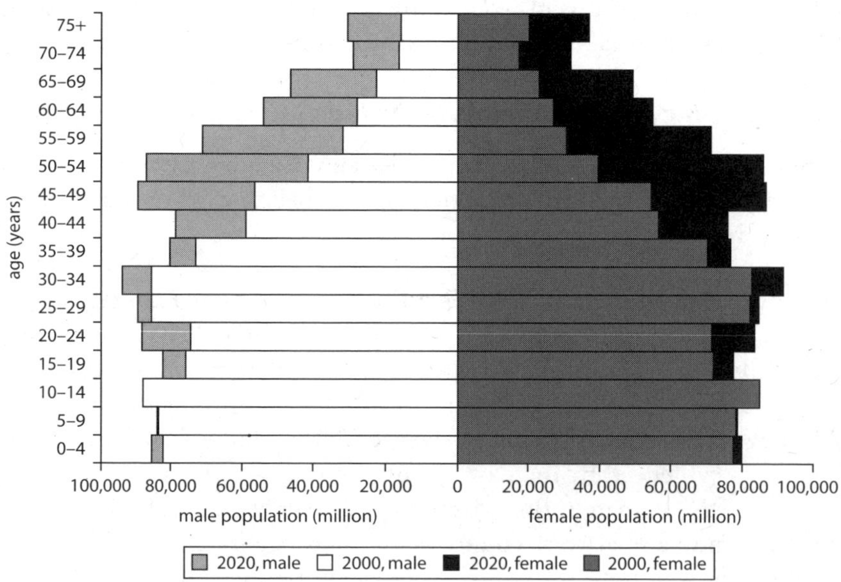

Source: World Bank 2008d.

dividend" whereby a healthy workforce can support economic expansion and help improve overall productivity. However, a less than healthy workforce will create greater pressures on the health and social protection systems.

Age-Dependency Ratio

The age-dependency ratio, when analyzed over time, also provides insight as to the demographic changes under way. The age-dependency ratio looks at the economically dependent part of the population (the combined segment of the population age 0–14 and over 65) compared to the economically productive population (those age 15–64). It is an important measure because, as the ratio increases, the pressure on workers to support individuals who are economically more dependent increases.

For the 22 countries in the region for which data were available, all except Timor-Leste exhibited a decline in the age-dependency ratio from 1960 to 2005 (table 2.2). Timor-Leste's ratio has increased from 78.8 percent to 91.2 percent over this period. In total, nine countries have experienced a drop of at least 40 percent in the age-dependency ratio, indicating less demand on the economically productive segments of the population. Notably, however, over the next 50 years, the age-dependency ratios for many East Asian and Pacific countries are expected to increase dramatically from their 2005 levels, as in the case of higher-income countries such as China, Japan, the Republic of Korea, and Singapore.

Epidemiologic Changes and Burden of Disease

Placed in a global context, East Asian and Pacific countries have fewer disability-adjusted life years (DALYs) per person than do other countries with comparable income levels (figure 2.16). This finding correlates with the higher literacy and education levels found in East Asia (figure 2.17). Table 2.3 provides the country-level detail behind the estimated total DALYs by cause for each country, as estimated by the World Health Organization (WHO) for 2002.[3] The burden of disease (BoD) figures indicate that for communicable diseases and for maternal, perinatal, and nutritional conditions, the BoD in DALYs is greatest in China (37,084,000) because of its large population; it is also high in Indonesia (14,371,000). For noncommunicable diseases (NCDs), China again exhibits the highest levels (133,056,000), followed by Indonesia (25,959,000), Japan (11,206,000), and the Philippines (8,635,000).

With an aging population, the role of NCDs in the overall disease burden profile can also be expected to increase. Hence, the region will effectively face greater challenges in meeting growing demands for care

Table 2.2 Age-Dependency Ratios in East Asia and the Pacific, 1960–2050

	Actual										*Projected*								
Economy	*1960*	*1965*	*1970*	*1975*	*1980*	*1985*	*1990*	*1995*	*2000*	*2005*	*2010*	*2015*	*2020*	*2025*	*2030*	*2035*	*2040*	*2045*	*2050*
Regional average	*78.5*	*82.0*	*81.0*	*79.9*	*70.7*	*60.3*	*54.9*	*52.8*	*50.1*	*45.2*	*41.62*	*41.39*	*43.92*	*45.68*	*47.99*	*51.82*	*55.53*	*57.3*	*59.0*
Cambodia	82.5	83.7	85.3	82.0	78.5	85.7	90.1	96.4	81.2	68.6	63.0	62.3	60.7	57.5	53.8	50.7	48.8	46.2	49.0
China	77.7	80.4	78.7	78.2	67.4	55.1	49.6	48.4	46.6	41.4	38.3	38.8	43.1	45.8	49.1	54.4	59.7	61.5	62.8
Fiji	102.0	96.8	85.0	74.0	72.1	71.3	69.4	63.5	60.2	58.9	53.1	50.9	49.3	48.5	48.6	49.0	48.9	50.6	51.8
Hong Kong SAR, China	77.6	77.6	69.4	55.7	47.0	44.7	42.8	40.9	38.6	37.2	33.8	35.7	40.5	48.1	56.1	60.7	64.4	67.3	70.2
Indonesia	76.5	81.3	83.5	82.0	78.3	72.4	65.6	59.5	54.3	51.3	48.6	46.0	43.4	42.4	42.9	45.4	48.0	50.7	53.4
Japan	56.1	47.5	45.1	47.5	48.4	46.7	43.7	43.9	46.7	50.7	55.1	61.2	64.0	65.1	67.3	72.0	81.2	87.6	90.8
Korea, Dem. People's Rep.	63.3	59.1	70.0	66.6	58.7	49.4	44.6	48.4	48.9	48.6	44.0	42.2	40.0	42.4	45.1	49.1	51.1	50.3	51.5
Korea, Rep.	82.7	87.0	83.0	70.5	60.8	52.1	44.6	41.3	39.3	39.0	36.9	36.1	38.8	45.9	53.9	61.4	69.0	74.7	81.2
Lao PDR	83.0	90.1	87.6	87.1	94.4	93.8	92.5	92.0	87.9	76.4	73.6	68.7	63.5	59.2	55.1	51.7	48.9	46.7	45.2
Malaysia	94.9	97.5	92.3	84.6	75.4	73.6	69.7	66.2	59.6	55.6	53.0	49.8	48.2	48.0	47.9	47.6	47.8	49.0	51.2
Micronesia, Fed. Sts.	95.8	102.2	97.1	106.8	103.6	96.6	91.1	88.4	78.2	73.7	73.8	71.6	66.7	60.0	55.6	57.6	52.9	54.0	57.1
Mongolia	85.7	86.9	87.6	87.5	85.6	83.0	84.2	74.4	62.2	48.8	47.0	43.7	40.8	39.8	40.5	42.1	44.7	47.5	51.0
Myanmar	79.0	85.7	84.1	83.2	79.7	75.0	68.2	62.1	55.6	48.9	45.6	42.7	42.0	42.7	43.6	44.9	46.7	49.6	53.0
Papua New Guinea	81.8	91.2	84.1	84.4	87.8	83.0	78.2	77.1	77.0	75.3	65.6	57.8	53.5	51.7	50.7	48.8	46.7	44.8	44.3
Philippines	95.6	96.7	93.2	89.7	86.2	82.6	79.0	74.5	70.3	66.6	59.6	56.4	54.5	51.3	48.7	46.9	46.1	46.8	48.5
Samoa	101.6	105.6	97.8	89.0	78.2	74.4	81.1	77.2	82.5	83.0	73.4	58.8	53.7	55.0	59.8	65.5	62.7	53.3	43.8
Singapore	82.8	86.4	72.8	58.6	46.6	42.0	37.1	39.9	40.7	39.0	34.3	35.4	41.6	51.2	60.2	64.9	64.7	62.6	62.7
Solomon Islands	83.3	93.0	94.2	105.1	103.8	102.7	93.3	87.3	81.6	76.8	69.9	65.3	58.4	53.0	49.0	45.9	45.3	43.1	42.9
Thailand	87.4	92.2	91.3	84.7	73.6	59.4	50.1	46.1	43.4	41.8	43.2	43.6	45.3	47.9	50.9	53.5	55.3	57.6	60.1
Timor-Leste	78.8	79.9	80.7	80.9	72.7	72.9	72.1	78.6	108.0	91.2	87.1	99.1	93.9	80.2	71.6	65.8	62.3	59.1	56.3
Tonga	101.9	100.3	96.7	99.6	89.5	81.9	78.0	81.7	78.2	78.1	63.1	58.5	57.6	55.4	47.8	55.6	53.3	50.0	50.9
Vanuatu	96.2	95.8	94.3	93.7	93.0	92.0	90.5	88.3	83.4	75.7	70.5	63.6	60.5	56.5	54.0	51.9	52.3	49.8	49.8
Vietnam	78.2	92.6	96.1	92.2	87.6	81.9	78.0	72.6	63.9	54.3	44.6	41.5	40.8	43.2	45.2	46.5	48.2	51.2	55.4

Source: World Bank's World Development Indicators database.
Note: Data are not available for American Samoa, Kiribati, the Marshall Islands, the Northern Mariana Islands, Palau, and Taiwan, China.

Figure 2.16 International Comparison of DALYs and Health Spending, 2002

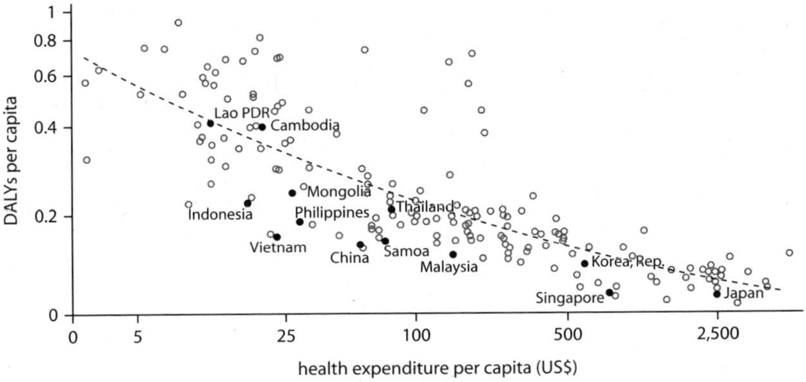

Source: Data from Mathers and Loncar 2005.
Note: Both axes are in log scale.

Figure 2.17 Adult Literacy Rate versus Income, 2005

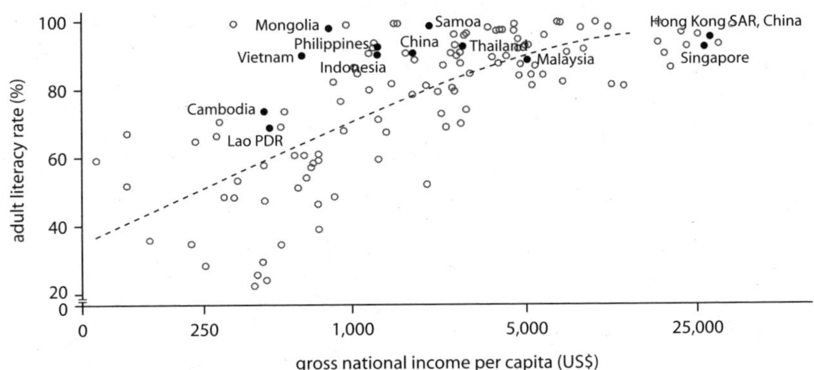

Source: World Bank's World Development Indicators database.
Note: Adult literacy is the average of available data for 2000 to 2005. Literacy data for Vietnam are for 1999. The *x* axis is in log scale.

for primary and secondary prevention and for treatment of chronic diseases. This trend will also lead to rapidly rising expenditures on health over the 20-year period from 2000 to 2020 (figure 2.18). China is one example where the progress of life expectancy over the past 20 years has been somewhat slower than in other countries with similar income levels. This slow progress can be attributed in part to the increased burden of NCDs (box 2.1).

Table 2.3 Estimated Total DALYs by Cause in East Asia and the Pacific, 2002

Economy	*Communicable, maternal, perinatal, and nutritional conditions*								
	Infectious and parasitic diseases	*Respiratory infections*	*Maternal conditions*	*Perinatal conditions*	*Nutritional deficiencies*	*Total from communicable diseases total*	*Noncommunicable diseases*	*Injuries*	*Total from all causes*
Cambodia	2,236	248	119	459	248	3,311	1,636	363	5,310
China	14,833	6,113	2,306	11,279	2,553	37,084	133,056	30,134	200,274
Fiji	15	6	2	7	13	43	108	12	163
Indonesia	7,689	1,413	865	3,029	1,375	14,371	25,959	6,054	46,384
Japan	263	317	53	18	99	750	11,206	1,341	13,297
Kiribati	3	1	0	3	1	8	15	1	24
Korea, Rep.	457	43	39	89	73	701	4,850	819	6,370
Lao PDR	594	202	76	368	105	1,345	622	261	2,228
Malaysia	384	86	35	86	106	697	2,440	369	3,506
Marshall Islands	2	1	0	1	0	4	8	1	13
Micronesia, Fed. Sts.	4	2	0	—	1	7	13	2	22
Mongolia	80	32	12	39	6	169	331	80	580
Myanmar	3,630	1,269	285	1,471	573	7,228	5,655	1,640	14,523
Palau	0	0	0	0	0	1	2	0	3

Papua New Guinea	448	109	38	187	84	866	578	162	1,606
Philippines	2,129	997	321	1,046	458	4,951	8,635	1,404	14,990
Samoa	4	1	1	1	1	8	19	2	29
Singapore	20	11	3	1	12	47	369	27	443
Solomon Islands	24	5	2	8	4	43	59	7	109
Thailand	2,838	331	101	288	243	3,801	7,260	1,694	12,755
Timor-Leste	62	20	1	10	4	97	39	17	153
Tonga	2	1	0	1	0	4	11	1	16
Vanuatu	7	1	2	2	1	13	23	3	39
Vietnam	2,337	460	192	744	573	4,306	7,334	1,721	13,361

Source: WHO burden of disease statistics.

Note: — = not available. Data are not available for American Samoa, the Democratic People's Republic of Korea, the Northern Mariana Islands, and Taiwan, China.

Figure 2.18 Expected Increases in Health Expenditures from 2000 to 2020 because of Population and Epidemiologic Dynamics

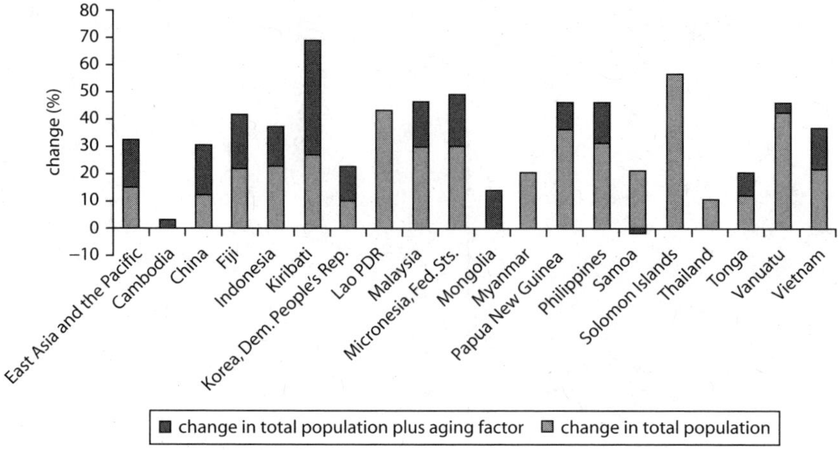

Source: Schieber 2006.

Millennium Development Goals

Although several countries have reached or will reach the human development targets established under the Millennium Development Goals, the difference in achievement across countries is stark (table 2.4). The middle- and near-middle-income countries do better than the low-income states, but performance is by no means uniform within these groupings. Within the first group, Indonesia, the Philippines, and Vietnam still have to catch up with the wealthier MICs. In the latter group, without concerted effort, Cambodia, Lao PDR, Timor-Leste, and several of the more fragile Pacific Island economies may fall short of some of the 2015 targets.

Health Financing Levels and Trends

Global health spending in 2002 was US$3.2 trillion, about 10 percent of the global GDP. Of this expenditure on health, only about 12 percent was spent in LMICs (Gottret and Schieber 2006). High-income countries (HICs) spend about 100 times more on health per capita (population weighted) than do LICs.

Box 2.1

China's Experience with Rising Levels of Non communicable Diseases

The most recent data show that NCDs caused 79 percent of all deaths in China in 2005. Injury caused another 11 percent of deaths. Deaths attributable to infectious diseases and illnesses related to maternal and child health accounted for only 10 percent.

The situation of NCDs will continue to worsen because of two factors. The first is demographics: 144 million people in China are more than 60 years of age, and by 2030, this figure will increase to 300 million. The second factor is epidemiologic: China has about 350 million smokers, and 540 million people inhale secondhand smoke, including 180 million children. In addition, some 160 million people have hypertension, and 160 million people have abnormal cholesterol levels. Half the burden is in rural areas.

Health costs of NCDs are high in China. In 2008, the Ministry of Health estimated that five NCDs—cancers, hypertension, diabetes, cerebrovascular diseases, and ischemic heart diseases—consume 21 percent of total national health expenditures. There is an impact on out-of-pocket costs as well; on average, one episode of inpatient care for any given NCD costs one-half of annual income per capita for urban citizens and one and one-half times annual income per capita for the rural population.

China has no current comprehensive national plan or effective programs for NCD prevention and control. Most interventions have concentrated on secondary or even tertiary clinical care stages and on urban settings, where the mix of services is not cost-effective.

Together, the combination of population growth, an aging population, and a shifting epidemiologic profile suggests that policy makers may need to be concerned about overall macrolevel efficiency of heath care expenditures. Demand for health care will grow significantly by 2020 because of population dynamics alone (figure 2.18) and will be even more explosive for changes in patterns of aging.

In East Asia and the Pacific, total health spending as a share of GDP was between 3 percent and 10 percent in 2005[4] (table 2.5). Total health expenditure as a share of GDP increased modestly per year on average in countries in the region between 2000 and 2005 (table 2.6). This increase in spending was driven largely by sustained increases in public sector spending in China, Japan, Malaysia, and Thailand. By contrast, increased donor spending in Cambodia, Lao PDR, and the Pacific Island countries

Table 2.4 Relative Performance against Selected Millennium Development Goals

Indicator	*Goal*	*East Asia and the Pacific*	*China*	*MICs*[a]	*LICs*[b]
Share of population below US$1 per day purchasing parity power poverty line (%)	15	9	10	8	17
Prevalence of underweight children under 5 years of age (%)	10	15	7	22	29
Net enrollment ratio in primary education (%)	100	93	98	93	94
Ratio of girls to boys in primary and secondary education (%)	100	99	100	97	97
Mortality rate of children under 5 years of age per 1,000 live births	20	33	24	26	93
Maternal mortality rate per 100,000 live births	63	117	45	279	425
Prevalence of tuberculosis per 100,000 people	0	136	99	213	241
Population with access to improved water sources (%)	85	79	77	84	65

Sources: ADB 2007; World Bank's World Development Indicator database.
a. Population-weighted group average for the following MICs and emerging MICs: Indonesia, Malaysia, the Philippines, Thailand, Vietnam, as well as the Pacific Island nations of Fiji, the Federated States of Micronesia, Kiribati, the Marshall Islands, Palau, Samoa, Tonga, and Vanuatu.
b. Population-weighted group average for the following low-income countries: Cambodia, Lao PDR, Mongolia, Myanmar, Papua New Guinea, the Solomon Islands, and Timor-Leste.

explains a large proportion of the growth in overall spending. Only in Vietnam, with the initiation of user fees, has the increase in overall health spending been driven by an increase in out-of-pocket (OOP) spending.

Nominal spending elasticities for selected years (1998–2004) for most countries are above 1.0, indicating that expenditures on health are growing faster than GDP overall (figure 2.19). Schieber and Maeda (1997) and later Gottret and Schieber (2006) have documented that income elasticities for health are above 1.0 globally and that elasticities tend to increase on average as national incomes rise.

Public versus Private Expenditures

The balance between public prepayment (tax or social insurance) and OOP payments varies across the region. East Asian and Pacific countries and territories generally conform with the stylized fact that reliance on OOP payments declines and government's share of total financing increases as national income rises (Musgrove and Zeramdini 2001). Globally, the public share of total health spending is 29 percent in LICs, 50 percent in

Table 2.5 Main Health Financing Indicators, 2000–07

Economy	*Total health expenditure per capita (current US$)*	*Total health expenditure (as a % of GDP)*	*Private health expenditure (as a % of GDP)*	*Public health expenditure (as a % of GDP)*
Cambodia	39.0	8.0	6.8	1.2
China	94.3	4.7	2.8	1.9
Fiji	133.6	3.7	0.8	2.9
Hong Kong SAR, China	1,360.0	5.2	2.4	2.8
Indonesia	16.0	1.2	0.5	0.7
Japan	2,358.0	8.0	1.5	6.5
Korea, Rep.	983.0	6.0	2.8	3.2
Lao PDR	18.0	3.6	2.9	0.7
Malaysia	229.1	4.3	1.9	2.4
Mongolia	37.0	4.1	0.2	3.9
Philippines	38.5	3.3	2.0	1.3
Samoa	128.7	5.4	2.1	3.3
Singapore	780.3	3.7	2.1	1.6
Taiwan, China	934.0	6.0	2.3	3.7
Thailand	116.6	3.6	1.3	2.3
Timor-Leste	45.0	13.7	1.8	11.9
Tonga	113.6	5.9	0.7	5.1
Vietnam	46.0	6.3	4.3	2.0

Sources: Country documents from task team leaders.
Note: Data reflect latest available year. Allocations apportioned to public sector financing are based on government revenue allocations; allocations apportioned to private sector financing are based on social health insurance + private health insurance + out-of-pocket payments + other. Data are not available for American Samoa, the Democratic People's Republic of Korea, the Federated States of Micronesia, Kiribati, the Marshall Islands, Myanmar, the Northern Mariana Islands, Palau, Papua New Guinea, the Solomon Islands, and Vanuatu. Total health expenditure per capita reflects 2001 data for Indonesia and 2002 data for Singapore. Total health expenditure as a percentage of GDP reflects 2002 data for Singapore, as obtained from Gottret and Schieber 2006.

MICs, and 65 percent in HICs (Gottret and Schieber 2006). Government share of total health financing ranged from 20 percent to 30 percent in low-income East Asian and Pacific countries such as Cambodia, Lao PDR, and Vietnam, compared to 50 to 60 percent in MICs such as Malaysia and Thailand, consistent with global trends (table 2.7).

OOP spending finances 70 to 80 percent of total expenditures in most LICs in Asia and 40 to 50 percent or less of expenditures in MICs and HICs. There are some exceptions. In Mongolia and the Pacific Island countries, the government is the main financier of health care regardless of the level of income, and it accounts for 80 percent or more of total spending. In Fiji, Samoa, and the Solomon Islands, OOP expenditures account for less than 20 percent of total expenditures. Potential

Table 2.6 Total Health Expenditure as a Share of GDP, 2000–05

	Share of GDP (%)					
Economy	*2000*	*2001*	*2002*	*2003*	*2004*	*2005*
Australia	8.3	8.4	8.6	8.6	8.8	8.8
Brunei Darussalam	2.5	2.6	2.6	2.5	2.2	2.0
Cambodia	5.8	6.2	6.3	6.8	6.6	6.4
China	4.6	4.6	4.8	4.8	4.7	4.7
Fiji	4.7	4.0	4.2	4.1	4.4	4.1
Indonesia	1.7	1.8	1.8	2.2	2.1	2.1
Japan	7.6	7.9	8.0	8.1	8.0	8.0
Korea, Dem. People's Rep.	3.6	3.5	3.5	3.5	3.5	3.5
Korea, Rep.	4.4	5.3	5.2	5.5	5.5	6.0
Lao PDR	3.2	3.3	3.3	4.4	3.9	3.6
Malaysia	3.3	3.5	3.5	4.7	4.5	4.2
Mongolia	5.6	6.0	6.0	5.4	5.0	4.3
Myanmar	2.1	2.1	2.3	2.2	2.2	2.2
Palau	9.7	9.1	10.1	11.5	9.7	9.6
Papua New Guinea	3.6	3.9	4.3	3.9	4.5	4.2
Philippines	3.5	3.2	3.0	3.3	3.3	3.2
Samoa	5.5	4.8	4.8	5.1	4.9	4.8
Singapore	3.4	3.7	3.7	4.2	3.7	3.5
Solomon Islands	5.2	5.4	5.0	5.2	6.0	4.3
Thailand	3.4	3.3	3.7	3.9	3.5	3.5
Timor-Leste	8.9	8.6	8.5	9.2	10.3	13.7
Tonga	5.7	6.8	5.9	5.5	5.3	5.0
Vanuatu	4.4	4.5	4.7	4.6	4.3	4.3
Vietnam	5.4	5.7	5.2	5.3	5.7	6.0
Average of total health expenditure	4.8	4.9	5.0	5.2	5.1	5.1
Weighted average of total health expenditure	4.4	4.4	4.6	4.7	4.6	4.6

Source: Authors' calculations.

explanations for this situation lie in the virtual absence of any significant private provision or financing in these sparsely populated countries. This factor, combined with relatively high levels of political commitment to providing health coverage, means that the government has little choice but to be the predominant financier and provider of health care.

Figure 2.19 Nominal Elasticity of Health Spending, 1989–2004

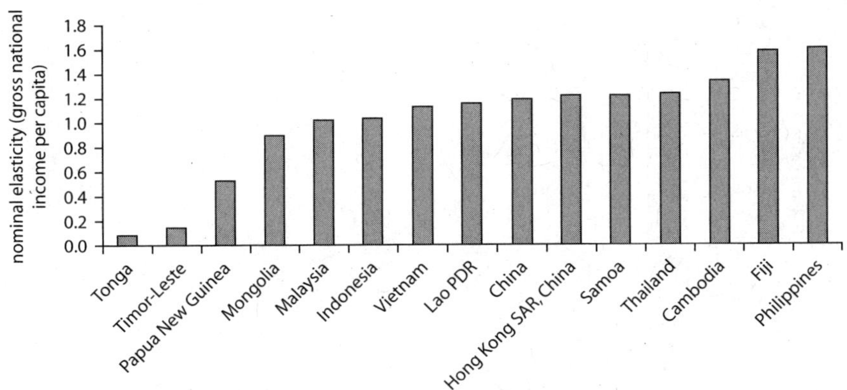

Source: World Bank 2008a, using WHO data.
Note: Insufficient trend data are available to calculate elasticities for American Samoa, the Democratic People's Republic of Korea, Myanmar, the Northern Mariana Island, and Taiwan, China.

In Mongolia, the ratios may be due to informal payments not being captured adequately through existing data systems.

Health Expenditures in East Asia and the Pacific versus Other Regions

In terms of GDP per capita and health expenditure per capita, East Asia and the Pacific is in a middle range compared to other regions (figure 2.20 and table 2.7). Eastern Europe and Central Asia, Latin America and the Caribbean, and the Middle East and North Africa do better on average on both indicators, whereas Sub-Saharan Africa and South Asia do worse. The figures in table 2.7 are consistent with other figures that show that outcomes are relatively good compared to relative expenditures across other regions. Total health spending as a share of GDP, however, is low. Public funding is also relatively low in the region, and financing is more reliant on OOP payments.

Total government revenues as a share of GDP are also low, suggesting the ability to raise revenues may be more limited in East Asia and the Pacific than in other regions. Public funding is also less dependent on external resources. This factor has implications for fiscal space analysis and further suggests public funding is relatively more dependent on political commitment given the relatively low ratios of revenues to GDP. The issues of fiscal space are taken up in more depth in chapter 4, which examines sources of financing for health care services. Finally, some caution is needed with these numbers. The numbers are population

Figure 2.20 GDP and Health Expenditure Per Capita, 2005

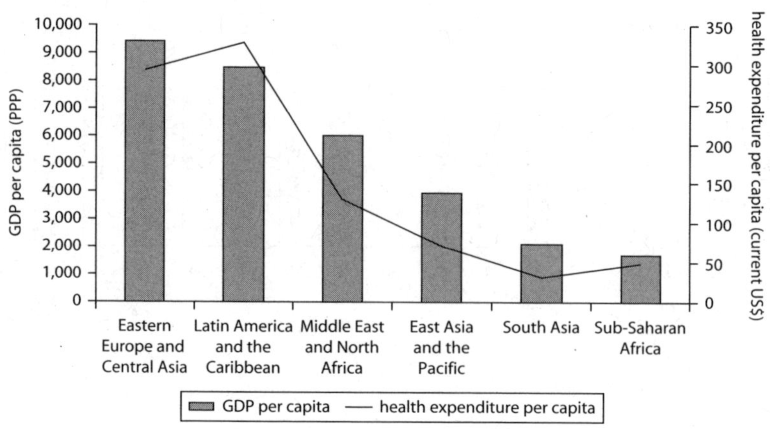

Source: Provisional data from the WHO National Health Accounts database; GDP data from the World Bank's Health, Nutrition, Population Hub database.
Note: PPP = purchasing power parity. Population-weighted averages are calculated to obtain GDP and health expenditure regional averages.

weighted; hence, in East Asia and the Pacific, these averages are heavily influenced by numbers from China.

Expenditures in East Asia and the Pacific Relative to Global Patterns of Expenditure

Per capita health expenditures in the region tend to match GDP per capita, although there are some exceptions, such as in Cambodia (figure 2.21). For the most part, countries in the region tend to be below the regression line relative to expected levels based on global experience. For instance, per capita health spending levels in Indonesia, Malaysia, and Thailand are lower relative to their income levels, whereas those in Cambodia and Vietnam are above the expected income levels.[5]

Government funding for health relative to income largely mirrors the pattern for total health spending (figure 2.22). Again, the regression line for global averages suggests that East Asian and Pacific countries generally commit less public funding to health relative to other countries in similar income categories. Japan, Mongolia, and Samoa are the only countries above the line. The reasons behind this finding are explored in greater depth in chapter 4.

Table 2.7 Regions of the World: Selected Economic and Development Indicators, circa 2005

Region or income class	GDP per capita (US$)	Health expenditures (population-weighted)								
		Health spending per capita (US$)	Total health spending (% of GDP)	Public spending (% of total)	OOP spending (% of total)	Total revenue (% of GDP)	Social security spending (% of total)	External resources (% of total)	Life expectancy	Mortality of children under 5 and infants (per 1,000 live births)
Region										
East Asia and the Pacific	1,662	71	4.4	40.6	50.10	18.70	17.70	0.50	71	28
Eastern Europe and Central Asia	4,690	313	6.7	67.8	27.00	31.80	37.80	1.40	69	26
Latin America and the Caribbean	4,701	332	7.4	51.0	36.90	24.10	17.00	0.40	72	30
Middle East and North Africa	2,149	129	6.0	53.0	42.80	33.50	12.10	1.00	71	39
South Asia	701	31	4.5	20.0	75.30	13.10	0.80	1.90	64	76
Sub-Saharan Africa	551	24	4.5	45.8	46.60	17.50	0.80	15.50	47	161
Income class										
Low income	613	28	4.6	24.2	70.00	12.90	0.92	5.80	59	99
Lower-middle income	2,029	109	5.6	46.6	43.80	25.90	15.00	0.50	71	32
Upper-middle income	6,137	408	6.7	59.1	30.80	30.80	30.90	0.90	70	24
High income	35,446	4,022	11.4	64.5	15.70	27.10	28.30	0.00	79	6

Sources: WHO National Health Accounts database; World Bank's World Development Indicators database.
Note: All regional and income class aggregated data are weighted by the series denominator. Sub-Saharan Africa GDP and health spending data exclude South Africa.

Figure 2.21 Total Health Spending versus Income, 2005

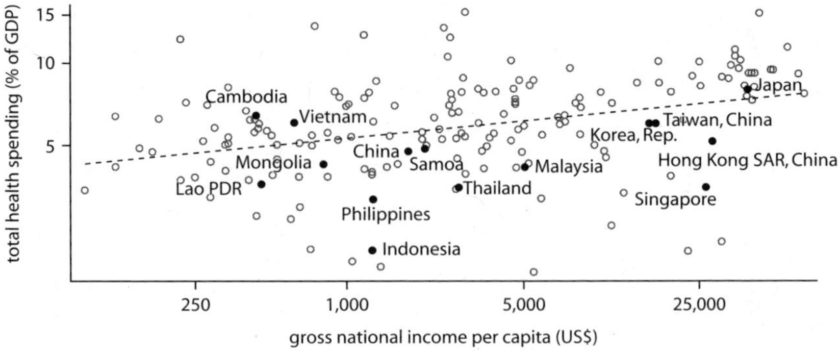

Source: World Bank's World Development Indicators database.
Note: Both axes are in log scale.

Figure 2.22 Government Health Spending versus Income, 2005

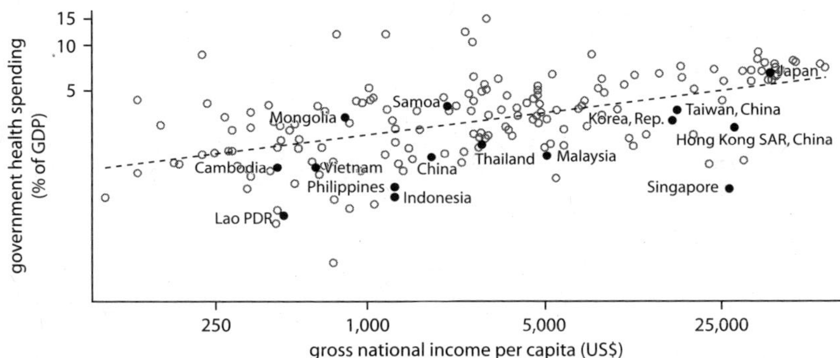

Source: World Bank's World Development Indicators database.
Note: Both axes are in log scale.

Linking Health Expenditures and Delivery of Services

Most LMICs in the region, as well as Hong Kong SAR, China, have direct provision of public sector health services. Under direct provision, the same organization—usually the government—integrates and manages financing and provision of health. Typically, the ministry of finance transfers grants to the ministry of health, which is the owner and financier of hospitals and health centers. In decentralized settings, the ministry of finance transfers block grants to local governments, which are responsible for making allocations to the health sector. In these countries, private sector provision exists in parallel and is concentrated in urban areas. Nongovernmental

Figure 2.23 Global Comparison of Hospital Beds to Population and GDP

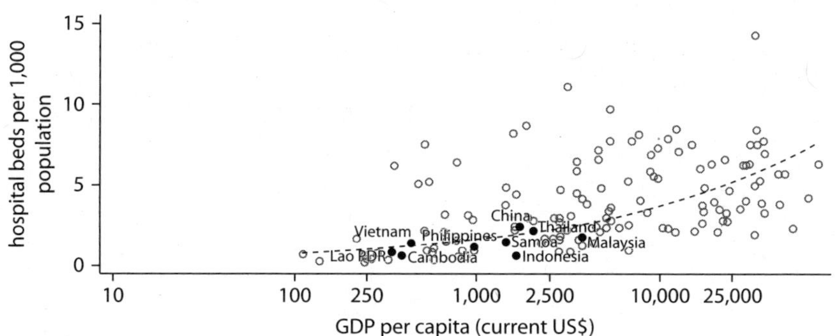

Sources: Bossert and others 2007; World Bank's World Development Indicators database.
Note: The *x* axis is in log scale. Data are for the latest year available.

and religious organizations provide health care, particularly primary care, in countries such as Cambodia and Papua New Guinea. Figures 2.23 and 2.24 show global comparisons of hospital beds, physicians, and health workers. There is significant variation across the region.

In LICs and MICs in East Asia and the Pacific, health facilities are managed by bureaucratic rules rather than on the basis of efficiency of operations. Hospital autonomy exists to a limited extent in Indonesia and Papua New Guinea, as is discussed in more depth in chapter 7. Typically, managers have little authority over spending and hiring decisions, and they have no managerial role in improving efficiency of care. Physicians and health workers are civil servants with job guarantees, and employees are promoted in accordance with civil service rules, without taking into account service performance and patients' satisfaction. Some health workers pursue their own interests, including receiving informal payments from patients to pay for nontaxable salary increases and "moonlighting" in private practice while on the public payroll.

Most HICs in the region have purchaser-provider split models with third-party payers that contract directly with both public and private providers. In the Republic of Korea, the private sector is the main provider of health care. These countries are also characterized by a higher degree of managerial autonomy.

Utilization Patterns and Treatment-Seeking Behaviors

Utilization patterns vary dramatically, with annual per capita visit rates for outpatient care ranging from two visits in China and to nearly 10 in

Figure 2.24 Global Comparisons for Physician and Health Workers to Population Trend Line, 2000–06

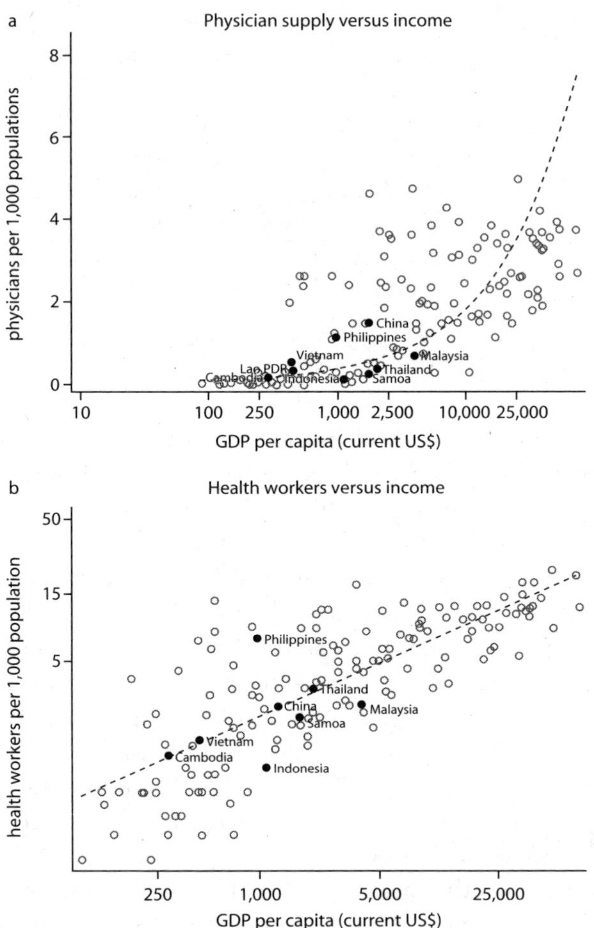

Sources: Bossert and others 2007; World Bank's World Development Indicators database.
Note: Both axes are in log scale. Data are for the latest year available.

Hong Kong SAR, China (table 2.8). Although per capita income is often observed as a key determinant of care-seeking behavior, it is not the only one. Visit rates in middle-income Indonesia, for example, are similar to those in HICs such as Japan. Similar variations are found in hospital admission rates. Table 2.8 provides an overview of health system indicators and characteristics. The data are missing in many of the cells; those cells with data show significant variation in the region on most of these indicators.

Table 2.8 Health System Characteristics

Characteristic	Cambodia	China	Fiji	Hong Kong SAR, China	Indonesia	Japan	Kiribati	Korea, Rep.	Lao PDR	Malaysia	Mongolia	Philippines	Singapore	Solomon Islands	Taiwan, China	Thailand	Timor-Leste	Tonga	Vietnam
Hospitals																			
Public (%)	—	—	—	76	—	20	—	10	—	—	29	38	45	98	15	—	—	—	—
Private (%)	—	—	—	24	—	80	—	90	—	—	71	62	55	2	85	—	—	—	—
Hospital beds																			
Total per 1,000 population	—	—	~2.0	5.2	—	12.9	1.5	7.9	1.2	—	—	—	2.8	—	5.9	—	—	2.9	—
Public per 1,000 population	0.6	2.5	—	4.1	0.4	—	—	—	—	1.4	7.4	0.5	—	—	1.9	1.6	—	—	2.0
Private per 1,000 population	—	0.1	—	0.4	0.2	—	—	—	—	0.4	—	0.5	—	—	3.8	0.4	—	—	—
Public (%)	—	—	—	86	58	33	—	10	—	75	86	50	81	—	32	—	—	—	—
Private (%)	—	—	—	14	42	67	—	90	—	25	14	50	19	—	68	—	—	—	—
Bed occupancy rate (%)																			
Total	75	—	—	—	—	83	—	77	—	—	—	—	—	—	—	—	—	—	95.8
Public	—	65.7	—	77.0	62.9	—	—	—	—	65.1	82.3	—	—	—	70.5	78.2	—	—	—
Private	—	46.6	—	63.5	49.6	—	—	—	—	—	78.6	—	—	—	66.3	54.9	—	—	—

(continued)

Table 2.8 *(continued)*

Characteristic	Cambodia	China	Fiji	Hong Kong SAR, China	Indonesia	Japan	Kiribati	Korea, Rep.	Lao PDR	Malaysia	Mongolia	Philippines	Singapore	Solomon Islands	Taiwan, China	Thailand	Timor-Leste	Tonga	Vietnam
Average length of stay (days)																			
Total	5.0	—	—	—	—	34.7	—	13.6	—	—	—	*2.95*	—	—	—	—	—	—	6.7
Public	—	9.2	—	6.9	5.1	—	—	—	—	4.4	9.5	n.a.	—	—	12.4	4.5	—	—	—
Private	—	8.9	—	3.0	4.2	—	—	—	—	n.a.	9.0	n.a.	—	—	8.5	3.0	—	—	—
Hospital admissions																			
Total per 1,000 population	—	—	~80	—	—	—	—	117.8	—	—	—	—	93.7	—	—	—	—	—	0.1
Public per 1,000 population	—	58.4	—	165.6	204.0	—	—	—	—	72.9	—	—	70.9	—	31.9	103.3	—	—	—
Private per 1,000 population	—	1.8	—	34.8	138.0	—	—	—	—	12.8	—	—	22.7	—	77	27.6	—	—	—
Public (%)	—	—	—	82.0	—	—	—	—	—	81.0	89.6	—	74.0	—	—	—	—	—	—
Private (%)	—	—	—	—	—	—	—	—	—	19.0	10.4	—	26.0	—	—	—	—	—	—
Physicians																			
Total per 1,000 population	—	1.51	—	1.58	0.20	2.02	0.23	1.60	0.40	—	—	—	1.50	—	1.40	—	0.10	—	0.50
Public per 1,000 population	—	1.30	—	0.70	—	—	—	—	—	0.50	—	0.04	—	—	0.35	0.24	—	—	—

Private per 1,000 population	—	0.2	—	1.0	—	—	—	—	—	0.3	—	n.a.	—	—	1.2	0.1	—	—	—
Nurses																			
Total per 1,000 population	—	—	—	—	12.9	6.4	—	1.9	1.0	—	—	—	—	—	—	—	2.2	—	0.6
Public per 1,000 population	—	1.0	—	3.0	—	0.3	—	—	—	1.9	—	0.1	—	—	1.2	1.4	—	—	—
Private per 1,000 population	—	0.1	—	2.2	—	—	—	—	—	0.5	—	—	—	—	3.0	0.2	—	—	—
Outpatient visits	—	1.8	—	9.2	12.2	13.8	—	8.6	—	4.8	5.7	—	—	—	14.7	2.1	1.3	—	1.9
Total per capita	—	—	2.0	—	—	—	—	8.6	—	—	—	—	—	—	—	—	1.3	—	1.9
Public per capita	—	1.7	3.1	2.2	8.1	—	—	—	—	1.8	—	—	—	—	1.5	1.5	—	—	—
Private per capita	—	0.1	0.8	7.0	4.1	—	—	—	—	3.0	—	—	—	—	13.2	0.6	—	—	—

Sources: For most economies, country documents from World Bank task team leaders; for high-income economies,Wagstaff 2007. World Development Indicators data (2004–06) are used for the following countries only: China (physicians per 1,000 population); Kiribati (physicians per 1,000 population and hospital beds per 1,000 population); Tonga (hospital beds per 1,000 population). Average length of stay data for the Philippines are based on PhilHealth data, not national data.

Note: — = n.a. (not applicable). Data reflect latest available year. Data are not available for American Samoa, the Democratic People's Republic of Korea, the Federated States of Micronesia, Myanmar, the Northern Mariana Islands, Palau, Papua New Guinea, and Vanuatu. The Marshall Islands and Samoa are excluded because either the public sector is the sole provider of health services or the provision of services in the private sector is negligible or unknown. In Kiribati and Tonga also, either the public sector is the sole provider of health services or the provision of services in the private sector is negligible or unknown.

Private Provision of Services

The region as a whole includes a large and growing private sector in terms of delivery of care. The private sector remains small in some economies, such as China, Lao PDR, and Vietnam. There is little involvement in hospital services in Hong Kong SAR, China. However, the private sector has grown significantly in Cambodia (mostly nongovernmental organizations), Indonesia, Mongolia, and Philippines over the past decade. The private providers are growing in places such as China and Vietnam as well. The private sector has a dominant role in delivery of care in middle- and upper-income economies such as Japan; the Republic of Korea; Singapore; Taiwan, China; and Thailand. Table 2.9 summarizes

Table 2.9 Public and Private Provision of Care, 2007 or Latest Available Year

Economy	*Public sector*	*Private sector*
Low income		
Cambodia	• 22% of the population uses public providers • 8% of the population seeks care in public hospitals	• Care is provided mainly by nongovernmental organizations, but also by for-profit and traditional medicine providers and by pharmacies • Role in service delivery (particularly for small, physician-owned facilities) is increasing • 48% of population uses private providers
Fiji	• Sector is well developed • 3.1 ambulatory care visits per capita are provided annually	• 0.75 ambulatory care visits per capita are provided annually • Number of private general practitioners and specialists is increasing • Emigration of private providers is occurring
Indonesia	• Sector comprises 7,100 health centers, 23,000 subcenters, and 4,000 mobile clinics	• Growth is rapid since the mid-1990s • Private hospitals (510 in 1998) account for 42% of patient bed days in general hospitals
Kiribati	• Government is the sole provider of health services	• Currently, no private sector providers exist • Efforts are being made to develop private pharmacies and medical practices • Traditional health system comprising traditional healers and using local medicines currently exists

Economy	*Public sector*	*Private sector*
Lao PDR	• System covers 93% of population • Sector is heavily assisted by donors and nongovernmental organizations • Sector comprises 4 central hospitals, 6 specialty centers, 17 provincial and regional hospitals, 141 district hospitals, and 740 health centers • 18,000 public health workers exist • Services are underused	• Sector (which includes 45 nongovernmental organizations) is small but is growing in urban areas • Sector delivers a large proportion of outpatient services • Sector comprises 2,000 private pharmacies, 500 private clinics, and 600 traditional medicine providers • Private hospitals are forthcoming
Marshall Islands	• Services are delivered through hospitals in urban areas and medical dispensaries in outer islands	• No private sector exists • Government is considering contracting the management of remote facilities to nongovernmental organizations
Mongolia	• Focus is shifting from hospital to primary care	• Remarkable growth has occurred • 683 private hospitals (2005) are registered • 200+ family group practices exist • Sector provides 13.9% of hospital beds (2006) • Sector accounts for 10.4% of private hospital admissions (2004)
Papua New Guinea	• Services are primarily provided by public sector	• Churches play a dominant role, running 45 health facilities and employing 23% of health workers. Churches account for 50% of ambulatory care visits • Nongovernmental organizations and church-sponsored organizations (small but increasing), corporate employers (only 50–60 full-time practitioners and 9 small private hospitals), and traditional healers also provide services
Samoa	• Primary provision of health services is through the National Health Service	• Small sector comprises private hospital and various private medical and dental practitioners, pharmacies, physiotherapists, and traditional healers • Nongovernmental organizations provide health care at the community level

(continued)

Table 2.9 *(continued)*

Economy	*Public sector*	*Private sector*
Solomon Islands	• Primary provision of health services is through the public sector • System has a primary health care orientation • Supply of financial and human resources is centrally controlled • Sector employs 89 doctors, 52 dentists, 53 pharmacists, and 620 nurses	• Sector has minimal involvement • Data are not available on the size of health workforce
Timor-Leste	• Health system is mixed, but the Ministry of Health has primary responsibility for service delivery and financing • Sector provides 80% of health services • Ministry of Health employs 1,718 health workers	• Private sector complements the public sector in providing services that the public sector cannot (ambulatory care) • Sector consists primarily of local and international nongovernmental organizations, mostly church affiliated • Sector includes traditional healers, private pharmacies, and drug shops • Size of private sector health workforce is unavailable
Tonga	• Small government clinics offer preventive and curative care • Secondary-level care is provided by Vaiola Hospital, Tonga's only referral facility, which is closely integrated with lower-level facilities	• Nominal private sector exists • Only 10 private clinics offer outpatient care • No private diagnostic or hospital services exist • All private providers are Ministry of Health employees working after hours • Foundation-based organizations play a minor role
Vanuatu	• Public sector offers inpatient and outpatient services • Network of 5 hospitals, 25 health centers, 80 dispensaries, and 180 health aid posts exists	• Private sector is limited to outpatient services
Vietnam	• Decentralized system exists, with services administered by the Ministry of Health (at the central level), provincial health offices, district health offices, and community health centers	• Small private sector has been expanding • Sector comprises private providers (18%), general practitioner clinics (16%), traditional medicine clinics (14%), private pharmacies (14%), and nursing homes (12%)

Economy	*Public sector*	*Private sector*
		• Sector accounts for 50% of outpatient visits • Sector consists of public providers working after hours and retirees from public sector • Number of private health workers is unknown
Middle income		
China	• Public provision has declined over time • Public providers compete with private providers in the market • Sector accounts for 96.2%, 97.1%, and 98.2% of all outpatient, inpatient, and emergency episodes • Conversion of facilities from public to private ownership is increasing	• Sector is increasing, with beginnings in 1980s
Malaysia	• Ministry of Health is the major provider of services, accounting for 75% of hospital beds and 80% of hospital admissions	• Sector accounts for 57% of outpatient visits and 18% of admissions, and its presence is increasing over time • Private providers account for two-thirds of physicians and specialist services • Government contracts with nonstate providers and outsources specific service areas
Philippines	• Sector provides subsidized public health services • Services are delivered by local government units • Central government controls regional and tertiary hospitals • Health workforce in 2005 comprises 2,967 government doctors, 1,946 dentists, 4,519 nurses, and 17,300 midwives • In 2005, the sector accounted for 38% of hospitals and 50% of hospital beds	• Sector manages hospital and physician clinics and diagnostic centers • In 2005, the sector accounted for 62% of hospitals and 50% of hospital beds • 66% of private facilities are primary care facilities • Health workforce data are not available • Few cases exist of local government units contracting out health service delivery for indigents to private facilities

(continued)

Table 2.9 *(continued)*

Economy	*Public sector*	*Private sector*
Thailand	• Ministry of Health is the principal agency for public service provision. Other ministries also provide services • Public hospital bed ratio is 1.64 • Bed occupancy rate is 78.2% • Average length of stay is 4.5 days • Sector has more physicians and nurses than does the private sector	• Sector plays a large role in service delivery • Private hospitals seek to increase their breadth of services • Most private hospitals are secondary-level facilities • Private hospital bed ratio is 0.41 • Bed occupancy rate is 54.9% • Average length of stay is 3 days
High income		
Hong Kong SAR, China	• Health care infrastructure is largely publicly funded and provided • Public services are commissioned, funded, and directly provided by the government, through the statutory Hospital Authority • 45.7% of registered doctors work in the Hospital Authority, 5.7% in the Department of Health, and 3.5% in the academic and subvented sectors • Sector accounts for 24% of outpatient visits • Sector accounts for 92% of total bed days	• Private services account for 74% of ambulatory care visits and 8% of inpatient bed days • Private services are funded through out-of-pocket payments and employer-provided insurance policies • Typically for middle- and upper-income groups, supplementary private insurance is provided by employers or self-purchased • Sector also provides Chinese medicine and other traditional or nonallopathic healers • Few experiments have occurred with public-private partnerships (for example, contracting out of some common, high-volume procedures such as cataract surgery to reduce excessively long waits) • 44.7% of registered physicians work in private practice as full-time private physicians • 12 private hospitals account for 8% of bed days • 50% of all specialists work in the private setting
Japan	• Health system mainly combines private provision of services with mandatory public health insurance • All residents are eligible to receive benefits from social health insurance • Providers are either office-based or hospital-based physicians	

Economy	*Public sector*	*Private sector*
	• Hospitals include privately owned hospitals, public hospitals run by the government (mostly at the local level), and university hospitals • Investor-owned for-profit hospitals are prohibited • More than 50,000 insurers, 9,000 hospitals, and 90,000 clinics exist, as well as a large number of doctors, dentists, and pharmacists • 13 million admissions and 4 billion outpatient visits (an average of 31.5 visits per person) occur annually	
Korea, Rep.	• Sector accounts for 7% of all local hospitals and 20% of all general hospitals	• Sector has continued to grow with the increase in per capita income and the expansion of health insurance coverage • Clinics are 100% private • 87% of the 7.1 hospital beds per 1,000 population are in private hospitals and clinics
Singapore	• Health services are provided through 3 cooperating ministries, as well as the private sector; the Ministry of Health is responsible for providing preventive, curative, and rehabilitative health services • Dual system of health service delivery exists • Public system is managed by the government • Private medical insurance is available • Private providers are required to publish price lists to encourage comparison shopping • Private sector is operated by private hospitals and general practitioners • System includes primary health services provided at outpatient polyclinics and private medical practitioner clinics and secondary and tertiary specialist care provided at public and private hospitals • Highly privatized health care system emphasizes individual fiscal responsibility • Private sector competes with the public health system, which helps to contain prices in both directions • Private practitioners provide 80% of primary health services, while government polyclinics provide the remainder • 80% of hospital care is provided by the public sector and the remainder by the private sector	
Taiwan, China	• 1.9 hospital beds exist per 1,000 population • 31.87 hospital admissions occur per 1,000 population	• Sector accounts for 85% of hospitals (547) and 66% of total hospital beds (hospital beds per 1,000 = 3.8) • 77.02 hospital admissions occur per 1,000 population • 19,135 clinics (facilities with < 10 beds) exist; nearly all are owned and operated by private practicing physicians as part of their medical practice

Source: Authors' compilation.

the key features of public and private sector provision in East Asia and the Pacific.

In terms of setting of care services, outpatient or primary care is sought at both public and private providers in most countries in the region. Inpatient care services are sought predominantly at public hospitals in LMICs in the region. Except in Thailand, private hospitals are used mostly by the richest 5 to 10 percent of households. Use of informal and unqualified providers is common in many LICs in East Asia and the Pacific. Traditional medicine—particularly traditional Chinese medicine providers—are sought out quite frequently in many economies in the region, including in high-income economies such as Taiwan, China. This issue of emergence of the private sector and related issues of governance and coordination across the public and private sectors and its relationship to financing of care is discussed further in subsequent chapters.

Notes

1. The United Kingdom's Department for International Development defines fragile states as those where the government cannot or will not deliver core functions to the majority of its people, including the poor (DFID 2005).
2. See the National Health Accounts database of the World Health Organization.
3. WHO burden of disease estimates for East Asian and Pacific countries are presented for 2002 (the latest available year) and are based on the Global Burden of Disease study (version 3). This summary represents WHO's best estimate, based on the evidence available in mid-2004, rather than the official estimates of member states. The burden of disease estimates for 2005 are not yet available.
4. The most recent year for which expenditure data are available for all of the countries in the region is 2005.
5. Health expenditure data are based on national health accounts in most cases. In some cases, these estimates may not include spending by the military and by other agencies whose primary objective is not to provide health care. Informal payments for health services, which are thought to be widespread, are included only to the extent that they are captured by household surveys. See appendix A for a review of national health accounts in the region.

References

ADB (Asian Development Bank). 2007. *Key Indicators of Developing Asian and Pacific Countries 2007.* Manila: ADB.

Bossert, Thomas, Till Bärnighausen, Diana Bowser, Andrew Mitchell, and Gülin Gedik. 2007. "Assessing Financing, Education, Management, and Policy Context for Strategic Planning of Human Resources for Health." World Health Organization, Geneva.

DFID (U.K. Department for International Development). 2005. "Reducing Poverty by Tackling Social Exclusion: A DFID Policy Paper." London, DFID.

Gottret, Pablo, and George Schieber. 2006. *Health Financing Revisited: A Practitioner's Guide*. Washington, DC: World Bank.

Mathers, Colin D., and Dejan Loncar. 2005. "Updated Projections of Global Mortality and Burden of Disease, 2002–2030: Data Sources, Methods, and Results." Evidence and Information for Policy Working Paper, World Health Organization, Geneva.

Musgrove, Philip, and Riadh Zeramdini. 2001. "A Summary Description of Health Financing in WHO Member States." CMH Working Paper 3, Commission on Macroeconomics and Health, Geneva.

Schieber, George. 2006. "Assessing Demographic and Epidemiologic Trends and Implications for Health Care Delivery and Financing." Presentation at the Europe and Central Asia/Middle East and North Africa Regional World Bank Conference, Istanbul, October.

Schieber, George, and Akiko Maeda. 1997. "A Curmudgeon's Guide to Health Care Financing in Developing Countries." In *Innovations in Health Care: Proceedings of a World Bank Conference, March 10–11, 1997*, ed. George Schieber, 1–40. Washington, DC: World Bank.

Wagstaff, Adam. 2007. "Health Systems in East Asia: What Can Developing Countries Learn from Japan and the Asian Tigers?" *Health Economics*, 16 (5): 441–56.

World Bank. 2006. *Repositioning Nutrition as Central to Development: A Strategy for Large-Scale Action*. Washington, DC: World Bank.

———. 2008a. *Good Practices in Health Financing: Lessons from Reforms in Low- and Middle-Income Countries*. Washington, DC: World Bank.

———. 2008b. "Health Financing in Lao PDR: Issues and Options." Overview Concept Note, World Bank, Washington, DC.

———. 2008c. *Regional Strategy: East Asia and Pacific Region*. Washington, DC: World Bank.

———. 2008d. "Timor-Leste: Health Sector Review." World Bank, Washington, DC.

———. 2009. *Regional Strategy Update: Navigating the Crisis, Securing the Future*. Washington, DC: World Bank.

CHAPTER 3

Importance of Investing in Health and a Framework for Managing and Using Funds

This chapter is a prelude to the rest of the book. It sets out the case for investing in health and explains why health financing is a key policy lever. It also describes the goals of health financing.

Health and Its Effects on Economic Growth

Countries in East Asia and the Pacific have an opportunity to use the current patterns of economic growth to advance their reform agenda, and the health sector presents one such opportunity. Strong cross-country correlations between (a) aggregate measures of health, such as life expectancy or child mortality, and (b) per capita income are well established.

The adage "health is wealth" is still, primarily, an intuitive proposition; however, a vast majority of researchers present theoretical and empirical evidence of the reverse proposition that "wealth is health." Consequently, contemporary discussions on health reforms typically see the delivery of health care as a cost that needs to be contained, hence implying that income is the instrument and health outcomes the end-points of development objectives (Suhrcke and others 2005). This view perhaps undermines the role that health plays in economic development. Notwithstanding widespread recognition that population health is an important factor in strengthening economies and reducing poverty, health and longevity remain predominantly a subject in the field of demography and epidemiology rather than mainstream economics.

A recent strand of literature, however, reflects significant changes in these perceptions: improvements in health and longevity are no longer viewed as a mere by-product of economic development. The argument is that improved health is one of the key determinants of, and a means to achieve, economic development and poverty reduction (Bloom and Canning 2005). Weil (2001) estimates the relationship between health and labor productivity using a population's adult survival rate. In his analysis, he finds that workers in a low-mortality country are about 68 percent more productive than workers in a higher-mortality country, and he estimates about 17 percent of the variation in output per worker across countries can be attributed to health differentials. In comparison, physical capital is estimated to account for 18 percent of the variation, and education, 21 percent. Sala-i-Martin (1997) found that initial health is one of the most robust predictors of subsequent economic growth.

Global cross-country analysis reveals that income elasticity for consumption of health services stands at around 1.2 for middle-income countries (table 3.1). This figure indicates that demand for health services grows at a rate 20 percent higher than the overall economic growth rate. Chapter 2 (in figure 2.19) showed that the patterns for East Asian and Pacific countries are similar—on a longitudinal basis—with most above 1.0 for 1989 to 2004.

Thus, more recent research seems to suggest that better health does not have to wait for an improved economy. Measures to reduce the burden of disease, to ensure that children have healthy childhoods, and to

Table 3.1 Global Averages of Nominal Elasticity of Health Spending on Income, 1989–2004

Category	*Elasticity of health spending on income (gross national income per capita)*
Low-income countries	0.85
Middle-income countries	1.17
High-income countries	1.26

Source: World Bank's World Development Indicators database, using World Health Organization data.
Note: Insufficient trend data are available to calculate elasticities for Afghanistan, Andorra, Côte d'Ivoire, Cuba, the Democratic Republic of Congo, the Democratic People's Republic of Korea, The Gambia, Iraq, the Republic of Korea, Mayotte, Myanmar, Serbia, Papua New Guinea, São Tomé and Príncipe, Somalia, and the Republic of Yemen.

increase life expectancy will, in themselves, contribute to creating richer economies (Alsan, Bloom, and Canning 2006).

Health Care Financing Function and Goals

Investing in health is not enough if such investments are not managed and allocated well. Before examining and assessing details of health financing in East Asia and the Pacific, one must develop a conceptual framework. Wagstaff and others (2009) have neatly summarized the World Health Organization (WHO) report on health systems (WHO 2000) and have provided a useful way of thinking about this issue.

Increasingly, health systems are seen in terms of *actors* performing *functions*, and these functions are seen as being geared toward the health system achieving *goals*. The overriding goal is better health, and the subsidiary goal in many countries is equity of health—not necessarily full equity but some acceptable level of inequality. A second basic goal is financial protection. The ability to buy food and shelter should not be compromised by unforeseen (and largely unforeseeable) health shocks that necessitate possibly large amounts of spending on health care. A third goal is responsiveness or patient satisfaction. It is important how well a health system responds to people's nonmedical expectations concerning areas such as being treated with dignity. The key actors in any health system include patients and households, health care providers, health financiers and insurers, and the government (WHO 2000).

The most basic function of any health system is delivering health care. This function entails delivering the right care, depending on the needs of the person, when the person needs it. Doing so requires resources: human resources (doctors, nurses, pharmacists, and managers); medicines and other consumables; equipment; and physical infrastructure. Creating resources (training doctors, developing and acquiring medicines, and investing in and maintaining equipment and infrastructure) is an important second function of any health system. Delivering health care and creating the necessary resources entail expenditures—often very large ones. Thus, financing health care—finding the money to pay for the whole enterprise and seeing that providers get paid—is a third function of any health system.

Health financing and resource allocation for services are critical dimensions of health policy in all countries of the world. Revenues for services need to integrate and interact with tax policy and with broader macroeconomic and fiscal goals. Typical sources of revenue include out-of-pocket payments, contributions to social insurance schemes, taxes and other government revenues, private insurance premiums, and development assistance.

Pooling and management of funds are a common theme in health financing; they are directly linked to one of the principal goals of health financing reform (and, indeed, of health systems more generally): improving protection against the financial risk of using health care services. Experience with reforms in other countries suggests that pooling has two aspects: (a) as a policy objective (that is, risk pooling) and (b) as a policy instrument (changes in the way that funds are accumulated in the health system). When patients pay providers directly out of pocket, there is no pooling of risk. If a village mounts a community insurance scheme, the households in the village pool their risk with one another. In a social insurance scheme, the risk pool is larger and more diverse. A tax-financed health system is also a mechanism by which risks are pooled.

Resource allocation and purchasing decisions also relate to policy decisions regarding both equity and efficiency. Such factors include who is covered, what services are covered, who can deliver services, and what incentive structure underlies the payment for services rendered. Patients and third-party payers (for example, insurers and ministries of health) can be thought of as buying services from providers. Purchasing encompasses a number of different aspects, such as who will determine what will be purchased (the provider or the purchaser), what basis will be used to make such decisions, who will deliver the service, and how the provider will be paid. These questions are equally important whether the services are of a public health nature (both population interventions and personal ones) or of a private nature.

Each of these functions is itself exceedingly complex; each not only needs to be performed well but must be performed in close coordination with the others. Overseeing the health system is the task of making sure the actors who perform the various functions do so in a competent and coordinated fashion. It is, in effect, another function of a health system. It is often thought of as one of stewardship.

According to the WHO definition, the purpose of health sector financing is to generate sufficient funds to motivate health care providers in a manner that would ensure society's access to individual and public health care and medical services (WHO 2000). The success of the financing process depends on the performance of these three important functions: revenue collection, pooling of resources, and purchasing of services and interventions (figure 3.1).

Figure 3.1 Flow of Funds and Functions for Health Financing

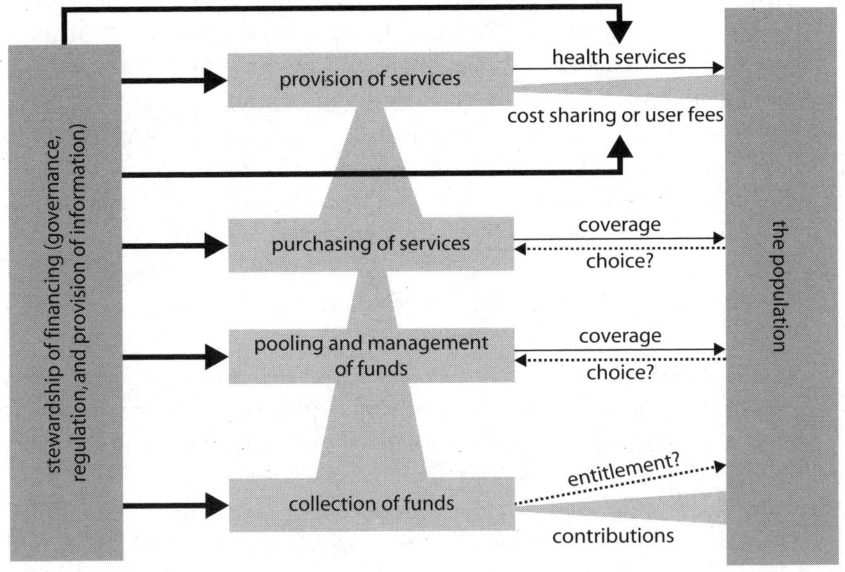

Source: Adapted from Kutzin 2010.

The next three chapters discuss the current systems in East Asia and the Pacific in terms of sources of financing (revenues), pooling and management, and resource allocation. For each of the three functions of financing, strengths and weaknesses are assessed and opportunities for restructuring are reviewed. International best-practice models are provided as examples of what policy makers may consider for future paths. Furthermore, these three chapters contain a discussion of the governance and regulatory arrangements in place in the current financing system.

An examination of the current financing systems suggests that opportunities exist to raise more revenues through public channels, to improve pooling, and to allocate resources more effectively. The book later integrates the discussion with conclusions and recommendations for consideration of changes in health financing.

References

Alsan, Marcella, David E. Bloom, and David Canning. 2006. "The Effect of Population Health on Foreign Direct Investment Inflows to Low- and Middle-Income Countries." *World Development* 34 (4): 613–30.

Bloom, David E., and David Canning. 2005. "Health and Economic Growth: Reconciling the Micro and Macro Evidence." CDDRL Working Paper, Center on Democracy, Development, and the Rule of Law, Stanford Institute on International Studies, Stanford University, Stanford, CA.

Kutzin, Joseph. 2010. "Conceptual Framework for Analyzing Health Financing Systems and the Effects of Reforms." In *Implementing Health Financing Reform: Lessons from Countries in Transition*, ed. Joseph Kutzin, Cheryl Cashin, and Melitta Jakab, 3–24. Copenhagen: World Health Organization, on behalf of the European Observatory on Health Systems.

Sala-i-Martin, Xavier. 1997. "I Just Ran Four Million Regressions." NBER Working Paper 6252, National Bureau of Economic Research, Cambridge, MA.

Suhrcke, Marc, Martin McKee, Regina Sauto Arce, Svetla Tsolova, and Jørgen Mortensen. 2005. "The Contribution of Health to the Economy in the European Union." Health and Consumer Protection Directorate-General, European Commission, Brussels.

Wagstaff, Adam, Magnus Lindelow, Shiyong Wang, and Shuo Zhang. 2009. *Reforming China's Rural Health System*. Washington, DC: World Bank.

Weil, David. 2001. "Accounting for the Effect of Health on Economic Growth." Brown University, Providence.

WHO (World Health Organization). 2000. *The World Health Report 2000: Health Systems—Improving Performance*. Geneva: WHO.

CHAPTER 4

Mobilization of Revenues for Health

Assessment of the Mix of Health Financing Revenues

The key health financing issues for low- and middle-income countries (LMICs) are how to mobilize sufficient resources to finance health services without resorting to excessive public sector borrowing and how to raise revenues equitably and efficiently. The process of achieving universal coverage through insurance is at varying stages of development across East Asia and the Pacific, as discussed in chapters 5 and 6 of this book. In LMICs, health care is almost exclusively financed by sources such as out-of-pocket (OOP) payments and general government revenues (GGRs). In high-income countries (HICs), social insurance is usually funded by employee and employer contributions, with state subsidies for low-income groups. There are exceptions to these patterns, and middle-income country (MIC) or HIC status is not always associated with universal coverage.

From a public finance perspective, all sources of revenues for health care should be judged by the following criteria (Gottret and Schieber 2006):

- Revenue adequacy and stability. The tax should raise a significant amount of revenue, be relatively stable, and grow over time.

- Efficiency. The tax should minimize distortions on labor markets and capital formation.
- Equity. The tax should treat all income groups fairly.
- Ease of collection. The tax should be simple to administer.
- Political acceptability. The use of taxes should be transparent to promote acceptability.

These criteria highlight the need to examine revenue sources for health in the context of the overall macroeconomic environment. Economic growth is a prerequisite for expanding the general revenue base, which is critical for increasing health expenditures. Increasing taxes to pay for health care, whether indirectly (for example, through income taxes) or directly (for example, through payroll contributions), could distort economic activity. Economic growth could be affected as a consequence.

The discussion in this section is grouped according to the three categories of high-, middle-, and low-income economies. The current mix of financing in each group is reviewed against a framework of global experiences as set out by Gottret and Schieber (2006) and against the public finance criteria.

High-Income Economies

Public prepayment, consisting of taxes and social insurance, is the largest source of health financing and expenditures in high-income East Asian and Pacific economies, as it is in many Organisation for Economic Co-operation and Development (OECD) countries. In East Asia and the Pacific, Japan, the Republic of Korea, and Taiwan, China, derive most of their health care resources from social security contributions, and Hong Kong SAR, China, derives its resources from direct and indirect tax payments in national health services. Singapore finances health care through government revenues and medical savings accounts. Figure 4.1 shows the shares of tax and social insurance financing across high-income economies globally. Notably, in HICs outside Asia, particularly in Europe, many health systems are predominantly tax financed. Moreover, in recent years, three of the oldest countries financed by social health insurance (SHI)—France, Germany, and the Netherlands—have reduced their reliance on payroll-based taxes (contributions) as sources of financing. By contrast, high-income economies in East Asia and the Pacific all rely primarily on social insurance financing, with the exception of Hong Kong SAR, China, and, to a lesser degree, Singapore.

Figure 4.1 Share of Tax and Social Insurance Revenues in Total Health Expenditure in High-Income Economies Globally

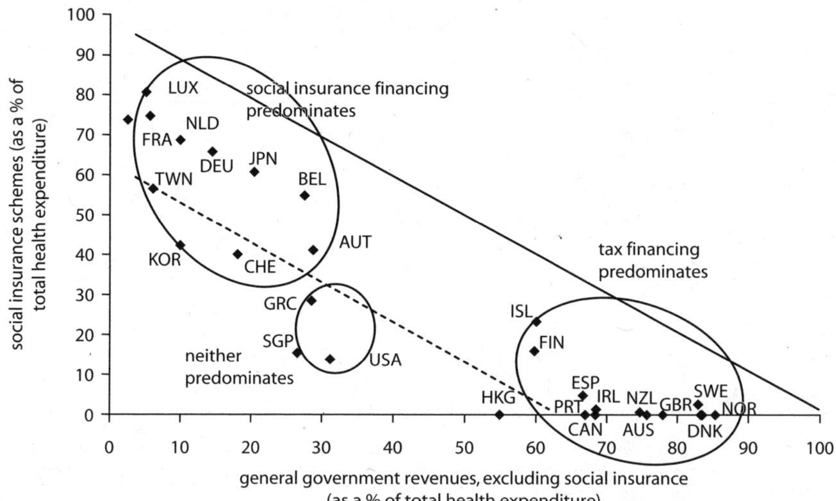

Sources: Gottret and Schieber 2006, except data for Hong Kong SAR, China, and Taiwan, China, which are from domestic health accounts estimates for 2007 (Hong Kong SAR, China) and Department of Health health and national health insurance statistics for 2006 (Taiwan, China).

Note: AUS = Australia; AUT = Austria; BEL = Belgium; CAN = Canada; DNK = Denmark; FIN = Finland; FRA = France; DEU = Germany; GRC = Greece; HKG = Hong Kong SAR, China; ISL = Iceland; IRL = Ireland; JPN = Japan; LUX = Luxembourg; NLD = Netherlands; NZL = New Zealand; NOR = Norway; PRT = Portugal; KOR = Republic of Korea; SGP = Singapore; ESP = Spain; SWE = Sweden; CHE = Switzerland; TWN = Taiwan, China; GBR = United Kingdom; USA = United States of America.

Compulsory social insurance contributions

In 2007, the share of compulsory payroll related social insurance contributions in total health expenditures was 41 percent in the Republic of Korea and 54 percent in both. Japan and Taiwan, China. Although Japan has historically relied primarily on compulsory social insurance contributions to finance health, the Republic of Korea and Taiwan, China, have moved to SHI only in the past few decades. The Republic of Korea was a predominantly privately financed system, with taxes as the second most important financing mechanism in the 1970s. Like Germany and several other European countries, the Republic of Korea started with a small scheme for industrial workers in 1977 and gradually extended the scheme to other populations. Similarly, National Health Insurance in Taiwan, China, was established in the late 1990s by merging the existing social insurance programs for health and expanding coverage to the uninsured.

Table 4.1 Sources of Financing for Health in High-Income Economies in East Asia and the Pacific, 2000–07

	Share of total health revenues (%)				
Source	*Hong Kong SAR, China*	*Japan*	*Korea, Rep.*	*Singapore*	*Taiwan, China*
Direct tax	33.3	19.5	4.8	—	3.7
Indirect tax	11.2	13.7	6.3	—	2.7
Nontax revenues	10.3	0.0	0.8	26.5	0.0
Social health insurance	0.0	54.0	41.1	15.5	54.3
Private insurance	12.5	12.8	3.4	—	11.4
OOP payments	31.8	0.0	37.7	58.0	25.4
Other	0.9	0.0	5.9	0.0	2.5
Total	100.0	100.0	100.0	100.0	100.0

Sources: Country documents.
Note: — = not available. Data reflect latest available period.

A large portion of prepayment revenues in social insurance systems is raised through wage-related contributions. In East Asia and the Pacific, as in Europe and elsewhere, contributions are shared between employers and employees. However, arrangements differ among countries. All individuals who are insured contribute at a uniform rate in the Republic of Korea and Taiwan, China, as has been the practice in Austria (since 2004), Belgium, France, Luxembourg, and the Netherlands. In Japan, rates differ according to employment status (Gottret and Schieber 2006).

In the Republic of Korea, the uniform premium rate of 4.48 percent of wages for all employed people is shared equally between employers (the government, in the case of civil servants) and employees. The premium basis for the self-employed depends on taxable income, assets, automobiles, sex, and age. The contribution rate is one of the lowest among OECD economies, but a low rate means that benefits are limited (see forthcoming volume of East Asia and the Pacific Country Health financing Profiles), as discussed in chapter 6 of this book.

In Taiwan, China, the premium is shared among employers, employees, and the government in the ratio of 60:30:10 (see forthcoming volume of East Asia and the Pacific Country Health Financing Profiles). Employers have to pay for the worker and 0.7 dependents, and workers have to pay the premium for themselves and a maximum of three dependents. Imposing a premium per insured employee penalizes workers with large families or with surviving unemployed parents. As the program ran into deficit in 2002, the government raised the wage contribution rate from 4.25 percent to 4.55 percent.

General revenues: Direct and indirect taxes

Hong Kong SAR, China, is the only high-income economy in East Asia and the Pacific that collects more than half of its publicly funded prepayment through general revenues rather than social insurance (table 4.1). In this respect, Hong Kong SAR, China, is similar to Iceland, New Zealand, Spain, and the United Kingdom. Notably, Iceland and Spain (both previously social insurance–financed countries) moved to tax financing motivated by the perception that tax financing was less regressive (Gottret and Schieber 2006). Progressivity of sources of health financing in East Asia and the Pacific is discussed in chapter 8 of this book. Direct and indirect general revenue taxes also contribute to overall sources of financing in the social insurance–financed countries in East Asia and the Pacific: about 33.2 percent in Japan, 11.1 percent in Korea, and 6.4 percent in Taiwan, China.

Voluntary insurance

Voluntary or private health insurance accounts for a relatively low share of overall health expenditures in high-income East Asian and Pacific economies. The relative shares are 12.8 percent in Japan; 12.5 percent in Hong Kong SAR, China; 11.4 percent in Taiwan, China; and 3.4 percent in the Republic of Korea. Voluntary health insurance in East Asia and the Pacific may be classified as duplicate, complementary, or supplementary (box 4.1).

Hong Kong SAR, China, has *duplicate health insurance,* which is typically available in national health systems with tax-financed schemes under which the amount or the quality of publicly provided health services is perceived to be insufficient or inappropriate. The main drivers are the length of waiting lists and the desire to choose providers, particularly in the private sector. The share of the population covered by voluntary health insurance in Hong Kong SAR, China, is 30 percent, compared to more than 40 percent in Australia and Ireland, and 35 percent in New Zealand (Gottret and Schieber 2006). Employer-provided medical benefits for private care typically form part of the remuneration package. Individually purchased insurance premiums vary greatly in design, ranging from capped indemnity plans to per diem cash rebates, mostly for hospitalization only.

Box 4.1

Types of Voluntary Health Insurance

Substitute health insurance: Provides an alternative to statutory schemes.

Supplementary health insurance: Covers services not included in the benefits package of statutory schemes and provides superior amenities.

Duplicate health insurance: Providesindividuals already covered by a given public health system with private alternative coverage for the same set of services, often furnished by different providers.

Complementary health insurance: Covers copayments or deductibles applicable to public health systems.

Sources: Gottret and Schieber 2006; OECD 2004.

Voluntary health insurance in the Republic of Korea and Taiwan, China, may be classified as *complementary health insurance.* This type of insurance accounts for much of the spending on private health insurance in OECD countries. In France, for instance, complementary health insurance is purchased to cover coinsurance rates ranging from 20 percent for inpatient treatment to 30 percent for physician fees. The main motivation, therefore, is to limit the financial risk posed by high use of services (Gottret and Schieber 2006). It is therefore surprising that the market for complementary health insurance is not significant in the Republic of Korea, a country with relatively high coinsurance rates.

Under Japan's social insurance system, individuals cannot opt out of the social insurance system. However, *supplementary health insurance* is available to cover additional related expenditures (such as costs of family visits to the hospital and income loss because of hospital stays). For each episode of disease, the patient can receive private health care services, if the patient can afford to pay for them. These services cannot be used or paid for under SHI. In such cases, none of the costs of services to treat the episode of illness will be covered by the scheme to which the patient belongs. These costs are considered OOP obligations (Hasegawa 2005).

Medical savings accounts

Under the Medisave program in Singapore, every employed citizen is required to deposit 6 to 8 percent of his or her income (depending on age) into an individual account managed by the state. The government invests the funds in the capital market and pays interest on the account at the prevailing market rate. This program is supplemented by a high-risk insurance scheme (Medishield), which is funded by contributions depending on age and can be financed from Medisave accounts. In addition, a fund (Medifund) financed by tax subsidies is used to support low-income individuals who do not have Medisave or Medishield (Gottret and Schieber 2006).

Out-of-pocket payments

The share of OOP payments in total health expenditure is relatively high in high-income East Asian and Pacific economies compared to other OECD countries (figure 4.2). The OOP payment share of total health expenditure was 32 percent in Hong Kong SAR, China; 38 percent in the Republic of Korea; and 35 percent in Taiwan, China, in 2005. Only in Japan is it relatively low at 13 percent. By comparison, the OOP share in most OECD countries was less than 30 percent in 2005. Switzerland (about 30 percent) has some of the highest shares of OOP payments in the OECD.

As is often the case in tax-financed countries, OOP payments in Hong Kong SAR, China, are predominantly used to pay for services obtained from private health care providers. Payments to private ambulatory care providers and traditional medical providers account for about

Figure 4.2 Out-of-Pocket Payments as a Proportion of Total Health Expenditure for High-Income Economies, 2005

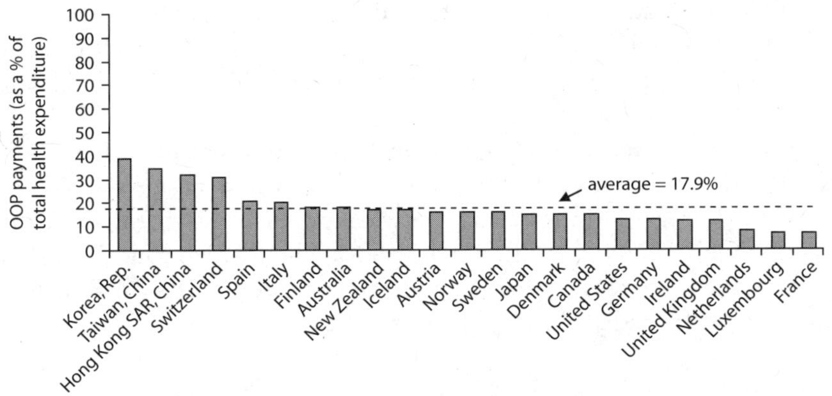

Sources: World Health Organization's National Health Accounts database, except data for Hong Kong SAR, China, and Taiwan, China. Data for Taiwan, China, are based on Department of Health statistics, but other sources vary.
Note: Data for Hong Kong SAR, China,are from 2004/05.

75.0 percent of all OOP payments. User charges from government providers are nominal and account for only about 6.5 percent of total OOP spending.

In social insurance–financed countries in East Asia and the Pacific, OOP payments consist of copayments, coinsurance, and deductibles. In the Republic of Korea, copayments are 20 percent for inpatient care and 30 to 55 percent for outpatient care. In addition, some services are not covered by SHI at all. It is estimated that the sum of copayments and direct OOP payments accounts for 40 to 50 percent of outpatient care costs and 60 to 70 percent of inpatient care costs in the Republic of Korea. In Taiwan, China, copayments for inpatient care are 10 percent if the length of stay is less than 30 days, and the copayment is higher for longer stays. In principle, OOP payments (especially copayments, coinsurance, and deductibles) prevent the moral hazard arising in HICs (Zweifel and Manning 2001). However, OOP payments are a regressive source of financing in high-income East Asian and Pacific economies, as will be discussed in more detail in chapter 8 of this book. Moreover, there are other ways aside from OOP payments to put health resources to more effective use (Gottret and Schieber 2006).

Middle-Income Economies

Efficient revenue mobilization should be a top priority in MICs to ensure funding is sustainable and matches long-term needs (Gottret and Schieber 2006). Because domestic revenue sources will need to supply the bulk of financing in MICs, tax-raising ability should increase and resources should be mobilized equitably and efficiently for health. These objectives can be achieved through better payroll collection, tax reform, and other structural reforms.

How are resources mobilized for health care in MICs in East Asia and the Pacific? There is wide variation across MICs in East Asia and the Pacific with regard to the balance between public prepayment and OOP payments as table 4.2 and figure 4.3 show. The relative contribution of each of these sources of financing in the context of MICs in East Asia and the Pacific is discussed in the next section.

Public sector prepayments for health care: General revenues and social insurance

MICs in East Asia and the Pacific have allocated a relatively high share of public resources to health compared to other MICs in recent years,

Table 4.2 Sources of Financing for Health Care in Low- and Middle-Income Countries in East Asia and the Pacific, 2000–07

	Share of total health revenues (%)												
Source	*Cambodia*	*China*	*Fiji*	*Indonesia*	*Korea, Rep.*	*Lao PDR*	*Malaysia*	*Mongolia*	*Philippines*	*Samoa*	*Thailand*	*Tonga*	*Vietnam*
Direct tax	—	3.4	—	12.5	4.8	—	30.9	23.6	11.7	—	22.8	—	—
Indirect tax	—	11.9	80.7	9.0	6.3	—	14.3	36.0	13.1	82.5	26.8	87.3	19.8
Nontax revenue	33.6	1.7	—	13.2	0.8	20.6	10.8	11.5	3.9	—	6.1	—	—
Social health insurance	—	23.0	2.2	21.3	41.1	—	0.0	24.0	11.0	0.3	8.0	0.0	12.6
Private insurance	0.0	4.0	—	6.0	3.4	0.4	6.0	—	6.3	17.1	8.4	0.0	1.9
OOP payments	66.4	49.0	17.7	38.0	37.7	73.6	33.0	5.0	48.4	—	27.7	12.7	60.5
Other	0.0	6.0	—	0.0	5.9	5.4	5.0	—	5.6	—	0.2	0.0	5.2
Total	100.0	99.0	100.0	99.0	100.0	100.0	100.0	100.1	100.0	99.9	100.0	100.0	100.0

Sources: Country documents.

Note: — = not available. Data reflect latest available period. Rows may not add to 100 percent because of rounding. American Samoa, the Democratic Peoples' Republic of Korea, the Federated States of Micronesia, Kiribati, the Marshall Islands, Myanmar, the Northern Mariana Islands, the Solomon Islands, and Vanuatu are excluded because of lack of data. For Mongolia, the 5 percent of health revenues generated from OOP payments includes only payments to public facilities and does not include informal payments, which have not been estimated.

Figure 4.3 Sources of Financing for Health Care in Low- and Middle-Income Countries in East Asia and the Pacific, 2000–07

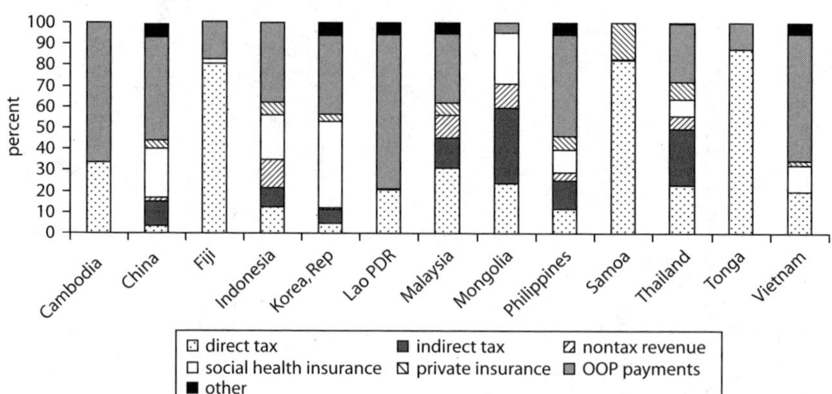

Sources: Country documents.
Note: Data reflect latest available period. American Samoa, the Democratic People's Republic of Korea, the Federated States of Micronesia, Kiribati, the Marshall Islands, Myanmar, the Northern Mariana Islands, the Solomon Islands, and Vanuatu are excluded because of lack of data. For Mongolia, the 5 percent of health revenues generated from OOP payments includes only OOPs from public facilities; it does not include informal payments, for which there is no estimate.

thanks in part to stronger economic growth. Overall public spending for health decreased in many countries in Eastern Europe and Central Asia during the 1990s as the region suffered an economic downturn (Langenbrunner 2005). By contrast, in East Asia and the Pacific, Mongolia, the Philippines, and Thailand have been successful in expanding insurance coverage by mobilizing additional tax and social insurance revenues. However, in Fiji, Malaysia, and Tonga, general revenue financing has almost exclusively financed universal coverage, regardless of the level of economic growth.

The share of public prepayment (taxes and social insurance) in total health expenditure varies considerably across the region. This share is 25 percent in Indonesia, 40 percent in China and the Philippines, 56 percent in Malaysia, 67 percent in Thailand, 70 percent in Mongolia, and more than 80 percent in Fiji, Samoa, and Tonga. Despite these variations, three groups of countries can be discerned: (a) those that rely primarily on tax financing, (b) those that rely on some mix of general revenues and social insurance, and (c) those in which prepayment is a small share and that rely primarily on OOPs (figure 4.4). By comparing global averages (figure 4.5), one sees that East Asian and Pacific countries rely more on GGR than on social insurance financing (see forthcoming volume of East Asia and the Pacific Health Country Profiles).

Figure 4.4 Share of Tax and Social Insurance Revenues in Total Health Expenditure for East Asia and the Pacific, 2005

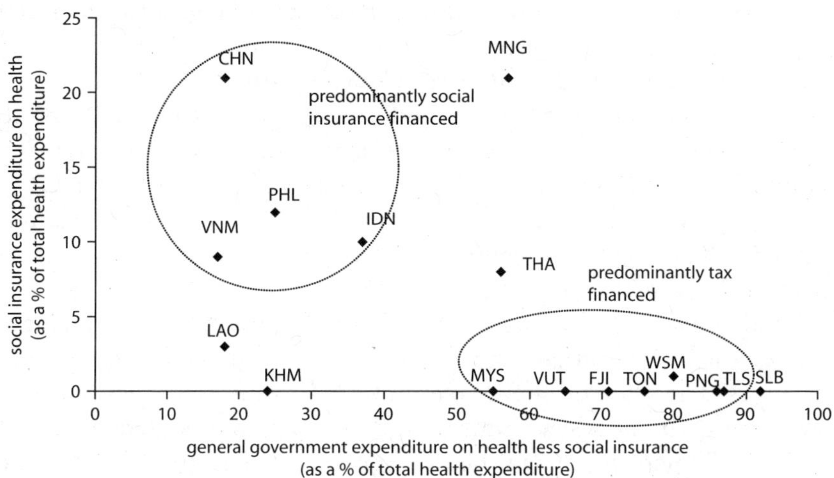

Source: Country documents.
Note: KHM = Cambodia; CHN = China; FJI = Fiji; IDN = Indonesia; LAO = Lao PDR; MYS = Malaysia; MNG = Mongolia; PNG = Papua New Guinea; PHL = Philippines; WSM = Samoa;SLB = Solomon Islands; THA = Thailand; TLS = Timor-Leste; TON = Tonga; VUT = Vanuatu; VNM = Vietnam. American Samoa and the Northern Mariana Islands are excluded because of lack of data.

Figure 4.5 Share of Tax and Social Insurance Revenues in Total Health Expenditure, LMIC Regional Averages, 2005

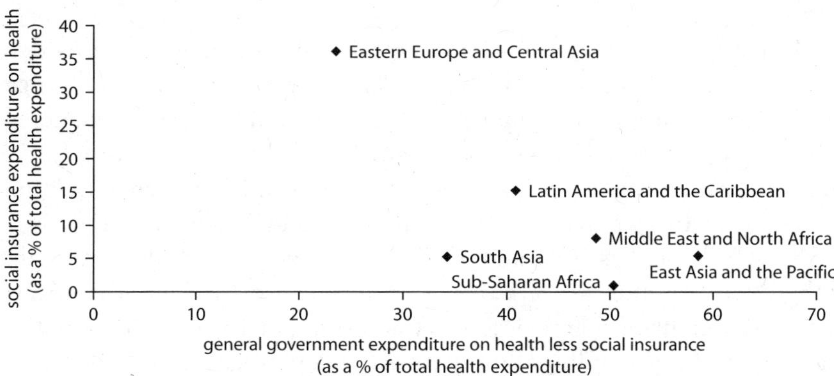

Source: World Health Organization's National Health Accounts database.

GGR accounts for a significant portion of public prepayment in MICs in East Asia and the Pacific, regardless of the type of health financing model or system. Fiji, Malaysia, Samoa, and Tonga have tax-financed systems in which GGR is the main source of financing, contributing

80 to 90 percent of public prepayments. In social insurance–financed countries, GGR is used to supplement payroll contributions in social insurance schemes and to subsidize insurance programs for the poor, the unemployed, and the informal sector. A large informal sector generally calls for a greater role for GGR in financing health care. A high level of political commitment (for example, in Mongolia and Thailand) to ensuring universal coverage enhances this role. Indonesia, Mongolia, the Philippines, and Thailand have social insurance systems; however, GGR still accounts for the largest share of public prepayment in those four countries. The share of social insurance contributions in public prepayment exceeds that of GGR only in China.

GGR consists of revenues from direct and indirect taxes and nontax sources such as royalties from the sale of minerals and other natural resources. The share of direct taxes in total GGR is highest in Malaysia (55 percent). In all other countries in this group, indirect taxes account for 50 to 70 percent of total GGR. Nontax revenues (remittances) are important in Indonesia and in Malaysia because of revenues from the sale of timber and minerals. Outside East Asia and the Pacific, countries such as Ecuador, Kazakhstan, Lithuania, and Ukraine rely primarily on general revenues. Meanwhile, some other countries with mixed or predominantly social insurance–financed systems are contemplating shifting from payroll-based contributions to general revenues. In doing so, they need to ensure that the GGR base is relatively predictable and stable.

The share of SHI contributions in total health financing varies widely across East Asia and the Pacific. In Fiji, Malaysia, Samoa, and Tonga, SHI accounts for a relatively minor share of total sources of financing. However, payroll-based social insurance contributions account for 32 percent of total public prepayment in Mongolia, 23 percent in China, and only 10 to 15 percent in the Philippines and Thailand.

Most MICs in East Asia and the Pacific have SHI for civil servants and other formal sector workers that is financed through payroll contributions. The contribution regimes vary across countries, with contribution rates in MICs generally falling within a wide range, from as low as 2 percent to as high as 18 percent (table 4.3). Rates tend to be higher in Eastern Europe than elsewhere (Langenbrunner and Adeyi 2003). By contrast, contribution rates in East Asia and the Pacific fall within a fairly narrow range of 2 to 10 percent.

The impact on labor and capital formation is difficult to assess, although it needs to be linked to overall social insurance contribution

Table 4.3 Characteristics of Sources of Financing for Social Health Insurance Systems in East Asia and the Pacific

Country	*Groups covered*	*Division of funds*	*Contribution shares (%)*			*Earnings limits on contributions*	*Rate structure of contributions*
			Employee	*Employer*	*State*		
Cambodia	The Ministry of Health developed a master plan for SHI in 2003, which was officially released in March 2005. Current plans call for a separate administrative structure for civil servants and formal sector workers.						
China	Employees of state and collective-owned units are covered.	Single fund	25	75	75	None	8% of basic salary
Indonesia	Formal sector employees are covered.	Separate funds for public and private sectors	22	22	78	None	2% (public sector) and 3% to 6% (private sector) of basic salary
Japan	The entire population is covered.	Separate funds by regions and company	50	50	0	None	3% to 9% of earnings depending on amount of earnings and family status
Korea, Rep.	The nonpoor population is covered.	Single fund	50	50	0	Upper limit abolished in 2002	3.7% of earnings
Lao PDR	Salaried employees in the private sector, civil servants, and low-income families are covered.	Separate funds by target group	50	50	0	None	4% of salary
Mongolia	The following groups are covered: employees of businesses and organizations; owners of businesses; self-employed persons; children	Single fund	50	50	0	None	6% to 4% of base salary (since the contribution rate decline in 2006)

(continued)

Table 4.3 *(continued)*

Country	*Groups covered*	*Division of funds*	*Contribution shares (%)*			*Earnings limits on contributions*	*Rate structure of contributions*
			Employee	*Employer*	*State*		
	under age 16 (secondary school pupils under age 18); university and college students and those attending day classes at vocational training and production centers; people with no other sources of income except a pension; mothers and fathers caring for children under age 2 (or twins under age 3); military personnel on active duty; herdsmen; people specified in article 12 of the Social Welfare Law; convicts serving their sentences; and others, except those prescribed in paragraphs 6.1.1 through 6.1.10 of the Social Welfare Law.						
Philippines	As of June 2002, target coverage is universal, but effective coverage is 48.8% of the population.	Single fund with separate programs for public employees and private employees, as well as for individually payingcitizens, retirees, and the indigent	50; 100 (individually paying citizens); 0 (the indigent)	50; 0 (individually paying citizens); 0 (the indigent)	0; 0 (individually paying citizens); 0 (the indigent)	Upper limit	2.5% of basic earnings

Taiwan, China	The entire population is covered.	Single fund	Varies according to occupation and income			Lower and upper limits	4.25% of upper bound of 29 earnings intervals
Thailand	Civil servants and formal sector employees are covered. The remaining inhabitants received universal coverage in 2001.	Single fund with separate programs for civil servants and private sector employees; others financed from taxes	33	33	33	Lower and upper limits	3% of earnings

Sources: Adapted from O'Donnell and others 2008.

House holds below the poverty line (4.6 percent) are covered by a tax-financed Medicaid scheme.

Of those covered, 23.9 percent are government employees, 55.4 percent are private sector employees, 11.2 percent are individually paying citizens, 7.8 percent are indigent, and 1.9 percent are retirees.

Retirees are covered, at zero premium, on the condition that they have at least 10 years of contributions.

For manual workers, for example, the contribution share is 30 percent for employees, 60 percent for employers, and 10 percent for state government employees. For low-income people, 100 percent is paid by the state.

In 2002, the rate increased to 4.55 percent, and the number of intervals was raised to 38.

The state pays a 100 percent flat-rate contribution for children under age 16 (secondary school pupils under age 18), persons with no source of income other than pension, mothers and fathers caring for their children under age 2 (or twins under age 3), military personnel on active duty, and persons specified in article 12 of Social Welfare Law.

rates. For example, in China, the social insurance scheme for urban formal sector employees, Urban Employee Essential Medical Insurance (UEEMI), is financed through contributions from both employers (6 percent) and employees (2 percent), with some regional variation in the contribution rates. However, the overall social contribution rates are a very burdensome 50 percent on average.

Health insurance schemes in China vary in their financing arrangements. Insurance schemes for formal sector employees and migrants (also UEEMI) and other urban residents (Urban Residents Essential Medical Insurance) are financed through employee contributions and government subsidies. The insurance scheme for rural households, New Cooperative Medical Scheme (NCMS), is financed through a flat-rate contribution from members (Y 10 or more, depending on how generous the county makes the scheme) and a government subsidy of at least Y 20 (Wagstaff and others 2009). The cost of the subsidy is borne entirely by local governments in China's richer provinces and is shared between central and local governments in China's poorer provinces. In addition, the Medical Assistance program, which provides financial assistance to specific vulnerable groups, is financed mostly by tax subsidies and is supplemented by lottery revenues, donations, and development assistance.

In Indonesia, the two social insurance schemes for formal sector workers, Askes and Jamsostek, are financed by contributions made by employees and employers (22 percent) and by the state (78 percent). The wage contribution rate is 2 percent for the public sector and 3 to 6 percent for the private sector. The National Health Insurance Program in the Philippines is financed through equal contributions from employers and employees at the rate of 2.5 percent of earnings. The self-employed can enroll by paying the premium in full. In addition, premiums for the indigent are paid by the state. In Thailand, the Civil Servants' Medical Benefit Scheme is noncontributory. For the social security scheme covering formal private sector employees, contributions from employers, employees, and government are set at 1.5 percent each of the employees' wages. The universal scheme covers the remainder of the population and is financed almost entirely by subsidies from GGR.In Mongolia, the contribution is shared equally by employees and employers. The state makes a flat-rate contribution for children and other vulnerable groups. Students, herdsmen, and insured inhabitants pay their own flat-rate monthly contribution in full. The health insurance law specifies that contributions paid by employees of businesses and organizations will not exceed 6 percent of wages and similar income. At present, the employer pays 2 percent and the employee pays 2 percent of wages as his or her health insurance contribution.

Private health insurance

The share of private health insurance in total health expenditure in middle-income East Asian and Pacific countries is relatively low compared to that in MICs in the other regions. The share ranges from 17.1 percent in Samoa to 8.4 percent in Thailand, 6.3 percent in the Philippines, 6.0 percent in Indonesia and Malaysia, and 4.0 percent in China (table 4.2). In Brazil, Chile, Namibia, South Africa, and Uruguay, private health insurance exceeds 20 percent. However, private insurance plays a small role in LMICs in other regions such as Eastern Europe and Central Asia and the Middle East and North Africa (Langenbrunner 2005).

The relatively minor role played by private health insurance in MICs in East Asia and the Pacific is somewhat surprising. First, the OOP share of total spending is relatively high, which in most other countries creates large demand for supplemental voluntary insurance. Second, a middle class, an important prerequisite for the development of private health insurance, has already been established in East Asia and the Pacific. Third, a viable financial market is another precondition for the development of private insurance entities because the reserves from premiums collected must be invested to ensure that profits cover resource outlays; this profit is critical for the sustainability of private entities (Gottret and Schieber 2006). This precondition has also been met. In East Asia and in the Middle East, a growing private insurance market has paralleled health development in the financial sector over the past decade (World Bank 2005).

Regardless of the magnitude of the share of private health insurance, regulatory oversight and management skills are necessary to ensure adequate fiduciary control and oversight. Private health insurance markets are still largely unregulated in East Asia and the Pacific and elsewhere. Moreover, the likelihood of risk selection within private health insurance markets has not been assessed and documented adequately in MICs. The lack of regulation, management skill, and actuarial sophistication contributed to the failures of private sector–based reforms in Latin America and Eastern Europe (Gottret and Schieber 2006).

In addition, private health insurance companies find it very difficult to operate in developing countries because of poor licensing standards and regulations for practitioners, clinics, and hospitals. This poor oversight makes overtreatment and fraudulent claims a threat to the financial survival of commercial insurance plans (Hsiao and Shaw 2007). When commercial insurance plans do exist, they usually operate like closed-panel health maintenance organizations with their own clinics and hospitals (or contract with only a few of the best hospitals in a country). Some private insurers insure only medical services abroad, especially in many of the Pacific Island countries.

OOP payments

The share of OOP payments in total health financing varies significantly across MICs in East Asia and the Pacific (table 4.2 and figure 4.6). OOP payments account for a very high share of total expenditures in China (49 percent), the Philippines (48 percent), Indonesia (38 percent), Malaysia (33 percent), and Thailand (28 percent). By contrast, OOP payments account for only 15 percent or less of total spending in Fiji, Samoa, and Tonga. Notwithstanding measurement errors in estimating the OOP share of total spending, it is clear that there is a great deal of heterogeneity in the OOP burden of health care spending among these countries. The very high shares in China, the Philippines, and Indonesia represent a large burden on household budgets in those countries. Chapter 8 of this book discusses the impoverishing effects of OOP payments and financial barriers to further explain these findings.

The nature and composition of OOP payments also vary across these countries. In Fiji, Malaysia, Thailand (since 2007), and Tonga (until 2008), user charges at government facilities have been minimal. As a result, OOP payments in these countries are composed primarily of payments to private providers, including the traditional medical and informal providers, and the purchase of drugs and supplies not available at the public facilities. In Indonesia, user charges at public facilities account for one-quarter of all OOP spending. Of total OOP spending, nearly half is for ambulatory care, and about one-third is for medicines.

In China and, to a limited extent, the Philippines, the share of OOP payments is high, not only because of a lack of insurance, but also because OOP payments in the form of coinsurance, deductibles, and copayments are considerable for those with insurance. In China, for instance, the share of inpatient OOP costs is 60 percent. In the Republic of Korea, Mexico, and Switzerland (the countries with the second highest rate), the OOP share of inpatient costs is 20 percent. The lack of insurance is only part of the reason the OOP burden is high. Flat-rate contributions (as in the case of migrants, informal sector workers, and

Figure 4.6 Out-of-Pocket Payments as a Proportion of Total Health Expenditure for Low- and Middle-Income Countries in East Asia and the Pacific, 2005

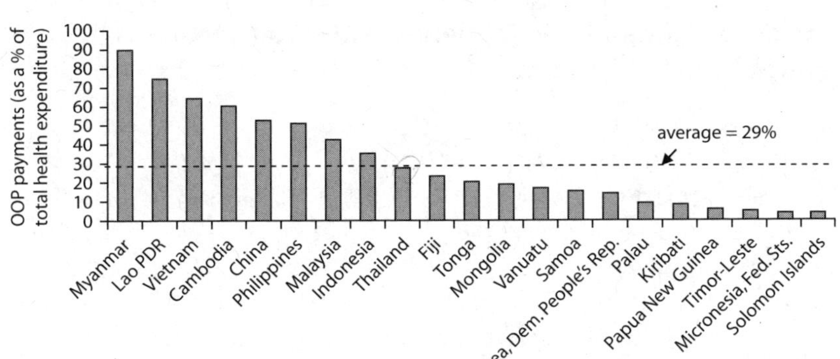

Source: World Health Organization's National Health Accounts database.
Note: American Samoa and Northern Mariana Islands are excluded because of lack of data.

NCMS enrollees in China and enrolled individuals in the Philippines) also impose a large burden on low-income households. Under NCMS in China, for instance, the effective coinsurance rate (after factoring in deductibles and ceilings) is very high (Wagstaff and others 2009). Exceptionally high costs of care relative to per capita income compound the problem caused by the high OOP burden. Box 4.2 explains why the expansion of NCMS in China has failed to reduce the OOP burden on households.

Informal payments are also common in East Asia and the Pacific, especially in China, Mongolia, Thailand, and Vietnam. However, the exact level of informal payments and their level relative to formal charges are unknown because of difficulties in collecting data on informal charges in household and provider surveys. What is known is discussed in more detail in chapter 7 of this book.

Low-Income Economies

LICs in East Asia and the Pacific, as elsewhere, are characterized by low health spending, heavy reliance on OOP financing, and limited domestic resource mobilization ability. On average, in East Asia and the Pacific, public prepayment revenues for health account for 30 percent or less of total health expenditure; most of the remaining 70 percent from private sources is in the form of OOP payments (table 4.2). Severe institutional, fiscal, economic, and political constraints underlie the limited potential for domestic resource mobilization in LICs (Gottret and

Box 4.2

Effect of China's New Cooperative Medical Scheme on Out-of-Pocket Spending

Despite its voluntary nature, China's New Cooperative Medical Scheme has already achieved high enrollment rates (about 80 percent of the population), including among the poor. Evidence shows that NCMS has increased outpatient visits and inpatient episodes at the township health center level. In situations in which care is often forgone because of financial and other barriers to access, NCMS has evidently helped to make medical care more accessible to households.

Nevertheless, household survey data do not reveal any effect of NCMS on OOP spending per ambulatory visit or inpatient episode. Although NCMS increased health care use, the program did not put any downward pressure on provider costs. As a result, OOP payments associated with copayments and deductibles have increased.

Source: Wagstaff and others 2009.

Schieber 2006). However, several LICs in East Asia and the Pacific are experimenting with new prepayment schemes such as the health equity funds in Cambodia and the Lao People's Democratic Republic. These schemes are discussed in more detail in the next section.

Prepayments for health care

Historically, GGR is the mechanism that has financed public prepayment for health care in low-income East Asian and Pacific countries. Low economic growth, weak tax administration capacity, and limited potential for increasing GGR have led to the imposition of fees. In recent years, a range of social insurance schemes and community-based insurance schemes has been introduced, partly to diversify the revenue base for health care (for example, SHI in Vietnam) and partly to provide low-income households with a means of financial protection in the face of rising user fees (for example, health equity funds in Cambodia and Lao PDR). Social insurance schemes are not as common in Papua New Guinea and the Solomon Islands, but they are being examined for their potential to reduce the burden on the public purse. Donor contributions to public prepayment of health care are increasingly common.

The public prepayment share ranges from 20 percent to 40 percent in Cambodia, Lao PDR, Timor-Leste, and Vietnam. The pattern is slightly different in Papua New Guinea and the Solomon Islands, where public prepayment accounts for over 70 percent of total health financing. In all of these countries, with the possible exception of Vietnam, donor financing accounts for over 50 percent of public prepayment. National health accounts (NHAs) are not available for many of these countries, and estimates of private spending are not always reliable. In Cambodia, for instance, OOP spending is thought to be underestimated by about 25 percent.

GGR financing is generated through taxes and nontax revenues, including royalties related to the sale of natural resources or minerals. Nontax revenues of this nature are particularly important in countries such as Papua New Guinea (copper and gold) and the Solomon Islands (timber). Given the narrow income tax base in most LICs, indirect taxes account for a larger share of tax revenues.

Social insurance contributions and shares vary among LICs in East Asia and the Pacific. Contributions are payroll-based in Lao PDR and Vietnam, and they account for 11 percent and 13 percent of total health financing, respectively, in each of these countries. In Lao PDR, the contribution rates vary with the type of scheme (table 4.3). The Civil Service Health Insurance is financed through a combination of contributions (6 percent of salaries) and open-ended government financing. The Social Insurance Fund is financed through contributions from both employees (4.5 percent of earnings) and employers (5 percent of earnings). Of the total 9.5 percent of earnings that is contributed to the Social Insurance Fund, 4.4 percent is allocated to the Social Health Insurance Fund. In Vietnam, the contribution rate for formal sector workers and civil servants is 3 percent of earnings, which is split between the employee (1 percent) and the employer (2 percent). The contribution rate for policy beneficiaries is 3 percent of the minimum wage, which is covered in the state budget at the local level. Provinces receive a 100 percent subsidy from the central government to cover the cost of this scheme.

Donor financing accounts for a significant share of health spending in LICs. Complete, consistent data on donor spending are, however, rarely available. Box 4.3 summarizes the level and composition of donor spending in Cambodia, one of the few countries for which such data are available. Donor funding may be quite critical for scaling up expenditures in LICs, but some serious problems are associated with it. Globally, the issues include a lack of predictability, an increased focus on specific diseases, a large number of new actors and donors, and a donor's

Box 4.3

Donor Financing in Cambodia

External aid for health is highly fragmented and is not closely aligned with stated health priorities. Donor financing is largely earmarked for disease-specific national programs (particularly from global health partnerships), which inhibits the flow of funds to where they are needed most. Total per capita health spending in 2005 amounted to US$37 per capita, or more than US$500 million nationally, which is equivalent to more than 8 percent of gross domestic product. Of this figure, donor financing amounted to US$8.30 per capita in 2005 (up from US$3.00 per capita in 2000), or 22.4 percent of total health spending. The remaining sources of health financing include OOP expenditures (US$24.90 per capita, or 67.1 percent of total health spending) and financing from the government's recurrent budget (US$4.00 per capita, or 10.8 percent of total health spending).

Donor aid for health has been increasing rapidly in recent years, largely as a result of disbursements from Japan, the United Kingdom, and the United States, as well as from the Global Fund to Fight AIDS, Tuberculosis, and Malaria. The depreciation of the U.S. dollar has further increased aid flows that are not denominated in that currency in U.S. dollar terms. The importance of donor aid in the Cambodian context illustrates the need for donor aid that is aligned and coordinated with the government. A 2006 OECD baseline survey of harmonization and alignment reveals a low level of donor alignment in Cambodia, although donors in health have increased efforts to coordinate their assistance. Seven major donors have indicated that they would support a program-based approach in health known as Sector Wide Management (SWiM). Four donors report that they will contribute to a program-based approach to combating HIV/AIDS, and nine donors will coordinate technical assistance under SWiM.

Source: World Bank 2008.

lack of accountability for the absence of results and progress (Gottret and Schieber 2006). Not only is donor funding unpredictable, but also commitments have generally proven to be bad predictors of actual disbursement. The focus on specific diseases risks neglecting broader health system issues such as human resource shortages and problems in the procurement and distribution of drugs.

Only a small share (20 percent) of global donor funding for health is provided as budget support. The remainder is provided as earmarked project support, off-budget support for disease-specific interventions, or even technical assistance that is not registered in the country's balance of payments (Gottret and Schieber 2006). Significant donor financing of health-related activities, particularly those outside the government's budget, may motivate ministries of finance to allocate domestic resources to uses other than health. Allocating resources to other areas is potentially a major risk for low-income, fragile states (such as Papua New Guinea, the Solomon Islands, and Timor-Leste), where the government revenue base is weak and donor financing is considerable. In the Solomon Islands, for example, where donor financing accounts for 50 percent of public spending on health, health receives low priority in the parliamentary resource allocation process.

Voluntary health insurance

Voluntary health insurance accounts for less than 5 percent of total health expenditures in LICs in East Asia and the Pacific. It is mainly used to supplement private care for middle- and high-income groups. In East Asia and the Pacific, private insurance is largely unregulated, as in LICs and MICs in other regions.

In LICs, a potential advantage of voluntary health insurance is that it could provide an opportunity for better-off inhabitants to opt out of the public system. This option alleviates demand pressures on the overcrowded public system; however, there is very little evidence of this strategy in practice. At the same time, opting out could skim off public revenues if premiums are paid through wage contributions and could effectively create a two-tiered system.

While private voluntary health insurance accounts for a relatively small share of expenditures in LICs, community-based insurance plans offered by nonprofit organizations are quite common. Community-based health insurance is effectively a voluntary health insurance scheme operated at the district level with flat-rate contributions that vary according to household size and area (rural or urban).

Although it is not a significant source of revenue, community-based health insurance has played an important role in scaling up SHI in some countries (Hsiao and Shaw 2007). China's previous community-based plan—the Cooperative Medical Scheme also helped in scaling up the current rural health insurance schemes. Historically, the Jyorei system (a late 19th-century, community-based financing scheme in Japan) played a critical role in scaling up social insurance, although full coverage was not achieved until the middle of the 20th century.

Out-of-pocket payments

OOP payments as a proportion of total health expenditure vary widely for LICs—from less than 10 percent in the Federated States of Micronesia, Kiribati, Palau, Papua New Guinea, the Solomon Islands, and Timor-Leste to 90 percent in Myanmar (figure 4.6). In Cambodia, OOP payments comprise official and unofficial user fees in the private and public sectors, cost of drugs in the private sector, and transportation costs for receiving health services. OOP payments comprise the major component of total health sector expenditures, and, in per capita per year, they appear to have risen in absolute terms between 2000 and 2005 according to the Cambodia Demographic and Health Surveys (from US$20.00 per capita per year to US$24.90). However, the reduction in public sector OOP costs is mostly in rural areas and is mostly due to reduced transport costs, with treatment costs remaining static.

OOP expenditures accounted for about 74 percent of total health expenditure in Lao PDR in 2005, according to NHA estimates in the World Health Organization's National Health Accounts database. Recent surveys indicate that the costs of health care can indeed be significant. For example, according to the Lao World Health Survey (WHO 2003), inpatient episodes cost between US$15 and US$90, depending on the level of care. Although various sources tell slightly different stories about the level and pattern of household expenditures, it is clear that health care costs can create a substantial burden for households.

There are no reliable estimates of OOP spending in Papua New Guinea and the Solomon Islands, although household surveys indicate that OOP spending is relatively low. This finding is not too surprising in the Solomon Islands, where there are no official user fees for health care, where free drugs are provided at all government facilities, and where the private sector is limited to a few private clinics in Honiara. Use of informal providers is also minimal according to the most recent household survey. It is, however, reasonable to expect the OOP share to be higher in Papua New Guinea, where official and unofficial fees are charged, use of informal providers (for example, witch doctors) is greater, and levels of private sector provision are higher than in the Solomon Islands.

In Timor-Leste, the 2006/07 Medium-Term Expenditure Framework noted the difficulties in estimating the level of private financing of the health sector. Although nongovernmental organization (NGO) clinics may cover up to 25 percent of all outpatient visits, donors currently fund many NGOs, and much of the NGO financing is, therefore, included in the external funding cited earlier. The 2001 Living Standard and

Monitoring Survey suggests that approximately US$2 per capita is spent annually by households on health services (including indirect costs). In addition, Café Timor, raises funds directly from its cooperative members (see forthcoming volume of East Asia and the Pacific Country Health Financing Profiles).

Analysis and Discussion

Fiscal Space for Health

The term *fiscal space for health* refers to the budgetary room available to increase government health spending without jeopardizing macroeconomic stability and distorting economic activity. The fiscal space for health is assessed by the following:

- Deriving implications for the health sector from the overall fiscal space framework
- Focusing on the extent to which health might be reprioritized within the government's budget
- Examining the pros and cons of sector-specific means for raising resources (for example, by use of earmarked taxes)
- Evaluating the use of sector-specific grants from international agencies such as the Global Alliance for Vaccines and Immunisation and the Global Fund to Fight AIDS, Tuberculosis, and Malaria
- Improving the efficiency of sector outlays

Analyses of fiscal space have shown that, although macroeconomic constraints are critical, there may be upper limits to increasing health spending in LICs without economic growth. With a ratio of government expenditure to gross domestic product (GDP) of about 30.0 percent and with the share of health at 15.0 percent of the budget, fiscal space is likely to be limited to about 4.5 percent of GDP. The current average of public expenditure on health is about 2.5 percent in LICs. In an average country with a GDP per capita of US$400 and a population of 44 million, increasing public expenditure on health from 2.5 percent to, for instance, 5 percent of GDP would raise per capita health spending by only US$10 per capita.

Improving the efficiency of sector outlays may generate fiscal space for health. Improvements in efficiency can increase effective fiscal space and attract additional resources from ministries of finance. Variations in health sector performance relative to income and health spending are often wide, both between and within countries (figures 4.7 and 4.8).

Figure 4.7 Performance Relative to Income and Health Spending, 2005

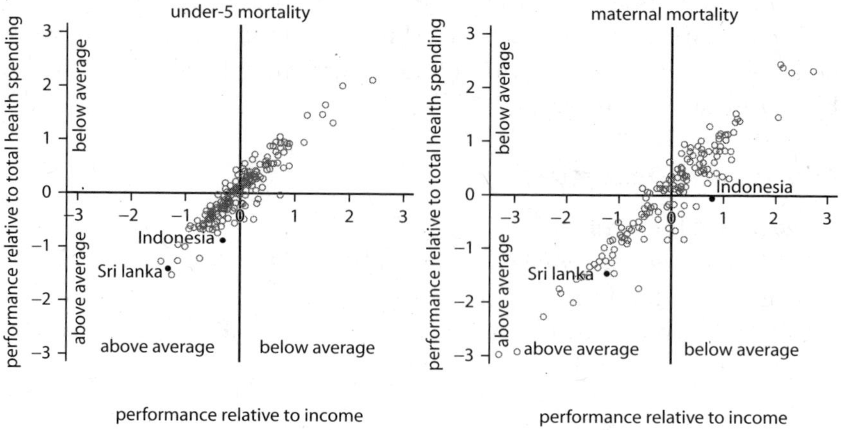

Source: World Bank's World Development Indicators database.

Figure 4.8 Variations in Infant Mortality across Countries and within Indonesia, 2006

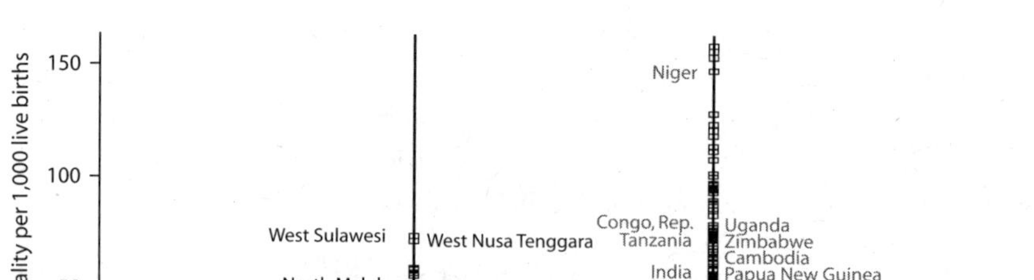

Sources: Statistics Indonesia and Macro International 2008; World Bank's World Development Indicators database.

These performance differentials suggest variations in the efficiency with which health sector outlays are used.

Current health financing reforms in East Asia and the Pacific are motivated by policy makers' concerns that current health care financing mechanisms are insufficient for meeting future health financing needs in a sustainable manner. Fiscal capacity and policy priorities are twin dimensions in improving levels of public prepayment for health. Overall levels of public prepayment tend to track with movements in a country's

Figure 4.9 Government Health Spending and Out-of-Pocket Payments in Asia, 2007

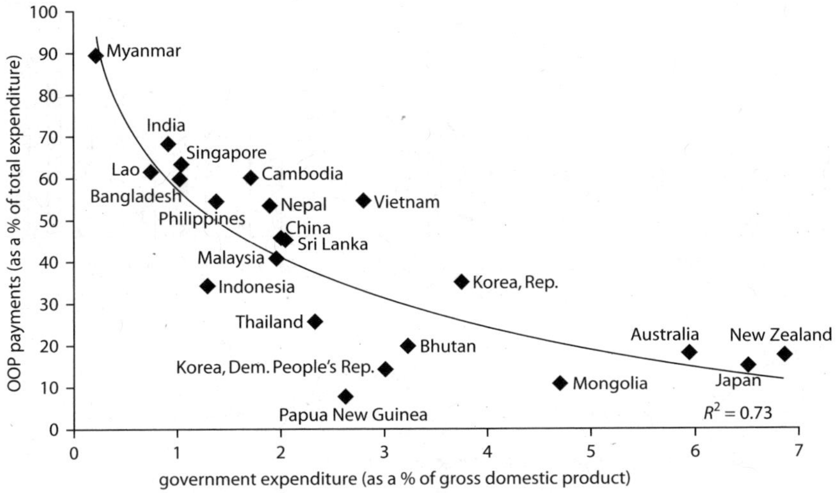

Sources: Kutzin 2009 using 2007 estimates from the World Health Organization.

GDP per capita. This correlation is true both globally and in East Asia and the Pacific (see figure 4.9). At the same time, there is significant variation in public spending as a share of GDP for countries with similar GDP. This variation may be due to variations either in fiscal capacity or in public sector priorities to invest in health spending as a share of the public budget. Analysts will want to disentangle these two factors to understand how much is due to fiscal context versus how much is due to public policy priorities.

Prepayments for Health

The two main types of prepayment in the region are general revenues and payroll taxes, although individual savings accounts are being used in China and Singapore under some insurance schemes. Economic growth and strong administrative capacity to raise taxes are critical for the sustainability of GGR financing. Economic growth is conducive to the collection of GGR because it expands the tax base and has a positive effect on tax collection. In general, the share of direct taxes increases as economies grow and the income tax base becomes broader.

General revenues

In LICs, the tax and nontax resource bases are low, and economic growth is weak (figure 4.10). The low ratios of tax to GDP imply that developing

Figure 4.10 Tax Revenue as a Share of Gross Domestic Product, 2006

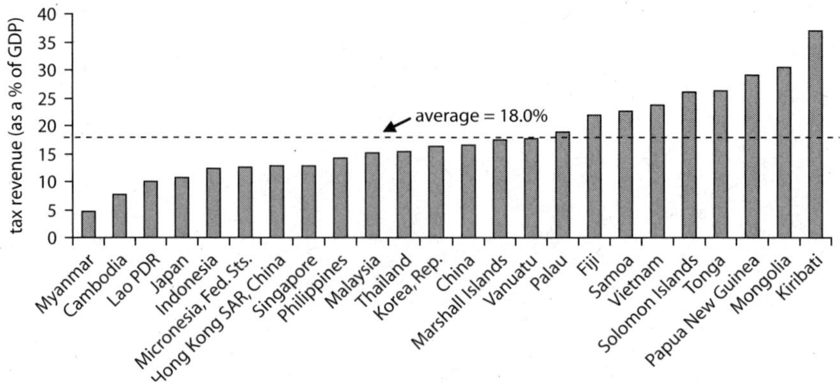

Sources: ADB 2007, except data for Myanmar, which comes from the World Bank's World Development Indicators database.
Note: Timor-Leste is excluded because of lack of data. Data for Thailand are for 2003.

countries have room to increase revenues from taxation to accommodate greater public spending, including spending on health. However, weak tax administration capacity remains a constraint. On average, central government tax revenue as a share of GDP in LICs is 14.5 percent, compared with 16.3 percent for lower-middle-income countries, 21.9 percent for upper-middle-income countries, and 26.5 percent in HICs (Gottret and Schieber 2006). However, even with economic growth, the GGR base may not be sustainable if the country's administrative capacity to raise taxes is weak and the country's governance is poor.

By contrast, most MICs have the infrastructure to raise general tax revenues, but the administrative capacity to raise taxes is weak. These countries lack appropriate tax structures and incentives, including clear rules and transparency. This problem impedes efficient collection of tax revenues. For instance, MICs in Latin America and the Caribbean have collected much less in total taxes relative to their per capita income than have European countries (Baeza and Packard 2006).

LMICs generally have a narrow, distorting tax base (Wagstaff 2007b). For instance, China's value added tax cannot be used to finance services, and China's real estate taxes are defined on a base that is narrower than it needs to be (Ahmad 2006). In many cases, tax reform is needed to broaden tax bases and to generate higher revenues at lower rates that do not discriminate against the various sources and uses of income (Gottret and Schieber 2006). Bolivia provides a good example of a country that raised tax revenues from 3 percent of GDP in 1983 to 17 percent by the end of 1987 (Wagstaff and Claeson 2004). The Bolivian tax reform replaced a highly complex tax system containing more than 100 taxes with a simple structure of six taxes.

Tax reform is desirable because it would result in efficiency gains, greater administrative simplicity, and horizontal equity. However, many practical difficulties are associated with tax reform, especially when institutional changes in tax authorities are required, when the rural and informal sectors are important, when the borders are large, and when the wealthy are politically powerful (Gottret and Schieber 2006). Governance of tax administration is also a critical issue. Corruption affects revenue collection agencies and mechanisms in countries such as Indonesia and the Philippines. Thus, poor governance often compounds weak administrative capacity.

Payroll taxes

The enabling conditions needed to ensure the sustainability of payroll tax–based schemes are an urban population, a growing economy, a large formal labor market, an administrative capacity for collection, good regulatory and oversight structures, and appropriate incentive structures. In MICs in East Asia and the Pacific, economic growth has been strong in recent years, but many of the other enabling factors are not present. In LICs in East Asia and the Pacific, economic growth is a constraint and may be more so in the near future because of the financial crisis and longer-term increases in the prices of food and oil.

The large rural populations in East Asia and the Pacific and the limited size of the formal labor market are impediments to reliance on payroll-based taxes (figure 4.11). The countries that chose payroll taxes as the primary source of funding in Europe, Central Asia, and Latin America generally benefited from having a large percentage of the working-age population employed in the formal sector (Ensor and Thompson 1998). Eastern European countries such as the Czech Republic, Estonia, Hungary, and the Slovak Republic, where payroll taxes are the predominant source of financing (Langenbrunner 2005), have a tradition of large state enterprises and civil service institutions. These entities are large formal sector employers and reliable sources of payroll contributions. In Latin America and the Caribbean, where payroll taxes also are significant, labor unions representing a large share of the formal workforce are actively involved in collecting and managing health insurance contributions. To cater to the informal sector, however, most countries in Latin America have had to maintain a parallel

Figure 4.11 Informal Sector as a Share of Total Employment in East Asia and the Pacific

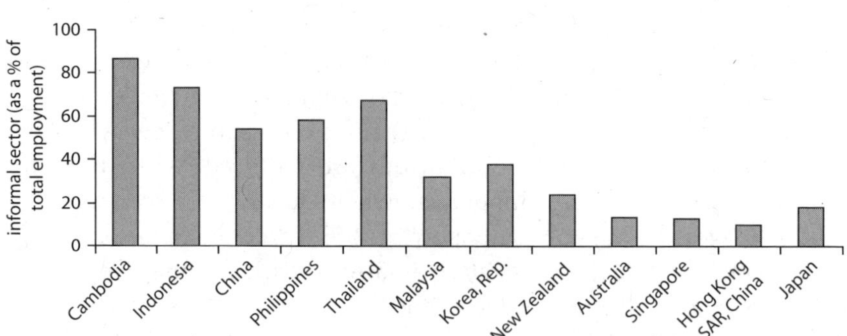

Sources: World Bank 2008; World Bank's World Development Indicators database.
Note: Informal sector workers are defined as self-employed workers in the nonagricultural workforce and agricultural workforce. Self-employed workers in the nonagricultural sector, as defined by the International Labour Organization, include employers, own-account workers, and unpaid family workers in the nonagricultural labor force. Gross domestic product per capita is 2000 data from the World Bank's World Development Indicators database, and percentages of nonagricultural employment are from ILO statistics.

tax-financed system with separate providers operated by their ministry of health (Wagstaff 2007b).

Payroll taxes can negatively affect job growth and capital formation. Payroll taxes place a tax on employers and can have a negative effect on future economic growth, which is, in turn, critical for expanding the revenue base. Nickell's (2004) review of labor markets in OECD countries found that tax rates are a significant factor in explaining differences in the amount of market work undertaken by the working-age population. According to the World Bank's World Development Indicators database, a 10 percent increase in tax rates could decrease labor inputs by 1 to 3 percent for the working-age population. Another recent study (Wagstaff 2009) analyzed the effects of adopting SHI instead of tax financing in OECD countries between 1960 and 2006. The study found that adopting SHI instead of tax financing increased per capita health spending by 3 to 4 percent, reduced the formal sector share of employment by 8 to 10 percent, and reduced total employment by as much as 6 percent.

The direct evidence of payroll taxes decreasing labor inputs in transition economies is less clear cut, but what is clear is that high payroll tax rates discourage firms and workers from entering the formal economy. Even in the context of the limited formal labor market, the collection of social insurance contributions is constrained by weak administrative capacity and the lack of good regulatory oversight and incentive structures.

Nonenrollment of formal sector workers in insurance schemes and evasion of payments among those who are enrolled means that the collection of social insurance contributions is no more efficient than the collection of tax revenues in most MICs. In urban China, for instance, only 24 percent of private sector employees and 50 percent of state-owned enterprise employees were enrolled in the new urban health insurance scheme in 2004 (Chen 2004; Wagstaff 2007b; Wu 2004). In Vietnam, only one-third of formal sector workers are enrolled in SHI (Nguyen 2006; Wagstaff 2007a).

Evasion exists even in countries where enrollment is mandatory, because workers and employers can take advantage of lax enforcement and not enroll in the scheme at all. In Indonesia, 86 percent of those eligible for coverage in the national scheme have taken advantage of an opt-out clause in the legislation (Hsiao and Shaw 2007). In Colombia, evasion in the contributory regime, caused by underreporting and nonpayment, is associated with revenue losses of about 3 percent of GDP (Escobar and Panopoulou 2003). In Eastern Europe and in the countries that made up the former Soviet Union, the introduction of SHI schemes did not actually result in additional revenues for health care; in Kazakhstan, only 40 percent of expected revenues were actually collected (Gottret and Schieber 2006).

It is not clear, therefore, that social insurance financed through payroll taxes represents a better alternative for mobilizing revenues for health care than does general tax financing in East Asia and the Pacific. It may be argued that rather than pay taxes individuals prefer to pay a social insurance premium that is virtually earmarked for health, because they do not trust the government to allocate the tax revenues for health care. Given the large share of social insurance contributions allocated to administrative expenses, it is uncertain whether the SHI system would do better than a tax-financed system at converting revenues to quality care. Moreover, the very governance issues that make citizens suspicious of the way their government allocates resources imply that the government may also be a weak regulator of an SHI scheme (Wagstaff 2007b).

Alternative sources of revenues?

Taxes on tobacco, cigarettes, and alcohol represent alternative sources of revenues with a relatively untapped potential in most of the region. As table 4.4 shows, the tobacco tax rate is less than 50 percent of the price

Table 4.4 Share of Smokers in the General Population and Tobacco Tax Rates in East Asia and the Pacific and the European Union

Country or region	*Year*	*Share of smokers*	*Share of tobacco taxesin the price of cigarettes*
Cambodia	2004	21.7	9
China	2002	31.4	21
Fiji	2002	15.0	—
Indonesia	2001	28.7	22
Japan	2006	27.0	5
Korea, Rep.	2005	29.1	10
Lao PDR	2003	35.7	32
Malaysia	2006	21.2	39
Mongolia	2005	24.2	31
Philippines	2003	23.6	41
Singapore	2004	12.6	69
Sri Lanka	2003	13.6	54
Thailand	2004	21.1	79
Vietnam	2003	17.5	32
EU-15 average	—	24.2	58

Sources: World Health Organization's Global Info Base and latest available national data for East Asian and Pacific countries; OECD Health Data 2008 and latest available data for European Union countries.
Note: — = data not available, * = average not computed because of different years for individual countries. EU-15 refers to the 15 countries that were members of the European Union prior to May 1, 2004: Austria, Belgium, Denmark, Finland, France, Germany, Greece, Ireland, Italy, Luxembourg, the Netherlands, Portugal, Spain, Sweden, and the United Kingdom. Data for Cambodia, Fiji, Indonesia, and Mongolia reflect the percentage of people who smoke 15 or more cigarettes a day. Data for Japan and the Republic of Korea reflect the percentage of people who smoke 20 or more cigarettes a day. Data for Lao PDR, Myanmar, the Philippines, Singapore, Sri Lanka, and Vietnam reflect the percentage of people who smoke 18 or more cigarettes a day. Data for Malaysia reflect the percentage of people who smoke 25 or more cigarettes a day. Data for Thailand reflect the percentage of people who smoke 11 or more cigarettes a day. Data for the EU-15 reflect the percentage of the population aged 15 years or older who are daily smokers.
a. Different years apply to different countries.

of cigarettes in all of East Asia and the Pacific, except Singapore, Sri Lanka, and Thailand. By contrast, in the 15 countries that were members of the European Union prior to May 1, 2004,[1] taxes on the price of cigarettes average 58 percent. However, the proportion of smokers in the population is quite similar in both regions.

So-called sin taxes, such as levies on alcohol and tobacco, have the added value of raising revenues while lowering health care costs, improving health status, and adding to labor productivity. Tobacco taxes are particularly beneficial. China, with its large population, is estimated to account for 30 percent of the world's tobacco consumption. Sin taxes are thought to be regressive, but lower-income groups are, in fact, typically more price sensitive.

Sin taxes that are earmarked for use only in a particular sector, such as health, can be inflexible and distortionary in overall fiscal policy. Although earmarked taxes generate fiscal space, they can displace existing general revenue funding, making the net impact on overall resources for health minimal. The amount of the revenue generated through the earmarked tax is often offset by an equivalent reduction in the general tax-funded proportion of the budget allocated to the health sector. Earmarked taxes can also reduce the ability of spending budgets to respond to changing public priorities and macroeconomic circumstances (McIntyre and Mooney 2007).

Improved revenue-raising capacity, although important, is only one factor and is not sufficient by itself for increasing allocations for health. Countries in East Asia and the Pacific generally commit less public funding to health relative to other countries in similar income categories. This practice is confirmed by figure 4.12, which shows that the health share of total government spending in East Asia and the Pacific is less than 15 percent, except in Japan, Palau, and Timor-Leste. In Cambodia, the Solomon Islands, and Timor-Leste, donor spending accounts for a very large share of total government spending on health.

Prioritizing health in the government budget is linked to difficult political economy considerations. Reducing unproductive expenditures to make space for health often involves difficult political trade-offs. The literature suggests that factors such as the level of democratization, income inequality, ethno-linguistic fractionalization, and initial levels of education are important determinants of the degree to which governments prioritize health.

Figure 4.12 Health Expenditure as a Share of Total Government Expenditure, 2005

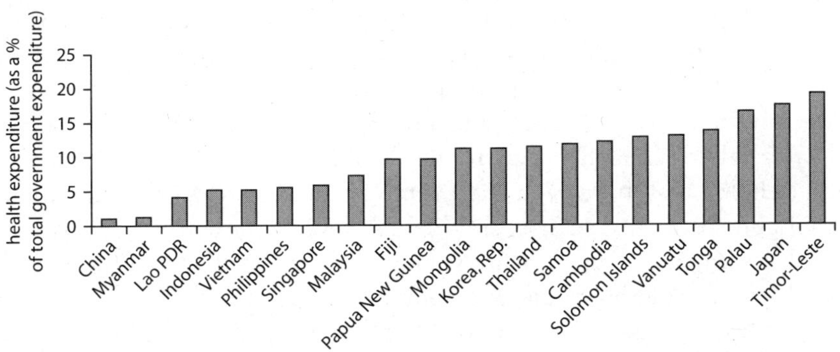

Source: World Health Organization's National Health Accounts database.

User Fees, Exemptions, and Targeting

In East Asia and the Pacific, charges are generally levied for most health services and medicines provided under the public or social insurance system. Immunization and family planning services are usually free, and primary care is also exempt from charges in some cases (for example, in the Philippines).

In an effort to target public spending to needy groups, most governments have exemption schemes in place for the poor, the elderly, and children (table 4.5). In Indonesia, ownership of a health card entitles households to free health care at public facilities. The card is allocated to households that village leaders identify as poor. Similarly, health equity funds in Cambodia and Lao PDR help poor households pay user fees and other costs associated with seeking care.

Poor implementation of fee waivers and related programs targeted to the poor often weaken the intended effects of these schemes (Arhin-Tenkorang 2001; Tien and Chee 2002). One reason is the shortage of medicines at public sector facilities. When users have to purchase drugs from private pharmacies, the waiver for drug fees becomes redundant. A second reason is a lack of accountability on the part of public providers to their users. In a context in which official fees exist and are accepted as the norm, providers can introduce informal fees that are not covered by the fee waiver schemes.

Impact of OOP Payments for Health Care

OOP payments are the principal means of financing health care throughout much of East Asia and the Pacific and place a significant burden on household resources in many LMICs. If payments for health are large relative to household resources, the disruption to material living standards could be substantial or even catastrophic. *Catastrophic payments* for health care are defined as payments in excess of a substantial proportion of the household budget, usually by 10 percent to 40 percent (Van Doorslaer and others 2006; Xu and others 2003). This measure does not, however, take into account the longer-term effects of health-related financial catastrophe on household welfare. For instance, households may borrow at high interest rates or forgo critical human capital investments, such as children's schooling, to pay excessively high health care bills. This measure simply analyzes health spending relative to the household budget at one point in time.

A recent cross-country study of equity in health care in East Asia and the Pacific (known as Equitap, or Equity in Asia-Pacific Health

Table 4.5 User Fees and Exemptions

Country	*Charged services*	*Free services*	*Income and poverty-related fee waivers*	*Nonpoor groups exempt from charges*
Cambodia	Fees for most services were introduced in 1996.	Prenatal care after the fifth visit and inpatient services for neonates born at some public hospitals are free.	The low-income population is exempt from user fees	n.a.
China	Inpatient and outpatient services (including medicines) are charged.	Vaccination, immunization, and family planning are free.	n.a.	Old Red Army soldiers and retirees are exempt.
Hong Kong SAR, China	Inpatient and outpatient care (including medicines) and dental services are charged.	Accident care and emergency care were free until December 2002.	Welfare recipients exempt	Civil servants and dependents (with reduced rate for inpatient care) and hospital staff members and dependents are exempt.
Indonesia	All medical care and medicines are charged.	No services are free.	The poor are exempt from all charges; indirect relation of inpatient charges to income through price discrimination	Charges are determined at the local government level. Some better-off local governments provide free health center care.
Korea, Rep.	All medical care and medicines are charged. Copayments under SHI are 20%, at most, for inpatient services and 30–55% for outpatient services depending on the institution. In addition, some services are not covered by SHI	No services are free.	None; SHI premium proportional to income but copayments and charges not related to income	The elderly (> age 65 years) pay half the deductible for outpatient services from clinics.

(continued)

Table 4.5 *(continued)*

Country	*Charged services*	*Free services*	*Income and poverty-related fee waivers*	*Nonpoor groups exempt from charges*
	and are paid for by OOP. The sum of copayments and OOP payments isestimated at 40–50% for outpatientservices and 60–70 % for inpatient services.			
Lao PDR	Fees were introduced in 1996. There are7 charged items in central, provincial, and district hospitals: medical records and other documents; supplies; laboratory, radiology, and other diagnostics; medicine; medical appliances; curative cost; and room and board.	Diagnostics and admission at health centers are free.	Low-income is population exempt	Government employees and their families, pensioners, monks, and students are exempt.
Malaysia	Inpatient, outpatient,primary, and dental care are charged, as well asx-rays and other diagnostics.	Family planning, vaccinations, immunizations, and outpatient pre- and postnatal care are free. Treatment of infectious diseases in third-class wards and dental care for pregnant women and preschool children are free.	Indigent population exempt by the authority of hospital directors (upper limit on charges for third-class ward patients)	The following groups are exempt: infants less than 1 year (outpatient); state rulers, governors, and their families; civil servants (including retirees) and their dependents; and local authority employees and their dependents.
Mongolia	For all inpatient services, patientsmake copayments of 15% and 10% for tertiary- and secondary-level services,	The following services are free: medical emergency and ambulance services; treatment of tuberculosis, cancer, mental illness, and infections; research service;	Poor exempt from user fees and copayments (no clear definition of poor)	The following groups are exempt: disadvantaged people; children under age 16; people with no other source of income except a pension;

	respectively. Some outpatient diagnostic and treatment services at the secondary and tertiary levels are also subject to user fees.	planned immunization; sanitation and disinfections of the sources of communicable diseases; medical examinations, tests, and treatments provided during pregnancy, delivery and postdelivery care under the instructions of medical institutions (only for reasons related to pregnancy and birth delivery); medical services provided to mothers and children; treatment of people who have been injured or fallen sick during natural calamities, accidents, or the outbreak of dangerous, infectious, or mass diseases; treatment of people who have been injured or have suffered an illness because of unavoidable danger and extreme necessity to save a life or to prevent a large scale of damages; expenses of diseases requiring lengthy rehabilitation; some costs of palliative care; and primary health care and services.		mothers and fathers caring for children under age 2 (twins under age 3); military personnel on active duty; persons specified in article 12 of the Social Welfare Law; pregnant mothers; women above age 55 and men above age 60.
Philippines	Inpatient services (including medicines) are charged.	Consultation and medicines at primary care facilities and hospitals and outpatient services are free (donations accepted). Shortages result in people often purchasing medicines privately.	The poor are considered charity patients and are exempt from hospital charges.	Elderly people (over 60 years) are exempt.
Taiwan, China	All medical care and medicines are charged. There is a fee	Family planning and vaccinations and immunizations are free.	Low-income exempt from National	Residents of remote areas are exempt.

(continued)

Table 4.5 *(continued)*

Country	*Charged services*	*Free services*	*Income and poverty-related fee waivers*	*Nonpoor groups exempt from charges*
	schedule for outpatient services. For inpatientservices, there is a copayment of 10% (5% if chronic) if the lengthofstay is less than 30 days. The rate increases thereafter.		Health Insurance copayments.	
Thailand	All medical care and medicines are charged. In October 2001, the government instituted a fixed fee (B 30) with a very minimal copayment.	Nonpersonal health care and Expanded Programme on Immunization vaccinations are free.	Poor exempt from user fees and copayments, as well as those "unable to pay" (informally)	Children (under age 12;), the elderly (over age 60), public health volunteers, and monks are exempt.
Timor-Leste	n.a.	All medical care and medicinesare free.	n.a.	n.a.
Vietnam	Fees for most services were introduced in 1989. Medicines are rarely provided free of charge.	Outpatient services at communal health centers are free.	Fee exemptions for individuals who have certification of indigence from their neighborhood or the People's Committee of their village	Families of health personnel, certain classes of patients (such as patients with disabilities or with tuberculosis), and orphans are exempt.

Sources: Akashi and others 2004; Patcharanarumol 2008; Van Doorslaer and others 2006.
Note: n.a. = not applicable.

Systems) (Van Doorslaer and others 2006) found that the proportion of households incurring catastrophic payments for health care is highest in Bangladesh, China, India, and Vietnam (figure 4.13). In Vietnam, for instance, OOP payments for health care exceed 25 percent of the nonfood budget for 15 percent of households. By contrast, in Malaysia, the Philippines, Sri Lanka, and Thailand, OOP payments exceed 10 percent of the nonfood budget for only 5 percent or less of all households. Among HICs, the incidence of catastrophic payments is highest in the Republic of Korea because of the high level of social insurance copayments. It is no coincidence that the frequency of catastrophic payments is higher in countries where there is greater reliance on OOP financing for health care.

The Equitap study also found that catastrophic payments in HICs tend to be evenly distributed or slightly concentrated on poor households. In most LICs, however, rich households have a higher propensity to incur catastrophic payments. This finding may reflect the inability of the poorest of the poor to divert resources from other basic needs and the possible forgoing of care by the poor. In countries such as China and Vietnam, where there were no fee waivers or exemptions for poor households at the time of the study, poor households were as likely or more likely to incur catastrophic payments.

Figure 4.13 Proportion of Households Incurring Catastrophic Payments

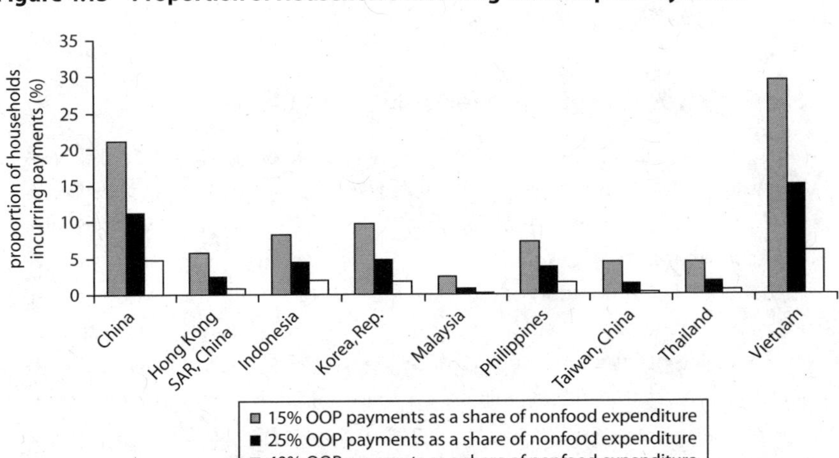

Source: Van Doorslaer and others 2006.
Note: Catastrophic payments are defined as OOP payments exceeding 15 percent of nonfood expenditure.

In the absence of health insurance and other social safety nets to protect against the catastrophic costs of health care, poor households that are faced with health shocks are vulnerable to further impoverishment. The Equitap study reassessed measures of poverty in 11 low- to middle-income countries in Asia by calculating total household resources both with and without OOP payments (Van Doorslaer and others 2006). The study found that more than 78 million people, representing about 3 percent of the total population in the 11 countries studied, fell below the extreme poverty threshold of US$1 per day when payments for health care were subtracted from the countries' resources. These findings lend support to earlier qualitative studies suggesting that health care payments cause impoverishment (Narayan and others 2000).

Households cope with catastrophic payments for health care by saving, selling assets, and reducing food consumption. Poor households hold more wealth in liquid form to protect themselves from income shocks (Gottret and Schieber 2006). Health shocks have a significant impact on households not only because of the large OOP payments associated with the care of the illness, but also because of income losses that occur when a working member of the family becomes ill. Box 4.4 provides recent evidence on the impact of health shocks in China and describes some household coping mechanisms. This issue of equity is also discussed in chapter 8 of this book.

Box 4.4

Health Shocks and Impoverishment in China

The OOP share of total health spending in China is one of the highest in Asia, having grown from 20 percent in 1978 to nearly 60 percent in 2000. The proportion of the population experiencing catastrophic health expenditures (defined as health expenses that are more than 25 percent of household consumption or more than 40 percent of nonfood consumption) is higher in China than elsewhere in Asia, and is concentrated among the poor. Health shocks can have devastating consequences for these households, as evidenced by the accompanying figure, which compares the effects of illness on a household to other types of shocks. The problem of large OOP costs for health care is compounded by the lack of any safety net scheme that protects families from not only the medical costs but also from the income losses associated with illness.

Impact of Illness on a Chinese Household Compared to Other Impacts, 1990s

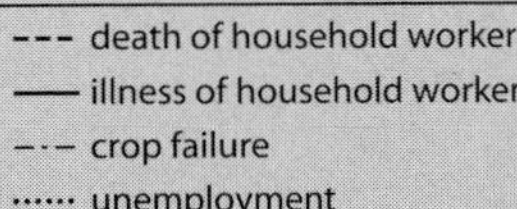

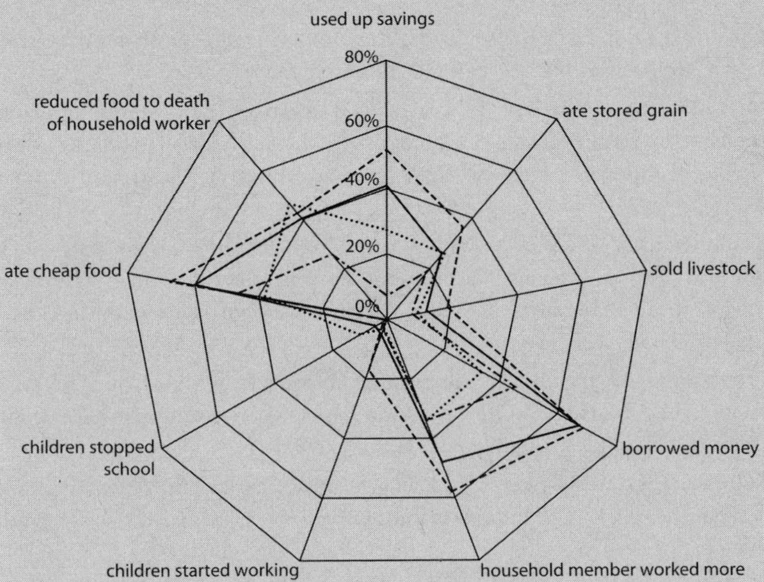

Source: Wagstaff and others 2009.

In rural China, household survey data conducted by the Ministry of Civil Affairs and the World Bank found that health shocks

- have larger effects on income than even crop failure, which is the most commonly reported shock;
- are more likely than crop failure to push households into poverty;
- are more likely than other shocks to result in households depleting their savings; eating stored grain; selling livestock, furniture, and other property; borrowing money; and making surviving household members work more; and
- have a longer-lasting impact than do other shocks

Source: Wagstaff and others 2009.

a. The substantial number of households that reported relying on savings confirms the widely held view that one of the factors behind China's high savings rate is the fear that Chinese families have of the financial consequences of health shocks.

Note

1. These countries were Austria, Belgium, Denmark, Finland, France, Germany, Greece, Ireland, Italy, Luxembourg, the Netherlands, Portugal, Spain, Sweden, and the United Kingdom.

References

ADB (Asian Development Bank). 2007. *Key Indicators of Developing Asian and Pacific Countries.* Manila: Asian Development Bank.

Ahmad, Ehtisham. 2006. "Taxation Reforms and Sequencing of Intergovernmental Reforms in China: Preconditions for a Xiaokang Society." In *Public Finance in China,* ed. Jiwei Lou and Shuilin Wang. World Bank: Washington, DC.

Akashi, Hidechika, Takako Yamada, Eng Huot, Koum Kanal, and Takao Sugimoto. 2004. "User Fees at a Public Hospital in Cambodia: Effects on Hospital Performance and Provider Attitudes. *Social Science and Medicine* 58 (3): 553–64.

Arhin-Tenkorang, Dyna. 2001. "Mobilizing Resources for Health: The Case for User Fees Revisited." CID Working Paper 81, Center for International Development, Harvard University, Cambridge, MA.

Baeza, Christian C., and Truman G. Packard. 2006. *Beyond Survival: Protecting Households from Health Shocks in Latin America.* Washington, DC: World Bank.

Chen, J. 2004. "A Ten-Year Review and Prospects of Chinese Medical Insurance System." *China Medical Insurance Research* 3: 6–8.

Ensor, Timothy, and Robin Thompson. 1998. "Health Insurance as a Catalyst to Change in Former Communist Countries?" *Health Policy and Planning* 43 (3): 203–18.

Escobar, María Luisa. and Panagiota Panopoulou. 2003. "Health." In *Colombia: The Economic Foundation of Peace,* ed. Marcelo M. Giugale, Oliver Lafourcade, and Connie Luff, 653–701. Washington, DC: World Bank.

Gottret, Pablo, and George Schieber. 2006. *Health Financing Revisited: A Practitioner's Guide.* Washington, DC: World Bank.

Hasegawa, Toshihiko. 2005. "Japan." In *Social Health Insurance: Selected Case Studies from Asia and the Pacific,* 19–20. New Delhi: World Health Organization Regional Office for South-East Asia and World Health Organization Regional Office for the Western Pacific Region.

Hsiao, William C., and R. Paul Shaw, eds. 2007. *Social Health Insurance for Developing Nations.* Washington, DC: World Bank.

Kutzin, Joseph. 2009. "Health Care Financing in Asia." Presentation to the World Health Organization, Manila.

Langenbrunner, John C. 2005. "Health Care Financing and Purchasing in ECA: An Overview of Issues and Reforms." World Bank, Washington, DC.

Langenbrunner, John C., and Olusoji Adeyi. 2003. "Decade of Experience: Lessons Learned, Implications for the Future." World Bank, Washington, DC.

Leung, Gabriel M., Keith Y. K. Ting, G. M. K. Yeung, E. S. K. Leung, Eva L. H. Tsui, D. W. S. Lam, Caroline S. H. Tsang, A. Y. K. Fung, and Su Vi Lo. 2008. "Hong Kong's Domestic Health Spending: Financial Years 1989/90 through 2004/05" Hong Kong Medical Journal 14, suppt 27: 2–23.

McIntyre, Di, and Gavin Mooney, eds. 2007. *The Economics of Health Equity.* Cambridge, U.K.: Cambridge University Press.

Narayan, Deepa, Raj Patel, Kai Schafft, Anne Rademacher, and Sarah Koch-Schulte. 2000. *Voices of the Poor: Can Anyone Hear Us?* New York: Oxford University Press.

Nguyen, Thi Kim Phong. 2006. "Extending Social Health Insurance to Informal Economy Workers: The Case of Vietnam." Presentation at the Conference on Extending Social Health Insurance to Informal Economy Workers, Manila. October 18–20.

Nickell, Stephen. 2004. "Employment and Taxes." CEP Discussion Paper 634, Centre for Economic Performance, London School of Economics, London U.K.

O'Donnell, Owen, Eddy Van Doorslaer, Ravi P. Rannan-Eliya, Aparnaa Somanathan, Shiva Raj Adhikari, Baktygul Akkazieva, Deni Harbianto, Charu C. Garg, Piya Hanvoravongchai, Alejandro N. Herrin, Mohammed N. Huq, Shamsia Ibragimova, Anup Karan, Soon-man Kwon, Gabriel M. Leung, Jui-fen Rachel Lu, Ohkusa Yasushi, Badri Raj Pande, Rachel Racelis, Keith Tin, Kanjana Tisayaticom, Laksono Trisnantoro, Quan Wan, Bong-Min Yang, and Yuxin Zhao. 2008. "Who Pays for Health Care in Asia?" *Journal of Health Economics* 27 (2): 460–75.

OECD (Organisation for Economic Co-operation and Development). 2004. "Proposal for a Taxonomy of Health Insurance." OECD, Paris.

Patcharanarumol, Walaiporn. 2008. "Health Care Financing for the Poor in Lao PDR." PhD thesis, University of London, London.

Statistics Indonesia and Macro International. 2008. *Indonesia Demographic and Health Survey 2007.* Calverton, MD: Statistics Indonesia and Macro International.

Tien, Marie, and Grace Chee. 2002. "Literature Review and Findings: Implementation of Waiver Policies." Partners for Health Reform*plus*, Washington, DC.

Van Doorslaer, Eddy, Owen O'Donnell, Ravi P. Rannan-Eliya, Aparnaa Somanathan, Shiva Raj Adhikari, Charu C. Garg, Deni Harbianto, Alejandro N. Herrin, Mohammed N. Huq, Shamsia Ibragimova, Anup Karan, Chiu Wan Ng, Badri Raj Pande, Rachel Racelis, Sihai Tao, Keith Tin, Kanjana Tisayaticom, Laksono Trisnantoro, Chitpranee Vasavid, and Yuxin Zhao. 2006. "Effect of Payments for Health Care on Poverty Estimates in 11 countries in Asia: An Analysis of Household Survey Data." *Lancet* 368 (9544): 1357–64.

Wagstaff, Adam. 2007a. "Health Systems in East Asia: What Can Developing Countries Learn from Japan and the Asian Tigers?" *Health Economics* 16 (5): 441–56.

——. 2007b. "Social Health Insurance Reexamined." Policy Research Working Paper 4111, World Bank, Washington, DC.

——. 2009. "Social Health Insurance vs. Tax-Financed Health Systems: Evidence from the OECD." Policy Research Working Paper 4821, World Bank, Washington, DC.

Wagstaff, Adam, and Mariam Claeson. 2004. *The Millennium Development Goals for Health: Rising to the Challenges.* Washington, DC: World Bank.

Wagstaff, Adam, Magnus Lindelow, Shiyong Wang, and Shuo Zhang. 2009. *Reforming China's Rural Health Care System.* Washington, DC: World Bank.

WHO (World Health Organization). 2003. *World Health Survey: Lao PDR 2003.* Geneva: WHO.

World Bank. 2005. *World Development Report 2005: A Better Investment Climate for Everyone.* Washington, DC: World Bank.

——. 2008. *Good Practices in Health Financing: Lessons from Reforms in Low- and Middle-Income Countries.* Washington, DC: World Bank.

Wu, R. 2004. "Try to Perfect the System." *China Medical Insurance Research* 1–2: 16–19.

Xu, Ke, David B. Evans, Kei Kawabata, Riadh Zeramdini, Jan Klavus, and Christopher J. L. Murray. 2003. "Household Catastrophic Health Expenditure: A Multicountry Analysis." *Lancet* 362 (9378): 111–17.

Zweifel, Peter, and Willard G. Manning. 2001. "Moral Hazard and Consumer Incentives in Health Care." In *Handbook of Health Economics,* vol. 1A, ed. Anthony J. Culyer and Joseph P. Newhouse, 409–59. Amsterdam: Elsevier.

CHAPTER 5

Pooling and Management of Funds

Pooling: Is It Important?

Health risks in any nation are highly skewed, with approximately 10 percent of the population, on average, consuming about 60 percent of total health expenditure. Approximately 30 percent of the population has no expenditure. The example of France is shown in figure 5.1. Universal social health insurance (SHI) or national tax-financed systems, when implemented well, pool risks from rich to poor, from healthy to sick, and from young to old (figure 5.2). This pooling can help improve equitable access to health services and can help prevent impoverishment from out-of-pocket (OOP) payments (figure 5.3).

Fragmentation of funds is both inequitable and inefficient, and pooling of funds would allow any country to achieve better spreading of risks, from rich to poor and from healthy to sick. The spreading of risks—from those with resources to those who need services—is the objective of insurance. A review of the current configuration of countries in the region suggests that this objective is not fully achieved, especially in low-income and middle-income countries (LMICs). At the same time, objectives are generally better met as countries move from low- to middle- and high-income status. Indeed, high-income countries (HICs) in the region serve as models for developing and transitioning economies.

Figure 5.1 Concentration of Total Health Expenditure in France, 2001

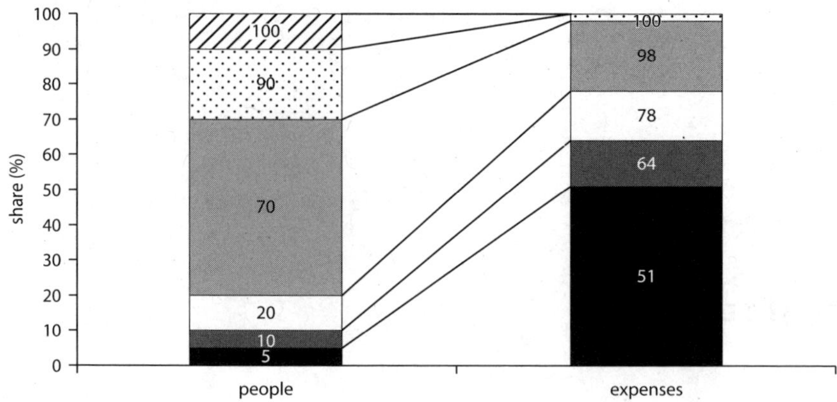

Source: Kutzin 2009.

Figure 5.2 Expenditures by Age Group for Organisation for Economic Co-operation and Development Countries, Normalized Gross Domestic Product Per Capita, 1999

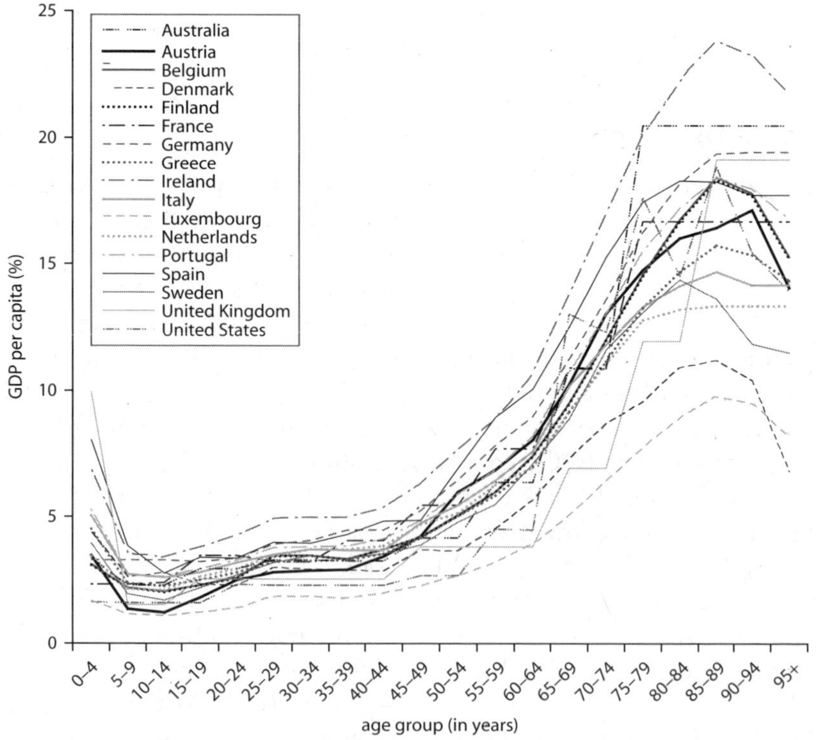

Sources: Dormont and others 2007 based on data from the European Network of Economic Policy Research Institutes' Ageing Health, and Retirement in Europe project and the Organisation for Economic Co-operation and Development.

Note: OECD = Organisation for Economic Co-operation and Development; GDP = gross domestic product.

Figure 5.3 Effects of Risk Pooling

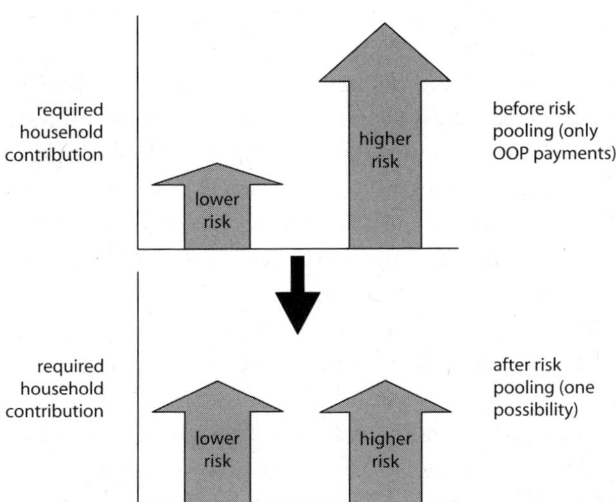

Source: Baeza and Packard 2006.

Each group of economies in the region is reviewed and assessed against the framework of global experience as set out by Gottret and Schieber (2006).

Pooling and Management of Funds in East Asia and the Pacific

High-Income Economies

Financing reforms in HICs should support the ultimate goal of universal coverage, either as nationwide SHI programs or as a tax-financed national health service (Gottret and Schieber 2006). Risk pooling and prepayment functions are essential because small, fragmented risk pools are insufficient. Pooling tends to become more centralized in HICs.

There is pooling across the higher-income economies in the region (Hong Kong SAR, China; Japan; the Republic of Korea; Singapore; and Taiwan, China) that has evolved and improved over time. In Hong Kong SAR, China, and in Singapore, there is a single budgetary pool similar to the United Kingdom's National Health Service. For example, in Hong Kong SAR, China, the Ministry of Health (MoH) receives an annual budget from the Treasury that is based on the MoH's spending history, with adjustments for inflation and any anticipated increase in the demand for care. Additional budgets also are provided for newly approved projects. Singapore, however, also relies on mandatory health savings accounts (HSAs) for outpatient care and catastrophic care. HSAs can pool funds for the individual or family over time, but these fail to pool across various groups of the population. However, a separate fund for poor populations has been established (Medifund) that is financed by the state (Hanvoravongchai 2002; Leung and others 2008).[1]

In the other three economies—Japan; the Republic of Korea; and Taiwan, China—an SHI system pools funds. Historically, these countries had multiple pools because SHI was initially a multiple insurer system based on occupation and residence. Only Japan retains a multiple insurer system (and multiple pools).

In the Republic of Korea, the National Health Insurance system started with more than 350 not-for-profit health insurance societies for three different groups of insured persons: industrial workers, government employees and teachers, and self-employed workers. It was phased in over 12 years, beginning in 1977, according to the size of the employer. Employers with 500 to 300 employees were the first participants, and then the system grew to include employers with 100 employees. The final stages included the self-employed in rural and urban areas. In July 2000, under strong political leadership, the societies were merged into a single scheme. The integration included 139 employee societies, 227 self-employed groups, and the government and private school programs. Inequity across income and occupation groups was a major concern leading to the reform. The financial merger was not fully implemented until July 2003. Administrative costs are much lower because of the integration of schemes—falling from an estimated 10.0 percent of all expenditures in 1994 to 0.4 percent in 2006 (figure 5.4).

Taiwan, China, achieved universal coverage in 1995 by merging three existing SHI schemes into a single fund. Before 1995, only 57 percent of residents had coverage through Labor Insurance (instituted in 1950),

Figure 5.4 Administrative Costs as a Proportion of Expenditures in the National Health Insurance System of the Republic of Korea, 1994–2006

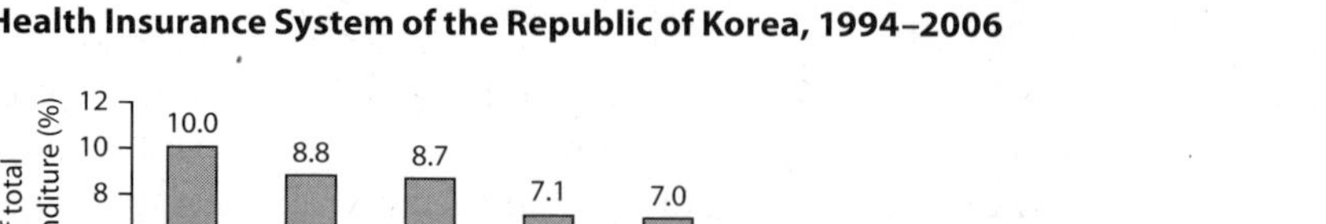

Source: Chun 2007.

Government Employee Insurance (instituted in 1958), and Farmers Insurance (instituted in 1989). The single-payer model was developed to better ensure access and to better control costs at a national (and global) level (Lu and Hsiao 2003). Claims processing was standardized. As in the Republic of Korea, administrative costs in Taiwan, China, are low, at an estimated 1.76 percent (Hu 2007).

In Japan, there are multiple pools under the SHI system. Both employer and community-based plans have evolved and become complex over time. The MoH regulates and, in some cases, operates insurance. There are three separate tiers of SHI plans, with many variations within each. The first two tiers are employer based, and the third is community based. The first tier features the public sector plan, plans for employees of large companies, and plans managed by the mutual aid associations for civil servants. There are currently 78 plans for civil servants and 1,600 plans for employees of large corporations. The second tier consists of one government (MoH) subsidy plan for small and medium-size enterprises. The third tier—so-called citizen health insurance for the self-employed and pensioners—consists of community-based plans, including 1,820 municipality-based plans and 166 occupation-based plans (for example, plans for carpenters, physicians, and dentists).

The contribution base and relative risks vary across Japanese plans and tiers, with the second and third tiers receiving substantial government subsidies for low-income beneficiaries. The second tier has a 14 percent subsidy, and the third tier has an average 30 to 50 percent subsidy for occupations, with up to an 80 percent subsidy for the poorest communities (Ikegami 2006). There are three equalization mechanisms across plans: (a) government subsidies for plans with low-income enrollees; (b) cross-subsidization across plans and a mandatory reinsurance fund for all plans (each plan contributes 80 percent of the total budget to a reinsurance fund, and medical claims exceeding a target level are then paid out of the reinsurance fund); and (c) a uniform fee schedule for providers (Ikegami 2008).

Middle-Income Economies

Globally, middle-income countries (MICs) are characterized by inequitable and ineffective financing systems that rely on large OOP expenses. Risk pooling typically needs to be consolidated to improve allocative efficiency, equity, and financial protection. The associated benefits are greater purchasing power and efficiency through lower transaction costs (Gottret and Schieber 2006).

Thailand is perhaps the best performer among East Asian and Pacific MICs. Thailand has public schemes and private insurance funds. It has legislated a process to move to a single-payer scheme, although it is not clear how long this process could take. The public funds pools include (a) the noncontributory Civil Servant Medical Benefit Scheme (CSMBS), which covers about 5.9 million government employees and their dependents (parents, spouses, and children younger than 20 years old); (b) the social security scheme introduced in the 1990s, or SHI, which covers about 8 million private sector employees (excluding dependents); and (c) the residual national universal coverage scheme (known as the 30 Baht Scheme), which covers people who are not eligible for SHI and CSMBS (about 48 million people, or most of the population). The 30 Baht Scheme replaces previous public health welfare schemes such as the Low-Income Scheme, the Voluntary Health Card, and the Welfare Scheme for elderly people and children younger than 12 years old. It also incorporats the previously uninsured into a single, unified scheme. In addition to these public schemes, private voluntary health insurance covers about 5 million people (see the forthcoming volume of East Asia–Pacific Country Health Financing Profiles).

China currently has a very fragmented system with four major schemes based on occupation, welfare level, and location (urban or rural). These four schemes include (a) formal urban sector workers and government workers (managed by the Ministry of Human Resources and Social Security, or MoHRSS); (b) informal and nonworking groups in urban areas, especially pensioners and children (managed by the MoHRSS); (c) a rural health cooperative scheme (managed by the MoH); and (d) the Medical Assistance program for the poor and vulnerable groups to supplement the basic package (managed by the Ministry of Civil Affairs). These schemes have expanded coverage considerably over the past few years but are vulnerable to adverse selection (the tendency of lower-risk groups—the young and the healthy—not to join), threatening their financial sustainability. Each scheme varies in its dimensions of management and benefits. There are also schemes for large state-run enterprises or sectors such as railroads and civil aviation. Finally, there is a supplemental, employment-based insurance program (Wagstaff and others 2009).

China's fragmentation is exacerbated by the partitioning of urban insurance into coverage for outpatient care through HSAs and coverage for inpatient care through the insurer. Furthermore, the schemes are vertically fragmented; the main schemes are being managed at local (county and municipal) levels. So, for example, the rural scheme pools funds and is managed at the district or county level. China has almost 3,000 counties, which have created literally thousands of risk pools across the country.

Pooling is also fragmented in Indonesia, which has a variety of insurance arrangements (figure 5.5). About 27 to 41 percent of the population is currently entitled to health insurance (depending on the source of the estimate), including formal sector workers under compulsory health programs and poor informal sector workers (originally under the Askeskin program). The 1992 law on health (Law No. 2/1992) allowed general and private insurance companies to operate in the health market. By 1997, 49 companies were selling health insurance, and an estimated 1.6 million people were covered by commercial indemnity health policies in 1998 (up from 450,000 in 1993). In 1993, PT Askes, the parastatal company that insures civil servants and their families,

Figure 5.5 Type and Coverage of Health Insurance Systems in Indonesia, 1999

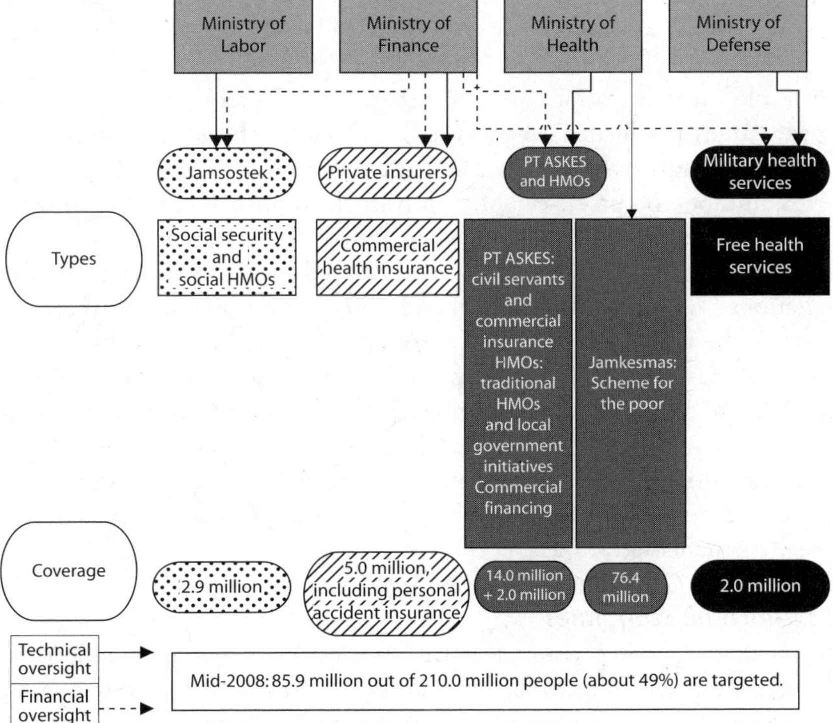

Source: World Bank staff based on Ministry of Health data.

also began marketing health insurance to the government and privately owned companies.

Since 2008, a new program called Jamkesmas (a community health insurance scheme replacing Askeskin) has provided health service access to poor and near-poor people by exempting user charges at the point of delivery. The current program target is 76 million poor people. Jamkesmas is a social aid program and is covered by the national budget. Separate government budgets provide free basic and referral health services for poor families, pregnant mothers (for deliveries), postpartum mothers, and infants, as well as assist in the development of health facilities (see the forthcoming volume of East Asia–Pacific Country Health Financing Profiles).

In the Philippines, pools of funds are split in the public sector with multiple private prepayment pools. The largest current program is the National Health Insurance Program, an SHI scheme that is estimated to cover 79 percent of the population. Of those covered, 42 percent are from the public and privately employed sectors, 36 percent are from the indigent population, 21 percent are individually paying members, and the remaining are nonpaying members. Public health facilities provide separate supply-side funding with subsidized public health services (for example, immunization, and micronutrient supplementation) and primary to tertiary health care services for a fee for those who can pay and for free for those who are poor and not yet enrolled in the SHI program.

A number of profit-oriented private insurance companies provide health benefits, including investor-based, HMOs, directed to the employed sector. In 2005, 17 investor-based health maintenance organizations (HMOs) operated in the Philippines. Although information is incomplete and unsystematic, several community-based health financing schemes exist that are designed to address problems related to inadequate or unaffordable services. These schemes take various forms, from single-purpose programs to multipurpose programs that address both health and other socioeconomic concerns. The schemes are often donor driven (see the forthcoming volume of East Asia–Pacific Country Health Financing Profiles).

Low-Income Economies

In most low-income countries (LICs), poverty magnifies the need for health care, while shrinking the capacity to finance it. The region has a number of countries struggling with various solutions to address the need for prepayment and financial protection. Many need to improve financial protection through appropriate prepayment and risk-pooling mechanisms that are adapted to country-specific circumstances. LICs face difficult trade-offs, and there are no "one-size-fits-all" solutions (Gottret and Schieber 2006).

Vietnam and Mongolia have each instituted new SHI programs, but neither has fully pooled funds yet. Vietnam depends on multiple pooling schemes (the national budget for supply-side subsidies and the two SHI schemes) and on private insurance and OOP spending at the local level.[2] Life insurers sell health insurance riders, and an estimated 2 million people are covered in this way (Wagstaff and others 2009; forthcoming volume of East Asia–Pacific Country Health Financing Profiles).

An SHI scheme is part of the Mongolian social security system, and the State Social Insurance General Office (SSIGO) is responsible for the management and administration of all social insurance schemes, including health insurance. The SSIGO operates under the auspices of the Ministry of Social Welfare and Labor. According to the Public Finance and Management Law, however, the MoH is the single purchaser. In effect, both the MoH and SSIGO engage in purchasing with separate pools of funds. There have been long-recognized issues with coordination, consultation, negotiation, and information sharing between these two main purchasers of health services. In terms of actual execution, however, both the state budget and health insurance are under the single Treasury system of the Ministry of Finance (see the forthcoming volume of East Asia–Pacific Country Health Financing Profiles).

Other LICs, such as Cambodia, the Lao People's Democratic Republic, and Timor-Leste, rely on donor pools of funds to provide prepayment or to directly deliver services. In Cambodia and Lao PDR, a number of interesting and important initiatives are being developed to provide new prepayment schemes—so-called health equity funds (HEFs)—and to better ensure access and financial protection (see Hawkins 2007; Sanigest International 2008; forthcoming volume of East Asia–Pacific Country Health Financing Profiles).

From 1975 to the late 1990s, the government funded health care in Lao PDR, and services were officially provided free of charge in public health facilities. However, budgetary constraints increasingly limited the types of care that the government could finance. Health insurance is still in the early stages of development and accounts for less than 20 percent of total funding. For most of the rural population working in the informal sector (80 percent of the population), it may take some time before health insurance is a widely available and accepted method to pay for health services (Schwartz 2006).

Lao PDR currently has a mix of insurance schemes that is heavily assisted by user fees, donors, and nongovernmental organizations (NGOs). This mix makes the public health sector highly vertical and fragmented. Insurance schemes include the Social Health Insurance Fund (SHIF), four different community-based health insurance (CBHI) schemes, and the Civil Servants Scheme (CSS). As in China, different schemes are managed by different ministries—SHIF and CSS by the Ministry of Labor and Social Security and the four CBHI schemes by the MoH. The HEF initiative, managed by the MoH, is designed to mitigate the impact of catastrophic health expenses and compensates facilities for services provided to low-income patients who are exempt from user fees.

Cambodia also has an HEF initiative that attempts to increase access to health services for the poor. Health equity funding is a social transfer mechanism designed to provide targeted income transfers to the poor for the purpose of pooling funds and to pay for health care in the public health system through providers contracted by the HEF. Funding is commonly provided by donors but may come from multiple sources, including the community and the government.

A number of donors, in collaboration with the MoH, have started implementing HEFs since 2000. The number of HEFs has been growing rapidly, with around 40 operational HEFs at the end of 2006 in 29 operational districts. The total target population of those HEFs is estimated at 432,000 preidentified beneficiaries, 89,000 direct beneficiaries, and close to 1 million potential beneficiaries. The relative performance of HEFs varies widely in terms of overall coverage and cost efficiency, as does their effect on use of health services. Administrative costs are considerable. On the whole, HEFs have been seen as a promising approach to protect the poor, and studies suggest that HEFs improve financial protection (Annear and others 2006). HEFs have existed mostly in the contracted districts, where there has been some degree of monitoring and supervision to ensure reasonably good quality of services. The government is trying to standardize some of the key practices such as preidentification of the poor.

International and local NGOs have introduced a number of CBHI schemes in Cambodia over the past several years. The basic design of CBHI is predicated on the principle of community-level risk pooling and prepayment for health care. CBHI is a private, nonprofit, voluntary insurance mechanism based on the sale of low-cost insurance premiums that provide the purchaser and his or her family with coverage for a stated list of medical services provided at contracted public health facilities (generally health centers and referral hospitals).

In 2006, the CBHI schemes had only an estimated 33,122 members from 7,012 households. It is argued, however, that CBHI has played an important role in developing Cambodia's understanding of the use of prepayment mechanisms for health and has laid much of the necessary conceptual groundwork for a broader pooled insurance system. All of Cambodia's schemes are supported by external premium subsidies or by funding for administration that the sponsoring NGOs and other donors provide. Issues remain, however, including the following:

- CBHI premiums are too expensive for poor households.
- Geographic coverage of voluntary CBHI schemes is very low.
- Risk pooling in small communities has proven difficult, if not economically unviable, in numerous international experiences.

The future of CBHI in Cambodia is most likely limited to the program acting as an agent of SHI rather than being a primary element in providing social protection to the population. Indeed, the MoH has developed a master plan for SHI (including CBHI) that was officially released in March 2005. The strategy advocates a three-pronged approach: (a) compulsory SHI through the social security framework for public and private sector salaried workers and their dependents, (b) funding of this framework by a payroll tax (based on a percentage of salary and shared by the employee and employer) for the formal sector, and (c) voluntary CBHI (Hawkins 2007; Sanigest International 2008).

Analysis and Discussion

The small and numerous pools in many countries limit the potential for cross-subsidy, while perhaps unnecessarily increasing administrative costs in very limited funding contexts. Many countries in the region, such as Indonesia, Mongolia, the Philippines, and Vietnam, have established a national SHI program as a way to pool funds. Cambodia is also developing this blueprint. Important challenges still exist, however, in implementing national SHI programs in LMICs. These challenges include the low tax base, limited formal sector employment, high administrative expenditures to establish new organizational structures, weak regulatory and enforcement environment for collection and claims-based systems, and highly mobile populations such as migrant workers.

Figure 5.6 Per Capita Expenditures: Urban versus Rural Insurance in China, 2007

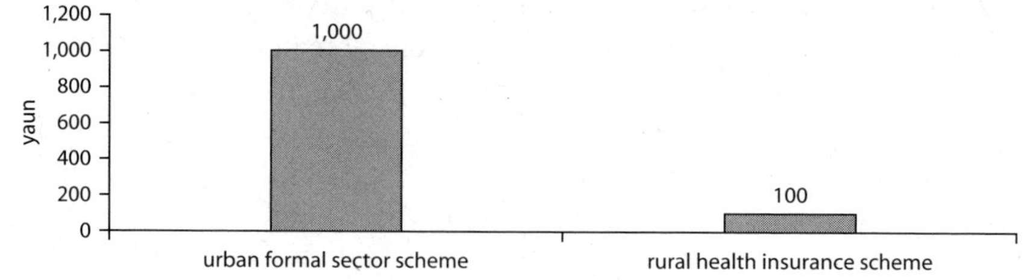

Source: Wagstaff and others 2009.

In some countries, such as Cambodia, current plans call for a separate administrative structure for civil servants and formal sector workers. This approach has been administratively unsuccessful in Thailand and in other countries with fragmented insurance pools. The decision is more political than technical. The government in Thailand, for example, has not been able to address the issue with civil servants politically.

Similarly, it is important to integrate poorer groups into the broader pooling of funds. HEFs are now well established institutionally in Cambodia and Lao PDR and could be used to make contributions to SHI for the poor. Similarly, in China, the Medical Assistance programs could be folded into larger social insurance pools. Perhaps China's biggest challenge will be to pool funds across geographic areas to spread the risk across urban and rural populations. The current per capita expenditure ratio of urban to rural areas is a profound 10:1 (figure 5.6).

Fragmentation can also involve segmentation in any country, leading to "inequity by design." Many LMICs, especially in Latin America, have experienced this problem. The lack of pooling is inefficient and increases administrative costs. Thus, more funds are wasted on administration than are used to provide high-quality services. Duplication of coverage and sometimes service responsibilities can be an issue. Relative lack of pooling further decreases the ability to leverage benefits from strategic purchasing. Multiple purchasers dilute incentives to increase provider performance.

Globally, there are various approaches to pooling, four of which are mentioned here:

- *Have a single pool.* Japan is an interesting model in the region. A single pooling fund was created in 1983 so that the multiple insurers that developed over time would share costs equally. This single pool pays for 70 percent of all costs (Ikegami 2006).

- *Adjust payments to insurance pools retrospectively, on the basis of relative risks.* This type of pooling is used in Germany.
- *Adjust premiums or payment rates.* Income-related contributions are paid into a risk-equalization fund, which equals 50 percent of the total insurance revenue. Premiums are based on community averages. This system is used in the Netherlands.
- *Pool either at the national level or at the regional or provincial level.* For example, Sweden and the United Kingdom pool at the national level, and Canada and Kazakhstan pool at the regional or provincial level.

Given that decentralization is a popular option in East Asia and the Pacific, several countries (including China and Indonesia) might find pooling at the national or regional (or provincial) level a useful model or interim model. Care would, however, need to be taken to ensure that pools would be large enough to cover population risks. Pooling size is less of an issue in more populous countries, but it may be an issue in less populous countries such as Cambodia. There is no "right" or "best" arrangement for the pooling of funds; as with all reforms, the essential starting point for decision makers is an understanding of existing arrangements. Both theory and evidence suggest, however, that from this starting point, reforms should aim to reduce the fragmentation of pooling. Options for reduction vary considerably across countries.

Countries with multiple pools should assess disparities across risk pools and develop a risk-adjustment mechanism across payers. Some regulatory framework and stewardship capacity would be needed, but establishing such a mechanism would increase equity, spread risks better, and encourage purchasers to better manage purchasing arrangements. It would create a virtual single pool for all. These types of mechanisms are technically achievable and are currently found in multi-insurer group systems in member countries of the Organisation for Economic Co-operation and Development (for example, Germany, Japan, and the Netherlands), as well as in MICs such as the Czech Republic and Morocco.

In effect, countries could create a virtual single pool among the multiple pools through the establishment of a redistribution fund. This single pool can be achieved through risk-adjusted allocations to various insurers. The experience of the Czech system is instructive. Czech reforms appear to have achieved success by subjecting the entire insurance pool to redistribution (thereby maximizing the scope for risk protection) and, at the same time, by lowering the benefits of risk selection for competing insurers. Retrospective risk adjusters can dilute insurer (purchaser) incentives to manage care and costs. Therefore, relative retrospective adjustments vary across countries and should be implemented prudently, allowing some opportunity for the purchaser to contain costs. The Czech Republic exemplifies a minimal retrospective risk adjuster (box 5.1).

Box 5.1

The Czech Republic Risk Adjustment Reforms

A law passed in 2003 in the Czech Republic introduced complete pooling of state contributions and all collected premiums that are redistributed between insurers on a capitation basis and adjusted for age and sex (according to 36 age and sex categories). Each insurer reports monthly the total amount of its collected premiums, as well as the number and age structure of its insured individuals. State payments for economically inactive citizens flow directly to a special account operated under the oversight of the insurers, the Ministry of Health, and the Ministry of Finance. The account's manager then calculates the total amount of income (collected premiums plus state payments) per standardized insured individual for the whole system and calculates the income of each insurer on the basis of the actual number of people insured and the age and sex structure. Within days, one-off payments between the insurers and the manager of the special account clear differences between the collected premiums and the income of a particular insurer after redistribution. Data provided by an individual insurer may be checked by the ministries or by a specialized task force consisting of representatives of all insurers. The data on redistribution results are also available to all insurers so that they can continuously follow the reports of their competitors.

In addition, because prospective risk adjustment systems fail to predict all variation in expenditures, the system includes an ex post partial compensation of expensive cases (a standardized methodology of accounting costs to insured individuals was issued with the 2003 law). If the annual costs of a client reach the limit of 25 times the average annual costs per client in the whole system, the insurer is compensated with 80 percent of the costs over that limit. Advances to cover expensive cases are divided between insurers according to historical numbers. Differences against the actual cost of expensive cases are set once a year when the prior year's financial results are published. In 2005, the compensation of expensive cases included 0.2 percent of the total population, and, redistributed 5.0 percent of total funds between insurers.

Source: Hrobon 2004.

Other countries have chosen to maintain multiple public funds, but they are introducing a unified regulatory framework to harmonize the rules that govern these funds. An example from the Middle East and North Africa is Morocco, which recently established a unified health insurance regulatory body. Lebanon is also proposing to harmonize payment systems across its various public funds. A number of other MICs with multiple public funds are opting to consolidate them to reduce the administrative complexities and costs. Examples of countries that have recently consolidated multiple health funds are: Estonia (from 22 to 7), the Kyrgyz Republic (from 7 to 1), Poland (from 14 to 1), and Tunisia (from 3 to 1) (Langenbrunner 2005; World Bank 2008).

Bureaucratically, there are also hurdles because in many countries, such as Cambodia, China, Lao PDR, and Mongolia, different government ministries manage different funds. A decision would need to be made in each country about whether the Ministry of Social Security or the Ministry of Health (or some other ministry) would bring various funds under one umbrella.

In the long term, governments with multiple pools might consider a unified single-pooled system for funding a core package of services for all citizens. This model is currently found in Canada; in Nordic countries, such as Norway and Sweden; in many Persian Gulf states such as Oman; and in the United Kingdom. The model would lower administrative costs and provide increased leveraging of the purchasing and commissioning of services.

The obstacles to full single pooling can pose both technical and political obstacles and might mean that this form of pooling would need to be done slowly over time. The opposition of Thailand's civil servants was noted earlier. Chile is one example of a country that implemented a set of reforms, including pooling, over a 15-year period (box 5.2), which is not unusual by global standards. Similarly, an LIC in Central Asia, the Kyrgyz Republic, pooled SHI and general revenue funds over a 12-year period, but only under long-standing pressure from donors, including the World Bank.

Governance will play an important role in pooling across funds. Savedoff and Gottret (2008) provide guidance from four case studies (Chile, Colombia, Estonia, and the Netherlands) on the types of governance arrangements needed for effective management of mandatory health insurance systems. Another study (World Bank 2008) analyzes nine good-practice cases of major health insurance expansions (Chile, Colombia, Costa Rica, Estonia, the Kyrgyz Republic, Sri Lanka, Thailand, Tunisia, and Vietnam) in terms of their common enabling

Box 5.2

Public Financing Reforms in Chile

In 1985, Chile implemented a radical reform of the health system (with structural reforms in the old-age pension system). The country separated the insurance and financial administration from public provision of health care services and created the National Health Fund (Fondo Nacional de Salud, or FONASA). FONASA was financed by a combination of general taxation (to subsidize the contributions for the poor, who are included in the pool from general taxation) and a 7 percent payroll tax contribution from formal sector workers (public and private). The reform aimed to consolidate all public financing for health in a single fund, reducing duplication and establishing the basis for implementing strategic purchasing in the public sector. FONASA consolidated the Ministry of Health financing (from general taxation) and the public Social Insurance Scheme for formal workers (abolished in 1985). As a result of subsequent reforms in the mid-1990s and a final set of legal reforms in 2004, FONASA has become the most important insurer in the country, covering almost 80 percent of the population. FONASA is mandated to collect and pool all public revenue for health and to use the revenue to purchase services from public and private providers. Implementation of FONASA reforms has taken more than 10 years. Consolidating all resources was a complex technical and political process. FONASA's consolidation as the health service purchasing agency in the public sector has been particularly complex and required substantial political and technical efforts in the 1990s.

Source: Baeza and Packard 2006.

factors. Gottret and Schieber (2006) also discuss the enabling conditions for successful National Health Service, SHI, CBHI, and private voluntary health insurance reforms.

Savedoff and Gottret's (2008) study responds to the lack of information concerning the key governance factors that affect the operation of health insurance funds. For example, although a good deal of material has been gathered concerning issues such as setting premiums and benefits and coverage rules, very little information exists on the more bureaucratic topics of supervisory boards, regulations, supervision, auditing, and accountability. Nevertheless, bureaucratic factors are the ones that largely influence performance and allow for dynamic "self-correction." The study details the major factors underlying coherent governance and accountability (table 5.1).

Table 5.1 Governance Factors

Dimension	*Features*
Coherent decision-making structures	Responsibility of health insurance objectives must correspond with decision-making power and capacity in each institution involved in the management of the system. All health insurance entities have routine risk assessment and management strategies in place. The costs of regulating and administering mandatory health insurance institutions are reasonable and appropriate.
Stakeholder participation	Stakeholders have effective representation in the governing bodies of health insurance entities.
Transparency and information	The objectives of health insurance are formally and clearly defined. Health insurance relies on an explicit and appropriately designed institutional and legal framework. Clear information, disclosure, and transparency rules are in place. Health insurance entities have minimum requirements about protecting the insured.
Supervision and regulation	Rules on compliance, enforcement, and sanctions for mandatory health insurance supervision are clearly defined. Financial management rules for health insurance entities are clearly defined and enforced. The health insurance system has structures for ongoing supervision and monitoring in place.
Consistency and stability	The main qualities of the health insurance system are stable.

Source: Savedoff and Gottret 2008.

The study highlights, in detail, good practices for implementing these governance and accountability principles according to the case studies and other global experience. The study also has some interesting observations on the focuses of governance arrangements (based on whether health insurance funds are unitary or have multiple competing funds) and on the appropriate roles of medical care providers:

- *Number of insurers.* With multiple and competing insurers, external oversight mechanisms can pay less attention to efficiency and management and focus more on consumer protection, inclusiveness, and preservation of competition through antitrust actions. In contrast, countries with a single health insurer need external oversight mechanisms that make the insurer responsible for integrity, quality, and productivity.
- *Provider-payer relationship.* The effect of including providers' representatives in decision-making bodies will depend on whether this relationship is antagonistic or collaborative. When providers are direct

employees of insurers, negotiations and oversight practices need to address civil service and labor regulation issues. Countries with independent providers need governance mechanisms for transparent negotiations of prices and payment mechanisms.

Notes

1. Implementation of the HSA system is not yet complete because the generation entering into retirement before 1984 could not accumulate capital stocks and is therefore financed by family members or by state assistance. For this reason, full implementation will not be achieved until 2030.
2. Formally, Vietnam has two insurance schemes: compulsory and voluntary. Both are run by Vietnam Social Security. The compulsory scheme includes two subschemes: (a) a mandatory wage tax–based SHI scheme for formal sector workers and civil servants (family members are not covered) and (b) a noncontributory scheme aimed initially at retired government officials, war veterans, members of parliament, Communist Party officials, and other special groups (such as children, pensioners, and the poor).

References

Annear, Peter L., David Wilkinson, Men Rithy Chean, and Maurits van Pelt. 2006. "Study of Financial Access to Health Services for the Poor in Cambodia: Phase 1—Scope, Design, and Data Analysis." AusAID, Phnom Penh.

Baeza, Christian C., and Truman G. Packard. 2006. *Beyond Survival: Protecting Households from Health Shocks in Latin America*. Washington, DC: World Bank.

Chun, H. R. 2007. "Lessons from South Korea's Health Insurance System." Presentation at the Health Financing Conference, sponsored by the government of the Islamic Republic of Iran, Tehran.

Dormont, Brigitte, Joaquim Oliveira Martins, Florian Pelgrin, Mark Suhrcke. 2007. "Health Expenditures, Longevity and Growth." Paper prepared for the 9th Annual European Conference of the Fondazione Rodolfo Debenedetti on Health, Longevity, and Productivity, Limon sul Garda, Italy, May.

Gottret, Pablo, and George Schieber. 2006. *Health Financing Revisited: A Practitioner's Guide*. Washington, DC: World Bank.

Hanvoravongchai, Piya. 2002. "Medical Savings Accounts: Lessons Learned from Limited International Experience." EIP/HFS/PHF Discussion Paper 52, World Health Organization, Geneva.

Hawkins, Loraine. 2007. "Health Financing Note: Cambodia." Background paper for the World Bank, Washington, DC.

Hrobon, Pavel. 2004. "Pooling across Health Insurance Funds in Czech Republic." PowerPoint presentation at the Health Financing Conference sponsored by the World Bank and the government of the Czech Republic, Prague, September.

Hu, Teh-Wei. 2007. "Recent Health Care Financing Reform in China and Taiwan." University of California, Berkeley.

Ikegami, Naoki. 2006. "Extending Social Health Insurance in Middle-Income Countries: Lessons from Japan." *Journal of Health Economics and Policy* 18 (1): 5–21.

———. 2008. "The Japanese Health Care System: Its Success and Challenges for the Future." *Harvard Health Policy Review* 9 (1): 110–18.

Kutzin, Joseph. 2009. "Health Care Financing in Asia." Presentation to the World Health Organization, Manila, March.

Langenbrunner, John C. 2005. "Health Care Financing and Purchasing in ECA: An Overview of Issues and Reforms." World Bank, Washington, DC.

Leung, Gabriel M., Keith Y. K. Tin, G. M. K. Yeung, E. S. K. Leung, Eva L. H. Tsui, D. W. S. Lam, Caroline S. H. Tsang, A. Y. K. Fung, and Su Vui Lo. 2008. "Hong Kong's Domestic Health Spending: Financial Years 1989/90 through 2004/05." *Hong Kong Medical Journal* 14 (suppl. 2): 2–23.

Lu, Jui-fen Rachel, and William C. Hsiao. 2003. "Does Universal Health Insurance Make Health Care Unaffordable? Lessons from Taiwan." *Health Affairs* 22 (3): 77–88.

Sanigest International. 2008. "Health Sector Note: Cambodia." Prepared under contract to the World Bank, Washington, DC.

Savedoff, William D., and Pablo Gottret, eds. 2008. *Governing Mandatory Health Insurance: Learning from Experience.* Washington, DC: World Bank.

Schwartz, J. Brad. 2006. "Health Equity Funds and Soft Loan Funds: Proposed System Design, Implementation Plan, and Evaluation Design." Primary Health Care Expansion Project, ADB Loan 1749-LAO (SF), Ministry of Health, Vientiane, Lao PDR.

Wagstaff, Adam, Magnus Lindelow, Shiyong Wang, and Shuo Zhang. 2009. *Reforming China's Rural Health Care System.* Washington, DC: World Bank.

World Bank. 2008. *Good Practices in Health Financing: Lessons from Reforms in Low- and Middle-Income Countries.* Washington, DC: World Bank.

CHAPTER 6

Resource Allocation and Purchasing

A Resource Allocation and Purchasing Framework

Elements of strategic purchasing are emerging in the region, but a significant agenda remains to capture value for money expended. The national health service–type systems and the insurance systems in many countries in the region have initiated activity, but often without coordination across public and private providers (as in, the Philippines and Timor-Leste), across levels of care (China), or across multiple insurers (the Lao People's Democratic Republic). Models and arrangements are often diluted, with both supply-side and demand-side financing, thereby not allowing the full effect of needed behavior change toward more cost-effective care provision.

Many countries have adopted a general framework for purchasing health services (Preker and Langenbrunner 2005) that specifies a number of purchasing components:

- *Core policy characteristics.* These "policy levers" can be used to allocate resources by purchasers across geographic areas or directly to providers.
- *Organizational characteristics.* Such characteristics include those of purchasers and providers and the incentive regimes within organizations.

Box 6.1

Core Policy Levers Related to the Uses of Financing

- Demand, or population coverage (for whom to buy)
- Supply, or benefits package (what to buy, in which form, and what to exclude)
- Factor and product markets, or contracting (from whom to buy, at what price to buy, and how much to buy)
- Prices and incentive regime, or provider payment systems (at what price and how to pay)

Source: Preker and Langenbrunner 2005.

- *Institutional characteristics.* These characteristics are embedded in the transactions that occur between different organizational units emanating from the government and across both public and private sectors. This area is similar conceptually to the *World Health Report 2000,* which discussed this area as stewardship of the health sector (WHO 2000).

A fourth component—and one that cuts across the three previous components—is management characteristics. This component is very much intertwined with the institutional environment (stewardship, governance, and autonomy). Management, organizational, and institutional characteristics are addressed separately in chapter 7. This chapter focuses on core policy levers that the government and purchasers might exercise.

In the short run, governments or purchasers can better focus on the core policy levers that they have at their disposal. These policy levers are outlined in box 6.1, and each is discussed in turn in this chapter.

For Whom to Purchase Services: Reaching All in the Health Sector

Many governments have made great strides in extending coverage step by step. For example, China has gone from near-zero coverage to almost universal coverage (more than 90 percent) for more than 700 million citizens living in rural areas since the early part of the 2000s. Nevertheless, challenges remain for covering all of the populations in East Asia and the Pacific. Universal coverage is the norm for all countries of the European

Union (EU) and the Organisation for Economic Co-operation and Development, with the exception of the United States. Approximately 10 to 60 percent of the population remains uncovered in several economies in East Asia and the Pacific, including high-income economies (figure 6.1).

In most of these economies, coverage appears to be linked to formalization of labor and payment of the payroll tax. In some cases, total social insurance tax may be high by international comparisons, such as in China, where it is 50 percent on average (although this figure varies across areas). Furthermore, the tax (where levied) is on income and not assets, and a cap prevents full recovery of payment for upper-income groups. A high tax may encourage underreporting of income for tax purposes in some countries. For example, in the Islamic Republic of Iran, average income reported for payroll tax purposes is only 1.2 times above minimum wage (World Bank 2007b).

A further issue involves payroll taxes and the link with formalization of the economy and longer-term management of macroeconomic growth in each of the region's economies. High payroll taxes may discourage job formation and capital investment and may drive private sector businesses underground, especially small and medium-size enterprises. Although the economics literature is mixed, high payroll taxes may distort labor and investment decisions in the formal sector. In the EU, for example, payroll taxes are much lower than in many economies in East Asia and the Pacific. The average for the 15 countries that were EU members prior to May 1, 2004,[1] is less than 10 percent, on average, with some countries, such as Denmark, having no payroll tax at all.

High payroll taxes discourage operators in the informal economy from coming into the formal sector and paying into the insurance schemes (Wagstaff 2007b). In East Asia and the Pacific, estimates of the

Figure 6.1 Uninsured Populations in East Asia and the Pacific: Selected Countries

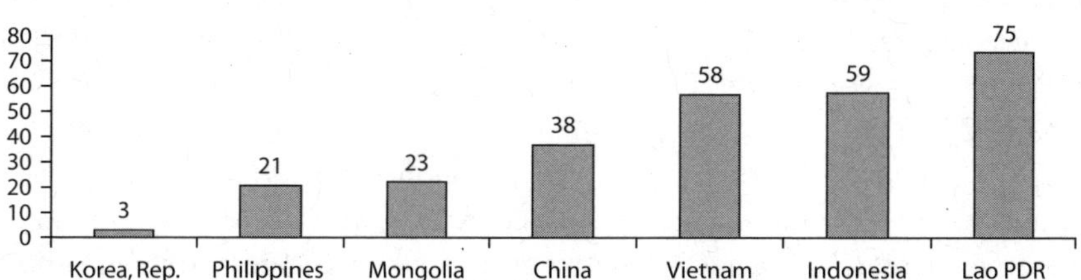

Source: Liu 2008; World Bank estimates based on the forthcoming volume of East Asia–Pacific Country Health Financing Profiles.

size of the informal economy vary from country to country but are high in some (for example, 63 percent in Indonesia and 70 percent in China). Governments with less than universal coverage may wish to consider other options for health revenues, especially if revenues for commodities such as oil (Indonesia) or other types of economic activity generate surplus general revenues (China) and especially if a high percentage of the private sector remains uncovered and without any insurance. General revenues or other types of taxes (for example, value added tax or tobacco tax) might be considered as an alternative to the payroll tax for private sector workers (see chapter 4). Alternatives are now being discussed, for example, in Vietnam related to its proposed new social health insurance (SHI) program (Lieberman and Wagstaff 2008).

Resource Allocation, Targeting, and Decentralization

Under a current insurance or allocation system arrangement, some insured groups and some regions may not be receiving equity of funding relative to need or demand; therefore, a mismatch of equity of access and equity to quality of services may exist. This inequity can especially be an issue in a region where so many countries—China, Indonesia, Malaysia, the Philippines, Thailand, and Vietnam—use some form of fiscal decentralization. Chapter 7 provides a summary of the level and experience of decentralization in the countries of East Asia and the Pacific.

In Vietnam, health disparities have apparently increased since decentralization, as exhibited by growth in the ratio of the highest to lowest regional infant mortality rate from 1.7 in 1989 to 3.6 in 2006. An important challenge facing Vietnam under decentralization is the wide disparity in economic development and poverty across regions and across provinces within a region (Capuno and Ohiri 2007). Table 6.1 illustrates this regional divide. In the Red River Delta and South East regions, for example, poverty rates in 2004 were at 12 percent and 5 percent, respectively, whereas the North West region exhibited a 59 percent poverty rate. This area also had the highest infant mortality rate in 2006.

In the Lao PDR, because of socioeconomic differences among the country's 18 provinces, health service delivery under decentralization became increasingly unequal between the more and less affluent areas (Phommasack and others 2005). Moreover, because the Ministry of Health (MoH) did not allocate health budgets centrally, mechanisms

Table 6.1 Selected Regional Indicators, Vietnam

	Real per capita household expenditure in January 2003 prices (D thousand)			*Regional poverty rates (%)*			*Infant mortality rate (deaths per 1,000 live births)*		
Region	*1998*	*2002*	*2004*	*1998*	*2002*	*2004*	*1998*	*2002*	*2006*
Red River Delta	1,996	2,296	2,696	29	22	12	26.5	20.4	10.6
North East	1,349	1,752	2,046	62	38	29	44.0	30.2	26.8
North West	1,064	1,241	1,427	73	68	59	—	40.5	34.1
North Central Coast	1,492	1,579	1,822	48	44	32	37.0	30.9	25.1
South Central Coast	1,799	2,039	2,375	35	25	19	40.6	23.6	19.0
Central Highlands	1,256	1,521	1,950	52	52	33	64.4	30.9	32.1
South East	3,072	3,554	4,175	12	11	5	23.6	18.9	11.5
Mekong River Delta	1,722	2,034	2,361	37	23	16	35.5	21.2	12.7

Source: Capuno and Ohiri 2007.
Note: — = not available.

were not created to ensure that resources for health targeted poor areas with greater need. In contrast, more affluent provinces were able to generate vast amounts of revenues, often leading to overspending (see the forthcoming volume of East Asia–Pacific Country Health Financing Profiles).

In China, as well, large disparities in funding relative to health outcomes and health service indicators remain. For example, the maternal mortality rate ranges from 9.6 deaths per 100,000 births in Shanghai to 11.0 in Guizhou and 399.0 in Tibet. The measles immunization rate is five to six times greater in western provinces than in eastern provinces. Malnutrition prevalence in rural areas is two to three times greater than in urban areas. In particular, a gender divide exists: girls suffer from less access to health services, which has implications for child mortality in females. Inequalities in health between rich and poor are increasingly evident. Children living in China's poorer central and western provinces are more likely to be malnourished than those living in richer eastern provinces, and rates of malnutrition have fallen faster among children living in cities than among those in rural areas. In part because of China's weak system of intergovernmental transfers (Wagstaff and others 2009), regional disparities are fostered by public health expenditures that are far lower in the provinces that may need resources the most (figure 6.2).

Figure 6.2 Government Health Expenditure Variations by Province, China

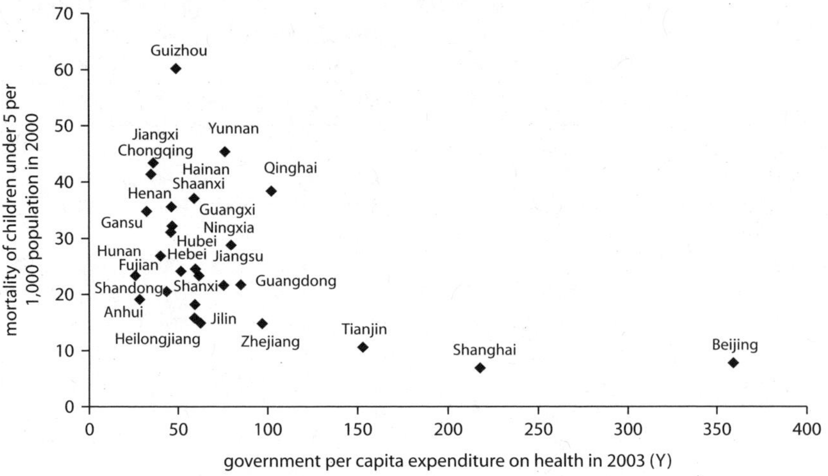

Source: Wagstaff and others 2009.

Similarly, variations in available funding exist at the local (county) level in China. Figure 6.3 shows intercounty variations in two provinces of relatively low per capita income levels (Jiangxi) and of relatively high per capita income levels (Jiangsu).

In the short term, the easiest technical approach for countries is a move toward more population-based allocation methods. Several countries in the EU representing various income levels—Lithuania, the Netherlands (through its all-payer insurance system), Poland, Sweden, and the United Kingdom—have in the past decade developed new geographic allocation formulas, which are based more on per capita or demand-side principles than on the older supply-side norms. Such a move would be useful for many countries in East Asia and the Pacific and could be done through risk adjusters in premiums or in the allocation and payment systems.

Internationally, most population-based formula funding mechanisms are based on the following formula for funding to region *i*:)

$$Allocation_i = PerCap \times POP_i \times (1 + a_i) \times (1 + n_i) \times (1 + c),$$

where *PerCap* is the per capita budget (total allocation divided by national population); *POP* is the population of each region; *a* is an adjuster for needs by age and gender (for example, areas with more

Figure 6.3 Per Capita Allocations for Health under China's New Cooperative Medical Scheme, 2003

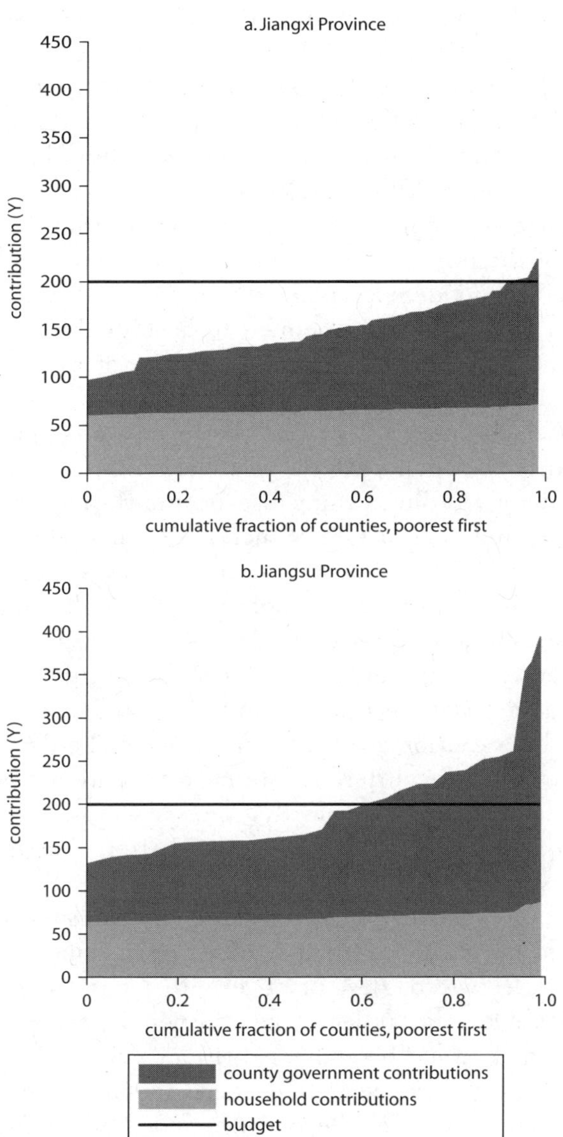

Source: Wagstaff and others 2009.

elderly or women of reproductive age than the national average, for example, would receive a higher allocation); n is an adjuster for health need (so an area with higher mortality or especially high morbidity might receive more funding); and c is an adjuster for cost (health care in a sparsely populated area, for example, might cost more to provide). All these elements are reflected in one of the original funding formulas developed in the 1970s for the United Kingdom's National Health Service—the Resource Allocation Working Party formula.

Defining need in a population usually begins with basing allocation on the size of the population and then adjusting for gender mix, age distribution, and nondemographic factors. Other things being equal, a population of 2 million is assumed to have double the needs of a population of 1 million. The second element of most funding formulas in health is some adjustment for differences across age groups and between men and women. The age for use of services generally follows a fairly common pattern: relatively high use occurs among children under five, diminishing use occurs during childhood and teenage years, and then a steady increase occurs for men, whereas women's use increases substantially during the reproductive years. International variations tend to emphasize local cultural and technological factors and also the age of relative life expectancy. In a small area, differences in age and gender can be extremely important. Between large populations (more than 500,000), however, the extent of demographic variation is usually quite small. The third part of the formula is to adjust for differences in need that are not explained by demographics on their own. Ideally, some objective and representative measure of need for services is required after adjusting for demographic characteristics.

In the first phase of developing a funding mechanism, a new regional formula could be introduced that is based on population, with levels adjusted to reflect need. Best practice is to focus on three to seven factors, or variables, that reflect need and policy priorities (table 6.2). For example, need could be addressed through age and gender adjusters because men and women, on average, require different levels of services as they grow older. Beyond age and gender adjusters, levels of poverty and rurality—as well as priority health outcomes such as infant mortality—could be used as proxies for need. Higher relative levels could determine correspondingly higher funding levels. After the formula is developed, it could be phased in over a period of several years. Implementing it all at once could create political opposition from

Table 6.2 Need Factors Used for Resource Allocation across Western Europe

Country	*Factors*
Belgium	Age, gender, unemployment, disability
Finland (to local government)	Age, disability, remoteness, local tax base
Germany	Age, gender
Netherlands	Age, gender, urbanization, funds income base
Switzerland	Age, gender, region, funds income
Need-based core indicators	
Denmark	Age, children of single parents
England	Age, standardized mortality ratio, unemployment, elderly living alone
France	Age
Italy (two-thirds)	Age, gender, mortality
Northern Ireland	Age, gender, mortality, low birth weight
Norway (50%)	Age, gender, mortality, elderly living alone
Portugal (15%)	Burden of illness: diabetes, hypertension, tuberculosis
Scotland	Age, gender, mortality, rural costs
Spain	Cross-boundary flows
Sweden	Age, living alone, employment status, housing
Wales	Age, gender, mortality, rural costs

Source: Ensor 2005.

wealthier regions; however, this change could be phased in over three to five years to allow regions to adapt to the new budget allocation formula. Some other factors must also be considered, such as each region's fiscal capacity to raise and manage funds on its own. The development and implementation of the formula would need to be concurrent, with a broader fiscal analysis related to national-regional fund flows.

In the longer term, a second phase would be to pool and mix funds from the insurance organizations for regional allocation, and a third phase might further refine the allocation formula for performance indicators such as improved primary care and outpatient services. Increasingly, countries in every part of the world are using this performance-based budgeting concept for health and other sectors, such as education and transportation. The second phase might also adjust for cross-boundary issues—for example, rural populations seeking care in high-end secondary and tertiary centers in large cities such as Vientiane or Jakarta. Some performance-based budgeting is to be developed in the Philippines under the current Health Systems Support project. Other countries, such as China, have expressed interest to the World Bank in moving to performance-based allocations.

What to Buy: Refining and Standardizing the Benefits Package

All countries would like to offer a comprehensive benefits package to all citizens, but budget constraints impose restrictions on what services can be bought. Defining the benefits package involves making decisions about who will benefit from publicly financed services (breadth of coverage), the types of services to be financed (depth of coverage), and the levels of out-of-pocket (OOP) contributions beneficiaries will need to make. These decisions are influenced by economic, social, and political factors specific to each country. In low- and middle-income countries, budget constraints become binding at relatively low levels of expenditure per capita—calling for rationing through user fees, the volume of services provided, or service quality. Difficult trade-offs have to be made for the poor and near-poor. The choice involves covering fewer poor and near-poor with a comprehensive package (deep coverage) or covering more of them with a less comprehensive package (broad coverage) (Hsiao and Shaw 2007).

The design and costing of a benefits package to which the insured are entitled is a central characteristic of SHI systems (Gibis, Koch-Wulkan, and Bultman 2004). In tax-financed systems, benefits packages are rarely defined explicitly. As countries have transitioned from tax financing to social insurance in East Asia and the Pacific, the definition of the benefits package has become one of the key elements of health financing reform. Table 6.3 summarizes the composition of the benefits packages across the region.

Low-Income Economies

In Cambodia, a health coverage plan adopted in 1995 defined the package of services that should be provided at each level of care. At the primary care level, health centers are to provide a minimum package of activities (one health center per 10,000–20,000 people), supplemented in remote areas by health posts. The complementary package of activities is provided at three levels of specialization through referral hospitals: the operational district level (one such hospital per 100,000–200,000 people), provincial level (typically providing general medicine, surgery, obstetrics, and pediatrics), and regional level. Additionally, national hospitals in Phnom Penh and Siem Reap provide a mix of secondary and tertiary services, and some provide clinical training, including medical specialization training. Many MoH facilities are not yet operating at the

Table 6.3 Benefits Packages in East Asia and the Pacific

Country	*Hospital care and nonhospital care*	*Preventive care*	*Drugs and supplies*	*Transportation and ambulance costs*
Low-income economies				
Cambodia	MoH provides nearly all public health services, including a minimum package of activities of specialty and clinic support services.	n.a.	MoH also provides equipment and drugs on the essential drugs list.	n.a.
	Complementary package of activities provides specialty services. Health equity fund (HEF) for the poor is designed to provide targeted income transfers for the purpose of paying for care in the public system, through providers contracted by the HEF. Community-based health insurance (CBHI; a private, nonprofit, voluntary insurance mechanism) provides the purchasers and their families coverage for a stated list of medical benefits delivered at contracted public facilities.	n.a.	n.a.	n.a.
Indonesia	Askeskin program for poor and near-poor households provides free inpatient (third-class beds only) and outpatient care at government facilities.	n.a.	Askeskin insurance program for poor and near-poor households provides drugs from a list of 500 items.	Askeskin insurance program for poor and near-poor households covers transportation and ambulance costs.
	Askes program for public sector workers provides free inpatient (all-class beds) and outpatient services at public facilities.	n.a.	Askes program for public sector workers provides drugs from a list of 1,200 items.	n.a.
	Jamsostek (for formal sector workers outside the public sector) provides medical services at public and private facilities with negotiated contracts with Jamsostek.	n.a.	n.a.	n.a.
	Private insurance companies are currently allowed to operate in the market and now cover 1.6 million individuals.	n.a.	n.a.	n.a.

(continued)

Table 6.3 *(continued)*

Country	*Hospital care and nonhospital care*	*Preventive care*	*Drugs and supplies*	*Transportation and ambulance costs*
Lao PDR	Public system covers 93% of the population and provides comprehensive services free of charge in public facilities.	n.a.	n.a.	n.a.
	SHI fund is a mandatory scheme covering salaried employees in the private sector that includes all health benefits offered in the public scheme.	n.a.	n.a.	n.a.
	Civil servants scheme for offers, for example, retirement pensions, survivors' benefits, employment injury and sickness benefits, and maternity benefits.	n.a.	n.a.	n.a.
	CBHI benefits include inpatient and outpatient care and cover members' dependents.	n.a.	n.a.	n.a.
	Private for-profit commercial insurance currently has a small presence in Lao PDR.	n.a.	n.a.	n.a.
	HEF for poor households provides treatment free of charge at public facilities. Benefits include comprehensive medical services.	n.a.	HEF provides drugs and laboratory tests at public facilities.	HEF provides transportation.
	Social health insurance fund and civil servants scheme provide free inpatient and outpatient care without limits on number of contacts or services.	n.a.	n.a.	n.a.
Mongolia	Mandatory SHI covers all types of employees, self-employed people, children under 16, students, people with no other sources of income, and social welfare beneficiaries. A wide range of services is covered, including inpatient and outpatient services.	n.a.	Mandatory SHI covers the cost of drugs on the reimbursement list.	n.a.

	Essential and complementary package of services provides an integrated package of health services across different levels of facilities and programs.	n.a.	n.a.	n.a.
Papua New Guinea	Benefits package is not explicitly defined. The majority of the population obtains most services at government and church-owned facilities.			
Timor-Leste	Basic package and hospital service package are provided, including rehabilitation for people with disabilities.	n.a.	n.a.	n.a.
Vietnam	SHI provides comprehensive benefits for formal sector workers and civil servants. Family members are not covered. Benefits package is the same for all members, covering most inpatient and outpatient services received at public facilities. Coverage includes the poor, ethnic minorities living in remote areas, and war veterans.	n.a.	n.a.	The poor incur transport costs.
	Commercial health insurance has been increasing, covering about 6% of the population. Many schemes focus on schoolchildren and university students.	n.a.	n.a.	n.a.
Middle-income economies				
China	Urban Employee Basic Medical Insurance is a mandatory scheme covering urban employees in the formal sector that funds both inpatient and outpatient care.	n.a.	n.a.	n.a.
	Urban Resident Basic Medical Insurance covers children, students, and unemployed urban residents not covered by Urban Employee Basic Medical Insurance. It primarily finances inpatient services.	n.a.	n.a.	n.a.
	Urban and Rural Medical Assistance is largely funded by the government to ensure access to care for the poor.	n.a.	n.a.	n.a.

(continued)

Table 6.3 *(continued)*

Country	*Hospital care and nonhospital care*	*Preventive care*	*Drugs and supplies*	*Transportation and ambulance costs*
	New Rural Cooperative Medical Scheme is mostly voluntary. In both urban and rural areas, it provides supplementary insurance to increase benefit coverage for the poorest populations. It covers inpatient care but coverage varies by county. Only one-fourth of counties cover outpatient expenses. Specific services (mainly outpatient) are not covered or only partially covered.	n.a.	n.a.	n.a.
Malaysia	Patients receive primary, secondary, and tertiary health care and dental services (for rural and urban populations, pregnant women, and schoolchildren) through the public system. Access is universal.	MoH services include preventive and promotive care and health education.	n.a.	n.a.
	Ministry of Defense hospitals and clinics serve army personnel and families and offer a wide range of services.	n.a.	n.a.	n.a.
	Department of Aborigine Affairs provides health services to the *orang asli* (aborigines), particularly those in remote areas.	n.a.	n.a.	n.a.
	Private health insurance is growing, as well as employer-based health care, managed care, and other contractual arrangements (through nongovernmental organizations).	n.a.	n.a.	n.a.

Philippines	National Health Insurance Program (NHIP) provides a unified benefits package for all members and their families, including inpatient and some outpatient services. It covers employed people in the government and private sectors, self-employed people, overseas Filipino workers, professionals in private practice, nonpaying members entitled to lifetime coverage (retirees, pensioners), and indigent members.	NHIP provides family planning services.	NHIP reimburses (up to a ceiling) for drugs and medicines, laboratory, and x-rays.	n.a.
	Indigent program (sponsored program) entitles members to free primary care consultations.	n.a.	Indigent program (a sponsored program) entitles members to free laboratory exams.	n.a.
	Employees' Compensation Commission provides public and private employees and their dependents with services in the event of a work-related injury, sickness, disability, or death. It covers all public sector employees, all employees in the private sector covered by the social security system, and Filipino sailors compulsorily covered under the social security system.	n.a.	n.a.	n.a.
	Private insurance and health maintenance organization, (HMOs) often cover inpatient and outpatient services and emergency care.	HMOs often cover preventive care.	n.a.	n.a.
	Private employers also provide a minimum set of health benefits (medical, dental, and covers occupational safety).	n.a.	n.a.	n.a.
	CBHI provides services that are inadequately provided or unaffordable. Benefits include surgery, room and board, and dental services.	n.a.	CBHI benefits include inpatient and outpatient drugs and laboratory work.	n.a.

(continued)

Table 6.3 *(continued)*

Country	*Hospital care and nonhospital care*	*Preventive care*	*Drugs and supplies*	*Transportation and ambulance costs*
	Universal coverage (through the 30 Baht Scheme) includes comprehensive primary, secondary, tertiary, and emergency care. It covers most of the population not eligible for SHI and CSMBS and replaces previous welfare schemes for low-income households and the elderly, among others.	Scheme covers prevention and promotion services.	Scheme includes medicines and supplies.	n.a.
	SHI covers hospitalization. SHI covers private employees (excluding dependents) on a mandatory basis for all private firms.	SHI covers health education.	SHI covers pharmaceuticals and medical supplies.	SHI covers ambulance costs.
High-income economies				
Hong Kong SAR, China	Citizens receive a wide range of services under the Hospital Authority at public facilities and associated ambulatory care clinics (for specialty services). Services include maternal and child health, student health, and health care for the elderly. Traditional Chinese medicine services are increasingly available in public facilities.	Department of Health also provides health promotion and public education services.	All inpatient pharmaceuticals are included in the standard per diem out-of-pocket charge; minimal copays for outpatient drugs.	n.a.
	Supplementary private insurance (either provided by employers or self-purchased) is typically enjoyed by middle- and upper-income households and is held by 30% of the population.	n.a.	n.a.	n.a.

Japan	SHI covers the same list of products and services for all providers and patients. Nearly all inpatient and dental care is covered.	n.a.	SHI covers the cost of drugs.	n.a.
Korea, Rep.	National Health Insurance (NHI) covers 97% of the population for a wide range of services (most inpatient and outpatient services) but not high-cost services. The benefits package is the same for the entire population.	n.a.	NHI includes drug treatment coverage.	n.a.
	Medical-Aid Program covers health services for 3% of the poorest people and people with disabilities through a tax-financed program.	n.a.	n.a.	n.a.
	Several commercial health insurance programs exist, and the private health insurance market is gradually expanding, covering about 20% of the population for high-cost services (for example, cancer-related treatments).	n.a.	n.a.	n.a.
Singapore	Government provides basic package of inpatient care.	n.a.	n.a.	n.a.
	Compulsory Medisave scheme covers 80% of hospital care and costly outpatient care.	n.a.	n.a.	n.a.
	MediShield covers amenities and catastrophic coverage.	n.a.	n.a.	n.a.
Taiwan, China	NHI provides comprehensive medical and dental services, Chinese medicine, and nurse home visits. Copayment exemptions are provided for individuals with catastrophic illnesses, children under age 6, users of maternal and preventive services, and low-income households.	NHI provides preventive care services.	NHI covers prescription drugs.	n.a.
	Essential and Complementary Package of Services provides an integrated package of health services across different levels of facilities and programs.	n.a.	Mandatory SHI covers the cost of drugs on the reimbursement list.	n.a.

Source: Authors' compilation based on the forthcoming volume of East Asia–Pacific Country Health Financing Profiles.
Note: n.a. = not applicable.

full standard of the minimum package of activities and complementary package of activities.

In Lao PDR, all services were officially provided free of charge in the public health system until 1996, when user fees were introduced. This change gave rise to a large number of social protection, or safety net schemes, with wide variations in benefit packages. The health equity funds (HEFs) target poor households, which are entitled to free treatment, drugs, and laboratory tests at public facilities, as well as transportation. Beneficiaries of the SHI fund and civil servants scheme are entitled to free outpatient and inpatient care, without any limits on the number of contacts or services provided. The benefits package for community-based health insurance (CBHI) scheme beneficiaries includes outpatient and inpatient care and referral mechanisms for hospital care (see the forthcoming volume of East Asia–Pacific Country Health Financing Profiles).

In Mongolia, health insurance was introduced mainly to fund personal health services, including outpatient and inpatient care at secondary- and tertiary-level hospitals and sanatoriums, as well as essential drug reimbursement for the population (see the forthcoming volume of East Asia–Pacific Country Health Financing Profiles). The Mongolian MoH recently adopted the concept of the essential and complementary package of services (ECPS) as an integral part of the Health Sector Strategic Master Plan for 2005 to 2015. The ECPS is a population-based approach to provide integrated packages of health services that improve the continuity of care at different stages of human development and across different levels of facilities and programs. The ECPS consists of services that fall under maternal health, child health, infectious disease, noncommunicable disease, and other areas.

In Papua New Guinea and most of the Pacific Island nations (Fiji, Samoa, the Solomon Islands, and Tonga), the benefits package is not explicitly defined. In almost all cases, the population can potentially obtain most services at government or church-owned health facilities. User fees are extensive in Papua New Guinea, but less so in the Pacific Islands.

In Timor-Leste, emphasis is placed on providing access to primary health care, with a focus on prevention. In 2007, the MoH outlined a basic services package that includes interventions to reduce child and maternal mortality and the spread of prevalent infectious diseases such as HIV/AIDS, sexually transmitted infections, tuberculosis (TB), and malaria, as well as several non–Millennium Development Goal interventions (dental, ophthalmology, mental health, and disability services). Complementing the basic services package is the hospital service package, which includes obstetrics and gynecology, neonatal and pediatric care, internal medicine, trauma and surgery, auxiliary services, diagnostic services, dental services, blood bank and transfusion services, rehabilitation of people with disabilities, and geriatric care (see the forthcoming volume of East Asia–Pacific Country Health Financing Profiles).

In Vietnam, benefits are comprehensive and mostly implicit; however, they are capped at D 7 million. Some groups, such as war veterans, enjoy benefits with no cap. Transportation costs for referrals are included for the poor (see the forthcoming volume of East Asia–Pacific Country Health Financing Profiles).

Middle-Income Economies

China has four main insurance schemes: (a) a rural scheme (Cooperative Medical Scheme, or CMS); (b) an urban scheme (Basic Medical Insurance); (c) a scheme for urban residents not in the formal sector or not employed; and (d) a medical assistance scheme for the poor. The benefits package across the four main insurance schemes in China is shallow and focused on catastrophic care, and it has a benefit ceiling as defined by costs of care. The ceiling varies by province and local areas (county) because management of funds is usually at the local (county) level. Resources also vary across localities. As a result, cost sharing is high under all of China's insurance schemes. The benefits package is the same for all in a locality regardless of income; hence, the poor also pay the same OOP expenses. Residents in both urban and rural areas have medical savings accounts to help with prepayment for health care costs, but the sick quickly deplete these savings, whereas the healthy carry significant surpluses.

Counties in China vary in what they cover under the rural CMS, but all cover inpatient care. Only one-quarter of counties, however, cover outpatient expenses on a pooling basis. The rest do not cover them at all (10 percent of counties), cover only catastrophic expenses (10 percent of counties), or cover them through a household account (Wagstaff and others 2009). The household's minimal contribution is placed in an account that can be used only by the household in question and only for outpatient care; no coverage is available beyond the contribution. Mostly, patients have to pay up front for inpatient care and get reimbursed later.

CMS revenues are small compared to rural average per capita health spending and, as a result, coverage is very shallow. Certain services (particularly outpatient) are not covered or are covered only partially. Deductibles are high, ceilings are low, and coinsurance rates are high. This situation causes considerable confusion among farmers about what can and cannot be reimbursed and how much will be reimbursed. Outpatients have received, on average, Y 200 per reimbursement episode, whereas inpatients have received, on average, nearly Y 700 per reimbursement episode. Inpatients, on average, spent six times out of pocket what they are reimbursed, revealing the shallow coverage of the scheme.

The SHI program implemented by the Philippines in 1999 provides a unified benefit package for all members that includes reimbursement up to a ceiling for drugs and medicines, laboratory and x-ray services, professional fees, room and board, surgical family planning, and some outpatient services. In addition to these benefits, the Indigent Program (now called the Sponsored Program) introduced additional benefits that entitled members to the following services from accredited rural health units or rural health centers: free primary consultation with the physician and free laboratory examinations. New health care packages have been introduced since 2000, including TB directly observed treatment (short course). Benefits outside of SHI vary according to program. The health maintenance organization (HMO) benefit packages commonly offer preventive health care, inpatient and outpatient services, and emergency care.

In Indonesia, entitlements vary with type of insurance coverage. The Askeskin program targets poor and near-poor households that are entitled to free inpatient (third-class beds only) and outpatient care services at government facilities; the program also covers transportation and ambulance costs, and a list of 500 drugs. Cost sharing is not required for Askeskin beneficiaries. Public sector workers are covered by a separate insurance program (Askes), which entitles beneficiaries to free inpatient (all classes of beds) and outpatient services at public facilities and a list of 1,200 drugs. Cost sharing under Askes is about 25 percent. Formal sector workers outside the public sector are covered by Jamsostek, which entitles members to medical care services at public and private facilities that have negotiated contracts with Jamsostek. The population not covered by any insurance scheme pays a wide range of user fees when seeking care at public hospitals. In recent years, districts governments have responded to political pressure to provide free services by introducing district-level health insurance programs.

In Thailand, the benefit package varies according to insurer. The Civil Servant Medical Benefit Scheme (CSMBS) benefits cover outpatient and inpatient services, medical and surgical services, emergency services, and drug expenses on a fee-for-service (FFS) reimbursement basis. The National Health Security Board, an independent governing board appointed under the National Health Security Act, is responsible for determining benefit packages for the universal coverage program known as the 30 Baht Scheme. The scheme's benefit package includes comprehensive primary, secondary, tertiary, and emergency health care; some high-cost medical treatments; and prevention and promotion services. Social security benefits include diagnosis, hospitalization, pharmacy and medical supplies, referral services and ambulance costs, and health education and immunization.

High-Income Economies

In Japan, SHI, by law, covers virtually the same list of products and services, and the reimbursement is the same for all providers and all patients, regardless of the scheme involved (see the forthcoming volume of East Asia–Pacific Country Health Financing Profiles). Patients can choose the provider they want, and providers have no reason to discriminate among patients. Almost all inpatient care, dental care, and drugs are covered by health insurance schemes in Japan. Therefore, insured people can receive those services with a 30 percent copayment (10 percent for people over 75 years old and 20 percent for those under 3 years old).

Malaysia has an implicit package, with primary health care recognized as the thrust of the Malaysian health care system, supported by secondary and tertiary care. Patients are navigated through this all-inclusive system by an effective national referral system. The MoH also provides comprehensive dental services to the population—particularly to the rural population, the urban poor, pregnant women, and schoolchildren. In addition, the Department of Aborigine Affairs provides health services to the *orang asli* (aborigine) population, particularly those who are not within reach of the MoH static and mobile outreach services.

In Hong Kong SAR, China, residents enjoy the full spectrum of Western allopathic care at public hospitals and associated ambulatory care clinics (mostly for specialty services) for a minimal copayment that is waived for the indigent (see the forthcoming volume of East Asia–Pacific Country Health Financing Profiles). All inpatient pharmaceuticals are included in a standard per diem OOP charge, whereas minimal copayments apply to outpatient drugs. Traditional Chinese medicine services have become increasingly available in public facilities since repatriation to China in 1997, but capacity remains very limited.

In Taiwan, China, the National Health Insurance (NHI) program provides a comprehensive benefit package that covers preventive and medical services, prescription drugs, dental services, Chinese medicine, and nurse home visits. The benefit package specified in the National Health Insurance Act lists the types of services not covered by NHI (see the forthcoming volume of East Asia–Pacific Country Health Financing Profiles). The NHI incorporates a copayment equivalent to US$2 for each outpatient visit to clinics and US$7 (US$12 without referral from a primary care doctor) for each visit to medical center outpatient clinics. In addition, a 10 percent coinsurance applies to inpatient services. However, the total amount that a patient has to pay for each admission is capped at 6 percent of the cost, and the total annual amount a patient has to pay is capped at 10 percent of the average national income per person. People with catastrophic illness (a disease type specified by the Bureau of National Health Insurance), children under the age of six, users of maternal and preventive services, and low-income households are exempt from the copayment requirement. Nonetheless, the copayment and coinsurance rates are regressive because they are fixed and do not vary according to a patient's income.

In Singapore, the government provides a basic package of inpatient care, but compulsory health savings accounts (Medisave) cover 80 percent of hospital care and expensive outpatient care, with annual limits. A voluntary enhanced benefit (MediShield) covers amenities and catastrophic coverage.

Analysis and Discussion

Given the low levels of health spending in low-income countries, a widely held view is that the state should first finance a small package of services for universal coverage. This coverage would essentially encompass public goods, goods with externalities, and other interventions with proven benefits. All other clinical care and catastrophic expenditures would be financed for the poor using some targeting mechanism (Gottret and Schieber 2006).

The *World Development Report 1993* (World Bank 1993) argued that such a package should be identified on the basis of which services are most cost-effective in maximizing the health status of the population. However, if the objective of the government is to maximize overall social welfare and not just health status, this approach may be inadequate

(Hammer and Berman 1995). For instance, such an approach does not take into account the insurance function played by public hospitals in developing countries, nor does it take into account the effect of private sector services or the marginal effect on health status of publicly sponsored interventions. Finally, current and past experiences from low-income countries suggest that targeting mechanisms (for example, user fee exemption schemes) are rarely perfect. A strategy of relying entirely on targeting mechanisms to deliver expensive hospital care services for the poor may not provide adequate financial protection.

In reality, decisions about which package of services the government should buy are made on the basis of not only economic criteria, but also social and political criteria. Although cost-effectiveness of spending is referred to frequently in policy documents in many of the low-income economies in East Asia and the Pacific, almost no country has a benefit package that was defined purely on this basis. Globally, tradition, corruption, and political pressures mean that increased health resources are often allocated to tertiary care centers and urban health facilities (Gottret and Schieber 2006). As chapter 8 shows, this strategy leads to a pro-rich distribution in the incidence of public subsidies.

In most tax-financed systems, both in Europe and in Asia, the benefits package is not explicitly defined. For instance, in the United Kingdom, the secretary of state for health is legally required to provide services by an act of Parliament (Gottret and Schieber 2006). High-income tax-financed systems in Asia, such as those in Hong Kong SAR, China, and in Malaysia, which are based on the United Kingdom's National Health Service, are no different. Low-income tax-financed systems in East Asia and the Pacific, such as those in the Pacific Island nations, also do not explicitly define benefits.

Although social insurance system services can be rationed by explicitly defining a benefit package, other forms of rationing are used in tax-financed systems. Queuing for government health services is a well-known form of rationing in Hong Kong SAR, China; Malaysia; and the United Kingdom. Another example is rationing through variations in service quality. In Hong Kong SAR, China, and in Malaysia, the relatively lower quality of services in the public sector means that the rich often opt out and use the private sector instead, which helps reduce demand pressure on public sector services.

The breadth and depth of coverage should be defined by the level of funding available, which ensures the financial sustainability of the system. The basic benefit package designed for the Kyrgyz Republic, for

Figure 6.4 New Benefits Package: Kyrgyz Republic

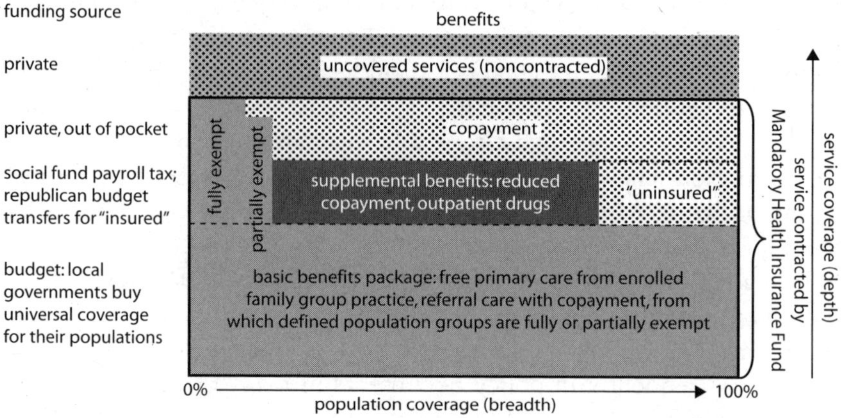

funding source
benefits
private
uncovered services (noncontracted)
private, out of pocket
copayment
social fund payroll tax; republican budget transfers for "insured"
fully exempt
partially exempt
supplemental benefits: reduced copayment, outpatient drugs
"uninsured"
budget: local governments buy universal coverage for their populations
basic benefits package: free primary care from enrolled family group practice, referral care with copayment, from which defined population groups are fully or partially exempt
service contracted by Mandatory Health Insurance Fund
service coverage (depth)
0%
100%
population coverage (breadth)

Sources: Kutzin, Ibraimova, Jakab, and others 2009; Kutzin, Ibraimova, Kadyrova, and others 2002.

example, was divided into three components that are paid by different funding sources (figure 6.4). The package across public funding groups should be standardized for equity reasons and should be transparent for both consumers and providers. This structure will help cut down on the use of informal payments, although the measure by itself will not be sufficient to eliminate informal payments. As the burden of disease increasingly shifts to noncommunicable and chronic diseases, preventive, promotive, and screening services become important. Providing early treatment can prevent longer-term complications and can help reduce costs overall.

After the package is standardized, it should be reviewed on an ongoing basis. A first step might be to develop a negative list to remove outdated technologies, devices, and procedures from the package. Any unnecessary services might be removed as well. Copayments and deductibles already exist, but reexamining their structure could generate new revenues and discourage overuse of certain types of services. Conversely, it could help address issues that increase OOP payments over time (as discussed previously) and issues of high OOP expenses for essential items such as pharmaceuticals, especially among the medically vulnerable and lower-income groups. This latter problem is discussed in more detail later in the chapter.

Governments or purchasers might also consider establishing a small organizational unit to formally and rigorously assess benefit issues as new technologies and procedures become available. The unit would develop assessments that were based on internationally recognized analytical methods, such as cost-effectiveness analysis, technology assessment, and evidence-based protocols. Traditionally, these types of analyses and assessments have not been part of the decision and policy process by insurance organizations. Each of these areas remains a challenge for many East Asian and Pacific economies.

East Asian and Pacific governments are firmly committed to providing public health services. Strong economic justification exists for government financing and provision. The prevention of communicable diseases such as measles, TB, and malaria generates large externalities, and many public health services represent public goods. Moreover, the technology and cost-effectiveness of public health interventions are for the most part well understood in East Asia and the Pacific.

Policy commitment and the availability of cost-effective interventions, however, do not necessarily translate to effective government financing and delivery of these services (Lindelow and Wagstaff 2007). This problem is evidenced by the response to the severe acute respiratory syndrome outbreaks in 2003, the subsequent avian influenza scare, faltering efforts to prevent chronic disease, and remaining weaknesses in communicable disease prevention across the region. In many countries, how public health is financed, how it is governed, and what organizational arrangements exist in public health are important factors underlying weaknesses in public health service delivery. Countries differ substantially in the role of different levels of government, in the role of SHI schemes in financing public health activities, and in their systems for performance measurement and accountability in public health. As a result, similar policies and levels of financing for public health can have very different effects in different contexts. Considerable variations exist in the share of government health spending allocated to public and preventive health services (figure 6.5).

In tax-financed systems, general revenues finance public health services, which are delivered through public delivery systems. Malaysia and Hong Kong SAR, China, are good examples of countries where the provision of preventive and promotive health services is integrated with the provision of curative care services. In Malaysia, the MoH's primary health care units fill this role. In Hong Kong SAR, China, maternal and child health clinics offer prenatal care in combination with services provided by the Hospital Authority obstetrics outpatient departments; postnatal checkups, which are provided at least once to more than 90 percent of all newborns; and well infant care, which extends through

Figure 6.5 Share of Government Health Spending Allocated to Prevention and Public Health

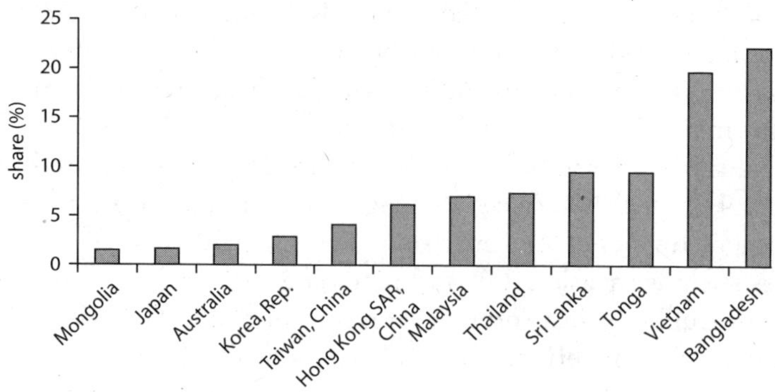

Source: Data from Fernando 2008.
Note: Data are for the most recent available year.

five years of age. Health clinics for the elderly provide annual health checks (including some basic blood tests) and limited primary care services for a nominal fee.

The Pacific Island nations, where health care is financed through a mix of general revenues and donor sources, were historically quite successful in ensuring wide coverage of public health services. In recent years, provision of public health services has deteriorated somewhat because of reductions in government allocations to public health and a failure to invest in improvements to the public health infrastructure. Papua New Guinea has responded only weakly to the growing threat of communicable diseases, including HIV and TB. In Timor-Leste, nongovernmental organizations (NGOs) have been instrumental in providing public health services, including maternal and child health, nutrition, malaria prevention, leprosy prevention and rehabilitation, health education and promotion, treatment of mental illnesses, first aid, HIV/AIDS prevention and treatment, and testing and treatment of sexually transmitted infections.

In social insurance–financed health systems in East Asia and the Pacific, public health tends to be financed through general tax revenues to ensure universal coverage. In Japan and the Republic of Korea, services for health promotion, prevention of disease, and maternal and child health are generally not covered by health insurance but are funded directly by the government. Similarly, in Mongolia, the government is responsible for providing public health services and treating diseases with public health impacts. These state budget or publicly funded services are available to all citizens regardless of their health insurance status. Preventive services in Vietnam are mainly provided through targeted national health programs, including programs aimed at controlling malaria, goiter, TB, leprosy, dengue fever, child malnutrition, and HIV/AIDS; the Expanded Programme on Immunization; community mental health care programs; and food hygiene and safety programs.

Decentralization in the health sector poses threats to the effective financing and provision of public health services, at least during the initial stages. First, where responsibility for financing public health is decentralized, local governments may underinvest in public health because they face a different set of incentives from the central government. Local governments may be incentivized to invest more in providing curative services that have the potential to generate user fee revenues and that are more popular with voters. Second, decentralization may lead to a breakdown of national public goods such as health information systems and disease surveillance. The public health system may not respond quickly and effectively to disease outbreaks as a result.

Many of these threats to public health provision were recognized when decentralization began in Indonesia in the late 1990s. Responsibility for strengthening the disease surveillance system, food and drug control, and public health service provision was vested with the central government through the MoH. However, success in institutionalizing these mechanisms at the central level was limited, at least in the first few years after decentralization (Rokx and others 2009). Evidence also exists that family planning services in Indonesia were disrupted when the National Coordinating Board for Family Planning (Badan Koordinasi Keluarga Berencana Nasional) was decentralized (ADB 2008).

From Whom to Buy: Contracting for Improved Cost and Quality

Through contracting, insurers and, more generally, purchasers can establish minimum standards—in terms of staff qualifications and infrastructure—that need to be met to be awarded a contract with the scheme. Purchasers can also establish service-specific standards, whereby providers are reimbursed for particular services only if they are performed by staff members with adequate qualifications and in a manner consistent with established practice protocols and prescription guidelines. At a second level, contracting can be used to develop benchmarks and performance standards with an organization such as a hospital or clinic. Such contracting could be used as part of the civil service code or outside it in the case of private organizations and NGOs.

Significant external contracting occurs with providers across most countries and income groups in East Asia and the Pacific. An important issue in contracting in many East Asian and Pacific economies is whether the payer is to contract with both the public sector and the emergent private sector. Progress in both public and private contracting can be found in Malaysia, Mongolia, and Thailand as well as in the high-income economies of Japan, the Republic of Korea, and Taiwan, China. Some countries, such as Mongolia and Thailand, also use the element of gatekeeping in contracts, making primary care providers responsible for encouraging the use of primary care and more cost-effective outpatient services.

High-Income Economies

In three high-income economies—Japan; the Republic of Korea; and Taiwan, China—the SHI system openly contracts with any licensed medical providers in the market place. The private sector dominates the hospital sector (about 90 percent) in both the Republic of Korea and Taiwan, China. None of the three high-income economies has a gatekeeping system, but penalty provisions can be used to terminate or temporarily suspend the contract in the case of fraudulent claims and unlawful practices (Gauld and others 2006; see also the forthcoming volume of East Asia–Pacific Country Health Financing Profiles).

Other economies appear less successful in coordinating and contracting across public and private sectors. In Hong Kong SAR, China, public sector services are commissioned, funded, and directly provided by the government through the statutory Health Authority (except for limited services). In recent years, a few experiments have been tried with private-public partnership initiatives. These initiatives have involved contracting out some common, high-volume procedures (for example, cataract surgery) to reduce excessively long queues. In the private outpatient sector, penetration of various forms of managed care, including contract medicine, prepaid plans, and preferred provider networks, is limited in extent and scope, although it has grown considerably in the past decade (Leung and others 2008).

Middle-Income Economies

Thailand uses a gatekeeping system with the civil service and formal private sector workers (SHI) schemes, requiring beneficiaries to register with specific health care providers. Public and private hospitals with more than

100 beds are considered eligible contractor providers for SHI members. Past experience indicates that private hospitals can play a major role as contractor providers for SHI. However, the government district health system (district hospital and affiliated health centers in a district) typically plays a significant role as the primary care contractor provider for civil service beneficiaries. The civil service and SHI schemes purchased services for their beneficiaries through annual contracts to a network of primary care contractors, typically the district health systems owned by the Ministry of Public Health in the case of civil service members, and contractor hospitals of more than 100 beds for SHI members (see the forthcoming volume of East Asia–Pacific Country Health Financing Profiles).

In Malaysia, the government contracts with many providers in the private sector, corporatized entities, and NGOs. The MoH has also outsourced services to private providers in the areas of radiotherapy and cardiothoracic and diagnostic imaging to increase access to specialized clinical care and reduce waiting times. Indeed, even the traditional medicine providers within the MoH facility are brought in on a contractual basis. Within the support services for health, the government has contracted out, among other services, the disposal of medical waste products, cleaning and laundry, pharmaceutical supply, food supply, security, and health education campaigns (see the forthcoming volume of East Asia–Pacific Country Health Financing Profiles).

In China, insurance schemes have already established contracts with providers, specifying the package of services to be delivered, payment methods, quality standards, drug lists, and other things. In some cases, contracts include provisions for terminating the contract if, for example, patients were not charged in accordance with the established price schedule (Liu 2008).

In a few isolated cases in the Philippines, some local health departments have contracted out the provision of health services to indigents to either private or public hospitals. These local departments have now shifted to enrolling the indigents in the SHI program. The local health department often contracts out non–health care services such as the training of government health workers and technical assistance to local governments (see the forthcoming volume of East Asia–Pacific Country Health Financing Profiles).

Low-Income Economies

Cambodia has used contracting extensively since 1998 (starting with an Asian Development Bank loan) as a way to improve service delivery and staff performance in health facilities in different local districts. The initial group contracted consisted of eight districts covering 1 million people. Three different models were piloted (using a randomized design) from that time until 2003: a contracting-in model (three districts), a contracting-out model (two districts), and a model that continued existing government policies (three districts).[2] The Belgian Development Cooperation Agency later introduced a different version of contractual agreements called the New Deal. The New Deal attempted to use the district rather than NGOs as the main management entity for the contracted units. The selection of contractors was done through a call for bids from NGOs to manage various districts using grants from donors.

The contracting model now in use is a hybrid of the previous pilots, in which an NGO contracts with MoH staff at the supervisory and service delivery levels. Civil service regulations apply to the staff, but NGOs can hire additional staff members when necessary. Data from one of the original eight districts (population 176,000) that used the contracting-in model revealed the output of services increased by 100 to 700 percent, depending on the type of service. Most notable were increases in prenatal care and deliveries (740 percent and 550 percent, respectively). Outpatient contracts showed the lowest increase—"only" 98 percent one year after implementation. The district population's OOP health expenditure was also shown to decrease, whereas staff salaries increased. Some providers faced decreasing income because they received less than they did from their earlier private practices, but they were willing to comply with the new system. In addition, contracted districts showed a more pro-poor distribution of resources than in noncontracted districts, but large discrepancies still existed, even within contracted districts.

Several reviews have analyzed the factors behind the success of contracting in Cambodia. In brief, these factors are as follows:

- Contracts have performance orientation and link funding to achieving predefined targets.
- The contractor brings in additional management expertise and skills.
- Additional financial incentives are paid to the staff.
- The government disburses the health facility operational budget in full and on time.
- The independent third-party role of the NGO is instrumental in monitoring performance, identifying problems, and lobbying the government and donors to address them.

A review of the outcomes associated with contracting indicates only mixed results: the high rate of administrative expenditure is the main problem. Evaluating six key outcome indicators—prenatal coverage, delivery in a health care facility, delivery with a trained staff, full immunization, vitamin A coverage, and birth spacing—indicates that results achieved are higher than the national average in about 50 percent of districts. In many cases, the target was not achieved even though the contracting model was in place. Administrative expenditure ranges from 19 percent to 46 percent in a summary review of contracting NGOs. The future participation of NGOs could be regulated by limiting overhead expenses through regulatory or contractual terms.[3]

The current contracting arrangements use several mechanisms to improve performance. These mechanisms include the following:

- An output- and outcome-oriented contract with performance incentives between the MoH and the NGO managing service delivery
- Increased financial and managerial autonomy for the districts
- An independent third-party role for the NGO in monitoring staff and services and in governance
- Improved management capacity
- Direct disbursement of a block grant to district level
- Salary supplements and staff performance management.

The NGOs involved differ in their approaches (Hawkins 2007; Sanigest International 2008).

In Mongolia, primary health care in urban settings is contracted out to medical practitioners (family group practices) assembled as cooperatives. There are 229 family group practices. These cooperatives are considered for-profit private entities, established on the basis of assets contributed by their members. However, confusion about their real status still exists because they do not have common assets and they are funded fully by the government subsidy, which conflicts with the budget law. The budget law defines an organization as public if it is fully funded by the state budget or general government revenue. Thus, the legal standing of the family group practices is still uncertain.[4] In addition, the government has in recent years decided to contract out certain support services, such as laundry, kitchen, cleaning, and security. The SHI organization also enforces contracts with public and private providers (sanatoriums and private hospitals) for the reimbursement of services delivered to insured persons; public providers have to conclude at least two contracts with respective organizations.

The Public Finance and Management Law (2002) requires all budget entities to have a service delivery contract or agreement with the relevant minister. At the end of every year, the health minister signs a contract with local government unit heads agreeing on the health sector budget and services to be provided in each local government unit. The health minister also delegates contracting authority to the state secretary to conclude agreements with tertiary-level hospitals and to local governors to conclude contracts with secondary- and primary-level public providers. When general agreements or contracts are concluded, outlining the overall services and funds for each provider, general managers conclude performance agreements with departmental managers and personnel internally within their organizations. The law brought a new management system for public entities where contracting is intrinsic to their functioning, but capacity is yet to be improved to ensure the effectiveness of this concept (see the forthcoming volume of East Asia–Pacific Country Health Financing Profiles).

In Vietnam, the SHI reimburses approved facilities, which include contracted private facilities. Enrollees may also use noncontracted facilities, including providers abroad, but reimbursement in this case is to the patient, who pays the facility and subsequently files a claim up to a ceiling amount based on the average facility cost (see the forthcoming volume of East Asia–Pacific Country Health Financing Profiles). In Lao PDR, in contrast, contracting is more limited. What contracting takes place is only between community-based schemes and facilities and providers (see the forthcoming volume of East Asia–Pacific Country Health Financing Profiles).

The public sector currently provides a majority of health services in Timor-Leste (Timor-Leste Prime Minister's Office 2008). Government services have been complemented by a significant private sector component—estimated at 25 percent of all services—to provide services that the public sector cannot (such as ambulatory care). These services are provided primarily through local and international NGOs (the latter often funded from abroad) and through private doctors, nurses, and midwives. The NGOs are often church affiliated (for example, Caritas, which is associated with the Catholic Church) and rely mostly on volunteer workers.

Although no formal contracts exist between public and private providers, the Timor-Leste government is working to strengthen public-private partnerships in health. Specifically, it aims to focus the public sector on those public goods it can effectively deliver, promote appropriate involvement of the private sector in the delivery of private goods such as ambulatory care, and strengthen collaboration between the public and private sectors in service delivery (World Bank 2008b). This strategy will entail further development of the relationship with local employer-labor groups and increased cooperation with church health facilities (for example, access to pharmaceuticals and basic health equipment to improve the quality of services in church facilities) (World Bank 2008b).

Analysis and Discussion

Contracting is common in the region, and some countries such as Cambodia have a rich contracting tradition. However, little exists in the way of contract evaluation in any of the region's economies or (outside of Cambodia) of selective contracting on the basis of quality and performance. More commonly, soft, relational contracts provide an expectation from both sides (purchaser and provider) that contracts will automatically be extended for ensuing years. Selective contracting is not easy, either politically or from a technical perspective, because it requires good and timely information about costs and quality of services delivered.

In the short term, economies with developing capacity may be encouraged along several lines:

- *Development of management and information systems facility pilots.* These pilot programs would adapt standard approaches to capturing clinical and cost information. This information could be used as the basis for negotiations with insurers or purchasers of services.
- *Development of a series of pilots that might focus on chronic health management areas such as asthma and diabetes.* Changing epidemiological patterns are emerging in many countries (for example, noncommunicable diseases in China, Thailand, and Vietnam). These pilots could be supported with good contracting rates of payment and associated quality and outcome indicators. Pilots could later be scaled up. These later pilots might be developed along similar disease-specific management lines, such as, diabetes, asthma, hypertension, and mental health services that promise more cost-effective provision. For example,

better management of diabetes might result in less renal failure and a less costly medical outcome for individuals and families. Disease management pilots are ongoing in Beijing (diabetes) and Nanjing (for mental illness), but little is known about those pilots (Liu 2008).

- *In geographic areas with few providers (rural areas), development of contracts that can still build in performance benchmarks for improved performance.* These benchmarks could be matched with performance payment bonuses of some type.
- *Development of more contracting internally to organizations such as hospitals and clinics.* Except perhaps in Vietnam, little has occurred in the region related to internal contracts with employees of public facilities. The contracts would be used in the first two or three years to assess performance and provide feedback. After three years, the contracts would be used to improve flexibility of inputs to better hire and fire personnel according to performance and input needs for care services.
- *Assessments of whether more countries should contract out selected services in their public facilities.* Countries such as Mongolia already do so. Contracted services include laundry, food, laboratory, and diagnostic services. Such assessments could continue to improve quality and cut costs.

Contracting out always requires some caution as well as the following criteria:

- A competitive environment
- Well-defined services
- Coordination with public sector activities
- Assessment of the quality of private management
- Specification of service standards
- Close monitoring of contract performance

Nevertheless, approaches given here might be expanded in the region, and selective contracting could be used in some initial countries.

How to Pay: Implementing New Incentive Payment Systems

East Asia and the Pacific has a rich variety of provider payment systems, and many economies appear to be in transition between systems (table 6.4). However, the multiplicity of forms and the variation across payers probably dilute the impact of these policy tools for encouraging

Table 6.4 Summary of Provider Payment Systems in East Asia and the Pacific

Country	*Primary care*	*Outpatient specialists*	*Hospitals*	*Pharmaceuticals*	*Payment pilots and other comments*
High-income economies					
Hong Kong SAR, China	Public: salary and one-line-item budgets Private: FFS	Public: salary and one-line-item budgets Private: FFS	Public: salary and one-line-item budgets Private: FFS	n.a.	No payment pilots
Japan	FFS and salary bonuses for physicians in sparsely populated areas	FFS and salary bonuses for physicians in sparsely populated areas	FFS Line-item subsidies to selected public sector facilities	FFS, physician based	Payment pilots: per diem for geriatric care; diagnosis-related groups (DRGs) for inpatient care
Malaysia	Public: salary Private: FFS	Public: salary Private: FFS	Soft budgets to facilities Providers: salary	n.a.	Payment pilots: FFS contracts to private physicians for rural posts and mix of FFS and salary for public providers
Korea, Rep.	FFS	FFS	FFS	Reforms in 2000 delinked physician and dispensing	Payment pilots: DRGs
Singapore	Health savings accounts	Health savings accounts	Line-item budgets and health savings accounts	Health savings accounts or consumer negotiated	n.a.
Taiwan, China	FFS	FFS	FFS	n.a.	Payment pilots: DRGs
Middle-income economies					
China	Health savings accounts and FFS	Health savings accounts, FFS for technology and equipment, and limited line-item budgets	Line-item budgets and FFS	Separate fee schedule, with pooled purchasing, and use controls	Payment pilots: several in urban and rural areas, including capitation, pay-for-performance, DRGs, and global budgets
Philippines	Capitation and FFS	Line-item and FFS	Line-item and FFS	n.a.	Development of DRGs for SHI fund

(continued)

Table 6.4 *(continued)*

Country	*Primary care*	*Outpatient specialists*	*Hospitals*	*Pharmaceuticals*	*Payment pilots and other comments*
Thailand	30 Baht Scheme: capitation SHI: capitation Civil service: FFS with demand-side controls	n.a.	30 Baht Scheme: Capitation SHI: global budget with case-mix adjusters Civil service: FFS with demand-side controls	n.a.	30 Baht Scheme and SHI use geographic-based global budget caps as a first step, and facility-based allocations follow
Low-income economies					
Cambodia	Varies by program: salary and line-item budgets in public programs; capitation, simplified case payments, and FFS in social insurance schemes				
Indonesia	Depends on scheme: line-item budgets and salary in public programs; FFS in private programs				
Lao PDR	Varies by program: salary and line-item budgets in public programs; capitation and FFS in social insurance schemes				
Mongolia	Risk-adjusted capitation	Flat payments	Flat payments based on 22 DRG categories in public facilities; adjustment for accreditation score for private providers	SHI reimburses at 50% to 70% of prices for drugs on essential drug list and drugs prescribed by designated outpatient providers	Public health programs based on global budgets
Papua New Guinea and Pacific Islands	Line-item budgets and salaries for providers				
Timor-Leste	Salary; bonuses in private sector	Salary; bonuses in private sector	Line-item budgets and salaries	n.a.	n.a.
Vietnam	Mix of line-item budgets and FFS (fee schedule has not been updated since 1995)			Hospitals negotiate drug prices with companies and pass on costs	Budget first allocated to provincial level; Plans to pilot DRGs

Source: Authors' compilation based on the forthcoming volume of East Asia–Pacific Country Health Financing Profiles.
Note: n.a. = not available.

efficiency and quality. Furthermore, economies tend to overrely on FFS systems.

Outside of high-income economies, FFS systems are often used in conjunction with supply-side financing and line-item budgets, as occurs in China, Lao PDR, and the Philippines. This mix of incentives can be toxic. Line-item budgets are often unresponsive to patient needs and demands. The FFS overlay can encourage unnecessary demand, often as a way of generating new revenues for underfunded line-item budgets or reallocating revenues across line-item budgets. The effects can fall on the purchaser in terms of unnecessary outlays or (as discussed in chapters 2 and 8) on consumers as OOP costs.

At the same time, many countries are now looking to move beyond FFS systems, especially as they start to address increased costs, making cost containment and efficiency areas of higher priority. New provider payment strategies or new provider payment pilots are emerging in several economies, regardless of income. Thailand is perhaps the regional leader in moving beyond FFS systems with a sophisticated mix of geographic caps, facility global budgets, and case-mix (often referred to as diagnosis-related groups, or DRGs) adjusters for hospital admissions.

High-Income Economies

Use of a national FFS schedule predominates among high-income economies of East Asia and the Pacific. The model fee schedule for the region is probably found in Japan, which has a common fee schedule across plans with an overall global cap to contain costs. High-technology services can be reimbursed for less cost to hold down volume. Historically, fees underreimburse high-technology services and overreimburse ambulatory care (Wagstaff 2007a). The fee schedule is composed of some 3,000 services or procedures and is revised periodically.

When reviewed, fees are reduced for services and drugs that have seen large volume increases, whereas those deemed important but underused may receive a fee increase. The fee-setting process is one of negotiation, with the MoH making the final decision with inputs from a 20-member advisory council. Strict billing limits help cap OOP expenses for consumers. Public sector hospitals, which have about one-quarter of the beds, receive general revenue subsidies (4 percent of all expenditures), and sparsely populated areas receive subsidies through, for example, physician salaries or fees.

The fee schedule in the Republic of Korea is determined by negotiations between representatives of provider groups and the SHI at the end of each year. When negotiations do not produce an agreement on the level of fees in time, the MoH determines the fee levels through a committee meeting. Negotiation between the two parties has rarely been successful, so the government has ultimately determined the fee levels (see the forthcoming volume of East Asia–Pacific Country Health Financing Profiles).

Three high-income economies have attempted to move beyond FFS systems for paying providers (Wagstaff 2007a). Japan has used a per diem method for geriatric hospitals and has piloted different versions of DRGs using a case-mix system of 2,552 groups since 1983. The Republic of Korea has launched a DRG program with 25 codes (nine disease categories covering 25 percent of inpatient cases) since 2001. Taiwan, China, has phased in DRGs for the 50 most common diseases and is experimenting with global budgets for hospitals.

A second important dimension of payment arrangements in high-income economies relates to pharmaceuticals. In many economies, including the high-income economies, drug prescribing and dispensing are not completely separated. In Taiwan, China, for example, physicians made significant profits from drugs because they were allowed to prescribe and dispense drugs freely, and the prices they charged enjoyed a significant markup over the wholesale prices they paid. This practice encouraged overprescribing of drugs and frequent but short office visits. In 1997, Taiwan, China, introduced a separation policy, which restricts physicians from dispensing medicines while prescribing for the same patients. However, because the policy allows physicians to hire in-house pharmacists, the desired policy effect of reducing drug expenditures has not been observed (Chou and others 2003).

The Republic of Korea introduced a separation policy in which physicians could not dispense drugs to outpatients, and pharmacists were banned from prescribing drugs. The objective was to cut expenditures and lower the unnecessary use of drugs. However, unintended consequences occurred, including hikes in professional service fees and prescription charges, induced demand for uninsured services (with prices not regulated under the fee schedule), and greater use of higher-priced branded drugs (Kim and Ruger 2008).

In Hong Kong SAR, China, the Health Authority receives a one-line tranche from the government budget that is negotiated annually. It then allocates a similar global budget, largely on a population per capita basis adjusted by simple case mix, to each of seven geographic clusters, which in turn fund different hospitals and departments offering patient care services. Public sector providers are all salaried employees and civil servants, and they are not permitted to undertake private work.

The Hong Kong SAR, China, private health care market is provided by full-time private physicians (about 45 percent of all physicians) and is mainly charged on a FFS basis. Charges are largely market driven with no uniform fees, except in the case of third-party payers that set their own standard payment schedules. The private primary care market is very competitive, although specialty services are much less so with a wide spread of charges. The FFS method predominates in the private inpatient market as well, because most patients either pay out of pocket or use indemnity insurance. Most Chinese medicine and allied health services also operate on an FFS basis (Leung and others 2008).

One of the perceived benefits of Singapore's health savings accounts is that they allow consumers not only to be price sensitive but also to directly purchase services from the provider. However, the evidence to date is that consumers often do not have appropriate information on costs and quality and therefore overbuy services not only in terms of use but also by mistaking price for quality, thus biasing purchased services toward high-end, high-technology care (Hanvoravongchai 2002; Yip and Hsiao 2008).

Middle-Income Economies

In Malaysia, the MoH previously had a soft budget, with the Treasury providing additional funds in times of unexpected or high volume. Health personnel within the government health care system are paid a salary but are allowed to do additional work when not on duty, both in private facilities and in the MoH during approved extended clinical hours on evenings and weekends. The MoH is currently piloting the provision of private wards in two public hospitals.

In an effort to overcome the problem of a labor shortage in the public sector, the Malaysian MoH procures the services of some private sector specialists and general practitioners. This effort is also aimed at encouraging the active participation of private providers in delivering health services to rural areas. Private sector providers work mainly on an FFS basis. Although not compulsory, the fee schedule developed by the Malaysian Medical Association apparently acts as a benchmark for prices charged by private practitioners. Some large employer groups and insurance companies may also set their own fee schedule and may define the benefits package that is covered (see the forthcoming volume of East Asia–Pacific Country Health Financing Profiles).

Thailand has developed sophisticated payment systems, but specific payment systems vary across pools of funds (purchasers). A global budget approach to providers in a geographic area is used by the 30 Baht Scheme and SHI. The SHI scheme applies capitation fees for outpatient and inpatient services, whereas the 30 Baht Scheme applies capitation fees for outpatient services and uses global budgets with DRG measures for inpatient services on a facility basis. The CSMBS uses an FFS fee schedule with demand-side controls (see the forthcoming volume of East Asia–Pacific Country Health Financing Profiles).

Thailand learned an interesting lesson in its evolution over time regarding different provider payment approaches. Thailand's first financing scheme, the Medical Welfare Scheme, reimbursed hospitals for the services they provided to beneficiaries, but the reimbursement levels were set below cost. Hospitals thus had no incentive to deliver quality care and would often charge insured patients extra to make up their losses. Moreover, the means-testing system used to identify those eligible for the program was unreliable.

Two health financing programs—the CSMBS for civil servants and the Social Security Scheme—provide case studies in different payment models. The CSMBS pays providers through an FFS payment mechanism. As a result, its beneficiaries have had a high hospital admission rate and a long length of stay. The Social Security Scheme pays providers through a capitation payment system (Wibulpolprasert and Thaiprayoon 2008). All beneficiaries are required to choose a hospital network and are permitted to receive care only from providers within that network. Hospitals receive capitation payments based on the number of beneficiaries. To combat problems of adverse selection and underprovision of expensive services, hospitals now receive extra payments for high-cost services, and capitation payments are now based on a formula that accounts for age and number of patients with chronic diseases.

As part of the 30 Baht Scheme, an autonomous purchasing agency, the National Health Security Office, was set up to contract with providers. Beneficiaries register with a provider network. Some of the details of the 30 Baht Scheme were not fully worked out until after implementation. For example, the switch in hospital payment from global budget to capitation met with significant resistance from providers. They first protested that the level of capitation was too low and lobbied successfully for adoption of a higher rate. Next, they asserted their power by effectively stealing control of the capitation funds in both rural and urban areas. In urban areas, large public hospitals were being squeezed by their new capitation-based budgets but refused to make the necessary staff cuts, opting instead to petition for more funds from the government budget. The government conceded and allowed the large provincial-level hospitals to control both budgets. Thus, the impact of the new capitation system on such hospitals was minimized because their prereform funding was restored.

The method by which the National Health Security Office contracted with providers also saw some changes, with both private and outpatient facilities now contracted directly. Originally, the fund copied the Social Security Scheme and contracted directly only with large public hospitals; smaller facilities and private providers were subcontracted. One of the problems with this method, however, was a disproportionate focus on inpatient care. In an effort to encourage the use of basic preventive care, it was decided in 2004 that both private and outpatient facilities could be contracted directly. The resultant gatekeeping system has been one of the most successful elements of the 30 Baht Scheme. Outpatient visits at health centers and smaller, district hospitals have increased, while outpatient visits to the larger, general hospitals have decreased.

Nevertheless, Thailand's referral system has seen some setbacks with the existing contractual arrangements. In the rural areas, purchasing power was given to small primary care units that were to act as fund holders, purchasing care from community hospitals as needed. Because the primary care units depend on physicians from these hospitals, however, the community hospitals have been able to leverage their power to control the purchasing behavior of the units. This factor has affected both the referral system, because the hospitals hold on to patients to keep the capitation funds, and the quality of care, because funds that should have gone to primary care units and district health offices are instead kept for the community hospitals (Hsiao and others 2008).

In the Philippines, the SHI organization (PhilHealth) contracts with local government units (those in rural areas) for primary care and a package of outpatient benefits. The payment is a block payment using capitation, although whether the basis of payment is per capita or some other input-based formula remains unclear. Public hospitals are provided line-item budgets from either the national government or the local government (for local government–owned hospitals), usually based on inputs such as bed capacity. Public sector physicians and specialists in hospitals and primary care facilities are paid salaries, although in some cases they are allowed to engage in private practice on a limited basis and charge for such work on an FFS basis.

On top of the line-item budget, hospital inpatient care is reimbursed by PhilHealth on an FFS basis up to some ceiling for specific items. PhilHealth has introduced an outpatient benefit package for indigent members, who are paid for on a per capita basis to the rural health unit where members are enrolled. Facilities in the private sector, either private hospitals or private clinics, are paid on an FFS basis with no uniform pricing scheme. No recent information is readily available, but when HMOs started in the 1990s, HMO doctors either were paid regular salaries or were accredited and compensated on an FFS basis, at rates negotiated by the HMO with individual doctors (see the forthcoming volume of East Asia–Pacific Country Health Financing Profiles).

In China, providers are still paid largely through a mix of government subsidies through line-item budgets and FFS payments. Subsidies take two main forms: (a) a general subsidy to cover part of salaries and other operational costs and (b) a specific subsidy for specific investments in infrastructure or equipment. The former are typically allocated according to criteria such as number of staff members and retirees or number of beds, with little or no regard to specific objectives or performance criteria.

Three separate fee schedules are used—for drugs, health services, and medical technology and equipment (Liu 2008). However, the fee schedule pricing is often below cost for basic services and above cost for specialized care. The idea is to encourage more access by patients to more basic and cost-effective services. However, the pricing schedule has reversed this behavior in that it gives providers an incentive for overprovision of more profitable specialized or curative services or antibiotics and underprovision of basic health services that are less profitable (Wagstaff and others 2009), thus resulting in the oversupply of care—especially drugs and high-technology care. Efforts to reform this system have been limited, and attempts to reduce the scope for facilities to retain financial surpluses and use them to pay staff bonuses linked to their contribution to the facility's revenues have yet to have much effect. Governance and regulation reforms have begun but have yet to have much effect (Wagstaff and others 2009).

Most urban and rural schemes have some mechanisms to control reimbursement expenditures. In urban areas, under the formal private sector workers' scheme, these mechanisms include (a) setting caps and limits on the rate of increase of the health care facilities revenues (for example, Shanghai); (b) limiting the cost per inpatient day (Nanjing, Zhenjiang, Guangzhou, Shenzhen); (c) use of DRGs (in Beijing, Nanjing has limited numbers of categories, Mudanjiang in Shandong has 329 categories); and (d) capitation case management for chronic disease patients (in Beijing, Nanjing) (Liu 2008). Typically, these control mechanisms have been associated with reductions in unit costs, but effects on quality have not always been evaluated (Wagstaff and others 2009). In other cases, the fee schedule regulations have not been removed, thereby preventing a larger "bundle" of services from being priced.

A small handful of rural insurance schemes have adopted alternative provider payment methods, including case-based payment for inpatient care and capitation or salary payment for outpatient care. Sometimes, these methods have involved the use of contracts to define explicit performance criteria, for example, specifying the package of services to be delivered and the payment methods and quality standards, especially the use of drug lists to control prescription practices. To date, no evidence exists on the effect of these rural reforms on cost and quality, although the evidence from urban reforms is encouraging. Rural areas also have reimbursement rules that specify lower rates for care delivered in higher-level facilities; most counties require members to use only certain approved facilities (Wagstaff and others 2009). New payment systems are being piloted in urban and rural areas (box 6.2).

Box 6.2

Provider Payment Pilots in Urban and Rural China

Traditionally, payments to urban hospitals by both self-paying patients and insurance schemes were based on the regulated price schedule. In the face of escalating costs, insurance schemes in some cities experimented with different forms of capped global budgets or payment per inpatient day with volume caps. When the Basic Medical Insurance (BMI) urban insurance scheme was introduced, the government established a national model for demand-side cost containment with health savings accounts but did not prescribe a particular method of provider payment. Most schemes have continued to pay hospitals on an FFS basis. Exceptions exist, however. Hainan Province, for example, implemented prospective payment—essentially a global budget with a small quality- and volume-contingent bonus—for six key hospitals in January 1997.

Average expenditure per admission fell below that of the other hospitals that had continued to be paid FFS, and the growth in spending on expensive drugs and high-technology services was reduced dramatically. Whether any adverse effect on quality occurred is not known. A similar approach to maintaining volume through a combination of global budget and contingent bonuses has been

(continued)

Box 6.2 *(continued)*

used in Qingdao. Jiujiang switched to a fixed charge per inpatient day in 1996. In 2001, the city switched again in an attempt to further curb expenditure growth, this time to capitation. After the switch to capitation, medical expenditure per insured inpatient fell from Y 2,320 to Y 1,778, and the share of drug spending in total spending fell from 76.5 percent to 59.8 percent. Zhenjiang, the other BMI pilot city, started out using a fixed charge per inpatient day, but in 2001 started to experiment with a DRG-based payment method for 82 diseases. In 2003, the average expenditure for diseases using the DRG payment method was 25 percent lower than the province average in hospitals at the same level.

In subsequent nationwide implementation of BMI, many cities followed the leads of Jiujiang and Zhenjiang, switching to payment methods other than FFS, including a fixed charge per inpatient. Interestingly, some providers in China have moved away from FFS toward prospective payment of their own volition. For example, some urban hospitals have introduced DRGs for self-paying patients, in the hope that the hospitals may be able to attract more business by developing a reputation for transparency and predictability in pricing. Implementation of DRGs has contained costs for care generally and has cut the proportion of drug expenditures. For example, in Jining Medical College Hospital, Shandong, for the five diseases monitored, total expenditure per case decreased by 30 to 50 percent following implementation of DRGs, drug expenditure per case fell by 34 to 64 percent, and average length of stay fell by 0.4 to 2.0 days. Less is known, however, about the effect on quality.

Following the lead of BMI, some provincial and local county rural insurance schemes have also adopted alternative provider payment methods. In some localities, this change has involved the introduction of capitation for primary care (Xinjiang Uyghur Autonomous Region and Hubei Province) and salary plus bonus payments (parts of Henan and Guizhou Provinces). Case-based payment for inpatient care has been piloted in Shaanxi and Gansu Provinces.

Source: Wagstaff and others 2009.

Some reforms to the price schedule have also occurred, aimed at reducing the distortions in it: prices of professional services have been increased, the price of high-technology care has been reduced, and a move has occurred toward a price ceiling system to encourage price competition. Although these reforms may have reduced the oversupply of high-technology care and drugs, they clearly have not eliminated it. Drug pricing policy has also been changed; the new policy involves the regulation of only selected drugs (10 percent by revenue), rather than the entire range as previously. These measures were expected to reduce drug prices through a combination of increased competitive pressure and more effective procurement. In practice, hospitals have often been able to maintain high drug revenues by increasing drug use and by shifting use from one drug to another (for example, regulated to unregulated and low margin to high margin) (Wagstaff and others 2009).

In Indonesia, schemes vary with provider payment systems. The civil service insurance scheme uses capitation, while others use line-item budgets and FFS payment (see the forthcoming volume of East Asia–Pacific Country Health Financing Profiles).

Low-Income Economies

Vietnam's health budget is allocated to the provincial level first, using population size and a regional adjustment coefficient. Providers are then paid on a mix of line-item budgets and a fee schedule. For example, the government provides line-item budgets to public health facilities to cover some inputs needed to provide preventive and curative services. The amount actually paid to a hospital is based on the number of planned beds; for preventive medicine, it is based on administrative norms (population), rather than outputs, workload, or quality of performance.

The government uses FFS for coverage of those under health insurance and for targeted groups such as the poor and children under six years of age. The fees in the fee schedule are a mixture of per item charges (for example, for tests) and per diem rates (for inpatient stays), with ranges for each type and variations according to the type of hospital (higher-class hospitals being able to charge more). The fee schedule, however, has not been updated since 1995, and new interventions were added at the prevailing price. Drugs are not included in the list of fees. Hospitals negotiate drug prices with pharmaceutical companies and pass on the costs to the patient or to the SHI.

Government decrees in 2002 and 2006 created more autonomy in facilities. Savings from fees could be used to increase staff incomes and reinvest in equipment. Current reviews have indicated that these changes have resulted in overinvestment in, and overuse of, high-technology services to generate more revenue from fee-paying patients and in deterioration in the quality of care to non-fee-paying patients (World Bank 2008a; see also the forthcoming volume of East Asia–Pacific Country Health Financing Profiles).

In Mongolia, the funding for primary health care providers is decided through a risk-adjusted capitation model. As is the case with primary-level providers, Mongolia's secondary and tertiary hospitals are funded by flat-rate payments for their inpatient and outpatient care. Since 2007, the hospitals are supposed to be funded by using a simple DRG system with 22 DRG classes. In reality, however, their funding is decided on the basis of the previous year's historical spending plus some percentage of increase that is then classified or divided into 22 DRG cases to define the respective contributions of the state budget and health insurance fund.[5] Payments from the health insurance fund for inpatient services of private health care providers and sanatoriums are calculated on the basis of the rate defined by the accreditation-level score of the respective provider multiplied by the average case-mix rate applied for public hospitals at a similar level.

The SHI fund reimburses designated pharmacies for providing essential drugs to the insured. Drugs on the essential list are reimbursable for pharmacies at a discounted rate (50 to 70 percent of prices are reimbursed), but only when the drugs are prescribed by family group practices (primary health care providers in urban settings) and health centers or hospitals (primary health care providers in rural settings). Public health national programs, research, professional training, health services during natural or unforeseen disasters, and infectious disease natural foci services are paid on the basis of a global budget from the central government budget (see the forthcoming volume of East Asia–Pacific Country Health Financing Profiles).

For its social protection schemes, Lao PDR uses various provider payment methods (Zweifel and Manning 2008). Providers rely on a mix of donations and NGO and community support on an ad hoc basis. Health centers must rely on multiple sources to cover operating costs because funds from districts are often limited. Salaries of public sector employees are covered by the central government budget, which transfers resources to the provincial level and then to the district level.

The SHI scheme pays public providers annually according to the capitation method, with additional capitation rates for chronic disease management. Recent developments include a refinement of the capitation payment to reflect the risk of populations affiliated with contract hospitals. Within the civil service scheme, FFS payments are being phased out; capitation will replace them, but the capitation rates are lower than FFS payments.

Under the community-based financing schemes, provider payment is by capitation, paid directly to the contracted hospitals, and the patient makes no copayments or other forms of cost sharing at the time of use. Reimbursement to health providers under the HEFs is on an FFS basis, except for cesarean sections, which are done on a flat, fixed-fee basis in

Vientiane province. The HEF currently represents a low proportion of the revenues of facilities (Zweifel and Manning 2008).

In Cambodia, donor funding is the source of two-thirds of public funding, but it appears to be poorly targeted. Over 60 percent of donor funds are allocated to HIV/AIDS, TB, and malaria programs, although prevalence of HIV/AIDS is relatively low; only a small share is allocated to basic health services, including maternal and child health and strengthening of local health systems.

Public expenditure growth over the past five years has been concentrated in specific input categories: medicines, commodities (financed predominantly from the government budget), and capital expenditure (financed predominantly by donors). The input mix of the budget is characterized by a very low share spent on salaries (under 15 percent of the government budget and 8.8 percent of all funds allocated in 2007). Salaries in Cambodia represent one of the lowest relative shares in developing countries. Spending on salaries as a percentage of recurrent government health spending has not increased since 2002.

Cambodia is experimenting with health service payment modalities in which money follows the patient, and first efforts are being made to provide appropriate incentives to health service providers. FFS and simplified case-based payments are prevalent among HEFs. Inappropriate care and overuse are known risks of these payment systems, but given the very low level of use of health services, these payment methods may be appropriate in the short term to increase use and productivity. Community-based health insurance schemes are using capitation models (Hawkins 2007; Sanigest International 2008).

Staffing controls in Timor-Leste are centralized, and expenditure on goods and services is tightly controlled at senior levels of the MoH and the Ministry of Planning and Finance. However, the recent creation of the Management Board for the National Hospital is an important step in the decentralization of authority within the hospital sector and could be accompanied by more flexibility in allocation (see the forthcoming volume of East Asia–Pacific Country Health Financing Profiles).

Timor-Leste's health professionals are salaried, although rates vary widely between the public and private sectors. Private sector health personnel earn significantly higher salaries than do government employees. Catholic Church–related organizations compensate doctors at similar rates as MoH physicians, but medical doctors at a clinic owned by international NGOs are paid twice as much as MoH doctors. The same holds true for nurses and midwives. In addition to monthly salaries, health professionals may qualify to receive bonuses, particularly nurses and midwives working for NGOs.

In the Pacific Islands and Papua New Guinea, countries generally use line-item budgets based on beds and salaries for providers.

Analysis and Discussion

Optimal payment systems do not exist, and payment systems and incentives need to be designed and developed to address the specific policy issues and objectives inherent in a nation's health care sector. Table 6.5 outlines the performance of various payment systems on various criteria.

The mix of incentives also needs to encourage the use of an overall mix of cost-effective services. The current mix of incentives in many of the countries of the region may be perverse. Because line-item budgets are frequently based on bed norms, they create incentives for hospitals to put patients in beds even if treatment is possible at lower-level facilities or on an outpatient basis (World Bank 2008a). The FFS overlay has also created incentives for facilities to increase the number of services provided, perhaps beyond what is necessary, and not, linked to performance and improved outcomes.

In many of the economies, the provider community strongly favors FFS payment for all types of services. This preference is understandable, because FFS payment tends to encourage higher volumes and higher expenditures on health services, thus increasing the flow of revenues to providers. At the same time, the FFS system has its place: it can be a

Table 6.5 Provider Payment Methods and Indicative Incentives for Provider Behavior

	Incentives for provider behavior		
Mechanisms	*Prevention*	*Delivery or production of services*	*Cost containment*
Line-item budget	+/−	−	+++
FFS	+/−	+++	−−−
Per diem	+/−	+++	−−−
Per case (for example, DRGs)	+/−	++	++
Global budget	++	−−	+++
Capitation	+++	−−	+++

Source: World Bank 2005.
Note: The number of plus (+) and minus (−) signs reflects potential for benefits and potential for unintended consequences, respectively.

powerful tool to deliver priority services and to reach special population groups such as the poor or those in remote regions. Thus, FFS payment may be prudent for use in Lao PDR for the poor and in remote areas of any country, whether it is Japan or Indonesia.

Purchasers and governments must, however, be very careful about adopting FFS payment for all services. Significant inflationary effects of FFS systems are well established—in Canada; the Czech Republic; parts of the Russian Federation; Taiwan, China; the United States; and other economies. Governments might want to be careful in considering FFS payment systems and to do so only in the context of an overall spending cap (as in Japan) or subject to very stringent administrative mechanisms that prevent increases in service volume.

On the outpatient side, the payment incentives might actually be reversed in many countries from the current structure of salary and line-item budgets. Primary and preventive services could move from salary and line item and be paid on an FFS basis to encourage use of priority services. Outpatient curative care, in contrast, might move to a capitation or fund-holding approach over time, which would discourage patterns of overuse for personal, curative services.

In EU countries, three models have dominated physician services historically: salary, capitation, and FFS models, or some combination of the three. In general, physicians in private practice are paid on an FFS basis, whereas salary or capitation or some combination tends to dominate as payment methods for service provision in the public sector. However, countries such as France and Germany pay on an FFS basis for all patients. But the FFS system in these countries differs from that in many East Asian and Pacific economies. Very importantly, FFS systems in these European countries are subject to an overall cap on total expenditures, and prices and volume are determined only within the target ceiling.

In the United Kingdom, in the early 1990s, some purchasing responsibility was allocated to selected general practice fund holders with at least 11,000 patients registered with them. Their budgets typically covered up to 20 percent of the total per capita allocation for each patient; the remainder rested with the health authority. Initially, 306 practices joined; by 1998, 3,500 general practice fund holders existed, covering 60 percent of the population.

The new Labour government abolished fund holding in 1997 and established a nationwide system of primary care groups or primary care trusts. Unlike fund holding—which was voluntary—membership in a primary care group was compulsory for all general practices. The average primary care group covered a population of 100,000, although variations around the average ranged from approximately 50,000 to more than 250,000 people. Over time, primary care groups have been converted into primary care trusts. These trusts are freestanding bodies with a budget for contracting and commissioning care, including inpatient care, covering average populations of 170,000 people and controlling about 75 percent of the overall national budget for health.

For facilities and inpatient care services, many East Asian and Pacific economies will probably need to move away from input-based budgeting for facilities. Often with a purchaser-provider split under insurance, the system of payment is then reoriented toward services or activities, as measured by outputs or even outcomes. The early experience in the 1980s and 1990s of many health insurance systems in Western Europe, North America, and Australia that were developing or using service-based systems of payment reinforces this trend. Today, more sophisticated purchasers increasingly attempt to link payment with service performance, service outputs, and ultimately, patient health outcomes (although the last is still not employed much). Such purchasers may also couple these performance-based mechanisms with demand-side mechanisms such as copayments or deductibles.

Case-mix groupings can be used as the basis for adjusting global budgets for hospitals and are often used for medical review and quality assurance as well. Case-mix groupings are composed of two streams of concurrent activity: (a) statistical and cost analysis and (b) clinical teams developing groupings based on both clinical coherence and relative resource homogeneity. These two streams are outlined in figure 6.6. Moving to global budgets would also be consistent with policies aimed at greater autonomy of providers (see chapter 7).

Like Thailand, some countries can eventually move to some combination of global budgets and case-mix-adjusted payment categories within the hospital sector. Most countries in Western Europe have moved to a performance-based approach, using some combination of payment per admission based on case-mix-adjusted DRGs while subject to some overall volume cap often termed a *global budget*. A global budget collapses all line items into one line item to provide maximum flexibility for resource use within an overall envelope of resources. Within this general model, some diversity of approaches to payment for inpatient services is in evidence throughout the EU, and most approaches have developed related to efficiency and cost-containment

Figure 6.6 Developing Case-Mix Groupings

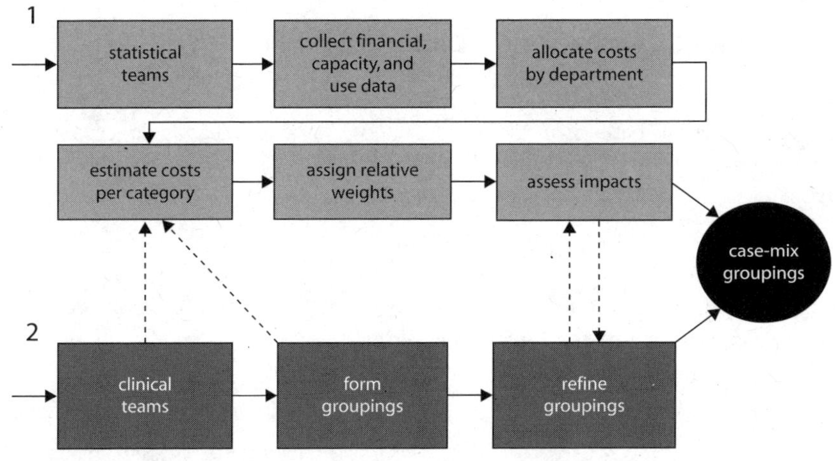

Source: Langenbrunner 2005.

objectives. Box 6.3 lists the steps for implementing a global budget for hospitals.

Uniform rates and incentives across all payers

Governments in East Asia and the Pacific with multiple sets of purchasers (for example, Cambodia, China, Indonesia, and Lao PDR) strongly need to consider a new and more consistent set of payment rules and systems across insurers. Variations across payers can distort (a) incentives providers face and (b) practice patterns by encouraging overuse of highly paid services by some payers. At the same time, variations across payers can discourage access for relatively poorly paid services and discourage equitable treatment for groups under some payers relative to others. New payment systems need to restructure incentives, but uniform rules across payers will help improve equity across groups.

Building and developing capacity

Payment systems are not developed and implemented overnight, and some testing and piloting might be initiated for countries either starting or scaling up new payment systems. These pilots could be done in selected provinces or districts and involve facilities developing improved costing and information systems. New payment systems require new types of skills, management systems, and institutions. Reliance on NGOs in managing HEFs and CBHI in lower-income countries, for example, is

Box 6.3

Steps for Implementing a Global Budget for Hospitals

1. Develop a baseline (1–3 years) database of patient use and costs.
2. Analyze use patterns, including patient flows across facilities and geographic areas.
3. Analyze expenditure patterns by
   - Demographics (age and sex)
   - Mix of patients (for example, by diagnostic categories)
4. Adjust per capita budgets for differences in costs across age or sex groups in a particular catchment area served.
5. Adjust budgets for differences in patterns of use.
6. Subtract from this base budget target levels of inappropriate and unnecessary patterns of care and associated costs (for example, inappropriate admissions, preadmission duplication of testing) and alternatives to hospital care (such as care on an outpatient basis or in day-care centers for "social cases").
7. Develop a draft budget of appropriate and necessary care, based on expected volume and case mix.
8. Develop a sharing agreement on who receives expected surpluses generated by new efficiencies, typically some portion to both facility and payer.
9. Develop rules for unexpected risk related to levels of patient demand or expenditures.
10. Conduct final negotiation and sign contract.

Source: Dredge 2009.

a short-term solution. More sustainable institutional arrangements need to be developed. These trends also put new demands on the stewardship role of the ministry of health in any particular country.

Demand-Side Financing (Purchasing)

Although purchasing services are primarily something done by a third party such as the MoH or a health insurance organization, consumers and households can be empowered to purchase services through two common mechanisms: conditional cash transfers (CCTs) and vouchers.

Implementing Conditional Cash Transfers

CCT programs were first implemented in Latin America in the late 1990s in an attempt to address high inequality and lack of access to health and educational services for the poor. In contrast to the more traditional supply-side mechanisms, such as investment in health centers and schools or general subsidies, CCTs, together with school vouchers and special health insurance schemes, offer a strategy of better targeting the poor through demand-side financing. By providing a cash transfer to poor households with children—on condition that they send their children to school and make regular health care visits—CCTs serve as a crucial instrument in removing opportunity costs for poor people as well as creating incentives for investing in their children's human capital.

Although the long-term effects of CCTs in health and education are still unclear, a few programs, such as Oportunidades in Mexico, have already demonstrated a decrease in infant morbidity and mortality rates. A significant short-term effect has become evident: the programs raise both health care use and school attendance rates. For example, in the case of Honduras, health clinic visits have experienced a 20 percent increase. In addition, CCTs have been demonstrated to cause a significant increase in consumption rates, with particular emphasis on nutrient-rich food such as meat, chicken, and milk. In the case of Familias en Acción in Colombia, a consumption increase of 9.3 percent in urban areas and 19.5 percent in rural areas was recorded (Gottret and Schieber 2006).

Several elements help determine whether a program will achieve the proposed health and nutrition objectives:

- An appropriate program design in accordance with the specific context of each country
- An effective targeting mechanism that adequately differentiates the poor from the nonpoor
- An efficient monitoring and enforcement of the conditions
- A sufficient amount of cash transfer to create a reasonable incentive for the target group to fulfill conditions
- A transparent and efficient administrative capacity.

It has been argued that the rise in educational attendance attributable to the CCT programs serves as a strong indirect contributing factor in improving health factors. In fact, educated women are widely believed to want fewer children and be more likely to use contraceptives. Furthermore, a historic correlation exists between (a) the education level of the mother and (b) the infant and maternal mortality or health status of the child (Oxaal 1997). In practice, fewer children would reduce the economic burden on the family. Educated women would also seek medical care sooner for themselves and their children and provide better care and nutrition.

In the case of Cambodia, the CCT program has already produced a positive effect on school enrollment, with an increase of 30 percent and a concomitant 43 percent increase for attendance (Doetinchem, Xu, and Carrin 2008). In Indonesia, two CCT programs are currently in the pilot phase; one is household based and the other is community based. Both CCTs share the same target indicators; however, other factors such as conditionality and size differ between the programs. Table 6.6 presents a more detailed description of the Indonesian CCT programs.

The effectiveness of CCTs in tackling both health and educational components strongly suggests CCTs as an adequate tool for demand financing. In fact, because of the strong evidence of CCTs as effective demand-financing mechanisms, they have grown in popularity and, since the emergence of such programs in Brazil and Mexico, have been implemented in several low- and middle-income countries, such as Bangladesh, Cambodia, Indonesia, and Kenya.

Perhaps the most crucial factor for ensuring the effectiveness of CCTs is to resolve the complicated balance between investing in demand and investing in supply financing. For CCTs to result in increased demand for health services, sufficient parallel investment in the quality and availability of health care must occur. Supply-side deficiencies that can affect the effectiveness of CCTs may include low administrative capacity and service quality, staff shortages or medical supply bottlenecks, and lack of physical infrastructure (clinics, schools, and transportation). Finally, a realistic and sustainable long-term plan must be in place, ensuring sufficient funding for the CCTs, because the programs demand high costs for an extended period of time to realize poverty objectives.

Providing Vouchers

Vouchers serve as an additional tool for demand financing by providing assistance to families with economic constraints through subsidies directed toward health and education. Voucher programs have been used in both health and education, but good impact evaluations are scarce. In health, sophisticated consumers who know what to buy and where to buy need to be created, as well as sophisticated risk adjusters to protect providers. Accessible information on the quality of services and providers is needed, which rarely exists even in member countries of the Organisation for Economic Co-operation and Development.

Table 6.6 Indonesian Household and Community CCT Programs

Elements	*Household CCT: Hopeful Family Program*	*Community CCT: Program Nasional Pemberdayaan Masyarakat Generasi*
Indicators targeted	Pregnant women receive four prenatal care visits. Women receive iron tablets during pregnancy. A skilled health professional attends births. Women receive two postnatal care visits. Children receive complete childhood immunizations. Infants receive monthly weigh ins. Children under 5 years of age receive vitamin A supplements. Children 6–12 years of age enroll at primary school. Children 6–12 years of age have 85% attendance record at primary school. Children 13–15 years of age enroll at junior secondary school. Children 13–15 years of age have 85% attendance record at junior secondary school. Household CCT includes option for children 16–18 years of age to go to informal junior secondary equivalency training (packet B).	
Size of transfer	Minimum Rp 200,000, maximum Rp 2,200,000 per household per year depending on family composition Average Rp 1,390,000	Average Rp 1,500,000,000 per subdistrict
Conditionality	Children under 6 years of age are required to visit a public health clinic. In case of private provision, the provider has to pass on the use record to the public clinic. Primary and junior secondary schools confirm 85% attendance rate. Providers send monthly a report to the district on whether conditions have been met. Next month's payment is reduced if conditions are not met.	Health service data are collected through village-level record keeping, and school attendance data are collected from regular classroom attendance records. Two versions are piloted. In one, the second year's block grant is independent of the first year's performance; in the other, it is not. For the latter, the second-year distribution of a portion of the block grant depends on village scoring on the 12 indicators. The budget is fixed at the subdistrict level (thus creating intervillage competition).
Targeting	Program focuses on income- and nutrition-poor subdistricts. Subdistricts that lack a supply of basic health and education services are excluded. Subdistrict quota depends on the number of poor in the subdistrict.	Jakarta and urban areas are excluded. Districts need to have the Kecamatan Development Program. Two richest districts in the province are excluded.

(continued)

Table 6.6 *(continued)*

Elements	*Household CCT: Hopeful Family Program*	*Community CCT: Program Nasional Pemberdayaan Masyarakat Generasi*
	Ministry of Social Affairs identifies beneficiaries through a proxy means test on unconditional cash transfer recipients and new candidates in areas where the unconditional cash transfer has too few recipients. Two richest districts in the province are excluded.	
Implementing agencies	Leading agency is the Ministry of Social Affairs. Post office transfers funds. Central Bureau of Statistics makes initial roster of beneficiaries.	Leading agency is the Ministry of Home Affairs (for Kecamatan Development Program). Leading agency is the Ministry of Public Works (for Urban Poverty Project).

Source: Adapted from World Bank 2007a.

Vouchers have been most often developed for the basic function of providing subsidies to poor individuals, but they can be applied for the achievement of more specific targets in health. Behavioral change in drug rehabilitation has been one objective of vouchers when applied as a reward for fulfilling certain requirements. Information gathering for research programs has also used vouchers for attracting volunteers and tracking patients.

A number of voucher programs have recently been implemented in East Asia and the Pacific. They include the following: Increasing Access to Mother and Child Care for Poor Households (China, 1999); Safe Motherhood Project (Indonesia, 1997); and Creating a Needle Exchange Program for Intravenous Drug Users (Vietnam, 2002). Under Indonesia's Safe Motherhood Project, village leaders organized and allocated booklets with vouchers (coupons). Women who participated in the program received different color-coded vouchers for various types of services, such as family health visits and normal obstetric delivery. Available data indicate that use of reproductive health services by beneficiaries has since increased.

An important difference between CCTs and voucher programs is that the conditions attached to CCTs could serve as an important factor in maximizing the effectiveness of the programs because many poor households might lack an understanding of the long-term benefits of participating in health and education schemes. In practice, determinants beyond monetary means, such as physical inaccessibility in the form of distance and poor transportation, also play a key role in whether higher-quality service reaches the target groups. Vouchers in developing economies are often funded at levels that are insufficient to enable poor people to access higher-quality health care or schools because most vouchers cover only a percentage of the cost.

Making Demand-Side Financing Cost-Effective

One important aspect in tackling high costs attached to CCTs lies in the type of demand-financing system responsible for reaching beneficiaries. Although significant initial costs will be necessary for most middle-income countries and for low-income countries, in particular, to make advances in payment technology and operations, significant cuts in disbursement and administrative costs should be expected in the longer term. In fact, the Mexican Oportunidades program experienced a reduction of administrative costs from 51.5 percent of its total budget in 1997 to 6.0 percent in 2003.

Beyond the monetary benefits of improved payment technology, evidence from Argentina, Brazil, and Mexico has shown amelioration in payment performance through the use of debit cards, along with more rapid and prompt disbursements. Greater accountability should also be expected, because financial data of transactions between municipalities will be electronically available for program managers. The high initial costs combined with the requirement of adequate institutional capacity mean many low-income countries are unable to adapt to the technological advances of middle-income countries. Instead, as in the case of Kenya, many low-income countries may have to rely on community monitoring.

Notes

1. These countries are Austria, Belgium, Denmark, Finland, France, Germany, Greece, Ireland, Italy, Luxembourg, the Netherlands, Portugal, Spain, Sweden, and the United Kingdom.
2. In the *contracting-out model,* the contractor has full responsibility for delivery of specified services in an outpatient department, directly employs a staff, and has full management control. Direct fund allocation is made in accordance with a bid. In the *contracting-in model,* the contractor provides management support to a civil service health staff, and recurrent costs are provided by the

government through normal channels. A budget supplement is provided from donor funds. Contractors have full management support over allocation and disbursement of the budget supplement but are obliged to follow government regulations with respect to government-provided resources.

3. A number of other shortcomings and recommendations for improvement have been noted, including the following:
   - Providers violating the private practice ban are not sanctioned.
   - The MoH and local health departments are at times unable to meet the obligation of providing adequate, quality staff members.
   - A conflict of human resource accountability sometimes occurred: the local health department was responsible for employees, but NGOs were supposed to manage them.
   - Primary care facilities did not have adequate autonomy.
   - Funding was inconsistent.
   - Contracting targets often did not match national targets. National programs still have a vertical approach, so they have limited coordination with outpatient departments.
   - Quality indicators should be included as performance targets and as criteria for monitoring performance. Practical assessment tools should be created.
4. However, it can be noted that their status is not that different historically from that of general practitioners in the U.K. National Health Service, who were legally independent contractors but were usually regarded as public sector doctors.
5. See Ministry of Health Order No. 279 of 2006.

References

ADB (Asian Development Bank). 2008. "Indonesia Health Care and Decentralization." Internal report, ADB, Manila.Capuno, Joseph J., and Kelechi Ohiri. 2007. "A Case Study of Vietnam's Recent Health Reform Strategies." World Bank, Washington, DC.

Chou, Y. J., Winnie C. Yip, Cheng-Hua Lee, Nicole Huang, Ying-Pei Sun, and Hong-Jen Chang. 2003. "Impact of Separating Drug Prescribing and Dispensing on Provider Behaviour: Taiwan's Experience." *Health Policy and Planning* 18 (3): 316–29.

Doetinchem, Ole, Ke Xu, and Guy Carrin. 2008. "Conditional Cash Transfers: What's in It for Health?" Technical Brief for Policy-makers 1/2008, WHO/HSS/HSF/PB/08.01, World Health Organization, Geneva.

Dredge, Robert. 2009. "Hospital Global Budgeting." In *Designing and Implementing Health Care Provider Payment Systems: How-To Manuals,* ed. John C. Langenbrunner, Cheryl Cashin, and Sheila O'Dougherty, 215–54. Washington, DC: World Bank.

Ensor, Timothy. 2005. "Geographic Resource Allocation: Global Experience and Implications for Uzbekistan." Paper prepared for the World Bank, Washington, DC.

Fernando, Tharanga. 2008. "Provision Data Tabulations from APNHAN-RCHSP Joint Asia-Pacific Health Accounts Data Compilation, Revision October 21, 2008." Institute for Health Policy, Colombo.

Gauld, Robin, Naoki Ikegami, Michael D. Barr, Tung-Liang Chiang, Derek Gould, and Soonman Kwon. 2006. "Advanced Asia's Health Systems in Comparison." *Health Policy* 79 (2–3): 325–36.

Gibis, Bernhard, Pedro W. Koch-Wulkan, and Jan Bultman. 2004. "Shifting Criteria for Benefit Decisions in Social Health Insurance Systems." In *Social Health Insurance Systems in Western Europe,* ed. Richard B. Saltman, Reinhard Busse, and Josep Figueras, 189–206. Maidenhead, Berkshire, U.K.: Open University Press.

Gottret, Pablo, and George Schieber. 2006. *Health Financing Revisited: A Practitioner's Guide.* Washington, DC: World Bank.

Hammer, Jeffrey S., and Peter Berman. 1995. "Ends and Means in Public Health Policy in Developing Countries." *Health Policy* 32 (1–3): 29–45.

Hanvoravongchai, Piya. 2002. "Medical Savings Accounts: Lessons Learned from Limited International Experience." EIP/HFS/PHF Discussion Paper 52, World Health Organization, Geneva.

Hawkins, Loraine. 2007. "Health Financing Note: Cambodia." Background paper for the World Bank, Washington, DC.

Hsiao, William C., and R. Paul Shaw, eds. 2007. *Social Health Insurance for Developing Nations.* Washington, DC: World Bank.

Hsiao, William, and others. 2008. "Social Insurance and Solidarity and East Asia Region." Paper prepared for the World Bank, Washington, DC.

Kim, Hak-Ju, and Jennifer Prah Ruger. 2008. "Pharmaceutical Reform in South Korea and the Lessons It Provides." *Health Affairs* 27 (4): 260–69.

Kutzin, Joseph, Ainura Ibraimova, Melitta Jakab, and Sheila O'Dougherty. 2009. "Bismarck Meets Beveridge on the Silk Road: Coordinating Funding Sources to Create a Universal Health Financing System in Kyrgyzstan." *Bulletin of the World Health Organization* 87 (7): 549–54.

Kutzin, Joseph, Ainura Ibraimova, Ninell Kadyrova, Gulaim Isabekova, Yevgeny Samyshkin, and Zainagul Kataganova. 2002. "Innovations in Resource Allocation, Pooling, and Purchasing in the Kyrgyz Health Care System." Policy Research Paper 21, Manas Health Policy Analysis Project, Bishkek. http://www.hpac.kg/images/pdf/RAPPRP21.E.pdf.

Langenbrunner, John C. 2005. "Health Care Financing and Purchasing in ECA: An Overview of Issues and Reforms." World Bank, Washington, DC.

Leung, Gabriel M., Keith Y. K. Tin, G. M. K. Yeung, E. S. K. Leung, Eva L. H. Tsui, D. W. S. Lam, Caroline S. H. Tsang, A. Y. K. Fung, and Su Vui Lo. 2008. "Hong Kong's Domestic Health Spending: Financial Years 1989/90 through 2004/05." *Hong Kong Medical Journal* 14 (suppl. 2): 2–23.

Lieberman, Samuel S., and Adam Wagstaff. 2008. *Health Financing and Delivery in Vietnam: Looking Forward.* Washington, DC: World Bank.

Lindelow, Magnus, and Adam Wagstaff. 2007. "Understanding System Level Constraints to Effective Prevention and Public Health Programs in the East Asia and Pacific Region: A Proposal for Funding from the GAVI Trust Fund." World Bank, Washington, DC.

Liu, Gordon. 2008. "Urban Health Insurance in China." World Bank, Beijing.

Oxaal, Zoë. 1997. "Education and Poverty: A Gender Analysis. BRIDGE Report 53, Institute of Development Studies, University of Sussex, Brighton, U.K.

Phommasack, Bounlay, Lathiphone Oula, Oukeo Khounthalivong, Inlavanh Keobounphanh, Thongvansy Misavadh, Loun, Phanpaseuth Oudomphone, Chanphomma Vongsamphanh, and Erik Blas. 2005. "Decentralization and Recentralization: Effects on the Health Systems in Lao PDR." *Southeast Asian Journal of Tropical Medicine and Public Health* 36 (2): 523–28.

Preker, Alexander S., and John C. Langenbrunner, eds. 2005. *Spending Wisely: Buying Health Services for the Poor.* Washington, DC: World Bank.

Rokx, Claudia, George Schieber, Pandu Harimurti, Ajay Tandon, and Aparnaa Somanathan. 2009. *Health Financing in Indonesia: A Reform Road Map.* Washington, DC: World Bank.

Sanigest International. 2008. "Health Sector Note: Cambodia." Prepared under contract to the World Bank, Washington, DC.

Timor-Leste Prime Minister's Office. 2008. "Meeting the Health Challenge." Prime Minister's Office, Dili.

Wagstaff, Adam. 2007a. "Health Systems in East Asia: What Can Developing Countries Learn from Japan and the Asian Tigers?" *Health Economics* 16 (5): 441–56.

———. 2007b. "Social Health Insurance Reexamined." Policy Research Working Paper 4111, World Bank, Washington, DC.

Wagstaff, Adam, Magnus Lindelow, Shiyong Wang, and Shuo Zhang. 2009. *Reforming China's Rural Health System.* Washington, DC: World Bank.

WHO (World Health Organization). 2000. *The World Health Report 2000: Health Systems—Improving Performance.* Geneva: WHO.

Wibulpolprasert, Suwit, and Suriwan Thaiprayoon. 2008. "Thailand: Good Practice in Expanding Health Coverage Lessons from the Thai Health Care Reforms." In *Good Practices in Health Financing: Lessons from Reforms in Low- and Middle-Income Countries*, ed. Pablo Gottret, George J. Schieber, and Hugh R. Waters, 355–84. Washington, DC: World Bank.

World Bank. 1993. *World Development Report 1993: Investing in Health*. Washington, DC: World Bank.

———. 2005. *World Development Report 2005: A Better Investment Climate for Everyone*. Washington, DC: World Bank.

———. 2007a. "Conditional Cash Transfers in Indonesia." World Bank, Washington, DC.

———. 2007b. *World Development Indicators*. CD-ROM. Washington, DC: World Bank.

———. 2008a. "Health Sector Transition in Vietnam: The Short- and Medium-Term Policy Agenda." World Bank, Washington, DC.

———. 2008b. "Timor-Leste: Health Sector Review." World Bank, Washington DC.

Yip, Winnie, and William C. Hsiao. 2008. "The Chinese Health System at a Crossroads." *Health Affairs* 27 (2): 460–68.

Zweifel, Peter, and Willard G. Manning. 2008. "Review of Ongoing Health Financing, Lao PDR, Vientiane, Lao PDR."

CHAPTER 7

Connecting Financing and Delivery of Services: Institutional and Organizational Characteristics in East Asian and Pacific Countries

Overview and Links to Health Care Financing

A variety of institutional and organizational characteristics have an important effect on the ability of financing, allocation, and purchasing arrangements to achieve their core objectives. Chapters 4, 5, and 6 examined the functions of health care financing, and chapter 6, in particular, focused on the technical contents of policy levers available to policy makers to ensure an optimal mix of services and to change provider behavior to improve performance. However, policy levers function only as well as the provider community can respond and organize care delivery in accordance with the priorities and principles of the purchaser.

This chapter first examines institutional characteristics, which are relevant because institutions structure the incentives that are embedded in the transactions occurring between and across different organizational units. Three characteristics in particular are worth exploring for their influence on, and confluence with, health care financing:

- Governance arrangements in providing oversight for health care financing functions and arrangements

- Governance of purchasing through different organizational arrangements on the delivery side
- Consumer pressure on financing and purchasing.

Where the three functions of financing (financing, pooling and management, and resource allocation and purchasing arrangements) are merged, the pressure exerted by these institutional characteristics will be on one organization (Langenbrunner 2005). However, chapter 5 pointed out that, in East Asia and the Pacific, a key health financing priority is to transition from fragmented systems with multiple pooling arrangements to universal coverage and coordination across pools. Institutional characteristics are critical for each step of this process.

This chapter then examines organizational characteristics, including organizational forms, incentives, and links. Although this book is not devoted to assessment of the delivery system, the role of health care financing includes strengthening cost-effective services, such as primary health care services, while constraining the use of outpatient specialist and hospital services to necessary levels. Key organizational characteristics that significantly affect the roles of health financing are reviewed, including (a) organizational forms, (b) incentive regimes facing these organizations, and (c) links in terms of horizontal and vertical integration or fragmentation. Many East Asian and Pacific countries are beginning to alter organizational characteristics through changes in the incentive regimes for hospitals.

The chapter begins with a discussion on historical developments related to decentralization, which is both an institutional and an organizational issue. Many East Asian and Pacific countries have recent experience with the decentralization of the financing and provision of health care services. Decentralization of provision is described, management and organizational models are reviewed, and performance to date is assessed. The chapter concludes by looking at current issues of governance, regulation, and quality, as well as related areas of patient satisfaction.

Decentralization and Organizational Issues in the Delivery Systems

The delivery of health care is often undertaken through a decentralized model, an important issue in many East Asian and Pacific countries. Decentralization is often discussed in terms of financing and delivery, but with financing it can lead to fragmentation and fracturing of the risk pool. At the delivery level, decentralization offers more promise as a way to provide greater satisfaction to patients and greater responsiveness to local care needs. Taken to its logical end, decentralization goes to the issue of provider autonomy, flexibility, and responsiveness.

The practical and production-related decisions of health services, including primary, secondary, and tertiary care, can be maintained at a central level through comprehensive planning and control systems. Alternatively, as witnessed in several East Asian and Pacific countries, responsibility for these functions can be devolved further to political or administrative authorities at lower levels (Saltman, Bankauskaite, and Vrangbæk 2007). Governance involves devolution (described in the following pages) and includes establishing the regulatory framework for the health system, including licensing and regulations, rules for contracting and coordination, surveillance and control of access, quality and service levels, incentives, and sanctions (Saltman, Bankauskaite, and Vrangbæk 2007). Following the discussion on devolution, the focus shifts to facility and provider levels.

Overview and Framework

The impetus for decentralization in East Asia and the Pacific stemmed from a variety of factors and motivations. In some instances, decentralization was not an end in itself but a means to achieving broader health sector reforms (Bossert 1998). In these settings, the objective was to decentralize both authority and fiduciary responsibility to provincial (and lower-level entities) to improve efficiency and health outcomes. In other settings, decentralization was sought to bring the delivery of services closer to the people to better respond to local needs. Other cases revealed political motivations for decentralization, such as the appeasement of provincial interests.

In many cases, decentralization was part of a broader public administration reform, with little scope for health. In fact, in only a few examples did the health sector take a lead role in decentralization. For many countries in East Asia and the Pacific, decentralization occurred in the context of economic and political crises, many in the aftermath of the East Asian financial crisis (1997), at which time per capita income, and with it public sector spending on health, declined dramatically. Decentralization often occurred within a climate of political uncertainty as well, as in the case of Indonesia following the overthrow of Suharto (1998) or in the context of weak governance and corruption in the Philippines in the wake of the Marcos regime.

Within the context of decentralization, there also has been a push for hospital, facility, and provider autonomy within the East Asian and Pacific countries cited previously. Using the Preker and Harding (2000) model, East Asian and Pacific countries undertaking structural reforms under decentralization can further examine how facilities have been given increasing levels of autonomy. Such facilities include quasi-private organizations susceptible to market pressures and fully autonomous private organizations.

Preker and Harding (2000) evaluate autonomy in organizational functions against the following five criteria (figure 7.1):

- *Decision rights*—the level of management autonomy a facility has in making decisions over production, input processes, outputs, and outcomes.
- *Income retention*—the ability of an organization to retain revenue or savings and the extent to which the organization bears responsibility for financial risks and losses.
- *Market exposure*—the extent to which facilities earn revenue in a market setting rather than through direct budget allocation.
- *Accountability*—the extent to which facilities are responsible and held accountable for their performance, either through direct hierarchical control by government or from rules, regulations, contracts, and independent boards.

Figure 7.1 Decentralization and Organizational Reform

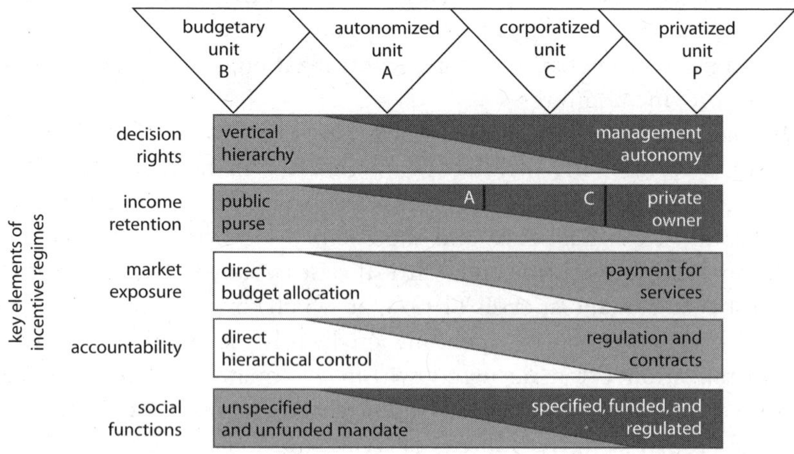

Source: Preker and Harding 2000.

- *Social functions*—functions that reflect the degree to which facilities are mandated to provide services of a particular social value to patients, particularly the poor.

Country Experience and Profiles

The following sections outline the key features of decentralization in selected East Asian and Pacific countries. The countries reviewed are Indonesia, the Philippines, Vietnam, Lao People's Democratic Republic, Papua New Guinea, China, Cambodia, Malaysia, Thailand, and the Pacific Island nations. Details are provided on the levels and changes in facility autonomy for countries undergoing decentralization, although data limitations prevent discussion of the Pacific Island nations. Remaining East Asian and Pacific economies are also summarized on dimensions of facility autonomy.

Indonesia

Decentralization of key government functions in Indonesia was legislated by Law No. 22 and Law No. 25 of 1999 and came into effect in January 2001. The devolution of health financing and service delivery bypassed provincial governments and devolved power primarily to subprovincial (that is, district) governments, with Regulation 25 facilitating implementation. Indonesia undertook a "Big Bang" approach, as opposed to the gradual, phased approach that occurred in Vietnam. Regional spending rose rapidly, central-level civil servants were reassigned, management of more than 16,000 public service facilities became the responsibility of the regions, and a new intergovernmental fiscal system was established. Such reforms have made Indonesia one of the most decentralized countries in the world (Rokx and others 2009).

With respect to institutional structures, Indonesia has experienced radical change. As an example, *kanwil* (central government offices located in provinces) and *kandep* (central government offices located in districts) have been transformed into provincial and district health offices. Little structural change has, however, occurred at the central level, which originally comprised four general directorates and, to date, has remained unchanged. Although initiated in 2001, the decentralization process as of 2008 has been described as incomplete, with basic administrative regulations of decentralization still undeveloped (see the forthcoming volume of East Asia–Pacific Country Health Financing Profiles).

Decentralization served as an opportunity for government to become more accountable and responsive to local needs; however, the ability to achieve these aims has been limited. Many provincial and district-level agencies lack the technical, managerial, and financial capacity to plan and manage health services (World Bank 2004). Furthermore, autonomous district governments lack adequate access to funds or expertise for infrastructure development (Gottret and Schieber 2006). The roles and responsibilities of each level of government—with regard to human resources, service delivery, and health financing—remain unclear, because decentralization legislation does not detail functional and operational responsibilities. As a result, there is no clear division of labor between provinces and districts.

In 1991, Indonesia initiated a program of hospital autonomy (Unit Swadana) that initially was designed to encourage hospitals to recover the costs of providing care. This program has not appeared to progress over time. Hospitals remain government-owned entities with strong oversight and control by the Ministry of Health (MoH) and by local and provincial entities reporting to the Ministry of the Interior. Moreover, hospital directors continue to be appointed by the MoH rather than by local authorities. Facilities do, however, have greater autonomy over the hiring and firing of nonpermanent, contract hospital staff members; most user fees; the assignment of beds for all fee levels; the purchase of drugs and supplies; and contracting with the private sector (Bossert and others 1997).

Under these reforms, hospitals have some control over the portion of the revenues generated by user fees that, in many instances, have amounted to 30 to 80 percent of facility income. Facilities can use a certain portion of these revenues for such things as salary top-ups, drugs, and contracting personnel, whereas equipment and construction costs are excluded. Annual hospital budgets outlining how the revenues from user fees will be spent must be submitted to the central authorities and are closely supervised by them (Bossert and others 1997).

Facilities earn revenue from user fees, as well as from local and national government subsidies. As a result, facilities are, to a certain extent, subject to limited market exposure and risk, which is mitigated by the issuance of government subsidies. To some degree, hospitals are held accountable for performance. For example, hospitals have been encouraged to improve the quality of care although, given data limitations, assessments of quality improvement are scarce. Some facilities have patient satisfaction surveys to measure quality, and hospitals have also been encouraged to become more cost-conscious and efficient.

Social functions and responsibility are an intrinsic part of government policy, because the MoH and the provinces control the number of beds assigned to the poor, which must be (at minimum) 50 percent of public hospital beds. The poor are often charged for these beds, although they are exempt from charges with a certification of indigence. Generally, however, these charges are controlled by the government and maintained at a low level. Facilities are to be reimbursed by local government for care provided to indigents, but such reimbursement does not consistently occur (Bossert and others 1997).

The Philippines

Decentralization in the Philippines occurred in the immediate aftermath of the Local Government Code (1991). This law called for a 10 percent reduction in the internal revenue allotment to local governments, resulting in a decline of local health spending in provinces and municipalities. The government launched decentralization in 1992, which led to the devolution of responsibility for basic health and social welfare services to local government units (LGUs), including both provincial and municipal governments (see the forthcoming volume of East Asia–Pacific Country Health Financing Profiles). This devolution occurred within a setting of 81 provinces, 150 cities, 1,500 municipalities, and more than 40,000 villages (*barangays*).

The devolution of health services to LGUs resulted in the provision of health services across three governmental levels: central, provincial, and municipal. The central level is responsible for regulation and provision of tertiary care, the provincial level is responsible for provision of secondary care, and the municipal level is responsible for the provision of primary care (see the forthcoming volume of East Asia–Pacific Country Health Financing Profiles). Some public health activities, although supported by deconcentrated entities, fell under the remit of the central level. Under this system, the number of key actors in health (including mayors and governors) increased, which has, in turn, heightened the need for improved coordination and monitoring.

As was the case in Indonesia, decentralization in the Philippines occurred in a "Big Bang" approach. In 1993, the Department of Health (DoH) devolved 46,080 out of 78,000 health personnel to LGUs, 595 out of 639 government hospitals, and all 12,580 rural health units and other primary health care facilities, which together accounted for 41.2 percent of the DoH's total budget. By 2004, LGUs contributed 14.4 percent of health spending nationwide, whereas the national government's share of health spending had fallen to a mere 15.9 percent (Capuno 2006).

The hospital system in the Philippines is composed of both public and private facilities. The public sector serves as the main provider of health care, with 703 public hospitals, and accounted for 52 percent of hospital beds in 2005. Seventy-two public hospitals are DoH managed, of which four are hospital corporations with individual charters. The remaining public hospitals are either teaching hospitals owned by local governments and run by state universities or military, police, and veteran hospitals (see the forthcoming volume of East Asia–Pacific Country Health Financing Profiles).

Although government legislation has called for increased hospital fiscal and management autonomy, this autonomy has been difficult to implement. Such reforms have yet to be implemented for facilities managed by the DoH or local governments (see the forthcoming volume of East Asia–Pacific Country Health Financing Profiles). Provincial and district hospitals are managed by provincial governments, whereas municipal governments oversee managed rural health units and *barangay* health stations (Batangan and others 2005). The DoH attempted, in 2001, to restructure 13 DoH-managed facilities into corporate entities, with the aim of improving efficiency in service delivery. This plan was never implemented in full and has resulted in the corporate restructuring of only four facilities.

Managers of most public hospitals have limited autonomy over budget allocations and human resource management (for example, hiring, firing, and performance management). The four corporatized hospitals, however, have a greater degree of autonomy (see the forthcoming volume of East Asia–Pacific Country Health Financing Profiles). Decision making is highly centralized, with the DoH serving as the lead agency in the sector, responsible for policy and regulatory functions for health services and management of specialty hospitals, regional hospitals, and medical centers (Batangan and others 2005). The DoH also exercises regulatory powers through the licensing of facilities and establishment of quality standards.

The main sources of financing for public hospitals include budgetary transfers from the DoH to local governments, revenue from social health insurance or private insurance, out-of-pocket (OOP) expenses, and special contributions from nongovernmental organizations (NGOs) and politicians (see the forthcoming volume of East Asia–Pacific Country Health Financing Profiles). Hence, public hospitals remain largely financed by line-item budget financing of inputs, which are typically determined by the number of beds and hospital staff members, as well as by historical budgets. Furthermore, public hospitals are allowed to retain revenues generated from insurance or from patient user fees, as noted in the hospitals' charters or provisions in national and local appropriation acts (see the forthcoming volume of East Asia–Pacific Country Health Financing Profiles). Generally, however, facilities have greater flexibility in using the income generated by the facilities themselves than in using budget allocations.

Market exposure is limited among public hospitals—with the exception being the four corporatized facilities—because most facilities, as noted previously, are largely supported through line-item budgets and income generated from user fees and other sources. Historically, hospitals had limited accountability for their performance. This situation has started to change, however, with the implementation of two performance-based funds to promote accountability. The Performance-Based Operation Fund provides incentives on the basis of administrative efficiency, utilization rate, quality of services, and implementation of social mandates. The Health Facilities Enhancement Fund was designed to fund infrastructure upgrades and equipment. In reality, however, this latter fund was released only to Amai Pakpak Hospital and was not based on performance. In terms of governance and regulations, the DoH has begun to create governing or oversight boards to further promote accountability and to assist hospitals in policy making and in making recommendations for appointments (see the forthcoming volume of East Asia–Pacific Country Health Financing Profiles).

Hospitals are mandated to provide free services to the poor, but this mandate is not tied to specific budget transfers or subsidies. In addition, a 1947 law stipulated that all public hospitals reserve 90 percent of beds as charity beds for free care. In reality, however, the poor often pay additional fees for services or medication, and an increasing number of patients must pay for their own health care services.

Vietnam

Decentralization in Vietnam occurred following the collapse of the agricultural financing system and after the economic reforms of the 1980s. Fewer funds were available for primary health services, which subsequently led to shortages of drugs and health workers. As a result, the quality of care deteriorated, and use of government facilities fell by more than 50 percent. In response, the government launched the Doi Moi economic reforms (1986). Under those reforms, budget support was cut, and facilities were allowed to charge patients directly, to retain user fee revenues, and (to a certain extent) to use those revenues to pay staff members (for example, to increase bonuses and hire contract staff).

Decentralization was implemented through state budget laws in 1996 and 2002 that assigned additional health tasks to provinces and districts. The laws delegated national authority to the local level, and at each level, budget preparation and implementation became the responsibility of the provincial People's Councils. Since 2004, the People's Councils have received greater authority to prioritize expenditures and determine sectoral allocations and transfers to lower tiers, with a stronger ability to mobilize resources.

Unlike in the Philippines and Indonesia, decentralization in Vietnam occurred gradually and had its beginnings even before 1996. Previous efforts had been significant, contributing to gains in the 1980s in the provision of primary care, as well as to increases in the combined province-commune share of government outlays by the early 1990s. Under this system, basic primary health care services became the responsibility of communes, including the network of village health workers. As such, provinces had a greater role in setting goals, developing plans, and using funds for national targeted programs. This system was beneficial because, although the disease burden varies greatly by region in Vietnam, provinces can better adapt to and address local needs.

In terms of governance, the central government plays a stewardship role, although the nature of its involvement varies by activity. For example, the central government remains active in policy formulation, the establishment of drug safety standards, the regulation of fees charged by public providers, the development of clinical guidelines for public facilities, and the licensing of private providers. The central government is not, however, active in the areas of quality assurance or other regulatory areas involving the private sector. The central government also fulfills a stewardship function with respect to local governments by providing guidelines and technical assistance for specific national programs. Its influence over decision making with regard to national programs is, however, weak.

Decentralization in Vietnam also included hospital autonomy under Decree 10 (2002). This autonomy was later revised in Decree 43, which granted facility managers greater authority over financial operations (for example, they had authority over budgets, as well as some discretion over pay and employment, user fees for nonbasic services, and domestic borrowing); management of human resources; organization of services; and choice of services offered. Under decentralization, however, the central government remains the owner of a vast network of facilities, but local governments also play a dominant role. In fact, the central government operates only 7 percent of beds and less than 1 percent of health facilities, whereas communes have the largest share (80 percent) of facilities, and provinces have the largest share (37 percent) of beds (see the forthcoming volume of East Asia–Pacific Country Health Financing Profiles).

Decree 10 required that service delivery units, including hospitals, across government become more financially self-sufficient. Service delivery units have since been encouraged to earn more income from clients and to use these extra revenues to top up staff salaries. Fiscal autonomy was further facilitated in 1989 with the introduction of user fees in government hospitals, thereby allowing state-owned hospitals to collect fees to cover part of the cost of treatment provided and thus to improve their financial status (Capuno and Ohiri 2007). Furthermore, facilities under Decree 43 were able to open bank accounts, borrow capital, receive tax reductions and exemptions, determine the use of all revenues, and set user fees (Capuno and Ohiri 2007).

Facilities under Decree 43 were given responsibility for a wide range of budgetary and other administrative functions. These functions included the power to (a) set management and operating expenditure norms for all units; (b) establish, merge, or dismantle subordinate units; (c) determine the size, composition, and assignment of permanent staff members; (d) hire temporary workers; (e) set wage levels and allowances according to guidelines; (f) determine recurrent and capital expenditures; and (g) adjust budgets across expenditure items. It can be argued that facilities experienced a great deal of market exposure. There further appears to be a great deal of accountability, because facilities are responsible and held accountable for their performance. For example, facilities are required to propose annual budgets to the People's Committees and to submit annual financial reports to relevant state agencies.

Social functions and responsibilities exist to better serve and protect the poor. The 1999 Health Card for the Poor program and later the Health Insurance program targeted the poorest and most vulnerable households. In the Health Card for the Poor program, each card entitled the beneficiary to free hospitalization in public health facilities. However, the Health Insurance program has covered less than 50 percent of the population, and poor and vulnerable groups remain outside coverage programs.

Lao PDR

From its inception in 1975, Lao PDR had a highly centralized administrative structure, in which the government was the sole provider of health services. Under this centralized system, provincial and district authorities merely administered the plans and budgets received from the central ministry (Phommasack and others 2005). Provinces sent funds to the central government, which then apportioned provinces with a budget according to needs.

An absence of skilled staff members and financial resources in the central government to manage service delivery, combined with local authorities' desire to become autonomous and self-sufficient, led to all sectors being decentralized to the provincial level in 1987 (Phommasack and others 2005). The provinces subsequently assumed responsibility for the planning, financing, administration, and provision of health services, including revenue generation, collection, and management (Phommasack and others 2005). In an effort to stimulate economic development under the so-called market-based New Economic Mechanism, each province subsequently retained its own revenue for public services across all sectors, including health, depending on provincial needs and priorities. As a result, local governments had to meet operating costs and recurrent expenditures of health facilities. Along with decentralization came efforts to privatize pharmacies and to allow some physicians to work in the private sector after hours.

Disparities across provinces have led Lao PDR to begin a process of recentralization, under Decree 73/PM. The central government currently plays a comprehensive role in health, particularly in the financing and provision of preventive and curative health services at the central, provincial, district, and village levels. At the central level, the MoH sets standards and formulates policy; regulates and implements donor-funded projects; manages vertical health programs in areas such as malaria, immunization, and food and drug regulation; and provides technical oversight to provincial health offices (PHOs).

PHOs continue to implement national health programs and donor-funded projects, operate provincial and regional hospitals, supervise district health offices (DHOs), and provide lower-level and in-service training. Provinces, under this system, are once again required to send revenue to the central government, which, in turn, determines the budget and allocations for each province. At the district level, DHOs supervise and manage the delivery of health services in district hospitals and health centers. Notably, however, given the strong provincial interests that have countered such reforms, actual implementation of recentralization has experienced delays.

The government is considering various options for hospital reform; however, this process remains at an early stage. Facilities at the district and provincial levels are supervised and managed by DHOs and PHOs, respectively. Although government regulations require facilities to remit financial surpluses, these regulations are not effectively enforced, and hospitals can use surpluses for capital investments, equipment purchases, and salary supplements. Given limited data availability, the degree of market exposure could not be ascertained. Market exposure is thought to be limited, given that hospital autonomy is still in its infancy. It appears that facilities are held accountable for their performance to their respective DHOs and PHOs, but more detailed information is not available to assess the extent to which strict accountability is in place.

Social functions and responsibilities, as through health equity funds, were piloted with NGO support in 2003 and have since been rolled out to 12 districts (out of 139). These initiatives aim to assist poor households in paying user fees and other costs associated with seeking care. However, the experience with health equity funds in Lao PDR has thus far been poorly documented.

Papua New Guinea

At the time of independence (1975), Papua New Guinea had a government-funded health system in place throughout the country. The system was supplemented by government-subsidized health services provided by various Christian missions. The centralized DoH managed the entire system, including hospitals, and delegated powers to regional, district, and line staff members, as well as to facilities. Papua New Guinea witnessed significant improvements in health outcomes, including marked declines in infant, child, and maternal mortality rates. Notably, however, these gains in health outcomes and health service indicators were not maintained in the postindependence period.

Following the establishment of the provincial government system in 1978, Papua New Guinea's health system became highly decentralized. Political responsibility for primary health care (including health centers and health posts) was devolved to 19 provincial governments. The revised decentralization arrangements embedded in the New Organic Law of 1995 called for provinces to assume responsibility for managing primary health care services, with local governments responsible for maintaining health facilities, while the national DoH retained the authority to develop policies and standards (Janovsky and Travis 2007).

The New Organic Law established the framework for local governments to assume responsibility for health centers and health posts. It also (a) established financing arrangements for provincial and local governments; (b) assigned provinces (and local governments) the administrative authority to create and execute budgets, with national sectoral (including health) departments providing only general policy oversight and monitoring and technical support; (c) removed provincial and local governments from being subject to the national government's finance management and audit acts and provided for provincial legislation instead; (d) required that national sectoral departments provide guidance to provinces in establishing provincial legislation for sector governance; and (e) created fragmentation in the responsibility and accountability for workforce employment and deployment (in the public sector) between national sectoral departments, provinces, and central agencies (ADB 2006).

Many provinces, however, failed to provide facilities with adequate resources, and many facilities neared collapse. The inadequate flow of financing to facilities, unequal allocation between provinces, and fragmentation of responsibilities led the government to recentralize control over provincial hospitals. This recentralization included the distribution of national DoH grants to church health services in 2003, a situation that occurred because provinces (on receipt of grants from the DoH) failed to distribute these grants to church health services as intended. Moreover, in 2007, the Provincial Health Authorities Bill was implemented, calling for a single health authority for primary and secondary care at the discretion of the provincial governor (Janovsky and Travis 2007). In essence, this law allows provincial health commissions to work closely with the central DoH. Although no such authorities have yet been created, policy makers are hopeful that the initiative can address many of the problems attributed to excessive decentralization.

The result of Papua New Guinea's recent reforms is a split between a public health system characterized by a decentralized primary health care system and a more centralized hospital system with conflicting functions. Hence, in terms of decision rights, provincial hospitals are the responsibility of the government (Janovsky and Travis 2007). Although facilities are allowed to generate revenues locally through user fees and community and business fundraising, the degree of facilities' residual claimant status and market exposure could not be assessed because of the limited availability of data (ADB 2006).

The level of market exposure for facilities is unclear based on the current level of data. In terms of accountability, facilities are managed by, and obligated to report to, a CEO (chief executive officer) and a hospital board. This accountability structure reportedly has improved the management of some of the larger hospitals, but administration and service quality continue to be problematic (ADB 2006). Information was not available to determine the degree to which social functions and responsibilities exist.

China

In 1978, China embarked on a major initiative known as the Open-Door Policy—including economic reform during its transition to a market-oriented economy. Government functions have since been decentralized, including the financing, organization, and management of health services. The result is a highly decentralized system where township, county, prefecture, and provincial governments raise and spend approximately 90 percent of government health funding. Interestingly, there is no political decentralization in the Chinese context, because local government is accountable to higher-level government officials (Uchimura and Jütting 2007).

Whereas central and provincial governments design broad policies and health sector strategies, counties have the responsibility to implement key health programs (table 7.1). Therefore, the fiscal and institutional capacity of the county government affects the provision of health services. Generally, counties rely on financial transfers from provinces to provide health services, creating equity concerns (as discussed in chapter 5). The central government has attempted to address the resulting inequalities between provinces through equalization grants, but these grants fall short of bridging the financing gap.

Table 7.1 China's Government and Health Administrative Structure

Government	*Health administration*	*Disease control and prevention*
Central	Ministry of Health	China CDC
Province (prefecture)	Provincial Health Bureau	Provincial CDC
County (township)	County Health Bureau	County CDC

Source: Uchimura and Jütting 2007.
Note: China CDC is the Chinese Center for Disease Control and Prevention. Similar agencies operate at the provincial and county levels.

Governance within the health sector occurs in a multiagency setting in which the role of the central government is ill defined. Public providers are not granted free reign over decision making because they are limited in hiring, firing, and other managerial decisions. Facilities are also limited in the prices they can charge. In the 1980s, the government budget for public hospitals was fixed under the then-recent reforms, and hospitals were forced to rely on charges to bridge their financing gap. With deregulation of the prices of certain services and certain drugs, hospitals were allowed to earn profits from sales of these services and drugs. Accompanying these changes was the introduction of performance-related pay for hospital doctors, now widespread in China, which sought to improve productivity and cost recovery.

The degree of facility market exposure is increasing. Facilities have become highly commercialized and profit oriented, characterized by widespread overprescribing and overcharging (Tandon, Zhuang, and Chatterji 2006; see also the forthcoming volume of East Asia–Pacific Country Health Financing Profiles). Because less than 10 percent of government health spending in China is provided by the central government, public facilities have been allowed to generate income by charging patients for drugs and services and to retain surpluses at the end of the year (Liu, Xu, and Wang 1996).

Deregulation of facilities may have eroded accountability to higher levels of government and the social responsibility of serving the poor. In China, hospital care is especially expensive, particularly with respect to per capita income. For example, a single inpatient admission requires OOP spending equivalent to nearly 60 percent of annual per capita consumption; this percentage has only increased between 1998 and 2003 (see the forthcoming volume of East Asia–Pacific Country Health Financing Profiles).

Cambodia

In 1994, the government of Cambodia proposed a health policy reform under the Health Coverage Plan. The aim was to reorganize and decentralize the health system, in terms of both service delivery and governance (Men and others 2005). Under this reform, implementation of health programs became the responsibility of district and provincial health departments rather than the centrally managed vertical programs of the MoH. Operational health districts were also established, with catchment populations of approximately 100,000 per district, each with a referral hospital and network of health centers (Men and others 2005).

Under the Guidelines for Developing Operational Districts (1997), the central MoH defines policies and strategies, undertakes national planning and supports provincial planning, defines legislation, and coordinates health activities (Men and others 2005). Each provincial health department serves as a link between the MoH and the operational health district by interpreting, disseminating, and implementing central policies through the development of provincial policy and operational planning. Furthermore, each operational health district implements operational plans to meet district health objectives by providing comprehensive services according to district needs. The provincial health department is responsible for planning and monitoring health services and coordinating resources across the province, whereas the operational health district coordinates the delivery of specific health services within the district (Men and others 2005).

Provincial governors and provincial departments of finance have recently strengthened their powers as signatories to the release of funds to provincial health departments. The Seila Program, a national program to alleviate poverty in rural areas and promote governance, has created development committees in more than 2,000 villages and 200 communes, which, in turn, support the development of systems and mechanisms for commune-level planning, financing, and implementation of development activities, including the construction of health facilities in rural areas. Village chiefs are often active as village health volunteers or as representatives in village health support groups. They provide information and feedback to health center management committees, which make local health financing decisions.

One particularly noteworthy form of decentralization is Cambodia's experimentation with various contracting mechanisms (as discussed in chapter 6). In the Cambodian context, decentralization reforms are ongoing and, in time, will entail delegation of responsibilities to provincial, district, and commune levels (see the forthcoming volume of East Asia–Pacific Country Health Financing Profiles). As such, the MoH plans to move from managing service delivery and financing to having a greater regulatory and enforcement role, engaging with lower levels of government on national health priorities, and strengthening their capacity of those entities to deliver services.

A 2006 policy on public service delivery called for increased autonomy of public service providers, including those in the health sector. This policy would entail the generation of hospital service revenues to complement government funding of health facilities, and would entail greater fiscal and administrative decentralization. Calmette Hospital in Phnom Penh serves as the only autonomous hospital to date; discussions are under way to expand this notion of hospital autonomy to other facilities.

Malaysia

The postindependence period of the 1960s was a turbulent time for local government authorities in Malaysia. Internal administrative and political problems facing local councils and Indonesia's violent confrontation with the newly formed Malaysian federation in 1964 led to the suspension of local government elections. Since then, local governments have yet to experience another election.

The problems faced by local government authorities in the 1960s were further compounded by the existence of various types of local councils and by the issuance of complex ordinances, enactments, bylaws, rules, and regulations. By the early 1970s, the proliferation of local government units had resulted in a large number of local administrative entities—up to 374 local governments for peninsular Malaysia alone. Hence, the government felt a need to reexamine and reform the local government system.

Local Government Act 124 (1976) restructured local authorities and sought to rationalize the lowest tier of government and improve its efficiency through decentralization of service delivery. Specifically, the law consolidated six forms of local authorities into just two—municipal councils and district councils. Under this legislation, local authorities were granted wide powers, including mandatory functions (such as those pertaining to public health) and discretionary functions.

During the past three decades, health and medical services have been gradually decentralized to the regions, states, and districts, with the aim of improving efficiency in the delivery of services (Merican and Yon 2002). During this decentralization process, the National Referral System, which places primary health care at the center of the health system, was implemented. The National Referral System is further supported by secondary and tertiary care facilities. Currently, the MoH is constitutionally responsible for planning and organizing medical care at the primary, secondary, and tertiary levels. Actual service delivery is conducted by both the public and the private sectors, including NGOs (Merican and Yon 2002).

Public hospitals, which largely fall under the remit of the MoH, are effectively not autonomous. Hospital directors negotiate annual budgets from the central office of the MoH. Hiring and firing of permanent staff members are conducted centrally, as are decisions on staff member postings to facilities and staff member promotions. Purchasing of drugs and major pieces of medical equipment is also conducted centrally. Nevertheless, hospital directors have some autonomy to shape service delivery and develop hospital services, but these decisions are negotiated centrally or with the state health director (when the decisions are large). Within the annual budget, the director has discretion on how the budget is used, within the recognized line item of spending; however, the director has less discretion to traverse line items (such as salary and assets).

The little revenue that is collected within the MoH structure is not retained at the facility level and is returned to the Ministry of Finance. The level of market exposure, or the extent to which facilities earn revenue in a market setting, appears to be limited. Facilities are ultimately held accountable by the central government and are responsible for achieving certain service agreements and performance targets. The degree to which social functions and responsibilities are in place is unclear.

Thailand

Historically, Thailand's strong central administration retained control over resources within the health sector. Although the role of subnational entities has increased over time, decentralization was not prioritized until the Seventh National Economic and Social Development Plan (1991–96), which emphasized the need to develop local infrastructure, provide credit to expand and improve local services, and assist local authorities in mobilizing capital and pursuing development projects. The Eighth Plan (1997–2002) advocated even stronger local institutions (World Bank 2005). Ultimately, decentralization occurred in the context of internal peace and stability, following armed conflicts with communist guerillas in 1985. This situation allowed for up to 12 percent of the national budget to be reallocated to social sectors, including health. The reallocation was accompanied by rapid economic growth from the mid-1980s to 1997, according to growth in exports and tourism (Tangcharoensathien and others 2007).

The 1999 Decentralization Act formally allowed a larger role for local government within the decentralized administration of the health system. It required the MoH to formulate detailed plans to devolve functions, facilities, and personnel to local administrative entities. During this decentralization process, the central government was to provide administrative assistance and technical support as needed. In terms of health sector administration, a steering committee on decentralization has been established at the central level to formulate policies and procedures to guide this process.

In an effort to decentralize the public health administration to regional organizations, the MoH has created regional health committees in 43 provinces. These committees are responsible for coordinating the formulation of policy, identifying resource requirements, and managing budgets and personnel (WHO 2007). Regional health committees are also responsible for allocating resources and for monitoring the outcomes of the regional public health administration. The committees are currently in the process of refining these operational procedures (WHO 2007).

Hospital autonomy was introduced as a means to improve efficiency in the use of resources within the public sector (Suriyawongpaisal 1999). Although no explicit policy on hospital autonomy exists, a detailed examination of regulations and management practices suggests that in certain dimensions, most notably finances and procurement, hospitals have substantial autonomy over operations; however, with regard to such issues as personnel management, hospitals have very little control (WHO 2007).

Although they are under central ministry control, health facilities (especially hospitals) have gradually acquired a greater degree of autonomy by raising their own revenues through user fees, donations, and insurance reimbursements. In some cases, such revenues account for more than 50 percent of the total annual budget that can be spent on activities perceived as priorities by the hospital or local administration (Janovsky and Travis 1998). Limited data prevent a full assessment of the current degree of market exposure, accountability, and social functions.

The future of decentralization in Thailand is a move to make facilities akin to autonomous, privatelike entities (Suriyawongpaisal 1999), which would entail governance by a board of directors. In terms of oversight, a provincial health board would be established to oversee essential functions and monitor performance of public health facilities, whereas the central MoH would focus on health policy development, health personnel development, allocation of capital expenditures, and development of the public and private sectors. Under this plan, staff member recruitment and positioning would be left to the discretion of hospital management under a regulatory framework established at the national level.

Pacific Islands

In the Pacific Island nations, the delegation of authority in the management of health services to local health departments has been sought to improve accountability and health sector performance. This delegation of authority was deemed necessary, given the large geographic barriers to receiving care and the population dispersion throughout the Pacific Islands (see the forthcoming volume of East Asia–Pacific Country Health Financing Profiles). It has been undertaken with a great deal of donor support within Fiji, Samoa, the Solomon Islands, Tonga, and Vanuatu. In many instances, such reforms have been accompanied by efforts to increase management at local levels as well.

The case of Fiji is particularly illustrative; decentralization has made remarkable progress through a two-phased approach. Responsibility for budgets and human resources was initially devolved from the Ministry of Finance and Planning and the Public Service Commission to the chief executive of the MoH (see the forthcoming volume of East Asia–Pacific Country Health Financing Profiles). Authority was subsequently delegated from the departmental secretary to the health system's four divisional directors (Western, Central, Eastern, and Northern). These changes have been facilitated by the large influx of donor aid (particularly from AusAID), as well as by a concerted effort to ensure local ownership of reforms (see the forthcoming volume of East Asia–Pacific Country Health Financing Profiles). In Kiribati, political administration and service delivery are decentralized, and line ministries and councils reportedly have few decision-making powers and little authority (WHO 2005).

Dimensions of Governance and Stewardship

Decentralization is an important element of institutional arrangements, but when thinking about financing issues, one may find it useful to analyze other critical issues related to governance and stewardship. Previous sections (chapters 4, 5, and 6) looked at issues of governance and collection, pooling, and allocation of funds. Here the focus is on anticorruption and the regulation of providers.

Good Governance and Corruption

Good governance is a crucial factor in providing an effective and accessible health service for citizens. However, in the absence of transparency, accountability, rule of law, regulatory quality, inclusiveness, and participation, the governing body is subject to ineffectiveness and corruption (Kaufmann, Kraay, and Mastruzzi 2003). Corruption can appear at the state level through senior officials and politicians (grand corruption), as well as at a lower level of administrative and public services (petty corruption) (World Bank 2004). Procurement fraud, misuse of facilities, informal payments, and absenteeism are all examples of common types of corruption that undermine effective financing and delivery of health care services.

Corruption is a worldwide concern in both developing and postconflict countries, where political instability, lack of adequate laws and regulations, and poor economic growth are present. Figure 7.2 displays government indicators considered crucial for good governance and the limiting of corruption levels in selected East Asian and Pacific countries. Corruption is regarded as a result of poor governance, and it also reduces opportunities for governments to improve service delivery (Lewis 2007). Many developing countries are unable to provide adequate resources for health financing. Corruption exacerbates revenue loss through evasion of taxes and mismanagement of public funds. As a result, fewer government resources are available for spending on health, education, and infrastructure. Upper-income countries do better on average with these indicators. Some low- and middle-income countries in the region do well with regulatory quality (Cambodia and Papua New Guinea), political stability (Vietnam), and government effectiveness (China and Malaysia).

Figure 7.2 Governance Indicators in East Asia and the Pacific, 2007

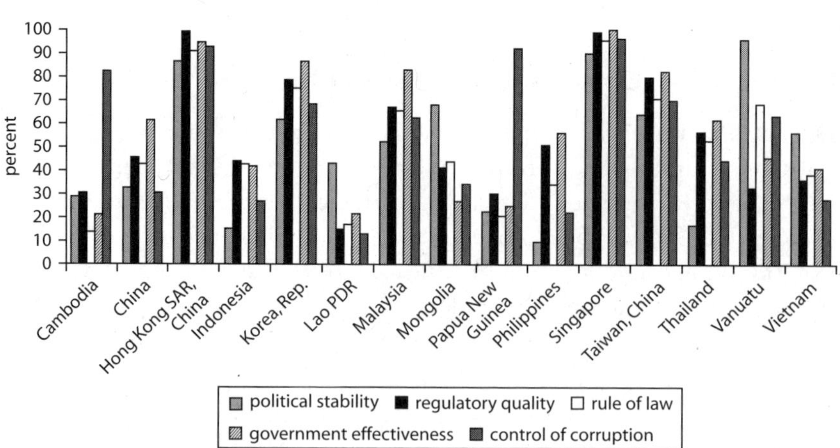

Source: World Bank's Worldwide Governance Indicators database.

Because of corruption in developing countries, the public's lack of trust in the health system results in less use of health services—which consequently affects the health of the population. Indeed, studies have shown a strong correlation between high mortality rates and elevated corruption (World Bank 2008). An effective government could help limit corruption and more efficiently allocate existing resources toward health services to help reduce child mortality rates. However, studies have found that, without a World Bank CPIA (Country Policy and Institutional Assessment) score of 3.25 or above—on a scale from 1.00 to 6.00—increased spending probably would not contribute to decreases in child mortality rates (Wagstaff and Claeson 2004). Figure 7.3 presents the CPIA scores for selected East Asian countries, measuring transparency, accountability, and corruption in the public sector.

The manner in which governments should tackle corruption greatly depends on the country specifics and the type of corruption that is most prevalent in a particular country. Increasing accountability, strengthening the voice of civil society, and overcoming institutional constraints, along with a competitive private sector, all play a decisive role in combating corruption (figure 7.4). Identifying the type, cause, and level of corruption within a specific country can be done through diagnostic surveys given to public officials, firms, and households. Depending on the outcome of the

Figure 7.3 CPIA Scores on Transparency, Accountability, and Corruption in East Asia and the Pacific, 2006

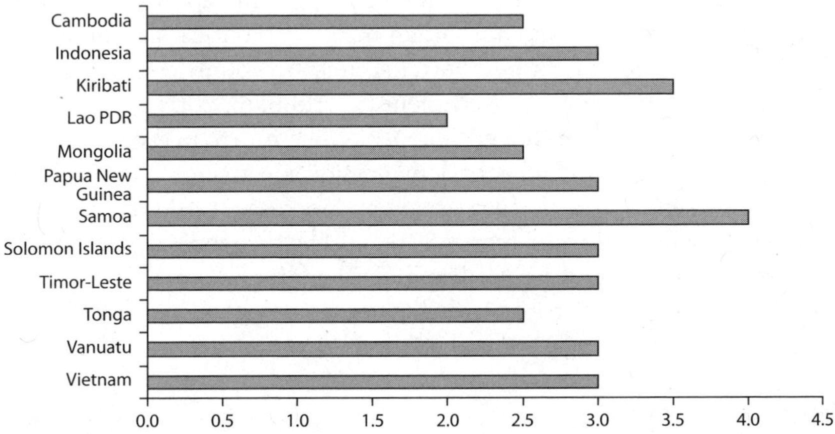

Sources: World Bank's World Development Indicators database; World Bank 2007.
Note: Scores of up to 6.0 are possible. The higher the score the better the performance on each indicator.

Figure 7.4 Means of Limiting Corruption in Service Delivery

Restricting corruption in service delivery

Institutional restraints
- Independent and effective judiciary
- Independent prosecution and enforcement
- Parliamentary oversight
- Watchdog enforcement agencies

Civil society participation and voice
- Freedom of information
- Public hearings on draft laws
- Role of media and NGOs
- Governance monitoring

Competitive private sector
- Incentive framework and policies
- Competitive restructuring of monopolies
- Regulatory reform
- Transparency in corporate governance
- Effective business association

Political accountability
- Political competition and credible political parties
- Transparency in party financing and public scrutiny
- Open parliaments, courts, and sunshine rules
- Asset declaration and conflict of interest rules

Effective public sector management
- Sound public expenditure management
- Merit-based civil service with monetized, adequate pay
- Decentralization with accountability and local capacity
- Public services that work
- Access to redress mechanism and legal system
- Tax and customs administration

Source: Adapted from World Bank 2004.

diagnostic survey, countries can better implement countermeasures to corruption. For example, in countries with extensive administrative corruption, improving financial accountability by setting up surveys to track expenditures would be an appropriate measure. Political accountability and decentralization might be a better strategy in countries experiencing state capture at the central government (World Bank 2004).

In February 2008, the Ateneo School of Government in the Philippines helped launch a new initiative for demand-side governance. This initiative attempted to enhance civic engagement and increase the demand on government accountability and responsiveness. The demand-side governance approach in the form of the Affiliated Network for Social Accountability for East Asia and the Pacific highlights one model for enhancing the role of citizens in promoting good and effective governance (see box 7.1).

Informal Payments

Informal payments constitute one aspect of corruption. Unofficial payments are given to medical personnel to receive better or more care,

Box 7.1

Demand-Side Governance: The Affiliated Network for Social Accountability

The Affiliated Network for Social Accountability in East Asia and the Pacific (ANSA-EAP) was launched in February 2008 and represents a new regional initiative in promoting good governance and development through increased social accountability. The network is based on ANSA-Africa, which was successfully implemented in 2007.

ANSA-EAP will build on experiences in the region and work toward improving current methodologies, such as citizen reports, participatory public expenditure tracking surveys, social audits, third-party monitoring, and social contracts. The network will provide a shared platform for trading information and experiences on social accountability in the region, along with technical assistance and the delivery of capacity-building initiatives for both civil society organizations and governments.

Establishing a practical conversation about the Asian perspective on various social accountability issues will help local institutions and members of society to realize the value of their participation in governance, ultimately improving the responsiveness of the government.

Source: World Bank 2008.

to jump queues, or to obtain medical supplies that should be free of charge. Informal payments are unaudited and do not constitute part of the national health care policy framework; therefore, they are part of an informal sector and can be considered a form of corruption. In terms of health financing policy, informal payments exacerbate the lack of pooling and dilute the incentives and purchasing effect of new payment reforms.

The frequency of informal payments within health services varies widely across the region, from 2 percent in Thailand to 74 percent in China and as high as 81 percent in Vietnam (Lewis 2006) (figure 7.5). Other countries in the region, such as Mongolia, have anecdotal reports of informal payments but to date these payments are not well documented. Determining the difference between a bribe and a gift is sometimes not easy. Similarly, measuring informal payments within a country can be a challenge and requires focused household surveys because the activities are not reported.

Figure 7.5 Informal Payments among Health Services in East Asia and the Pacific

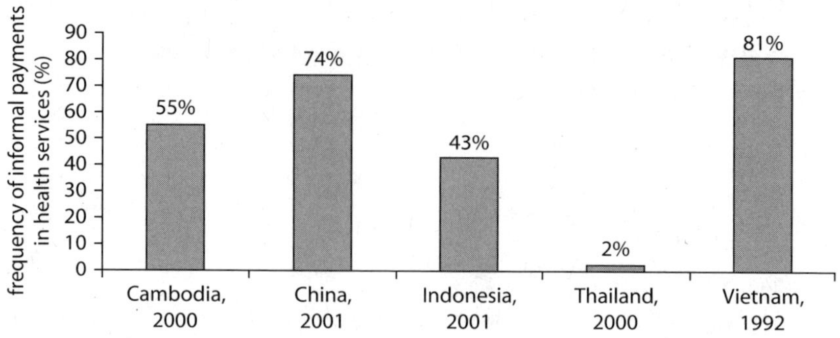
frequency of informal payments in health services (%)
90
80
70
60
50
40
30
20
10
0
55%
74%
43%
2%
81%
Cambodia, 2000
China, 2001
Indonesia, 2001
Thailand, 2000
Vietnam, 1992

Sources: Bloom, Han, and Li 2001; Lewis 2006.

The issue of informal payments is further complicated because in some countries informal payments could be accepted, although in other countries they are considered illegal. However, despite the differences in culture between countries, informal payments undermine the provision of efficient and equitable health care financing (Lewis 2000). In some countries, the high levels of informal payment costs can surpass the annual income of poor families—resulting in debt accumulation and ultimately forcing the sale of assets to cover medical costs. In a study in China, informal payments or so-called red envelopes were estimated to represent 90 percent of the monthly incomes of one-half of households surveyed (Bloom, Han, and Li 2001).

State, or public sector, monopoly has been considered a factor that promotes the payment of bribes by limiting the choice of service providers. A case study in Bolivia has demonstrated a correlation between lower informal payments and the provision of alternatives to government services and more competition in service delivery (Gray-Molina, de Rada, and Yañez 2001). Salary regulation that does not fully reflect market values is also pertinent to reducing informal payments because low government salaries can incentivize health care providers to accept additional bribes or gifts to improve their income. Nevertheless, salary regulation may need to be combined with a variety of incentives to be effective. Incentives could include performance-based compensation for high productivity and quality care provision, along with clear rules, norms, and, most important, accountability. Cambodia and the Philippines are two examples of countries that have implemented a form of performance-based incentive to improve effectiveness and reduce corruption in the health care system (Vian 2007).

Worker Absenteeism

Absenteeism is one more dimension of governance in East Asia and the Pacific that dilutes the financing and provision of health care services. The absence of doctors and health clinic workers compromises equity and reduces the effectiveness of public health spending. In many East Asian and Pacific countries (for example, China, Lao PDR, and Vietnam), wages represent a large proportion of government expenditure. Absenteeism directly affects the effectiveness of public health spending when important services do not reach beneficiaries.

Absenteeism is of particular concern in rural areas, with recent data suggesting absenteeism rates as high as 40 percent in primary health care facilities in Indonesia and 19 percent in Papua New Guinea (Chaudhury and others 2006; World Bank 2004). Absenteeism is of great concern in many developing countries globally and across different sectors (table 7.2). The literature suggests that doctors who grew up and trained in rural areas are more likely to practice there after graduating. One issue for the region may be the lack of qualified and motivated health personnel in rural areas correlated with high percentages of medical practitioners who are, instead, born and educated in urban areas. Another key contributing factor to absenteeism could be the alternative income opportunities available while absent, such as personal tutoring or private practice.

The lack of highly qualified and motivated health personnel in rural areas highlights the importance—as a first step—of ensuring that sufficient health care training is available in those areas. There also need to be sufficient compensation structures that are competitive with private

Table 7.2 School and Health Center Absenteeism Rates in Selected Countries

	Absence rates (%)	
Country	*Primary schools*	*Primary health centers*
Bangladesh	16	35
Ecuador	14	—
India	25	40
Indonesia	19	40
Papua New Guinea	—	19
Peru	11	25
Uganda	27	37

Sources: Chaudhury and others 2006; World Bank 2004.
Note: — = not available.

sector salaries and urban physician levels of compensation. A study in West Papua, where the vacancy rate is 60 percent, found that significant wage increases would be needed to attract qualified doctors (World Bank 2004). Of course, adequate salary rates alone are not the panacea; living amenities and performance-based opportunities for compensation and advancement may also be needed to reduce absenteeism.

Dual Practice

Health workers may combine public sector medical work with private sector work where a fee is required for service. This type of medical practice could be referred to as *dual practice* and is closely related to the issues of absenteeism and informal payments. Because health workers prefer to undertake additional work in their private sector practice to better meet their income needs, under-the-table payments and absenteeism often result.

In many East Asian and Pacific countries, the private sector plays an increasingly dominant role in health care financing (see chapter 2). For example, the share of beds in private hospitals in Thailand grew from 5 percent in 1970 to 14 percent in 1989. In Indonesia, 50 percent of all hospitals are privately run. In Malaysia, the proportion of physicians engaged in private practice increased from 43 percent in 1975 to 70 percent in 1990. Low salaries in the public sector may encourage privatization and dual practice in private clinics. In fact, the proportion of total income generated for dual-practicing medical personnel from private sector activities is 55 percent in Thailand and 90 percent in Cambodia (Human Resources for Health 2004).

Predatory behavior (where self-gain is pursued), conflict of interest, absenteeism, and redirection of publicly provided resources to the private sector are examples of issues that are exacerbated by dual practice. All of these practices affect the quality of, and accessibility to, the public health care system (Mathers and Loncar 2005). When medical personnel engage in predatory behavior, competition for time in the public health care system will, of course, lead to absent nurses and doctors. Access to health care for the poor can be affected. In Indonesia, the majority of qualified doctors are employed by the government but also practice privately in the evenings, particularly in urban areas (WHO 2000). Papua New Guinea is experiencing a public-private and rural-urban brain drain, hampering the provision of accessible and equitable health care in provincial centers (Thomason 1994). Private sector health care in Thailand and Vietnam is believed to be largely run by government doctors (WHO 2000). In Thailand, private practice by obstetricians from the public sector has been particularly common (Hanvoravongchai and others 2000). In Vietnam, public hospital facilities have often been used for prescribing and selling drugs privately by government personnel (Chen and Hiebert 1994).

Government responses to dual practice vary across countries, with dual practice accepted in some countries and strictly prohibited in others. Country context may be important in reducing dual practice. In countries with a high level of human capacity and resource availability in their health system, such as France and Italy, dual practice is encouraged, with certain safeguards and regulatory systems (Bridge Europe 2006). However, in many developing countries, dual practice may significantly undermine the provision of quality health services, particularly in rural areas.

Discussing the issue of dual practice openly is a necessary first step in directing the appropriate countermeasures. When health workers are unable to dedicate 100 percent of their time to public health because of inadequate financial compensation or insufficient equipment, this issue should be openly confronted. In many East Asian and Pacific countries, a simple tool, such as increasing salaries, may not be plausible because salary scales in some cases would need to increase fivefold to remove the financial incentives for extra private income activities. Furthermore, raising salaries alone is unlikely to significantly reduce dual practice, but should be combined with specific work benefits and career development opportunities and should be restricted to personnel within the public sector (Ferrinho and others 2004).

Consumer or Patient Voice and Provider Responsiveness

The lack of accountability by policy makers and providers to consumers, especially the poor, lays the groundwork for much of the poor health care provision and absent personnel in East Asian and Pacific countries, as in many other developing countries globally. Unless poor people have the chance to adequately express their need to policy makers, and as long as policy makers cannot guarantee that service providers supply their required quality deliverables to the people, absenteeism and other forms of corruption are likely to continue.

In Cambodia, policy makers managed to successfully communicate the required services to the NGO that was contracted to deliver the services; however, in many countries this accountability relationship is flawed. In addition to the government interventions mentioned previously, increasing individuals' power to choose by allowing enhanced competition between health services providers could help improve overall care and reduce absenteeism, because providers must improve care to attract patients. Government subsidies in the form of vouchers may be one option for providing poor people with the means to access alternative health care and to improve their choices.

Regulation of Providers

There is clear variation in the regulatory framework for health care providers, even across high-income economies (table 7.3). Of course, the regulatory framework is important in thinking about facility autonomy as well as associated governance and stewardship issues. The summary information presented in the table is not sufficiently detailed for a country-by-country analysis, but it provides a snapshot of levels of regulation, and, variation in regulation across the region. Table 7.3 is limited in its ability to measure effectiveness of the regulation. Legislation and regulation must be assessed with concrete implementation measures as well.

A recent study by Tangcharoensathien and others (2009) on dimensions of regulatory tools and mechanisms revealed a wide variation in political, administrative, and information constraints in 32 developing countries. Countries surveyed in East Asia and the Pacific included Cambodia, Lao PDR, Papua New Guinea, the Philippines, Thailand, and Vietnam. As a general pattern, low-income countries (LICs) faced greater political constraints; middle-income countries (MICs) reported issues with accreditation and registration of providers and lack of policing of conduct by health professional groups. Both groups reported intense administrative constraints, although the information constraint was not perceived as a major concern. Not many countries reported empowerment of consumers as a high policy concern. Fewer than half of the respondents reported a relatively strong institutional capacity in regulatory implementation, especially regarding setting and enforcement of prices (responses correlate with levels of national income), distribution of providers (mostly LICs), and consumer empowerment (mostly MICs). The issue of price controls related to multiple insurers and purchasers as well as to high levels of OOPs. The capacity to set rules was perceived as stronger than the capacity to enforce and monitor regulatory performance.

In general, LIC respondents gave high marks to engaging with the private sector for social marketing and tertiary care services, but lower

Table 7.3 Regulation of Providers in East Asia and the Pacific

Economy	*Regulatory framework*
Low-income economies	
Cambodia	Regulatory framework is weak. One-half of private facilities operate without a license. Public sector providers can work in the private sector.
Fiji	Status is unknown.
Indonesia	District and provincial health offices are responsible for licensing hospitals and clinics. Licensing and regulatory mechanisms are weak, with limited funding to support efforts.
Kiribati	No formal coordination exists between the traditional health system and the formal health system.
Lao PDR	Status is unknown.
Marshall Islands	Status is unknown.
Mongolia	Status is unknown.
Papua New Guinea	National DoH sets standards for hospitals and district services for the public and private sectors. All facilities and health workers (public or private) must register with government bodies. Churches Medical Council has the most developed arrangements for working with the public sector. No other associations for nonstate providers exist.
Samoa	Efforts are under way to promote public-private partnerships in health. Government is exploring contracting out to NGOs.
Solomon Islands	Status is unknown.
Timor-Leste	No formal contracts exist between the public and private sectors, but the government is strengthening public-private partnerships.
Tonga	Public providers are allowed to practice in the private sector. Government is reviewing private sector policy and may increase private participation. Sales of drugs in private clinics are banned.
Vanuatu	Status is unknown.
Vietnam	Status is unknown.
Middle-income economies	
China	Private sector is heavily regulated. Local governments influence hiring and firing decisions. Government administrative health departments are responsible for accreditation and quality assessment. Government is creating a more formal regulatory framework for accreditation.
Malaysia	MoH serves as the legislative, regulatory, and enforcement body of public and private services. MoH is responsible for registration and accreditation of personnel and facilities in both sectors.

(continued)

Table 7.3 *(continued)*

Economy	*Regulatory framework*
Philippines	Central government licenses facilities and establishes quality standards. Facility reporting on patient activities is no longer required by private or public facilities since devolution in 1992. DoH no longer has direct administrative supervision over devolved facilities.
Thailand	Status is unknown.
High-income economies	
Hong Kong SAR, China	Public sector providers—those in the Hospital Authority and DoH—are salaried employees and civil servants who are not permitted to undertake private work. Food and Health Bureau of the Government Secretariat oversees the entire health system. Public health and health protection functions, and some limited forms of direct service delivery (mostly preventive in nature), fall under the purview of the DoH, which reports directly to the Food and Health Bureau. Hospital Authority is a public statutory body established outside of the civil service, and it has its own board; however, it is directly funded solely by the government and is accountable to the Food and Health Bureau. Hospital Authority self-regulates, whereas the DoH has regulatory oversight of private hospitals and clinics. So far, no formal, uniform accreditation framework applies across all sectors and settings, but private hospitals have recently submitted themselves for voluntary, commercial-based quality assessment. Members of health care professions are under the purview of the relevant statutory licensing boards.
Japan	Laissez-faire policy exists toward service delivery, in contrast to the country's highly regulated financing system. Patients have freedom of choice in selecting facilities; therefore, clinics and hospitals compete for patients. Physicians in clinics do not have access to hospital facilities and must refer all patients for care that cannot be provided on their premises. Hospitals employ their physicians on fixed salaries and maintain large outpatient departments from which they admit their patients. The fee-for-service system operates under a minutely defined price schedule set by the government, and neither insurers nor providers have the freedom to negotiate individually a different fee schedule. All providers are paid exactly the same amount, inclusive of physician expertise, the facility characteristics, or geographic location.

Table 7.3 *(continued)*

Economy	*Regulatory framework*
Korea, Rep.	Status is unknown.
Singapore	Health care regulatory framework consists mainly of two parties: the regulator (comprising the MoH and its statutory boards) and the regulated (comprising public and private providers). MoH formulates national health policies, coordinates the development and planning of the private and public health sectors, and regulates health standards. All hospitals, clinics, clinical laboratories, and nursing homes are required to maintain a good standard of medical services through licensing by the MoH. Health care professionals are regulated by their relevant professional bodies.
Taiwan, China	DoH takes full responsibility for the health affairs of citizens, in terms of promoting medical, health care, and disease prevention; it is also responsible for food, drug, cosmetic management, and health insurance affairs. The Bureau of National Health Insurance, a quasi-governmental agency, serves as the only administration that operates the National Health Insurance Program.

Source: Authors' compilation.

marks for ambulatory care. The MIC respondents saw the private sector as a key partner for social marketing and pharmaceuticals (especially in rural areas). Stewardship functions were seen as key to better engaging and coordinating across public and private sectors.

Medical Tourism

Large investments in health care technology and training of medical personnel have facilitated a medical market for high-quality, yet relatively low-cost, care in developing countries in the region. Expensive care or long waiting lists combined with low-cost travel and increasing incomes in richer countries have contributed to an escalating flow of patients to poorer countries for medical procedures. In 2006, the global market for medical tourism was estimated to be worth US$60 billion and is predicted to reach US$100 billion by 2012 (Hansen 2008). At the moment, Asian countries are generating approximately US$1.3 billion in revenues from medical tourism. This growth is expected to continue with a compound annual growth rate of 19 percent, resulting in estimated revenue of US$4.4 billion by 2012 (Teh 2007).

As a result of the financial crisis in 1997, many private hospitals in East Asia began pursuing health revenues beyond their borders. However, despite the leading role of the private sector, a well-functioning partnership between the private and public sectors is essential for continued growth in medical tourism. As the success and future potential of the private sector to attract foreign patients to East Asian countries became apparent, government participation was intensified to maximize the direct gain from increased health revenues along with the benefits to tourism overall (Yoosuf 2004).

Increased employment opportunities generated by medical tourism will demand an increased supply of highly skilled human capital. An important role of governments will be to ensure sufficient resource allocation toward the training of medical personnel, to meet the increasing demand generated from the inflow of foreign patients.

Medical Costs, Quality, and Availability of Care

The high cost of medical procedures in many countries remains a primary reason that medical tourists are attracted to East Asian countries. In the United States, in particular, a heart surgery may cost US$50,000, whereas the price for the same procedure would be US$20,000 in Singapore and US$12,000 in Thailand (Teh and Chu 2005). In many European countries with universal health care, high costs are less of an issue; long waiting lists are the primary, recurring reason wealthy individuals who are able to pay for immediate health services may seek overseas treatment.

A growing number of private hospitals in East Asia and the Pacific are providing high-quality care in line with Western health care standards. However, despite an increase in success stories from medical tourism destinations, recent reports suggest a great discrepancy in the quality of care among various hospitals (Kaiser Family Foundation 2008). Hence, quality of care remains a central concern. For that reason, hospitals seeking to attract medical tourists must make considerable efforts to improve quality and establish their international credibility. The Joint Commission International, endorsed by the World Health Organization, provides quality assurance and safety control of health services for hospitals globally. By 2007, approximately 140 hospitals in 26 countries worldwide had been accredited by the Joint Commission International, including 30 hospitals in East Asia and the Pacific.

Telemedicine

Investment in medical technology, along with an explosive growth in information and telecommunication technology, has laid the groundwork for an emerging market in East Asia and the Pacific within medical care, known as telehealth, or telemedicine. By providing clinical consultations, diagnosis, or even laboratory samples for analysis through electronic mediums and regular mail, telemedicine may offer a cost-effective and speedy alternative for countries suffering from expensive care or long waiting lists. Developing countries in East Asia are directing increased attention to telemedicine, with new facilities emerging in India, Malaysia, the Philippines, and Thailand. Networks of telemedicine units and hospitals are also forming in the region to accommodate the new market of telemedicine (Janjaroen and Supakankunti 2002).

Country Profiles

Malaysia, Singapore, and Thailand are currently the three industry leaders for medical tourism in East Asia and the Pacific. It is estimated that Thailand will attract as much as 47 percent of the US$4.4 billion revenues that are expected to be generated from medical tourism in East Asia and the Pacific by 2012, making Thailand the primary destination for medical tourism in the region (Thailand Report 2007). The Philippines represents the fifth-largest medical tourism destination in Asia, although Taiwan, China, has also made serious attempts to enter the forefront of the medical tourism industry.

Thailand

A growing private sector has served as the main actor in achieving success in attracting foreign patients in Thailand. Beyond low prices for medical procedures, Thailand offers a variety of attractive qualities such as low-cost living, a tourist-friendly culture, and a relaxing environment for recuperation. Until now, the majority of medical treatments for foreign visitors have been primarily focused on lower-value treatments such as cosmetic surgery, dentistry, Lasik (refractive eye surgery), and general medical checkups. To stay ahead of the competition, particularly that of Singapore, a few Thai hospitals have begun to invest in so-called higher-value treatments, including hip replacement, organ transplant, and heart bypass.

In 2004, the percentage of revenue generated from foreign patients was reported to constitute 18 percent of the total health care revenues in

Thailand. The impressive growth of Thailand's medical tourism industry has attracted the interest of the initially passive government, resulting in several initiatives to support and promote the growing industry. Examples include simplification of visa procedures for travel to Thailand and plans for a 10-year investment of US$10 billion to US$15 billion for the construction of new hospitals (Teh 2007).

Malaysia

Malaysia has emerged as a major player in attracting medical tourism, with price advantages similar to those of India and Thailand. Malaysian hospitals recorded a 25 percent increase in foreign patients in the decade leading up to 2004. They offered medical services to approximately 130,000 medical tourists, generating US$27.6 million in revenues and making medical tourism the fastest-growing sector of the tourist market (Bookman and Bookman 2007). Unlike Thailand, Malaysia has experienced an initially higher level of government involvement and control in promoting the emergence of the medical tourism sector.

In an attempt to catch up with Singapore and Thailand, Malaysia has launched several marketing mechanisms aimed at attracting foreign patients. Indonesian patients currently represent nearly 70 percent of medical tourists in Malaysia. However, increased marketing toward other regions has contributed to a greater diversification of patients (Ganesan 2008).

Singapore

Singapore has marketed itself as the center for top-quality care, while still offering a considerable price advantage over medical costs in the United States and other Western countries. A focus on biomedical research, along with investment in the latest medical equipment, has enabled Singapore to provide the most advanced treatments and therapies. Low levels of corruption, political stability, cleanliness, and a modern infrastructure reinforce Singapore as a trusted center of medical quality. Competitors in the region such as India and Thailand still contend with urban slums and civil unrest. Singapore reportedly attracts more than 200,000 international patients each year, with 20 percent growth projections.[1]

The Philippines

In 2004, government-led agencies, including the DoH, Department of Tourism, and Department of Trade and Industry, joined together with the private sector to create the Philippine Medical Tourism Program. This program combines medical care from both public and private hospitals with various wellness services, vacation opportunities, sightseeing tours, and shopping packages. In 2007, the Philippines attracted an estimated 200,000 foreign patients from various parts of the world (PNA 2007).

Challenges for Medical Tourism

Achieving international credibility as a provider of safe, high-quality care remains a main priority for all developing countries aiming to solidify and further improve their positions as leading medical tourism destinations. Although many hospitals have already gained international acceptance for medical excellence, reports of uneven quality of care among various hospitals could sustain purchasers' skepticism. Large distances of travel could also deter patients from considering treatment abroad. It has been argued that there is an enhanced risk of developing complications such as venous thrombosis or infections as the result of long flights after procedures (Kaiser Family Foundation 2008). By offering medical packages, including vacation and wellness treatments of sufficient recuperation time for particular procedures, hospitals could better contain postprocedure risks.

Despite the apparent advantages of revenue generation, the new growing market does raise issues of equity, and the effect of less than equal access to affordable and high-quality health care for the local population. Increasing government focus toward meeting private hospitals' demands may result in the diminution of necessary funding and personnel for serving the host country's own citizens. The evidence base does not yet exist to suggest that increased revenues generated by medical tourism in East Asia and the Pacific have resulted in the reallocation of sufficient resources toward improving coverage, access, or quality health care for the local population. Medical tourism is covered in more detail in appendix B.

Analysis and Discussion

Decentralization has played a prominent role in East Asia and the Pacific in both financing and delivery, but with very mixed results. This section reviews experience and country profiles to date, but the evidence shows little or no improvement in effectiveness or equity in these countries. Indeed, although the objective was to encourage innovation and improve responsiveness to local needs, the outcome has often been to fracture the risk pool and create inequities across localities. The appropriate role of different levels of government has been ill or poorly defined.

The response in many cases, not surprisingly, has been to recentralize. Some case examples include Lao PDR and Papua New Guinea. More recently, China has taken steps to recentralize under its current efforts to develop a health care reform plan announced in early 2009. In other cases, the push for new forms of social health insurance has effectively meant that financing of health care must be pooled and recentralized. Discussion and dialogue are now occurring in a number of countries, including China, the Philippines, and Vietnam. In other cases, new forms of insurance, such as the health equity funds in Cambodia and Lao PDR, may encourage greater pooling and centralization of financing.

In all cases reviewed, full autonomization across all dimensions of hospitals (facilities) has not yet occurred in any country (Preker and Harding 2000). Most efforts are in the early stages of development and will require some greater focus and development in the future. At this stage, autonomization has most often been used to increase user fees rather than to encourage better management and quality of services. Equity of user fees is often an issue (as in China or Vietnam), whereas social objectives are often not explicit. Efficiency objectives are limited by the facility's ability to make its own internal decisions about cost structure as well as by a general lack of accountability and risk.

The issues of autonomization in the last analysis suggest that payment reforms may not be as successful in the near future without greater autonomy at the facility level. As in some other regions, such as Eastern Europe, payment reforms may not have the intended effect on behavior if the management space and flexibility are not present in the delivery sector. Thus, payment reforms and payment reform plans will need to assess this "enabling factor" carefully either before or during implementation.

As for governance and regulation, an important agenda remains unfulfilled in East Asia and the Pacific in the areas of financing policies and reform and government oversight. Government is the natural lead actor for stewardship and oversight. Although some other functions can be, and in some countries are, discharged with negligible government involvement, oversight cannot be discharged. Indeed, the more health system functions that the government leaves to other actors, the greater challenge it faces vis-à-vis increased oversight. Leaving health care delivery to private nonprofit providers or to autonomous public sector hospitals means that the government workload switches from line management of treatment facilities to the creation and operation of an effective oversight system. Leaving social health insurance to an "autonomous" health insurance agency, as has been done in many countries, requires the government to establish clear rules setting out the degree of freedom of the insuring agency in different areas, while retaining a voice in agency governance without interfering in its day-to-day decisions.

In public health, government oversight now emphasizes clarifying core functions, identifying the activities needed to perform those functions, and identifying the actors to perform them. Countries and international organizations have differed on core public health functions, but definitions commonly include prevention and control of disease and injuries, protection against environmental hazards and other health risks unrelated to disease, and public health disaster preparedness and response. Public health functions are sometimes defined more expansively to include, for example, quality control and assurance, equity, and human resources (Bettcher, Sapirie, and Goon 1998; Garcia-Abreu, Halperin, and Danel 2002; Public Health Functions Steering Committee 1994; Rojas 2002). Although there may be a case for government intervention to address these issues, they are arguably a function of the health system as a whole and not specifically a public health function.

Other actors, such as associations of health professionals, have important supporting roles to play. Such associations engage in self-regulation and set codes of professional conduct. Ensuring delivery of high standards of care is a benefit to all members. Quality and accreditation compose a more formal approach. The World Bank is now launching a new lending program in Indonesia to develop an accreditation process for doctors, nurses, and midwives. As discussed in earlier sections, insurers have financial and nonfinancial incentives to ensure that the revenues they collect are used to buy quality health care at reasonable cost. If given the space, they too can become important forces in system stewardship.

Households have a role to play, with one obvious example being litigation. The United States, as perhaps the most litigious country in the world, sees thousands of patients every year take providers to court for alleged malpractice. China, as one example in East Asia and the Pacific, is increasingly relying on courts to raise issues of public safety and standards for care and for inputs such as drugs and food. Courts are not the only venue in which households can make their voices heard. In many countries, consumer groups act as health system watchdogs, providing information to households on insurance policies, hospital quality, drug safety, and so on. Some countries explicitly tell patients what their rights are in the health sector through, for example, a patients' charter.

Many health insurance organizations in Eastern Europe and Central Asia have an ombudsman to referee patient complaints. Members of the public often get involved in helping to oversee the operation of a specific facility—sitting on a hospital board, for example, as a representative of the local community. The media and the polling booth are other channels through which the public can exercise health system oversight (Wagstaff and others 2009). At the same time, the 32-country survey discussed previously reveals consumer empowerment as underdeveloped and underappreciated by LICs and MICs.

The role of these actors and the coordination of financing policies in the region could be an important story over the next few years.

Note

1. Data are from the Health Tourism in Asia website at http://www.healthtourisminasia.com.

References

ADB (Asian Development Bank). 2006. *East Asia Health Financing Study.* Manila: ADB.

Batangan, Dennis B., Chona Echavez, Anthony A. Santiago, Amparo C. de la Cruz, and Engracia Santos. 2005. "The Prices People Have to Pay for Medicines in the Philippines." Institute of Philippine Culture, Ateneo de Manila University, Manila.

Bettcher, Douglas W., Stephen Sapirie, and Eric H. Goon. 1998. "Essential Public Health Functions: Results of an International Delphi Study." *World Health Statistics Quarterly* 51 (1): 44–54.

Bloom, Gerald, Leiya Han, and Xiang Li. 2001. "How Health Workers Earn a Living in China." *Human Resources for Health Development Journal* 5 (1–3): 25–38.

Bookman, Milica Z., and Karla R. Bookman. 2007. *Medical Tourism in Developing Countries.* New York: Palgrave Macmillan.

Bossert, Thomas. 1998. "Analyzing the Decentralization of Health Systems in Developing Countries: Decision Space, Innovation and Performance." *Social Science and Medicine* 47 (10): 1513–27.

Bossert, Thomas, Soewarta Kosen, Budi Harsono, and Ascobat Gani. 1997. "Hospital Autonomy in Indonesia." Working Paper 39, Harvard School of Public Health, Cambridge, MA.

Bridge Europe. 2006. Quarterly newsletter of WHO/Europe, World Health Organization.

Capuno, Joseph J. 2006. "Social Health Insurance for the Poor: Programs of the Philippines and Vietnam." *Philippine Journal of Development* 33 (1–2): 1–30.

Capuno, Joseph J., and Kelechi Ohiri. 2007. "A Case Study of Vietnam's Recent Health Reform Strategies." World Bank, Washington, DC.

Chaudhury, Nazmul, Jeffrey S. Hammer, Michael Kremer, Karthik Muralidharan, and F. Halsey Rogers. 2006. "Missing in Action: Teacher and Health Worker Absence in Developing Countries." *Journal of Economic Perspectives* 20 (1): 91–116.

Chen, Lincoln C., and Linda G. Hiebert. 1994. "From Socialism to Private Markets: Vietnam's Health in Rapid Transition." Working Paper 11, Harvard Center for Population and Development Studies, Harvard School of Public Health, Cambridge, MA.

Ferrinho, Paulo, Wim Van Lerberghe, Inês Fronteira, Fátima Hipólito, and André Biscaia. 2004. "Dual Practice in the Health Sector: Review of the Evidence." *Human Resources for Health* 2 (14). doi:10.1186/1478-4491-2-14.

Ganesan, Vasantha. 2008. "Medical Tourism Revenue Seen Growing 30pc Yearly." *New Straits Times*, March 10. http://www.malaysiahealthcare.com/medicaltourism.htm.

Garcia-Abreu, Anabela, William Halperin, and Isabella Danel. 2002. *Public Health Surveillance Toolkit*. Washington, DC: World Bank.

Gottret, Pablo, and George Schieber. 2006. *Health Financing Revisited: A Practitioner's Guide*. Washington, DC: World Bank.

Gray-Molina, George, Ernesto Pérez de Rada, and Ernesto Yañez. 2001. "Does Voice Matter? Participation and Controlling Corruption in Bolivian Hospitals." In *Diagnosis Corruption*, ed. Rafael Di Tella and William D. Savedoff, 27–55. Washington, DC: Inter-American Development Bank.

Hansen, Fred. 2008. "A Revolution in Healthcare: Medicine Meets the Marketplace." *Institute of Public Affairs Review* 59 (4): 43–45.

Hanvoravongchai, Piya, Jongkol Lertiendumrong, Yot Teerawatananon, and Viroj Tangcharoensathien. 2000. "Implications of Private Practice in Public Hospitals on the Cesarean Rate in Thailand." *Human Resource for Health Development Journal* 4 (1): 2–12.

Human Resources for Health. 2004.

Janjaroen, Wattana S., and Siripen Supakankunti. 2002. "International Trade in Health Services in the Millennium: The Case of Thailand." In *Trade in Health Services: Global, Regional, and Country Perspectives,* ed. Nick Drager and Cesar Vieira, 87–106. Washington, DC: Pan American Health Organization and World Health Organization.

Janovsky, Katja, and Phllida Travis. 1998. "Decentralization and Health Systems Change: Case Study Summaries." World Health Organization, Geneva.

———. 2007. "Non-state Providers of Health Care in Papua New Guinea: Governance, Stewardship and International Support." World Health Organization, Geneva.

Kaiser Family Foundation. 2008. "Medical Tourism Business Projected to Grow Eightfold by 2010, Study Finds." *Kaiser Daily Health News Daily Report,* September 28. http://www.kaiserhealthnews.org/daily-reports/2008/september/23/dr00054607.aspx?referrer=search.

Kaufmann, Daniel, Aart Kraay, and Massimo Mastruzzi. 2003. *Governance Matters III: Governance Indicators for 1996–2002.* Washington, DC: World Bank.

Langenbrunner, John C. 2005. "Health Care Financing and Purchasing in ECA: An Overview of Issues and Reforms." World Bank, Washington, DC.

Lewis, Maureen. 2000. "Who Is Paying for Health Care in Eastern Europe and Central Asia?" World Bank, Washington, DC.

———. 2006. "Governance and Corruption in Public Health Care Systems." Working Paper 78, Center for Global Development, Washington, DC.

———. 2007. "Governance and Corruption: Why Does It Matter for Health and Pharmaceuticals?" Presentation at the World Health Organization's Good Governance for Medicine Global Stakeholders Meeting, Bangkok, December 3–5.

Liu, Xingzhu, Lingzhong Xu, and Shuhong Wang. 1996. "Reforming China's 50,000 Township Hospitals: Effectiveness, Challenges, and Opportunities." *Health Policy* 38 (1): 13–29.

Mathers, Colin D., and Dejan Loncar. 2005. "Updated Projections of Global Mortality and Burden of Disease, 2002–2030: Data Sources, Methods, and Results." Evidence and Information for Policy Working Paper, World Health Organization, Geneva.

Men, Bunnan, John Grundy, Jeff Cane, Lon Chan Rasmey, Nguon Sim An, Sann Chan Soeung, Karl Jenkinson, Marian Boreland, Jim Maynard, and Beverley-Ann Biggs. 2005. "Key Issues Relating to Decentralization at the Provincial Level of Health Management in Cambodia." *International Journal of Health Planning and Management* 20 (1): 3–19.

Merican, Ismail, and Rohaizat bin Yon. 2002. "Health Care Reform and Changes: The Malaysian Experience." *Asia-Pacific Journal of Public Health* 14 (1): 17–22.

Phommasack, Bounlay, Lathiphone Oula, Oukeo Khounthalivong, Inlavanh Keobounphanh, Thongvansy Misavadh, Loun, Phanpaseuth Oudomphone, Chanphomma Vongsamphanh, and Erik Blas. 2005. "Decentralization and Recentralization: Effects on the Health Systems in Lao PDR." *Southeast Asian Journal of Tropical Medicine and Public Health* 36 (2): 523–28.

PNA (Philippines News Agency). 2007. "Medical Tourism Earned $200M." Asia Pulse, November 27.

Preker, Alexander S., and April Harding. 2000. "The Economics of Public and Private Roles in Health Care: Insights from Institutional Economics and Organizational Theory." World Bank, Washington, DC.

Public Health Functions Steering Committee. 1994. "Vision Statement." American Public Health Association, Washington, DC.

Rojas, Ricardo. 2002. "Guidelines for the Surveillance and Control of Drinking Water Quality." Pan American Center for Sanitary Engineering and Environmental Sciences, Lima.

Rokx, Claudia, George Schieber, Pandu Harimurti, Ajay Tandon, and Aparnaa Somanathan. 2009. *Health Financing in Indonesia: A Reform Road Map.* Washington, DC: World Bank.

Saltman, Richard B., Vaida Bankauskaite, and Karsten Vrangbæk. 2007. *Decentralization in Health Care.* European Observatory on Health Systems and Policies, Open University Press, Maidenhead, Berkshire, U.K.

Suriyawongpaisal, Paibul. 1999. "Potential Implications of Hospital Autonomy on Human Resources Management: A Thai Case Study." *Human Resources for Health Development Journal* 3 (3): 15–18.

Tandon, Ajay, Juzhong Zhuang, and Somnath Chatterji. 2006. "Inclusiveness of Economic Growth in the People's Republic of China: What Do Population Health Outcomes Tell Us?" *Asian Development Review* 23 (2): 53–69.

Tangcharoensathien, Viroj, Supon Limwattananon, Walaiporn Patcharanarumol, Chitpranee Vasavid, Phusit Prakongsai, and Suladda Pongutta. 2009. "An Assessment of Performance of Health Regulation in Low and Lower Middle-Income Countries." Presentation for the Prince Mahidol Award Conference, Bangkok, January 28–30.

Tangcharoensathien, Viroj, Phusit Prakongsai, Supon Limwattananon, Walaiporn Patcharanarumol, and Pongpisut Jongudomsuk. 2007. "Achieving Universal Coverage in Thailand: What Lessons Do We Learn?" Commission on Social Determinants of Health, World Health Organization, Geneva.

Teh, Ivy. 2007. "Healthcare Tourism in Thailand: Pain Ahead?" *Asia Pacific Biotech News* 11 (8): 493–97.

Teh, Ivy, and Calvin Chu. 2005. "Supplementing Growth with Medical Tourism." *Asia Pacific Biotech News* 9 (8): 306–11.

Thailand Report. 2007. "The Medical Tourism Boom." *Thailand Report*, February 1.

Thomason, Jane. 1994. "A Cautious Approach to Privatization in Papua New Guinea." *Health Policy and Planning* 9 (1): 41–49.

Uchimura, Hiroko, and Johannes Jütting. 2007. "Fiscal Decentralisation, Chinese Style: Good for Health Outcomes?" Working Paper 264, Organisation for Economic Co-operation and Development, Paris.

Vian, Taryn. 2007. "Review of Corruption in the Health Sector: Theory, Methods, and Interventions." *Health Policy and Planning* 23 (2): 83–94.

Wagstaff, Adam, and Mariam Claeson. 2004. *The Millennium Development Goals for Health: Rising to the Challenges*. Washington, DC: World Bank.

Wagstaff, Adam, Magnus Lindelow, Shiyong Wang, and Shuo Zhang. 2009. *Reforming China's Rural Health Care System*. Washington, DC: World Bank.

WHO (World Health Organization). 2000. *The World Health Report 2000: Health Systems—Improving Performance*. Geneva: WHO.

———. 2005. "Strategy on Health Care Financing for Countries of the Western Pacific and South-East Asia Regions (2006–2010)." Regional Office for the Western Pacific, WHO, Nouméa, New Caledonia.

———. 2007. *Country Health System Profile: Thailand*. Geneva: World Health Organization.

World Bank. 2004. *World Development Report 2004: Making Services Work for Poor People*. Washington, DC: World Bank.

———. 2005. *World Development Report 2005: A Better Investment Climate for Everyone*. Washington, DC: World Bank.

———. 2007. *IDA Resource Allocation Index (IRAI)*. Washington, DC: World Bank.

———. 2008. *Good Practices in Health Financing: Lessons from Reforms in Low- and Middle-Income Countries*. Washington, DC: World Bank.

Yoosuf, Abdul Sattar. 2004. "South-East Asia Regional Perspective." In *Trade and Health: Compilation of Presentations Made at the Inter-regional Workshop, New Delhi, October 2004*, 140–43. New Delhi: World Health Organization Regional Office for South-East Asia.

CHAPTER 8

Assessing Performance in East Asia and the Pacific: Efficiency and Equity of Health Financing

This chapter examines the performance of East Asian and Pacific countries in terms of allocative and technical efficiency of spending, equity in financing and service delivery, and incidence of public subsidies for health care. Two of the major goals of health policy are (a) minimizing costs, subject to the attainment of specified health outcomes (or using the optimal mix of inputs to achieve these outcomes) and (b) pursuing equity in terms of both financial protection against unpredictable, catastrophic medical care costs and access to health services. The allocation decisions of health policy makers have important implications for efficiency and equity. Demand for health care is virtually unlimited and, therefore, presents an important set of issues in any country. In low-income countries (LICs), where budget constraints are likely to persist even if expenditures are increased, equity and efficiency goals become even more critical to making the best use of available resources.

Efficiency

Efficiency is typically defined as the maximizing of outputs from inputs. It consists of two components: allocative efficiency and technical efficiency. *Allocative efficiency* is achieved when available resources are directed toward a mix of interventions that have the greatest marginal effect on health outcomes. *Technical efficiency* is achieved when the health system either maximizes outcomes given the resources it uses (staff members, equipment, and purchases of goods and services) or minimizes the use of those resources given what it produces. Another definition of allocative efficiency is "doing the right things"; another definition of technical efficiency is "doing things right." When combined, allocative and technical efficiency are often referred to as *economic efficiency*.

Allocative Efficiency

In practice, allocating health care resources to the most cost-effective set of interventions is regarded as a means to improve allocative efficiency (Liu 2003). The Disease Control Priorities Project (Jamison and others 2006) provides evidence on the cost-effectiveness of different types of interventions. Such evidence indicates that preventive and public health interventions are generally more cost-effective than curative care interventions. Thus, it is argued that allocative efficiency can be achieved by shifting resources toward greater provision of preventive and public health services relative to curative, mostly hospital-based services. In the absence of detailed information on the cost-effectiveness of the package of interventions that is delivered in a country, researchers often use the share of expenditures attributable to inpatient and outpatient curative care and medical goods relative to public health as a proxy for allocative efficiency (Kutzin 1995).

Table 8.1 shows the relative shares of expenditures on curative care and public health in a sample of economies in East Asia and the Pacific. One clear pattern that emerges is that high-income economies spend less on preventive and public health services relative to others. Among low- and middle-income countries (LMICs), there appears to be little correlation between the share of spending allocated to public health and good health performance.

Information on the relative shares of hospital and nonhospital expenditures does not provide sufficient evidence to make conclusions about the level of allocative efficiency. On the one hand, no evidence shows that providing a cost-effective package of services, such as the one defined in the *World Development Report 1993* (World Bank 1993), leads to better outcomes at lower cost. On the other hand, some of the best health outcomes in East Asia and the Pacific are found in countries with a relatively high share of hospital spending, such as Hong Kong SAR, China; Japan; and Sri Lanka. In short, there is little or no knowledge

Table 8.1 Government Expenditures on Curative versus Preventive and Public Health Expenditures in East Asia and the Pacific, Various Years

Territory	*Year*	*Inpatient curative care*	*Outpatient curative care*	*Medical goods dispensed to outpatients*	*Prevention and public health services*
Australia	2005	70.4	70.4	12.4	2.1
Bangladesh	2004	30.6	14.9	—	22.3
China	2003	75.0	25.0	—	—
Hong Kong SAR, China	2004	38.7	29.7	0.7	6.2
Japan	2004	24.9	31.3	16.4	1.6
Korea, Rep.	2006	29.8	31.5	24.8	2.9
Malaysia	2006	29.9	36.3	0.3	7.0
Mongolia	2002	65.4	18.4	4.0	1.5
Nepal	2003	28.0	1.8	—	—
Sri Lanka	2006	49.4	15.1	4.6	9.6
Taiwan, China	2005	32.1	53.9	2.7	4.1
Thailand	2005	37.4	40.5	*	7.4
Tonga	2004	23.6	6.7	24.7	9.6
Vietnam	2005	41.1	36.1	*	19.8

Source: Fernando and Rannan-Eliya 2008.
Note: — = not available * = category not estimated separately in the national health accounts available for this country.

about the relative ratio of hospital to nonhospital spending that implies allocative efficiency.

A second problem with assessing allocative efficiency by using cost-effectiveness criteria is that this method assumes that maximizing health outcomes is the only objective of a health system. In practice, health systems have multiple objectives. The government of Indonesia's goal is not only to maximize health outcomes, but also to provide insurance against financial catastrophe associated with health care costs. The importance of these goals may diminish the usefulness of allocative efficiency criteria in determining health policy (Hammer and Berman 1995).

Technical Efficiency

To optimize the use of resources available for the health sector, countries need to clearly understand the health system production function and maximize the effect of inputs to improve outcomes (Gottret and Schieber 2006). If health facilities are underused, overstaffed, and equipped with nonessential technical equipment (factors that lead to low marginal products of inputs), technical inefficiency is likely.

In LMICs, technical efficiency is measured using fairly basic methods such as ratios of inputs and service indicators as well as unit costs. Such microlevel measures can lead to an incomplete characterization of efficiency, because these measures tend not to control for quality of health care and differences in input costs that are due to cost-of-living differences (for example, rural-urban differences in costs that are not intrinsically related to the health system). However, measurement of technical efficiency is well developed in Organisation for Economic Co-operation and Development (OECD) countries and has led to a large body of evidence on the efficiency and productivity of health service delivery in these countries (Hollingsworth 2008).

In the absence of better data, this chapter compares bed occupancy and case flow in public hospitals in a sample of East Asian and Pacific and OECD economies to examine differentials in public hospital performance. Using the characterization of hospital efficiency introduced about 20 years ago by Pabón Lasso (1986), figure 8.1 shows the average bed occupancy rate (the percentage of beds occupied on average per year) and average case flow (the number of cases per bed per year) in each country. The vertical and horizontal lines show the average bed occupancy rate and the average case flow respectively. The vertical and horizontal lines also cut through the mean values of the occupancy rate and, turnover ratio, respectively, dividing the plane into four zones.

Some countries in the region, including China and Indonesia, perform poorly on both occupancy rate and bed turnover. Others, such as Mongolia, perform well on occupancy, although unnecessary admissions are thought to be quite high in Mongolia because of the lack of good primary care (World Bank 2008b). Hospitals in regions that fall in zone III (high occupancy and high turnover ratio relative to the mean) are argued to be more efficient than hospitals in regions in the other three zones.

Equity

If distributional issues in the health sector were not addressed, health outcomes would primarily benefit the rich, while largely bypassing the poor (Gwatkin and others 2007). Many countries in East Asia and the Pacific that have made significant progress toward achieving the

Figure 8.1 Pabón Lasso Diagram for East Asian and Pacific and OECD Countries

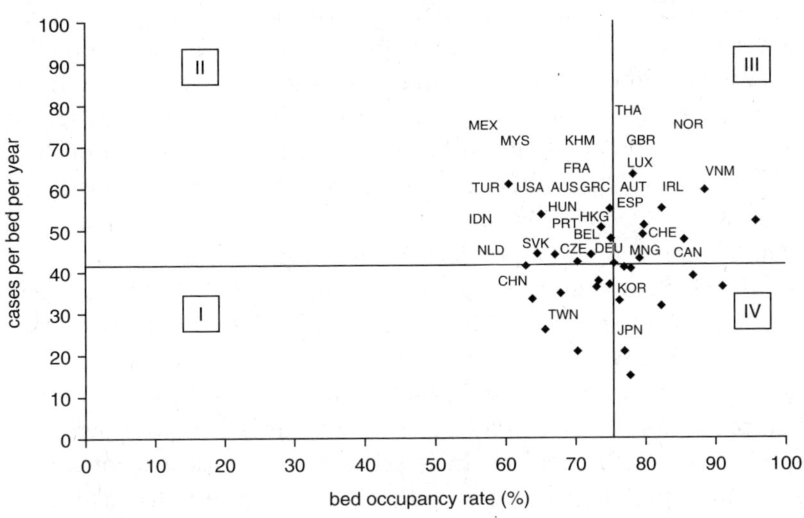

Sources: For OECD member countries, OECD 2008; for other countries, various sources as cited in World Bank 2009.

Note: AUS = Australia; AUT = Austria; BEL = Belgium; KHM = Cambodia; CAN = Canada; CHN = China; CZE = Czech Republic; FRA = France; DEU = Germany; GRC = Greece; HKG = Hong Kong SAR, China; HUN = Hungary; IDN = Indonesia; IRL = Ireland; JPN = Japan; KOR = Republic of Korea; LUX = Luxembourg; MYS = Malaysia; MEX = Mexico; MNG = Mongolia; NLD = Netherlands; NOR = Norway; PRT = Portugal; SVK = Slovakia; ESP = Spain; CHE = Switzerland; TWN = Taiwan, China; THA = Thailand; TUR = Turkey; GBR = United Kingdom; USA = United States of America; VNM = Vietnam. Data reflect latest available period (2003–06).

Millennium Development Goals are still characterized by large income inequalities in outcomes. Underlying this problem are large inequalities in the financing and delivery of health care.

Equity in Health Financing

Greater equity in health care financing is a relevant health systems goal because it has implications for the distribution of both health and income. The distribution of health may be affected by financial disincentives for the use of health care. This problem may occur, for example, if large out-of-pocket (OOP) payments result in high levels of forgone care, as was discussed earlier in the case of Indonesia. The distribution of income may be altered by taxes and social insurance contributions if, for instance, the rich pay disproportionately more of the taxes that are used to finance health care. Living standards may also be disrupted by direct payments for health care that diminish household resources available for meeting the demand for other goods (O'Donnell and others 2008).

The incidence of the health care financing burden in high-income economies in East Asia and the Pacific is similar to that in European countries (O'Donnell and others 2008; Wagstaff and Van Doorslaer 1992; Wagstaff and others 1999) and includes health systems financed through general revenues and social insurance. Among prepayment methods, tax financing is the most progressive, and social insurance is slightly regressive. Direct OOP payments are proportional (for example, in Hong Kong SAR, China) or regressive (for example, in Japan and Taiwan, China). Figure 8.2 provides a summary of these results.

Tax financing is even more progressive in LMICs in East Asia and the Pacific, because it reflects the narrow tax base (O'Donnell and others 2008). Direct taxes are more progressive than indirect taxes. Social insurance is progressive because its coverage is generally limited to skilled, professional groups such as civil servants. Direct payments are also progressive in all LMICs in East Asia and the Pacific, except China. This finding implies that, compared to the poor, the rich make more direct OOP payments for health care relative to their ability to pay.

In East Asia and the Pacific, the distribution of prepayment expenditures tends to be less pro-poor as economies become more developed. There are two factors underlying this tendency. First, as the economy grows, reliance on OOP payments falls and social insurance is typically established. Social insurance tends to be broadly proportional or regressive because contributions are levied as a fixed percentage of earnings.

Figure 8.2 Progressivity of Taxes, Social Insurance Payments, and OOP Financing in East Asia and the Pacific

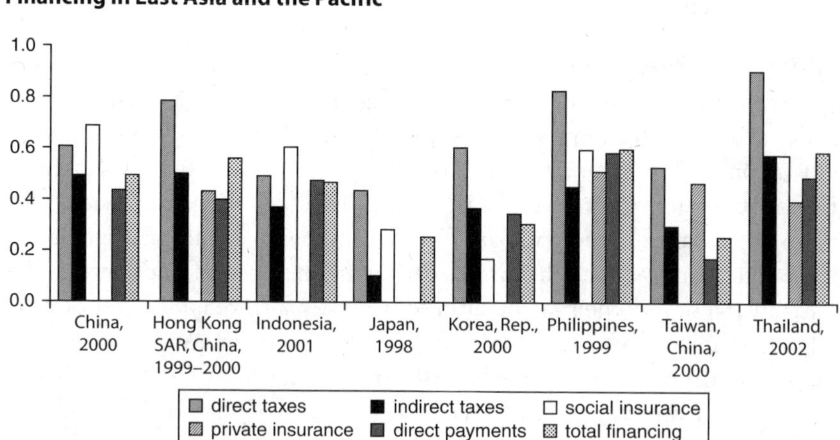

Source: O'Donnell and others 2008.

Second, although economic development broadens the tax base and allows for greater reliance on tax financing, direct taxation becomes less progressive because of the broader tax base. Similarly, social insurance contributions are spread more evenly across the population as the system moves from partial to universal coverage.

Likewise, the incidence of OOP payments is less concentrated on the rich as economies become more developed (O'Donnell and others 2008). In high-income economies, OOP payments are regressive because social insurance copayments are incurred across the full range of the income distribution. By contrast, OOP payments in Hong Kong SAR, China, are more concentrated on the rich because they are mainly for private care consumed largely by the rich. In LMICs, OOP payments are concentrated on the rich, who consume the more expensive private sector services. The poor, who cannot afford to pay for most private sector services, either forgo care or go to less expensive public sector providers.

When direct, OOP payments for health care account for a large share of health financing, as is the case in many LMICs, the distribution of financing also affects living standards and the distribution of health care use. In these settings, equity in financing and use need to be examined together.

Equity in Use of Health Care

In assessing equity in the delivery of health care, a core distributional concern is whether the principle of horizontal equity or "equal treatment for equal need" is met. This assessment requires standardizing for differences in need, which is difficult to do using most survey data in LMICS. In most surveys, the self-reported health measures typically used in horizontal equity analysis (Van Doorslaer and others 2000) to standardize for need often do not show the same socioeconomic gradients that are apparent in more objective measures of health (Baker and van der Gaag 1993; Wagstaff 2002). This discrepancy may be due to socioeconomic differences in health expectations.

In East Asia and the Pacific, evidence on horizontal equity is available only for Hong Kong SAR, China; Japan; the Republic of Korea; and Taiwan, China. For most other countries, inequalities in use of services can be presented without standardizing for need.

Inequalities in Health Care Use

Inequalities exist in the use of maternal and child health services in East Asian and Pacific countries, but they are less pronounced than in comparable LMICs in the Asian region as a whole. Medical treatment of fever among children under age five is usually a good indicator of access to formal health services. There are sharp disparities in the likelihood of getting medical treatment for child fever in Indonesia, the Philippines, and Vietnam, but less so in Cambodia and the Solomon Islands (figure 8.3). Similarly, there are large differentials in the likelihood of seeking prenatal care from a medically trained professional and in the likelihood of delivering with the assistance of a skilled provider in Cambodia, the Philippines, and Vietnam, but less so in Indonesia and the Solomon Islands (figures 8.4 and 8.5).

Significant evidence exists of pro-rich differentials in health care use in East Asia and the Pacific. Use of public sector inpatient services is strongly pro-poor in Hong Kong SAR, China; moderately pro-poor in Malaysia and Thailand; and pro-rich in China, Indonesia, and Vietnam (O'Donnell and others 2008). Use of outpatient care services,

Figure 8.3 Socioeconomic Inequalities: The Share of Children under Five Receiving Medical Treatment for Fever, 2000s

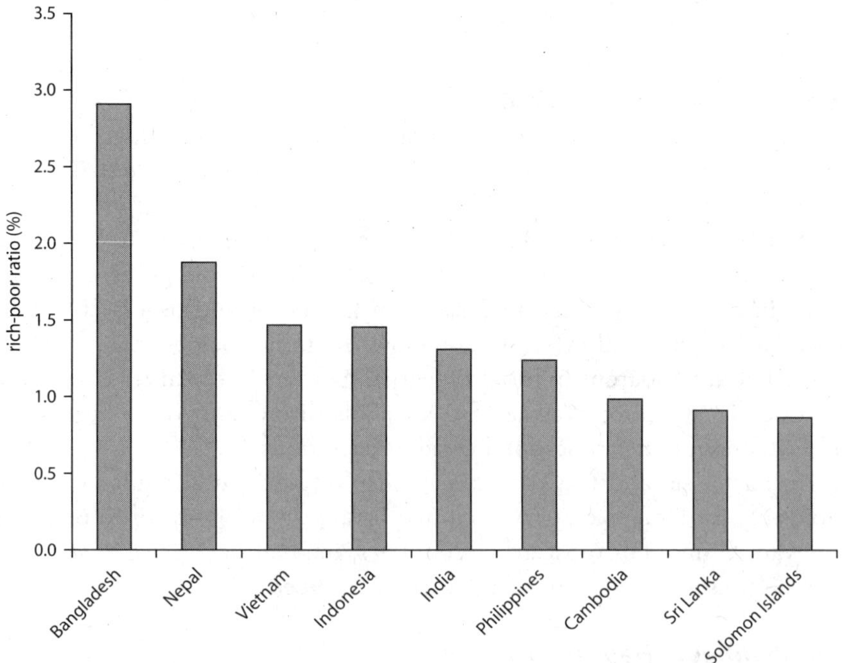

Sources: Gwatkin and others 2007. Data for the Solomon Islands are for 2008 and were provided by the Ministry of Health; data for Sri Lanka are for 2009 and were provided by the Department of Census and Statistics.

Figure 8.4 Socioeconomic Inequalities: Prenatal Care Visits to Medically Trained Personnel

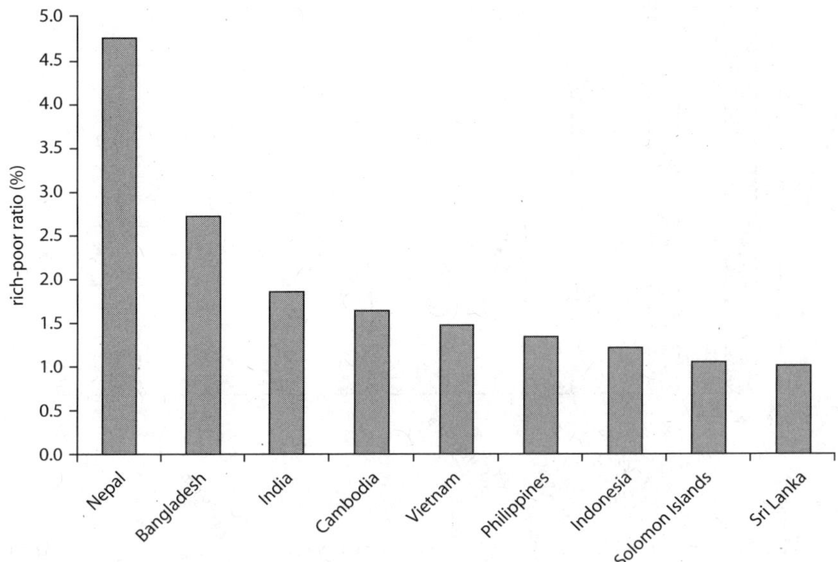

Sources: Gwatkin and others 2007. Data for the Solomon Islands are for 2008 and were provided by the Ministry of Health; data for Sri Lanka are for 2009 and were provided by the Department of Census and Statistics.

particularly nonhospital outpatient care services, is moderately pro-poor or proportionate to income in most countries (figure 8.6).

Assessment of horizontal equity in Hong Kong SAR, China; the Republic of Korea; and Taiwan, China, confirms that the distribution of health care use after standardizing for need is indeed more pro-rich than before such standardization (Lu and others 2007). The distributions presented in figure 8.6 did not standardize for need; however, a horizontal equity interpretation can be placed on the unstandardized distribution of health care in these countries. Because it is reasonable to assume that the poor are in worse health and in greater need of health care (Gwatkin and others 2007), distributions strongly disfavoring the poor imply a high degree of inequity.

The assessment by Lu and others (2007) in Hong Kong SAR, China; the Republic of Korea; and Taiwan, China, as well as a study in Japan by Ohkusa and Honda (2003) show significant differences in equity across these countries and services. Deviations in the degree to which health care is distributed according to need are measured by an index of horizontal inequity (HI) (table 8.2). In Hong Kong SAR, China, there

Figure 8.5 Socioeconomic Inequalities: Deliveries Attended by Medically Trained Personnel

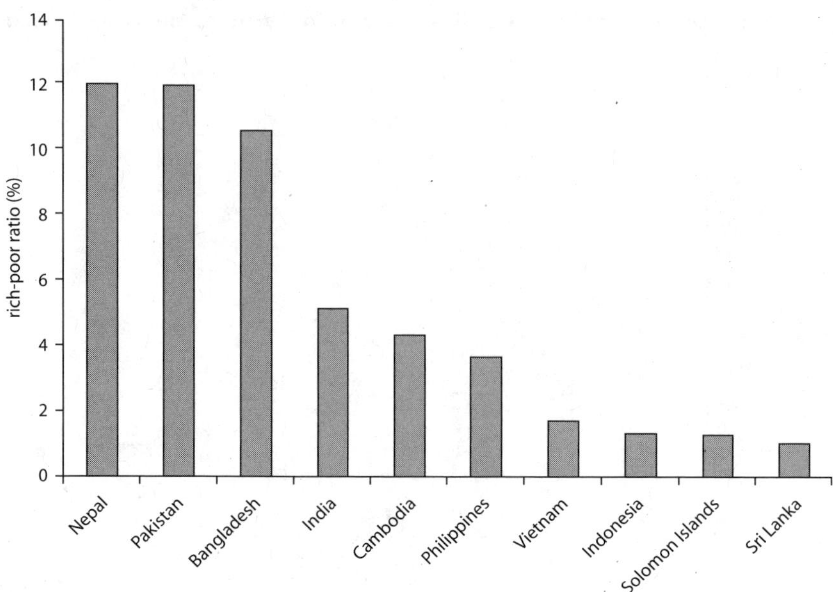

Sources: Gwatkin and others 2007. Data for the Solomon Islands are for 2008 and were provided by the Ministry of Health; data for Sri Lanka are for 2009 and were provided by the Department of Census and Statistics.

Figure 8.6 Distribution of Public Health Services in East Asia and the Pacific

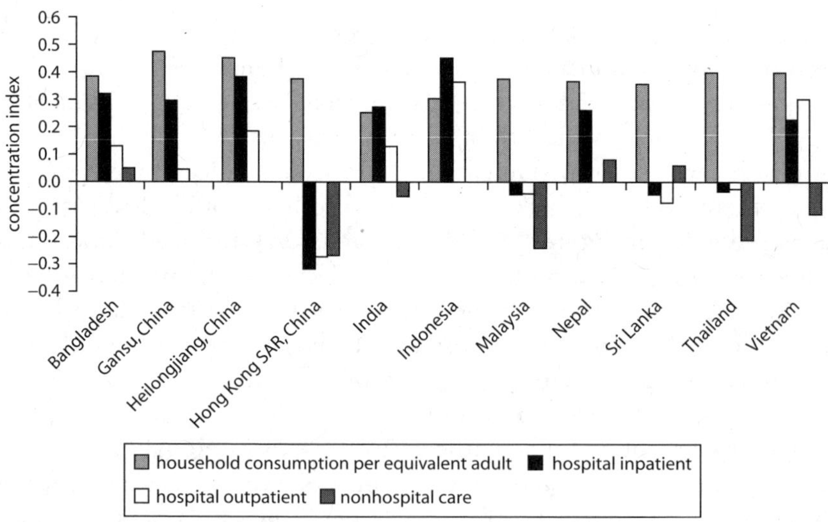

Source: O'Donnell and others 2008.

Note: A negative concentration index indicates a pro-poor distribution of subsidies, whereas a positive concentration index indicates pro-rich subsidies. A concentration index of zero indicates that the distribution of subsidies is proportional.

are pro-rich inequities for general practice (GP) visits and dental services, but not for specialist visits. The Republic of Korea has maintained equal-treatment-for-equal-need policies across all services, although the rich have preferential access to high levels of outpatient care. In Taiwan, China, the rich are slightly more likely to use outpatient services than the poor, but GP visits and dental services are evenly distributed. The distribution of hospital admissions is proportional or pro-poor in all three countries. A similar analysis, which compared horizontal equity in health care use in Japan to that in other OECD countries, found that there is no inequity in outpatient or inpatient use in Japan, although OOP payments show significant pro-rich inequity (Ohkusa and Honda 2003).

Explaining Inequalities in Health Care in East Asia and the Pacific

In LICs, inequalities in access to services are caused by deficiencies in both the breadth and depth of coverage. Chapter 6 discussed variations in benefits across and within countries in the region. Globally, social insurance–financed systems in which universal coverage has not been achieved, is characterized by formal sector employees enjoying more comprehensive coverage than others. Unemployed people and agricultural and informal sector workers either have no coverage (as in China, Indonesia, and Vietnam) or have shallow coverage that entitles them to a less comprehensive benefits package (for example, in China and the Philippines).

In tax-financed systems in which universal coverage has not been achieved, the poor face significant financial barriers to access in the form of formal and informal user charges at public health facilities. This challenge exists, for example, in Cambodia, Indonesia, the Lao People's Democratic Republic, and Papua New Guinea. Targeted fee waiver and exemption schemes (for example, health cards in Indonesia) and health equity funds (for example, in Cambodia and Lao PDR) are established to help the poor overcome financial barriers to access. However, there is little compelling evidence of the success of these targeting mechanisms in improving equity in access to care.

In high-income economies, where universal coverage has been achieved, inequalities still exist because of shallow coverage. Some of the more catastrophic expenditures may be outside the domain of health insurance, or there may be wide variation in benefits packages offered under different insurance schemes. In countries where the social insurance law mandates the same benefits for all (for example, in Japan),

Table 8.2 Income-Related Inequality and Inequity in Annual Per Capita Health Care Use: Probability of Use and Volume of Use.

	Hong Kong SAR, China						*Korea, Rep.*						*Taiwan, China*					
Service	*Prob.**	*C*	*HI*	*Total number*	*C*	*HI*	*Prob.**	*C*	*HI*	*Total number.*	*C*	*HI*	*Prob.**	*C*	*HI*	*Total number*	*C*	*HI*
Outpatient visits																		
Western doctor	0.18	0.0185	0.0927	8.27	0.0241	0.1037	0.16	−0.0921	−0.0090	9.76	−0.0975	−0.0234	0.35	−0.0180	0.0209	8.39	−0.0581	0.0014
General practitioner	0.15	0.0581	0.1144	6.99	0.0573	0.1181	—	—	—	—	—	—	—	—	—	—	—	—
Specialist	0.03	−0.2013	−0.0177	1.27	−0.1580	0.0243	—	—	—	—	—	—	—	—	—	—	—	—
LTM practitioner	0.03	0.0574	0.1195	2.55	0.0237	0.1237	0.02	−0.0178	0.0862	1.38	−0.0321	0.0726	0.08	0.0426	0.0675	2.19	0.0232	0.0507
Dental	0.31	0.2612	0.2698	1.14	0.2266	0.2386	0.02	0.0283	0.0333	1.12	−0.0155	−0.0262	0.09	0.0738	0.0830	2.58	0.0171	0.0272
Hospital services																		
Emergency room	0.01	−0.2226	−0.1751	0.22	−0.2518	−0.2013	n.a.	n.a.	n.a.	n.a.	n.a.	n.a.	0.10	−0.0198	0.0218	0.14	−0.0202	0.0403
Inpatient admissions	0.07	−0.0502	0.0638	0.14	−0.0954	0.0468	0.10	−0.0744	−0.0627	0.07	−0.0734	−0.0506	0.07	−0.1165	−0.0381	0.09	−0.1309	−0.0236

Source: Lu et al. (2007).

Note:— = not available; n.a. = not applicable; C = concentration index; LTM = licensed traditional medicine; Prob. * = probability of use of outpatient visits and inpatient admissions in the previous year (including individuals with zero consumption); total number = total number of visits, admissions, and hospital days per person per year.

there are fewer inequities. Any improvement to the benefits package must be provided to everyone. This equity also prevents the demonstration effect (seen in other countries) in which some benefits go first to individuals with a generous health insurance plan, causing the less privileged to pressure the system for benefits to be extended (Campbell and Ikegami 1999). Similarly, in high-income tax-financed economies where universal coverage has been achieved (for example, in Hong Kong SAR, China, and in Malaysia), inequalities are not as widespread because there are fewer restrictions on access to services. As noted earlier, these tax-financed economies have no explicit benefits package, and the goal is to provide universal coverage for all services that the public sector can afford.

Notably, there are no significant inequities in the use of specialist care services in high-income East Asian and Pacific economies. In the Japanese health system, there is no difference between specialists and general practitioners; therefore, no inequities exist in the use of either provider. In Hong Kong SAR, China, use of specialist outpatient services in the public sector is heavily concentrated on the poor, whereas private care is almost equally concentrated on the rich (Leung and others 2008). In the Republic of Korea and Taiwan, China, little distinction is made between specialist and general practice (GP) services.

However, using 1996 household survey data and after adjusting for insured individuals' need of care, Van Doorslaer and Masseria (2004) found evidence of pro-rich patterns of specialist care use among the insured in OECD countries. Higher-income groups use more specialist care than would be expected on the basis of their need for care. Similarly, household surveys from Switzerland indicate that service use for GPs and hospitals is distributed equally across income groups, whereas the distribution of specialist visits is significantly pro-rich.

Regardless of the economy's income level, equity is of particular concern when OOP payments are high and when the lack of single-risk pools allows various income groups to pool among themselves in fragmented risk pools and private insurance. These concerns are the case in, for example, Cambodia, China, Indonesia, the Republic of Korea, Lao PDR, and the Philippines. In Europe, the experience with voluntary insurance in France shows that complementary insurance negatively affects equity in health. People in low-income categories are more likely (54.5 percent in France) to be excluded from voluntary insurance than people in high-income categories (World Bank 2008a). Equity is less of a concern in countries like Japan where individuals cannot opt out of the insurance system and where providers are not permitted to charge prices set outside the insurance system (see the forthcoming volume of East Asia–Pacific Country Health Financing Profiles).

Supplementary private health insurance (as found in Hong Kong SAR, China; Japan; and Malaysia) does not threaten equity in access because it does not involve opting out of the main risk pool. These countries have universal coverage, and OOP payments are nominal. The need for supplementary health insurance arises from a desire among the rich to cover additional related expenditures (as, in Japan) or to buy more expensive services from the private sector (as, in Hong Kong SAR, China, and in Malaysia). For each episode of disease in Japan, the patient can receive private health care services (which the patient is not allowed to use or pay for under social health insurance programs) if he or she can afford to pay for them. In such cases, none of the costs of services to treat the episode of illness will be covered by the scheme to which the patient belongs. These costs are considered OOP obligations (Hasegawa 2005).

Distribution of Public Subsidies for Health Care

Benefit incidence studies in Asia have typically found that public health spending in LMICs is not pro-poor (Filmer 2003; Mahal and others 2000; van de Walle 1995). Public subsidies for inpatient care are especially pro-rich. Although confirming the earlier findings, results of a recent systematic benefit incidence analysis of 10 Asian economies (O'Donnell and others 2008)[1] also found that in some Asian economies the distribution of public subsidies is quite pro-poor. Those results are presented and discussed in this chapter.

The most pro-poor distribution of public health subsidies is in Hong Kong SAR, China. Although to a lesser extent than in Hong Kong SAR, China, total public health spending is pro-poor in middle-income Malaysia and Thailand and in low-income Sri Lanka. In all other countries included in this study (O'Donnell and others 2008), public health subsidies were found to be strongly pro-rich, which is consistent with the findings of earlier studies. The study also found that, although public health subsidies are typically not pro-poor, they reduce inequality in all other countries in East Asia and the Pacific (figures 8.7 and 8.8).

A second finding of this study (O'Donnell and others 2008) is that subsidies for public hospital care are less targeted on the poor than are

Figure 8.7 Distribution of Public Subsidies for Hospital and Nonhospital Care

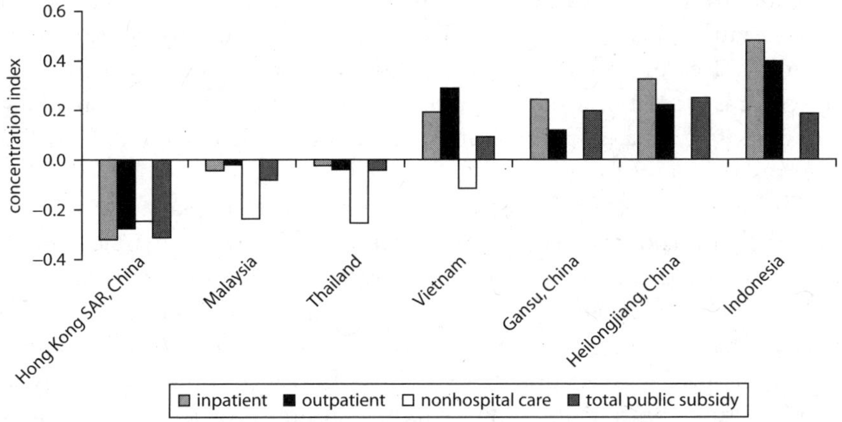

Source: O'Donnell and others 2008.
Note: A negative concentration index indicates a pro-poor distribution of subsidies, whereas a positive concentration index indicates pro-rich subsidies. A concentration index of zero indicates that the distribution of subsidies is proportional.

Figure 8.8 Distribution of Public Subsidies for Hospital and Nonhospital Care (Kakwani Indexes)

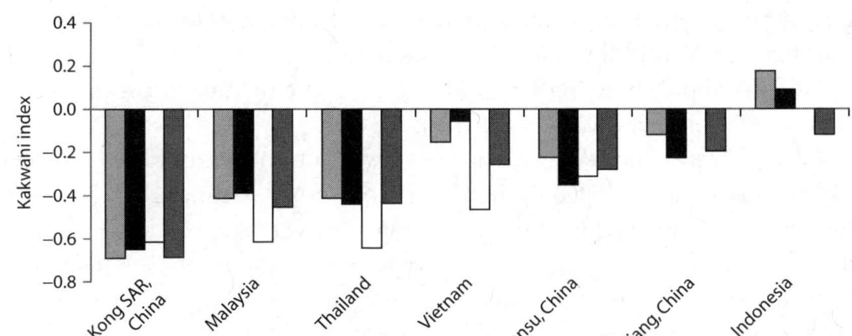

Source: O'Donnell and others 2008.
Note: A negative concentration index indicates a pro-poor distribution of subsidies, while a positive concentration index indicates pro-rich subsidies. A concentration index of zero indicates that the distribution of subsidies is proportional.

subsidies for nonhospital care. Spending on hospital inpatient and outpatient care is significantly pro-rich, whereas spending on nonhospital care is fairly pro-poor. Because the greater share of the subsidy goes to hospital care, pro-rich spending dominates the overall distribution. By contrast, spending on hospital care is strongly pro-poor in Hong Kong SAR, China, and moderately pro-poor in Malaysia and Thailand (figures 8.7 and 8.8).

The level of national income is one potential explanation for the unusually pro-poor distribution of subsidies in Hong Kong SAR, China; Malaysia; Sri Lanka; and Thailand. Targeting the poor is successful in richer countries because they can afford a universal public health care system that is funded by general taxation with minimal user charges. This practice does not apply to Sri Lanka, however. Moreover, Malaysia and Sri Lanka have historically exhibited similar pro-poor distributions of public subsidies since the 1960s, when these countries were at a much lower level of income (Alailima and Mohideen 1983; Hammer, Nabi, and Cercone 1995; Meerman 1979).

An alternative explanation for the pro-poor distribution of public health subsidies lies in the types of private sector alternatives available to the rich. Long waiting times and minimal amenities create incentives for the rich to opt out of the public sector. These incentives become stronger as the economy grows (as in Malaysia and Thailand, for example) and the number of middle- and higher-income groups with the desire and the means to purchase higher-quality care in the private sector increases (Hammer, Nabi, and Cercone 1995).

Clear discrepancies between the distributions of public and private hospital care exist only in Hong Kong SAR, China; Malaysia; Sri Lanka; and Thailand. In those economies, private sector care is clearly distributed in favor of the rich, whereas care in the public sector tends to be pro-poor or distributed equally between the rich and the poor. In those four economies, the combination of a universal public provision, a private sector offering an attractive alternative to the basic package, and incomes that make demand for this alternative effective leads to redistribution through public provision in precisely the way that theory predicts (Besley and Coate 1991). The health system in Hong Kong SAR, China, is perhaps the best example of this alternative in practice (box 8.1). By contrast, in Indonesia, the distribution of private sector care is only slightly more pro-rich than is care in the public sector.

Such findings suggest that effective targeting of public spending on health care depends not only on policies concerning the public health

Box 8.1

The Mixed Public-Private Health System in Hong Kong SAR, China

In Hong Kong SAR, China, payments for health care are highly concentrated on the rich, whereas benefits are strongly pro-poor. As a consequence, there is a significant net redistribution of public health care from the rich to the poor. Public health care is skewed partly toward the poor, not only because allocations are made according to need, but also because the rich opt out of the public sector and consume most of the private care.

Overall, there is horizontal inequity favoring the rich in general outpatient care and (very marginally) in inpatient care. Pro-rich bias in the distribution of private care outweighs the pro-poor bias of public care. A lesser role for private finance may improve horizontal equity of use but would also reduce the degree of net redistribution through the public sector.

system, but also on the scale and the allocation of public spending. Another important factor is the broader course of economic development that influences the supply and demand for private health care as well as the incentives and opportunities for the rich to opt out of the public sector, thereby releasing resources for the poor (O'Donnell and others 2008).

The extent to which the public subsidy is targeted at the poor also depends on the policy for charging users because the price effect on use may vary with income (Gertler and van der Gaag 1990; Mocan, Tekin, and Zax 2004) and also because exemptions may shield the poor, raising the subsidy to them. In any case, the implementation of fee exemption schemes is fraught with problems (Arhin-Tenkorang 2001; Tien and Chee 2002). Table 4.5 (chapter 4) summarizes user fee charges and exemptions in each country. It is no coincidence that the countries with the most pro-poor public subsidies for health are also the ones with the most extensive range of services available at zero or nominal cost to the user.

Note

1. The 10 economies were Bangladesh; China (two provinces: Gansu and Heilongjiang); Hong Kong SAR, China; India; Indonesia; Malaysia; Nepal; Sri Lanka; Thailand; and Vietnam.

References

Alailima, Patricia J., and Faiz Mohideen. 1983. "Health Sector Commodity Requirements and Expenditure Flows." Report prepared for the National Planning Department, Colombo.

Arhin-Tenkorang, Dyna. 2001. "Mobilizing Resources for Health: The Case for User Fees Revisited." CID Working Paper 81, Center for International Development, Harvard University, Cambridge, MA.

Baker, Judy L., and Jacques van der Gaag. 1993. "Equity in Health Care and Health Care Financing: Evidence from Five Developing Countries." In *Equity in the Finance and Delivery of Health Care: An International Perspective*, ed. Eddy van Doorslaer, Adam Wagstaff, and Frans Rutten. Oxford, U.K.: Oxford University Press.

Besley, Timothy J., and Stephen Coate. 1991. "Public Provision of Private Goods and the Redistribution of Income. *American Economic Review* 81 (4): 979–84.

Campbell, John C., and Naoki Ikegami. 1999. *The Art of Balance in Health Policy: Maintaining Japan's Low-Cost Egalitarian System*. Cambridge, MA: Cambridge University Press.

Fernando, Tharanga, and Ravi P. Rannan-Eliya. 2008. "Evaluation of the 2005, 2006, and 2007 Regional Health Accounts Data Collections in the Asia-Pacific Region." Presentation to the Fourth Organisation for Economic Cooperation and Development–Korea Policy Centre–Asia-Pacific National Health Accounts Network Meeting of Regional Health Accounts Experts, Asia Pacific National Health Accounts Network, Seoul, July 8–10.

Filmer, Deon. 2003. "The Incidence of Public Expenditures on Health and Education." Background Note for the *World Development Report 2004: Making Services Work for Poor People*, World Bank, Washington, DC.

Gertler, Paul, and Jacques van der Gaag. 1990. *The Willingness to Pay for Medical Care: Evidence from Two Developing Countries*. Baltimore, MD: Johns Hopkins University Press.

Gottret, Pablo, and George Schieber. 2006. *Health Financing Revisited: A Practitioner's Guide*. Washington, DC: World Bank.

Gwatkin, Davidson R., Shea Rutstein, Kiersten Johnson, Eldaw Suliman, Adam Wagstaff, and Agbessi Amozou. 2007. *Socioeconomic Differences in Health, Nutrition, and Population within Developing Countries: An Overview*. Washington, DC: World Bank.

Hammer, Jeffrey S., and Peter Berman. 1995. "Ends and Means in Public Health Policy in Developing Countries." *Health Policy* 32 (1–3): 29–45.

Hammer, Jeffrey S., Ijaz Nabi, and James A. Cercone. 1995. "Distributional Effects of Social Sector Expenditures in Malaysia 1974–89." In *Public*

Spending and the Poor, ed. Dominique van de Walle and Kimberly Nead, 521–54. Baltimore, MD: Johns Hopkins University Press.

Hasegawa, Toshihiko. 2005. "Japan." In *Social Health Insurance: Selected Case Studies from Asia and the Pacific,* 19–20. New Delhi, India: World Health Organization Regional Office for South-East Asia and World Health Organization Regional Office for the Western Pacific Region.

Hollingsworth, Bruce. 2008. "The Measurement of Efficiency and Productivity of Health Care Delivery." *Health Economics* 17 (10): 1107–28.

Jamison, Dean T., Joel G. Breman, Anthony R. Measham, George Alleyne, Mariam Claeson, David B. Evans, Prabhat Jha, Anne Mills, and Philip Musgrove, eds. 2006. *Disease Control Priorities in Developing Countries.* 2nd ed. New York: World Bank and Oxford University Press.

Kutzin, Joseph, ed. 1995. "The Consequences of Health Financing Change: A Framework for Analysis." World Health Organization, Geneva.

Leung, Gabriel M., Keith Y. K. Tin, G. M. K. Yeung, E. S. K. Leung, Eva L. H. Tsui, D. W. S. Lam, Caroline S. H. Tsang, A. Y. K. Fung, and Su Vui Lo. 2008. "Hong Kong's Domestic Health Spending: Financial Years 1989/90 through 2004/05." *Hong Kong Medical Journal* 14 (suppl. 2): 2–23.

Liu, Xingzhu. 2003. *Policy Tools for Allocative Efficiency of Health Services.* Geneva: World Health Organization.

Lu, Jui-fen Rachel, Gabriel M. Leung, Soon-man Kwon, Keith Y. K. Tin, Eddy Van Doorslaer, and Owen O'Donnell. 2007. "Horizontal Equity in Health Care Utilization Evidence from Three High-Income Asian Economies." *Social Science and Medicine* 64 (1): 199–212.

Mahal, Ajay, Janmejay Singh, Farzana Afridi, Vikram Lamba, Anil Gumber, and V. Selvaraju. 2000. "Who 'Benefits' from Public Sector Health Spending in India?" National Council for Applied Economic Research, New Delhi, India.

Meerman, Jacob. 1979. *Public Expenditure in Malaysia: Who Benefits and Why.* Oxford, U.K.: University Press.

Mocan, Naci H., Erdal Tekin, and Jeffrey S. Zax. 2004. "The Demand for Medical Care in Urban China." *World Development* 32 (2): 289–304.

O'Donnell, Owen, Eddy Van Doorslaer, Ravi P. Rannan-Eliya, Aparnaa Somanathan, Shiva Raj Adhikari, Baktygul Akkazieva, Deni Harbianto, Charu C. Garg, Piya Hanvoravongchai, Alejandro N. Herrin, Mohammed N. Huq, Shamsia Ibragimova, Anup Karan, Soon-man Kwon, Gabriel M. Leung, Jui-fen Rachel Lu, Ohkusa Yasushi, Badri Raj Pande, Rachel Racelis, Keith Tin, Kanjana Tisayaticom, Laksono Trisnantoro, Quan Wan, Bong-Min Yang, and Yuxin Zhao. 2008. "Who Pays for Health Care in Asia?" *Journal of Health Economics* 27 (2): 460–75.

OECD (Organisation for Economic Co-operation and Development). 2008. *Health Expenditure and Utilization Data*. Paris: OECD.

Ohkusa, Yasushi, and Chika Honda. 2003. "Updated Horizontal Inequity in Health Care Utilization in Japan: Comparisons with OECD Countries Using an Original Survey." ISER Discussion Paper 0585, Institute of Social and Economic Research, Osaka University, Osaka, Japan.

Pabón Lasso, Hipólito. 1986. "Evaluating Hospital Performance through Simultaneous Application of Several Indicators." *Bulletin of the Pan American Health Organization* 20 (4): 341–57.

Tien, Marie, and Grace Chee. 2002. "Literature Review and Findings: Implementation of Waiver Policies." Partners for Health Reform*plus*, Washington, DC.

van de Walle, Dominique. 1995. "The Distribution of Subsidies through Public Health Services in Indonesia, 1978–87." In *Public Spending and the Poor: Theory and Evidence*, ed. Dominique van de Walle, and Kimberly Nead, 226–58. Baltimore, MD: John Hopkins University Press.

Van Doorslaer, Eddy, and Cristina Masseria. 2004. "Income-Related Inequality in the Use of Medical Care in 21 OECD Countries." OECD Health Working Paper, Organisation for Economic Co-operation and Development, Paris.

Van Doorslaer, Eddy, Adam Wagstaff, Hattem van der Burg, Terkel Christiansen, Diana De Graeve, Inge Duchesne, Ulf-G. Gerdtham, Michael Gerfin, Jose Geurts, Lorna Gross, Unto Häkkinen, Jürgen John, Jan Klavus, Robert E. Leu, Brian Nolan, Owen O'Donnell, Carol Propper, Frank Puffer, Martin Schellhorn, Gun Sundberg, Olaf Winkelhake. 2000. "Equity in Delivery of Health Care in Europe and the US." *Journal of Health Economics* 19 (5): 553–83.

Wagstaff, Adam. 2002. "Poverty and Health Sector Inequalities." *Bulletin of the World Health Organization* 80 (2): 97–105.

Wagstaff, Adam, and Eddy Van Doorslaer. 1992. "Equity in the Finance of Health Care: Some International Comparisons." *Journal of Health Economics* 11 (4): 361–87.

Wagstaff, Adam, Eddy Van Doorslaer, Hattem van der Burg, Samuel Calonge, Terkel Christiansen, Guido Citoni, Ulf-G. Gerdtham, Michael Gerfin, Lorna Gross, Unto Häkinnen, Paul Johnson, Jürgen John, Jan Klavus, Claire Lachaud, Jørgen Lauritsen, Robert Leu, Brian Nolan, Encarna Perán, João Pereira, Carol Propper, Frank Puffer, Lise Rochaix, Marisol Rodríguez, Martin Schellhorn, Gun Sundberg, and Olaf Winkelhake. 1999. "Equity in the Finance of Health Care: Some Further International Comparisons." *Journal of Health Economics* 18 (3): 263–90.

World Bank. 1993. *World Development Report 1993: Investing in Health.* Washington, DC: World Bank.

———. 2008a. *Good Practices in Health Financing: Lessons from Reforms in Low- and Middle-Income Countries.* Washington, DC: World Bank.

———. 2008b. *Mongolia Public Expenditure Review.* Washington, DC: World Bank.

———. 2009. *Health Financing in Indonesia: A Reform Road Map.* Washington, DC, World Bank.

APPENDIX A

National Health Account Activity in East Asia and the Pacific

The development of national health accounts (NHAs) in East Asia and the Pacific is relatively advanced in comparison with other regions. Most major countries in East Asia and the Pacific have established or are currently in the process of establishing NHA systems, although few have yet to fully institutionalize an NHA. In most countries in the region, the ministry of health tends to commission NHA studies, and the actual production of accounts is conducted by public sector research agencies (Fernando and Rannan-Eliya 2008). Health ministries tend to be the most common source of financial support for NHA whereas external donors and agencies play a more minor role.

Country Typology

This book presents findings from a preliminary World Bank survey of NHA activity within official World Bank member countries in the region, as well as the East Asian "Tiger" economies (Japan; Hong Kong SAR, China; the Republic of Korea; Taiwan, China; and Singapore). This survey captures both financial and technical support received from the World Bank, as well as NHA activity supported by other international organizations. The economies surveyed have been categorized into the following typology, depending on their level of NHA development and institutionalization:

Group I consists of economies with permanent NHA systems where annual (or semiannual) updates are routinely generated and where multiyear estimates are available. Group I consists of Organisation for Economic Co-operation and Development (OECD) states (Japan and the Republic of Korea), as well as China; Hong Kong SAR, China; the Philippines; Taiwan, China; and Thailand (Fernando and Rannan-Eliya 2008).

Group II economies are those that have conducted at least one round of an NHA. These countries are Indonesia, Malaysia, Mongolia, Myanmar, Papua New Guinea, Samoa, Tonga, and Vietnam. Countries such as Indonesia had previously generated annual estimates, but these estimates were not in line with official NHA frameworks and classifications.

Group III economies are those that have an interest in producing NHA estimates but have not yet initiated an official process to establish an NHA system. This category includes those economies conducting public accounting and audit exercises, often with World Bank support. Group III comprises Cambodia, the Federated States of Micronesia, Fiji, the Lao People's Democratic Republic, the Marshall Islands, Singapore, and Timor-Leste.

Group IV includes countries with no interest in conducting NHA or where NHA studies are not feasible. Kiribati, the Solomon Islands, and Vanuatu are in this group.

Group V consists of those economies where the status of NHA activity is unknown. This group comprises American Samoa, the Democratic People's Republic of Korea, the Northern Mariana Islands, and Palau.

Table A.1 summarizes the number of countries that fall into each major category cited, and table A.2 provides the country-specific detail of NHA activity. Among the 29 East Asia and Pacific countries surveyed, 7 have either institutionalized NHAs or conducted multiple rounds of NHA estimates, whereas 22 countries have conducted only one round of NHA estimates or have not conducted NHAs at all. Hence, many countries have yet to institutionalize NHA and therefore implement and support the routine collection of national health expenditure data. Of the 29 East Asia Pacific countries, 11 have received World Bank support for NHA or other public sector accounting activities, as illustrated in table A.3.

Table A.1 Typology as Applied to East Asian and Pacific Economies

Typology	*Number of economies*	*Economies*
Group I	7	China; Hong Kong SAR, China; Japan; the Philippines; the Republic of Korea; Taiwan, China; and Thailand
Group II	8	Indonesia, Malaysia, Mongolia, Myanmar, Papua New Guinea, Samoa, Tonga, and Vietnam
Group III	7	Cambodia, the Federated States of Micronesia, Fiji, Lao PDR, the Marshall Islands, Singapore, and Timor-Leste
Group IV	3	Kiribati, the Solomon Islands, and Vanuatu
Group V	4	American Samoa, the Democratic People's Republic of Korea, the Northern Mariana Islands, and Palau
Total	29	

Sources: World Bank interviews and surveys; external interviews and surveys; APNHAN.
Note: Typology includes official World Bank member economies as well as the East Asian "Tigers."

An evaluation of regional health account activity for 2005, 2006, and 2007 highlights key trends in terms of coverage for the three data collection efforts conducted over that period. Table A.4 from Fernando and Rannan-Eliya (2008) highlights the coverage by economy of the system of health accounts (SHA) tables for expenditure information reported by the territories participating in the three rounds of data collection. Tables A.5 to A.7 contain the details of the International Classification of Health Account (ICHA) variables reported by economy. Among the OECD territories, Australia notably provided data tables for all four years. Among the World Health Organization (WHO)–Asia-Pacific National Health Accounts Network (APNHAN) countries, Bangladesh, Sri Lanka, Thailand, and Vietnam were best able to produce (or are expected to produce) the tables requested. In terms of the Regional Centre for Health and Social Policy territories, Hong Kong SAR, China, was able to provide the three core tables requested for 2002 to 2004; in contrast, Taiwan, China, provided a smaller set. The data provided here indicate that a large proportion of non-OECD territories in the region have the ability to report health accounts at the appropriate level of detail required by OECD, Eurostat, and WHO SHA questionnaires, although doing so will require extensive staff inputs and quality assurance of the data reported by countries (Fernando and Rannan-Eliya 2008). In the future, emphasis can be placed on further institutionalizing data collection efforts so that they are conducted on a routine basis.

Table A.2 Detail of Health Expenditure Resource-Tracking Work in East Asia and the Pacific

Country	*Typology*	*World Bank support?*	*Health expenditure resource-tracking activity*
American Samoa	Group V	No	NHA status is unknown.
Cambodia	Group III	Yes	Although completion of an NHA is reflected in the national health policy, Cambodia lacks the capacity to begin conducting an NHA. U.K. Department for International Development funds may be available initially through the Health Economics Unit of the Ministry of Health. The World Bank supports capacity building in public sector accounting and audit, public expenditure tracking surveys in health, and sectorwide planning.
China	Group I	Yes	Two NHA studies have been completed, analyzing data for 1990 to 2003. The first round covered 1990 to 1995, and the second round covered 1990 to 2002/03. The Bank has worked extensively with the China National Health Economics Institute, which is responsible for conducting China's NHA, in the context of ongoing rural health reform analytical and advisory activities. The Bank's NHA work in China has had three broad strands, some still ongoing: (a) reviewing China's NHA data and methods, (b) updating and preparing detailed NHAs for two provinces, and (c) studying the financing and organization of public health functions at the county level.
Fiji	Group III	No	NHA status is unknown. Fiji has expressed interest to the Bank in conducting an NHA.
Hong Kong SAR, China	Group I	No	NHAs are institutionalized. In fact, Hong Kong SAR, China, produced annual estimates of national health expenditures before it adopted a formal NHA system. Hong Kong SAR, China, developed and reported its first set of domestic health accounts (DHA1) in 1998 as part of a consultancy to review the local health system. The project was carried out by the Institute of Policy Studies of Sri Lanka, under contract to the Harvard School of Public Health. The University of Hong Kong was commissioned by the Health, Welfare, and Food Bureau in 2003 to update the DHA1 for fiscal years 1997/98 to 2001/02 (DHA2) and, in addition, retrospectively updated DHA1 estimates for fiscal years 1989/90 to 1996/97, thereby creating a 13-year series of health accounts compatible with the OECD system of health accounts (SHA). The next DHA (DHA3), covering 2002/03 to 2004/05, was prepared by the University of Hong Kong in 2008.

Table A.2 *(continued)*

Country	*Typology*	*World Bank support?*	*Health expenditure resource-tracking activity*
Indonesia	Group II	Yes	The first round of NHAs has been completed. This round, which analyzes data for 2001 and 2002, was supported by the World Health Organization. The NHA is self-managed by the government. Notably, the Bank has supported the establishment of provincial and district health accounts under the Health Workforce and Services project.
Japan	Group I	No	Three rounds of OECD SHA-based health accounts were been conducted in 2000, 2002, and 2007.
Kiribati	Group IV	No	NHA status is unknown. Kiribati may be too small to support permanent NHA capacity. A regional NHA solution should be explored.
Korea, Dem. People's Rep.	Group V	No	NHA status is unknown.
Korea, Rep.	Group I	No	Initial efforts to develop an NHA were made in the 1990s by various independent researchers and research institutions, including the Korea Development Institute. These efforts were then followed by a more formal publication of NHA by the Korea Institute of Health Service Management in 1998. After the Republic of Korea joined the OECD, the Korea Institute of Health and Social Affairs, at the OECD's request, produced formal NHA estimates for 1985 to 2002. These estimates are based on the OECD SHA. Overall, there have been three rounds of OECD SHA-based health accounts—for 2001, 2002, and 2007.
Lao PDR	Group III	Yes	As of March 2005, there was no official decision to develop an NHA. The Bank is supporting capacity building in public sector accounting and audit, public expenditure tracking surveys in health, and sectorwide planning.
Malaysia	Group II	No	The first round of NHAs has been completed, analyzing data for 1997 to 2002. Financial support was received from national resources and technical assistance from the Institute of Policy Studies of Sri Lanka and from Harvard in 1996. The NHA has been partly funded by the United Nations Development Programme and the government of Malaysia. Efforts to promote NHA institutionalization commenced in early part of decade.
Marshall Islands	Group III	Yes	As of March 2005, no official decision to develop an NHA had been made. The Bank supports capacity building in public sector accounting and audit, public expenditure tracking surveys in health, and sectorwide planning.

(continued)

Table A.2 *(continued)*

Country	*Typology*	*World Bank support?*	*Health expenditure resource-tracking activity*
Micronesia, Fed. Sts.	Group III	Yes	As of March 2005, no official decision to develop an NHA had been made. The Bank supports capacity building in public sector accounting and audit, public expenditure tracking surveys in health, and sectorwide planning.
Mongolia	Group II	Yes	The first round of NHAs has been completed, and the second round is in progress. In 2003, the first round (1999–2002 data) was completed with Bank funding under a project titled Capacity Building for Public Expenditure Management in the Health Sector. The project, which used an Institutional Development Fund grant, involved collaboration with the Asia-Pacific National Health Accounts Network (APNHAN), and used the OECD SHA format and mapping. The second round was due at the end of 2006 and has received technical assistance from the Bank and WHO.
Myanmar	Group II	No	The first round of NHAs has been completed and analyzes data for 1999 to 2001. WHO provided financial support and technical assistance.
Northern Mariana Islands	Group V	No	NHA status is unknown.
Palau	Group V	No	NHA status is unknown. As of March 2005, no official decision to develop an NHA had been made.
Papua New Guinea	Group II	No	The first round of NHAs has been completed, analyzing data for 1998 to 2000. Financial support was received from the Asian Development Bank and technical assistance from the University of Philippines School of Economics. AusAID also supported the effort. Note: A household expenditure survey to collect additional data was planned in 2003 and 2004 but had not been undertaken as of December 2005.
Philippines	Group I	No	NHAs have been produced (without Bank support) since the late 1990s by the National Statistical Coordination Board. Since 1997, NHAs have been a regular activity of the board.
Samoa	Group II	Yes	Three rounds of NHAs have been completed: 1999/2000, 2001/02, and 2003/04. The second round (2001/02) was part of a health sector project financed by the Bank and the International Development Association.
Singapore	Group III	No	As of December 2005, an NHA had been under consideration in Singapore. It may be supported internally.
Solomon Islands	Group IV	No	As of December 2005, no official decision to develop an NHA had been made. The Solomon Islands may be too small to support permanent NHA capacity. A regional NHA solution should be explored.

Table A.2 *(continued)*

Country	*Typology*	*World Bank support?*	*Health expenditure resource-tracking activity*
Taiwan, China	Group I	No	NHAs have been institutionalized. In fact, Taiwan, China, produced annual estimates of national health expenditures prior to adopting a formal NHA system. The Office of Statistics in the Department of Health is the official agent primarily responsible for compiling and estimating the health expenditures for Taiwan, China, and has routinely published the health data since 1991. To increase the comparability of data with the international community, the department contracted Professors William Hsiao at Harvard University and J. Rachel Lu at Chang Gung University to establish an NHA system in 1999 that was based on the OECD standard. So that the data collection process would be easier, a task force composed of representatives from the Directorate-General of Budget, Accounting, and Statistics (the responsible agent for compiling and releasing annual household survey data on family income and expenditure); health departments of local governments; and the Bureau of National Health Insurance was formed. Specific problems were tackled and consensus was reached at the three task force meetings, which were chaired by the vice minister of health. The NHA project also engaged an expert consultant, Dr. Ravi Rannan-Eliya, to validate the private sector estimates and review the final estimates. The research project was finally completed in the summer of 2000. The final report containing the estimated figures, methodology, technical notes, and worksheets was transferred to the Department of Health at the completion of the project. Annual estimations are to be updated and maintained by the Office of Statistics using the newly developed NHA methodology.
Thailand	Group I	No	NHAs have been institutionalized. The first round of NHAs has been completed, analyzing data for 1994 to 2001 and applying the OECD SHA methodology. This effort was a locally initiated and financially supported project by the Health, Science, Research Institute. The International Health Policy Program–Thailand has updated the 12-year series of NHA data from 1994 to 2005. National AIDS accounts have also been conducted for 2000 to 2003.
Timor-Leste	Group III	Yes	As of December 2005, there has been no official decision to develop an NHA. However, the government has asked for assistance in conducting an NHA, which may now be supported by a non-Bank-financed grant from the European Commission.

(continued)

Table A.2 *(continued)*

Country	*Typology*	*World Bank support?*	*Health expenditure resource-tracking activity*
Tonga	Group II	Yes	The first round of NHAs was completed in 2004, analyzing data for 2001 and 2002. In 2003, the Bank provided funding for an NHA under the Tonga Health Sector Support project (approved July 2003).
Vanuatu	Group IV	No	As of December 2005, no official decision to develop an NHA had been made. Vanuatu may be too small to support permanent NHA capacity; hence, a regional NHA solution should be explored.
Vietnam	Group II	Yes	Two rounds of NHAs have been completed. The first round analyzed data for 1998 to 2000. The second round analyzed data for 2001 to 2003. In 2001, the Bank supported an NHA under the National Health Sector Support project, which was financed by the Bank and the International Development Association.

Sources: World Bank interviews and surveys; external interviews and surveys; APNHAN.
Note: Includes official World Bank member economies and the East Asian "Tigers."

Table A.3 World Bank–Supported NHA or Public Sector Accounting Activity in East Asia and the Pacific

Typology	*Number of economies*	*Economies*
Group I	1	China
Group II	5	Indonesia, Mongolia, Samoa, Tonga, Vietnam
Group III	5	Cambodia; Lao PDR; Marshall Islands; Micronesia; Timor-Leste; Micronesia, Fed. Sts.
Group IV	0	n.a.
Group V	0	n.a.
Total	11	

Sources: World Bank interviews and surveys; external interviews and surveys; APNHAN.
Note: Includes official World Bank member economies and the East Asian "Tigers."

Constraints

Constraints to further development and institutionalization of NHAs are numerous and include a lack of financial and human resources,an absence of routine data collection mechanisms, and a lack of demand for an NHA at the central level because ministries fail to understand its usefulness (table A.7). In addition, site visits and interviews have revealed that externallyfunded consulting groups have conducted multiple

Table A.4 Coverage of SHA Tables in the Three Regional Health Account Data Collections, 2002–05

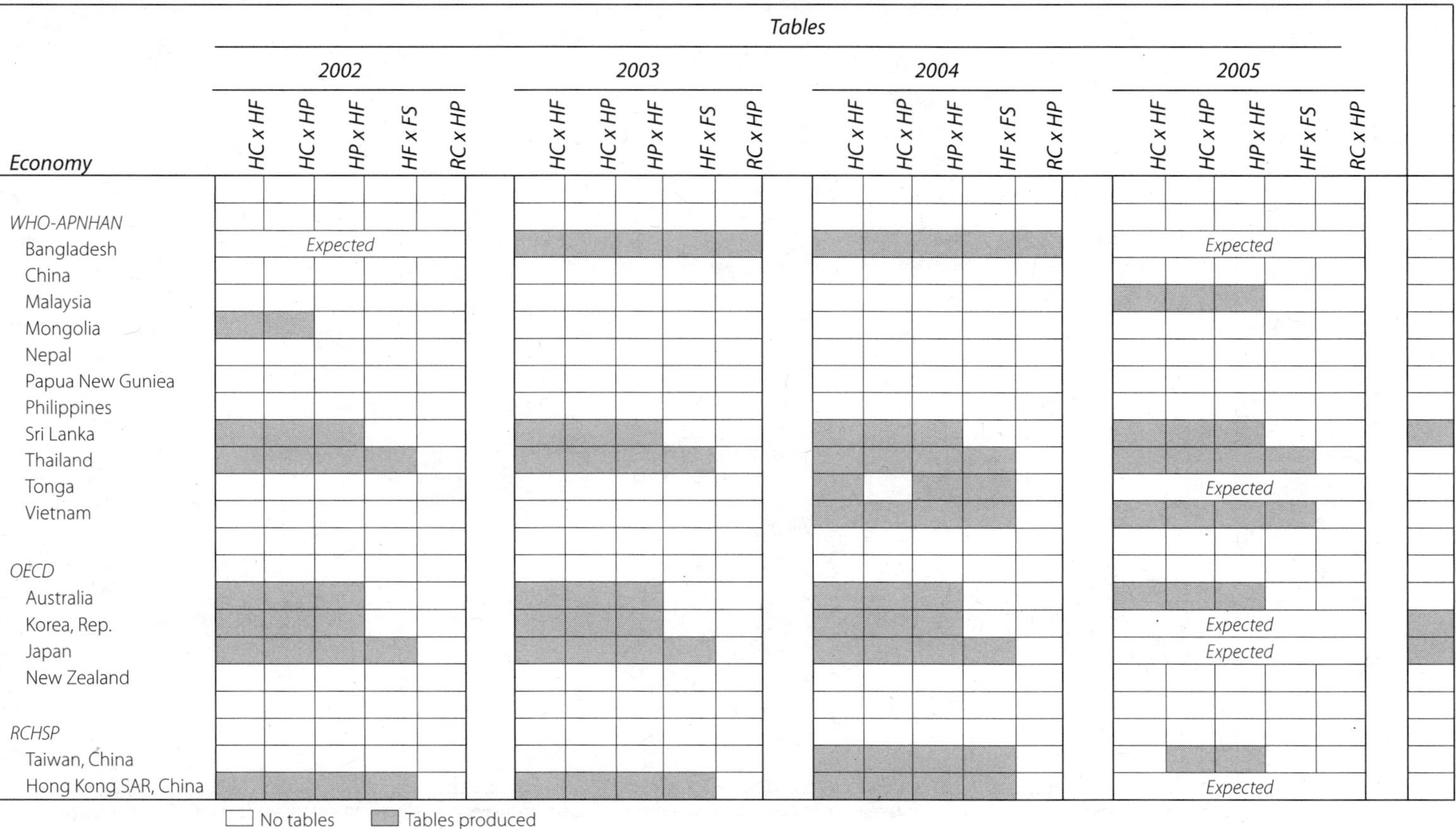

Economy	2002 HC x HF	2002 HC x HP	2002 HP x HF	2002 HF x FS	2002 RC x HP	2003 HC x HF	2003 HC x HP	2003 HP x HF	2003 HF x FS	2003 RC x HP	2004 HC x HF	2004 HC x HP	2004 HP x HF	2004 HF x FS	2004 RC x HP	2005 HC x HF	2005 HC x HP	2005 HP x HF	2005 HF x FS	2005 RC x HP	
WHO-APNHAN																					
Bangladesh	*Expected*					■	■	■	■	■	■	■	■	■	■	*Expected*					
China																					
Malaysia																■	■	■			
Mongolia	■	■																			
Nepal																					
Papua New Guniea																					
Philippines																					
Sri Lanka	■	■	■			■	■	■			■	■	■			■	■	■			■
Thailand	■	■	■	■		■	■	■	■		■	■	■	■		■	■	■	■		
Tonga											■		■	■		*Expected*					
Vietnam											■	■	■	■		■	■	■	■		
OECD																					
Australia	■	■	■			■	■	■			■	■	■			■	■	■			
Korea, Rep.	■	■	■			■	■	■			■	■	■			*Expected*					■
Japan	■	■	■	■		■	■	■	■		■	■	■	■		*Expected*					■
New Zealand																					
RCHSP																					
Taiwan, China											■	■	■	■			■	■			
Hong Kong SAR, China	■	■	■	■		■	■	■	■		■	■	■	■		*Expected*					

□ No tables ■ Tables produced

Source: Fernando and Rannan-Eliya 2008.

Note: FS = financing sources; HC = health care (functions); HF = health financing agents; HP = health providers; RC = resource costs, RCHSP = Regional Centre on Health and Social Policy.

Table A.5 Regional Health Account Data Collections: Variables of ICHA–Health Financing Agents, by Economy, 2006–07

				Bangladesh	*China*	*Hong Kong SAR, China*	*Mongolia*	*Nepal*	*Philippines*	*Sri Lanka*	*Taiwan, China*	*Thailand*	*Tonga*	*Vietnam*	*Total economies*	*SHA reporting economies*	*Australia*	*Japan*	*Korea, Rep.*	*Number of economies*
HF.1			General government												11	7				3
	HF.1.1		General government (excluding Social security) = territorial government												9	7				3
		HF.1.1.1	Central government												7	5				3
		HF.1.1.1.1	Ministry of health												7	5				2
		HF.1.1.1.2	Other ministries												7	5				2
		HF.1.1.2	State or provincial government												3	3				3
		HF.1.1.3	Local or municipal government												7	5				2
	HF.1.2		Social security funds												7	5				2
HF.2			Private sector												9	7				3
	HF.2.1		Private social insurance												4	4				1
	HF.2.2		Private insurance (other than social insurance)												7	4				3
	HF.2.1; HF.2.2		Private insurance												8	6				3
	HF.2.3		Private households out-of-pocket expense												11	8				3

		HF.2.3.1	Out-of-pocket excluding costsharing												2	2				3
		HF.2.3.2–.2.3.5	Costsharing: central government; state or provincial government; Local or municipal government; Social security funds												0					3
		HF.2.3.6–.2.3.7	Costsharing: private insurance												0					1
		HF.2.3.9	All other costsharing												0					1
	HF.2.4		Nonprofit institutions serving households												9	7				1
	HF.2.5		Corporations (other than health insurance)												9	6				3
HF.3			Rest of the world												6	5				0
			Current health care expenditure HF.1–.3												11	8				3

☐ No tables ■ Tables produced

Source: Fernando and Rannan-Eliya 2008.
Note: HF = health financing agents.

Table A.6 Regional Health Account Data Collections: Variables of ICHA–Health Providers, by Economy, 2006–07

				Bangladesh	*China*	*Hong Kong SAR, China*	*Mongolia*	*Nepal*	*Philippines*	*Sri Lanka*	*Taiwan, China*	*Thailand*	*Tonga*	*Vietnam*	*Total economies*	*SHA reporting economies*	*Australia*	*Japan*	*Korea, Rep.*	*Number of economies*
HP.1			Hospitals	■	■	■	■	■		■	■	■		■	9	7	■	■	■	3
		Of which	Government sector	■						■	■				3	3				0
		owned:	Private sector	■				■		■	■				4	3				0
	HP.1.1		General hospitals	■		■	■			■	■	■	■		7	7	■	■		2
	HP.1.2		Mental health and substance abuse hospitals			■				■	■				3	3	■	■		2
	HP.1.3		Specialty (other then mental health and substance abuse hospitals)	■		■	■			■	■	■			6	6	■	■		2
HP.2			Nursing and residential care facilities			■	■			■	■	■		■	5	5	■	■	■	3
		Of which	Government sector							■	■				1	1				0
		owned:	Private sector							■	■				1	1				0
	HP.2.1		Nursing care facilities			■				■	■				2	2	■	■	■	3
	HP.2.2		Residential mental retardation, mental health and substance abuse facilities			■									1	1				0
	HP.2.3		Community care facilities for the elderly			■									1	1			■	1
	HP.2.9		All other residential care facilities			■									1	1				0
HP.3			Providers of ambulatory health care	■	■	■	■	■		■	■	■			8	6	■	■	■	3

		Of which	Government sector												3	2					0
		owned:	Private sector												2	2					0
	HP.3.1		Offices of physicians												6	6					3
		Of which	Government sector												4	4					0
		owned:	Private sector												3	3					0
	HP.3.2		Offices of dentists												5	5					3
		Of which	Government sector												4	4					0
		owned:	Private sector												3	3					0
	HP.3.3		Offices of other health practitioners												6	6					2
		Of which	Government sector												3	3					0
		owned:	Private sector												3	3					0
	HP.3.4		Outpatient care centers												4	4					2
		Of which	Government sector												2	2					0
		owned:	Private sector												1	1					0
	HP.3.5		Medical and diagnostic laboratories												6	6					1
		Of which	Government sector												3	3					0
		owned:	Private sector												3	3					0
	HP.3.6		Providers of home health care services												3	3					3
	HP.3.9		Other providers of ambulatory health care												5	5					3
		HP.3.9.1	Ambulance services												2	2					2
		HP.3.9.2	Blood and organ banks												2	2					0
		HP.3.9.9	Providers of all other ambulatory health care services												3	3					0

(continued)

Table A.6 *(continued)*

				Bangladesh	*China*	*Hong Kong SAR, China*	*Mongolia*	*Nepal*	*Philippines*	*Sri Lanka*	*Taiwan, China*	*Thailand*	*Tonga*	*Vietnam*	*Total economies*	*SHA reporting economies*	*Australia*	*Japan*	*Korea, Rep.*	*Number of economies*
HP.4			Retail sales and other providers of medical goods												8	7				3
		Of which	Government sector												3	2				0
		owned:	Private sector												2	2				0
	HP.4.1		Dispensing chemists = pharmacies												6	6				3
		Of which	Government sector												4	4				0
		owned:	Private sector												3	3				0
	HP.4.2		Retail sales and other suppliers of optical glasses and other vision products												4	4				3
	HP.4.3		Retail sales and other suppliers of hearing aids												2	2				3
	HP.4.4–.4.9		Retail sales and other suppliers of medical appliances; all other miscellaneous sales and other suppliers of pharmaceuticals and medical goods												5	5				3
HP.5			Provision and administration of public health programs												6	6				3
		Of which	Government sector												4	4				0

		owned:	Private sector												2	2				0
HP.6			General health administration and insurance												7	7				3
		Of which	Government sector												2	2				0
		owned:	Private sector												3	3				0
	HP.6.1		Government administration of health												7	7				2
	HP.6.2		Social security funds												4	4				2
	HP.6.3		Other social insurance												2	2				0
	HP.6.4		Other (private) insurance												4	4				2
	HP.6.3–.6.4		Providers of private insurance												2	3				1
	HP.6.9		All other providers of health administration												4	4				1
HP.7			Other industries (rest of the economy)												4	4				1
	HP.7.1		Establishments as providers of occupational health care services												2	2				1
		Of which	Government sector												2	2				0
		owned:	Private sector												2	2				0
	HP.7.2		Private households as providers of home care												1	1				1
	HP.7.9		All other industries as secondary producers of health care												3	3				1
HP.9			Rest of the world												4	4				1
			Current health care expenditure HP.1–.9												11	8				3

☐ No tables ■ Tables produced

Source: Fernando and Rannan-Eliya 2008.
Note: HP = health providers.

Table A.7 Regional Health Account Data Collections: Variables of ICHA–Health Financing Agents, by Economy, 2006–07

				Bangladesh	China	Hong Kong SAR, China	Mongolia	Nepal	Philippines	Sri Lanka	Taiwan, China	Thailand	Tonga	Vietnam	Total economies	SHA reporting economies		Australia	Japan	Korea, Rep.	Number of economies
HC.1; HC.2			Services of curative and rehabilitative care												7	7					3
HC.1			Services of curative care												5	5					2
HC.2			Services of rehabilitative care												5	5					1
	HC.1.1; HC.2.1		Inpatient curative and rehabilitative care												7	7					3
	HC.1.1		Inpatient curative care												8	6					3
	HC.2.1		Inpatient rehabilitative care												3	3					1
	HC.1.2; HC.2.2		Day cases of curative and rehabilitative care												2	2					1
	HC.1.2		Day cases of curative care												1	1					0
	HC.2.2		Day cases of rehabilitative care												1	1					1
	HC.1.3; HC.2.3		Outpatient curative and rehabilitative care												7	7					3
	HC.1.3		Outpatient curative care												6	5					3
		HC.1.3.1	Basic medical and diagnostic services												7	7					3
		HC.1.3.2	Outpatient dental care												7	7					3
		HC.1.3.3	All other specialised health care												6	6					2
		HC.1.3.9	All other outpatient curative care												6	6					1

	HC.2.3		Outpatient rehabilitative care												2	2				0
	HC.1.4; HC.2.4		Services of curative home and rehabilitative home care												3	3				2
	HC.1.4		Services of curative home care												2	2				2
	HC.2.4		Services of rehabilitative home care												1	1				1
HC.3			Services of long-term nursing care												4	4				3
	HC.3.1		Inpatient long-term nursing care												2	2				3
	HC.3.2		Day cases of long-term nursing care												1	1				1
	HC.3.3		Long-term nursing care: home care												1	1				3
HC.4			Ancillary services to health care												6	6				3
	HC.4.1		Clinical laboratory services												4	4				1
	HC.4.2		Diagnostic imaging												3	3				1
	HC.4.3		Patient transport and emergency rescue												3	3				3
	HC.4.9		All other miscellaneous ancillary services												2	2				1
HC.5			Medical goods dispensed to outpatients												7	7				3
	HC.5.1		Pharmaceuticals and other medical nondurables												9	8				3
		HC.5.1.1	Prescribed medicines												4	4				3
		HC.5.1.2	Over-the-counter medicines												4	4				3
		HC.5.1.3	Other medical nondurables												4	4				2
	HC.5.2		Therapeutic appliances and other medical durables												7	7				3
		HC.5.2.1	Glasses and other vision products												4	4				2

(continued)

Table A.7 *(continued)*

				Bangladesh	*China*	*Hong Kong SAR, China*	*Mongolia*	*Nepal*	*Philippines*	*Sri Lanka*	*Taiwan, China*	*Thailand*	*Tonga*	*Vienam*	*Total economies*	*SHA reporting economies*		*Australia*	*Japan*	*Korea, Rep.*	*Number of economies*
		HC.5.2.2	Orthopedic appliances and other prosthetics	■		■				■		■			4	4			■		1
		HC.5.2.3	Hearing aids	■											1	2		■	■	■	3
		HC.5.2.4	Medicotechnical devices, including wheelchairs												0	0					0
		HC.5.2.9	All other miscellaneous medical durables			■				■					2	2		■	■	■	3
HC.6			Prevention and public health services	■		■	■			■	■	■		■	7	7		■	■	■	3
	HC.6.1		Maternal and child health; family planning and counseling	■		■	■			■			■	■	6	6		■	■		2
	HC.6.2		School health services	■		■				■			■	■	5	5			■		1
	HC.6.3		Prevention of communicable diseases	■		■	■			■				■	5	5		■	■		2
	HC.6.4		Prevention of noncommunicable diseases			■	■			■			■	■	5	5		■			1
	HC.6.5		Occupational health care	■		■				■			■		4	4			■		1
	HC.6.9		All other miscellaneous public health services	■		■	■			■				■	5	5		■			1
HC.7			Health administration and health insurance	■		■	■			■	■	■		■	7	7		■	■	■	3

	HC.7.1		General government administration of health	6	6	3
		HC.7.1.1	General government administration of health (except social security)	5	5	2
		HC.7.1.2	Administration, operation, and support activities of social security funds	2	2	2
	HC.7.2		Health administration and health insurance: private	4	4	2
		HC.7.2.1	Health administration and health insurance: social insurance	2	2	0
		HC.7.2.2	Health administration and health insurance: other private	3	3	2
HC.9			Not specified by kind	2	2	0
			Current health care expenditure HC.1–.9	11	8	3
HC.R.1			Capital formation of health care provider institutions	7	7	3
			Total expenditure HC.1–.9; HC.R.1	6	6	3
HC.R.2			Education and training of health personnel	2	2	1
HC.R.3			Research and development in health	2	2	2
HC.R.4			Food, hygiene, and drinking water control	2	2	1
HC.R.5			Environmental health	2	2	1
HC.R.6			Administration and provision of social services in kind to assist living with disease and impairment	1	1	2

(continued)

Table A.7 *(continued)*

				Bangladesh	*China*	*Hong Kong SAR, China*	*Mongolia*	*Nepal*	*Philippines*	*Sri Lanka*	*Taiwan, China*	*Thailand*	*Tonga*	*Vienam*	*Total economies*	*SHA reporting economies*	*Australia*	*Japan*	*Korea, Rep.*	*Number of economies*
	HC.R.6.1		Social services of long-term care (long-term care other than HC.3)												0					0
	HC.R.6.9		All other services classified under HC.R.6												0					0
HC.R.7			Administration and provision of health related cash benefits												1	1				0
Memorandum items																				
M.1(HC)			Other (non-health care/health-related) goods and services												0					2
M.2(HC)			Total pharmaceuticals and other medical nondurables (including inpatient and other ways of provision)												0					3
M.3(HC)			Total of ancillary services (including inpatient)												0					0

☐ No tables ▨ Tables produced

Source: Fernando and Rannan-Eliya 2008.
Note: HC = health care (functions).

rounds of NHAs but have failed to build local capacity in terms of, for example, systems and staff training.

In light of these constraints, identifying the basic criteria needed to support NHA institutionalization is important. Box A.1 highlights the more salient preconditions necessary at the country-level for NHA institutionalization. However, the criteria described are necessary but

Box A.1

Country-Level Criteria for Institutionalization of NHAs in Low- and Middle-Income Settings

The following criteria have been identified as useful in contributing to NHA institutionalization at the country level:

- Identification of the right "home" for the NHA (for example, the central bureau of statistics, ministry of finance, or ministry of health), contingent on where the greatest capacity lies for routine collection of nationally relevant and internationally comparable health expenditure data. Australia, Mexico, and Thailand are examples of countries that have met this criterion.
- Ability of selected health expenditure resource-tracking methodologies to cross-apply to either an SHA or an NHA so that national efforts can be used in conjunction with other global resource-tracking efforts. In two years time, with the completion of the SHA II revisions conducted by WHO, all methodologies should cross-apply to SHA II.
- Identification of the preferred timing for institutionalization of the NHA (for example, during a World Bank Country Assistance Strategy review, during a Medium-Term Expenditure Framework exercise, or during the planning or evaluation stages of health financing reform).
- Provision of incentives, both nationally and globally, for countries to institutionalize NHAs.
- Availability of funding (for example, through a donor-coordinated funding mechanism).
- Illustration of ways to apply NHA estimates for advocacy purposes by non-government organizations and civil society to hold governments and donors accountable.
- Identification of ways to enhance coordination among donors to minimize conflicting or duplicative demands on countries for health expenditure data.

Sources: World Bank interviews and surveys; external interviews and surveys.

not sufficient conditions for successful institutionalization. Importantly, success requires political will and ownership over the NHA development process. Without country ownership and, hence, demand for an NHA, the likelihood of an NHA being conducted as a one-off activity (rather than as part of a systematic, routine data collection exercise) is bound to increase.

Reference

Fernando, Tharanga, and Ravi P. Rannan-Eliya. 2008. "Evaluation of the 2005, 2006, and 2007 Regional Health Accounts Data Collections in the Asia-Pacific Region." Presentation to the Fourth Organisation for Economic Co-operation and Development–Korea Policy Centre–Asia-Pacific National Health Accounts Network Meeting of Regional Health Accounts Experts, Asia-Pacific National Health Accounts Network, Seoul, July 8–10.

APPENDIX B

Medical Tourism in East Asia and the Pacific

Emergence of Medical Tourism in East Asia and the Pacific

Large investments in health care technology and training of medical personnel have facilitated the development of a medical market in East Asian and Pacific countries with high-quality, low-cost care relative to members of the Organisation for Economic Co-operation and Development. Expensive care and long waiting lists, combined with low-cost travel and increasing incomes in richer countries, have contributed to an escalating flow of patients to poorer countries for medical procedures. In 2006, the global market for medical tourism was estimated to be worth US$60 billion and is predicted to reach US$100 billion by 2012 (Hansen 2008).

Trading of health services is not a new concept and was, as early as 1973, recognized as a commercial activity by the International Union of Travel Officials. However, the liberalization of trade has significantly increased the spread of information, products, and services and has contributed to an explosive growth in the trade of health services in developing countries (Bookman and Bookman 2007).

As a result of the East Asian financial crisis in 1997, many private hospitals in Asia began pursuing health revenues beyond their borders—particularly in Thailand, where the private sector initially led the growth of medical tourism. The Bumrungrad Hospital in Bangkok has been recognized as a main source for growth in attracting overseas patients and for spurring the emergence of medical tourism in Thailand. Asian countries are currently generating approximately US$1.3 billion a year in revenues from medical tourism. This growth is expected to continue with a compound annual growth rate of 19 percent, resulting in an estimated revenue of US$4.4 billion by 2012 (Teh 2007).

However, despite the leading role of the private sector, a well-functioning partnership between the private and public sectors is essential for continued growth in medical tourism. Involvement of the government through the ministries of health, tourism, transportation, and trade plays a crucial role in promoting a successful and sustainable medical tourism industry.

Government Involvement

As the success and potential of the private sector to attract foreign patients to Asian countries became more apparent, government participation intensified to maximize the direct gain from increased health revenues and to maximize the overall benefits of tourism (Yoosuf 2004). In Malaysia, the government supported the development of the medical tourism industry by establishing the National Committee for the Promotion of Health Tourism. Similarly, the governments of Hong Kong SAR, China, and Singapore have launched an intensive marketing campaign that promotes their medical capabilities and targets foreign countries (Teh and Chu 2005). In early 2006, the Philippine government initiated a national campaign in an attempt to promote the country as a central provider of medical care and wellness in East Asia. In the same year, a bill establishing the Medical Tourism Bureau was proposed in the House of Representatives to administer the growing market of medical tourism in the country (Tagpuan Tambayang Pinoy 2007).

The increase in employment opportunities generated by medical tourism demands a greater supply of highly skilled human capital. An important role of governments is to ensure sufficient resource allocation for the training of medical personnel to meet the increasing demand generated from the inflow of foreign patients. According to the Ministry of Health, between 1999 and 2006, Malaysia saw an increase in the number of doctors from 15,503 to 21,937, although no data are available on what proportion of this increase was generated as a direct response to medical tourism.

Avoiding bottlenecks and fostering an environment for business are other central roles for governments, achieved through sufficient development of infrastructure (including communication, transportation, banking, water, and sanitation) as well as balanced taxation that does not stifle investment. An appropriate level of taxation will promote a high level of investment while distributing revenues to the public sector and ensuring access to health care for the local population. It should be noted, however, that in many countries with a low appetite for taxes, increasing taxes might be politically unpopular, thereby limiting the government's capability to redirect resources to the public sector. Furthermore, by reducing legal and regulatory barriers and providing adequate subsidies, the government will encourage trade and investment in the private sector. For instance, through the 2004 Investment Priorities Plan, the Philippine government effectively stimulated investment incentives for the medical tourism industry by reducing tariffs on hospital equipment imports (Global Nation 2004). In 2005, the Malaysian government announced the extension of venture capital funds by US$260 million for small and medium-size enterprises related to the national medical tourism market (*Travel Daily News* 2005).

Enabling Attributes of East Asia and the Pacific

Several characteristics of East Asian and Pacific countries make them attractive locations for medical tourists.

Medical Costs and Availability of Care

The high cost of medical procedures in many other countries remains one of the main reasons medical tourists are attracted to Asian countries. These costs are particularly high in the United States, where the average heart surgery could cost US$50,000, while the price for the same procedure would be US$20,000 in Singapore and US$12,000 in Thailand (Teh and Chu 2005). Table B.1 further displays the significant cost benefits of medical procedures in East Asian countries compared to Western countries such as the United States.

The 44 million uninsured people in the United States who are forced to pay out-of-pocket for medical treatments compose a primary market pursuing medical procedures overseas. In addition, given the millions of underinsured people (resulting from partial coverage or ineligibility for certain medical procedures), U.S. insurance companies have begun

Table B.1 Comparison of Costs for Medical Procedures

	Costs (US$)			
Procedure	*Thailand*	*Malaysia*	*Singapore*	*United States*
Mastectomy	9,000	—	12,400	24,000–34,000
Coronary artery bypass surgery	12,000	7,000–10,700	20,000	122,000–177,000
Hip replacement	12,000	4,600–6,100	12,000	44,000–63,000
Knee replacement	10,000	4,600–5,500	13,000	41,000–59,000

Sources: Association of Private Hospitals of Malaysia 2008; Raad 2008.
Note: — = not available.

to include options for overseas treatment. For example, in early 2007, the BlueCross BlueShield Association began a partnership with the Bumrungrad Hospital in Thailand and World Access (a medical travel service organization) to promote lower-cost overseas medical care. Although BlueCross Blue Shield does not cover the cost of medical care in Thailand, the partnership will provide U.S. patients with hospital information, travel and accommodation arrangements,and prenegotiated discount rates at an affiliated hospital (Reese 2007).

In many European countries with universal health care, high costs are less of an issue; avoiding long waiting lists is the primary reason that wealthy individuals who are able to pay for immediate health services seek overseas treatment. Unavailability of certain medical procedures in one's home country provides an additional reason to pursue health care beyond national borders. It should be noted that, conversely, unavailability of medical procedures is one of the main reasons that patients from developing nations seek treatment in richer ones. One such example is the stream of patients from Tonga to New Zealand.

Quality Health Care

A growing number of private hospitals in East Asia and the Pacific are offering high-quality care, perhaps in line with Western health care quality. The success rate for coronary bypass surgery in India has been reported to be as high as 98.7 percent, compared with 97.5 percent in the United States (Hansen 2008), although data are not risk adjusted. However, despite an increase in success stories from medical tourism destinations, recent reports suggest a great discrepancy in quality of care among various hospitals (Kaiser Family Foundation 2008). Hence, quality of care remains a central concern for foreign patients considering pursuing care beyond their countries' borders. For that reason, hospitals seeking to attract medical tourists make considerable efforts to improve their quality of care and establish their international credibility.

The World Health Organization endorses the Joint Commission International (JCI), which provides quality assurance and safety control of health services for hospitals around the world. The JCI is an affiliate of the Joint Commission Resources, which accredits more than 90 percent of U.S. hospitals and is composed of a 16-member task force from all regions of the world to guarantee international applicability.

Although the JCI accreditation standards are similar to those carried out by the Joint Commission in the United States, they are adapted to the local cultures, laws, and regulations of any specific country. To earn a three-year accreditation by the JCI, hospitals must fulfill 300 standards and 1,200 measurable elements observed through scores and surveys. At the end of the three-year period, hospitals must undergo a full on-site survey that uses a systems approach (tracer methodology) and is conducted by a team of doctors, nurses, and administrators from the JCI during a period of three to five days (Timmons 2007).[1] By 2007, approximately 140 hospitals in 26 countries worldwide had been accredited by the JCI, including 30 hospitals from East Asia and the Pacific (table B.2).

Although the JCI cannot fully guarantee the safety of patients seeking medical care abroad, the accreditation process does reduce risk through quality controls, enhancements of patient care, and safety precautions. In addition, JCI-accredited hospitals are required to involve patients in the care procedures and to communicate in a language that the patient can understand. Patient confidentiality and privacy are required, along

Table B.2 Number of Hospitals Accredited by the JCI in East Asia and the Pacific, 2008

Country	*Number of accredited hospitals*
China	3
Hong Kong SAR, China	2
Indonesia	1
Korea, Rep.	1
Malaysia	1
Philippines	2
Singapore	13
Taiwan, China	3
Thailand	4

Source: Data from Joint Commission International.

with the transfer of information and recommendations to the patient for potential follow-up care in his or her home country (Timmons 2007). Moreover, the JCI and several other nonprofit organizations, such as the Medical Travel Authority and the Medical Tourism Association, provide information on their websites regarding available treatments and prior outcomes and provide interviews with former medical tourists. These materials facilitate increased trust in the organization's health care services, thereby enhancing the probability that patients will engage in medical tourism.

Significant time and resources must be allocated for training medical workers for the international medical services trade. Sustaining a high number of students in tertiary education is a central focus for Asian countries to maintain their competitiveness in the global market. A good working relationship between the public and private sectors is central to reaching the appropriate level of human capacity. Such a relationship is particularly important in Malaysia, where government expenditures on tertiary education represent 33.3 percent of the total government budget on education. Moreover, medical personnel from Asian countries are also trained abroad. Many Asian countries support their medical students in obtaining medical expertise from Europe or the United States on the condition that they will return to work in their home countries when they complete their studies (Bookman and Bookman 2007). Because it has U.S.-trained medical personnel, the Bumrungrad hospital in Thailand promotes itself as an American-managed hospital; thus, it overcomes credibility concerns regarding quality care for foreign patients.

Telemedicine

Investment in medical technology, along with an explosive growth in information and telecommunications technology, has laid the ground for an emerging market within medical care that is becoming known as *telehealth*, or *telemedicine*. Telemedicine facilitates medical education and furthers treatment and diagnosis across borders and countries, bringing a new dimension to medical practice. By providing clinical consultations, diagnosis, or even laboratory samples for analysis through electronic mediums and regular mail, telemedicine offers a cost-effective and speedy alternative for countries suffering from expensive care or long waiting lists. The telemedicine alternative has created not only an opportunity for foreign patients to pursue medical care without leaving their country or even their city, but also a new frontier of medical practice that could potentially create an additional source of revenues for developing countries.

Developing countries in Asia are paying increased attention to telemedicine, with new facilities emerging in India, Malaysia, the Philippines, and Thailand. Networks of telemedicine units and hospitals are forming in East Asia and the Pacific to accommodate the new telemedicine market. In Thailand alone, 17 national telemedicine units are currently linked to 3 public teaching hospitals, 20 community hospitals, 7 provincial hospitals, and 14 regional hospitals (Janjaroen and Supakankunti 2002).

Although telemedicine is different from medical tourism, it could serve as an important entry point for many patients who are initially hesitant to receive care in foreign countries. Repeated treatment and diagnosis by telemedicine providers from foreign countries could significantly reduce patients' existing barriers, such as concern about the quality of care or lack of familiarity with doctors and hospitals overseas, and could ultimately spur the development of medical tourism.

Scope of Medical Tourism in East Asia and the Pacific

Malaysia, Singapore, and Thailand are currently the three major leaders in the medical tourism industry in East Asia and the Pacific. Although estimates of the scope and market share of medical tourism vary among sources, one report estimates that Thailand will attract as much as 47 percent of the US$4 billion in revenues that are expected to be generated from medical tourism in East Asia and the Pacific by 2012, making Thailand the most popular destination for medical tourism in the region (*Thailand Report* 2007).

The competition for medical tourists among East Asian countries is likely to intensify as new medical destinations emerge. The Philippines represents the fifth-largest medical tourism destination in East Asia, trailing Thailand, India, Malaysia, and Singapore, respectively. Taiwan, China, has also made serious attempts to enter the forefront of the medical tourism industry. In 2007, Taiwan's Department of Health (DoH) declared its aspiration to generate NT$7 billion (about US$216 million) from foreign patients within the next three years (Jaw-Pyng and Wu 2007).

Thailand

A growing private sector has served as the main actor in achieving success in attracting foreign patients to Thailand. Of the 1,200 hospitals in Thailand, 471 are private and most are located in Bangkok (Mongkolporn 2005). The Bumrungrad hospital has been recognized as a major leader in attracting medical tourism to Thailand and was the first hospital to be accredited by the JCI. Bumrungrad hospital's 554 beds and its capacity to receive about 3,500 patients per day have made it the largest hospital in Southeast Asia (*Thailand Report* 2007).

In addition to low prices for medical procedures, Thailand offers a variety of attractions, such as low-cost living, a tourist-friendly culture, and a relaxing environment for recuperation. Thailand has been particularly successful in attracting foreign patients from around the world relative to Australia, Malaysia, and Singapore, which have depended heavily on a concentrated source of patients (predominantly from Indonesia). As figure B.1 displays, Japan has the largest share of foreign patients in Thailand (with 131,584 patients in 2002), followed by the United States, the United Kingdom, other Asian countries, Germany, and the Middle East (Mongkolporn 2005).

Most medical treatments for foreign visitors have, until now, been primarily focused on lower-value treatments such as cosmetic surgery, dentistry, Lasik (refractive eye surgery), and general medical checkups. To stay ahead of the competition, particularly that of Singapore, a few hospitals (such as Bumrungrad and Bangkok general hospitals) are investing in so-called higher-value treatments, including hip replacement, organ transplant, and heart bypass.

Because of its great success, medical tourism has been transformed from an alternative economic activity to an important source of revenue for Thailand. In 2004, foreign patients reportedly contributed 18 percent

Figure B.1 Foreign Patients Treated in Thailand, 2002

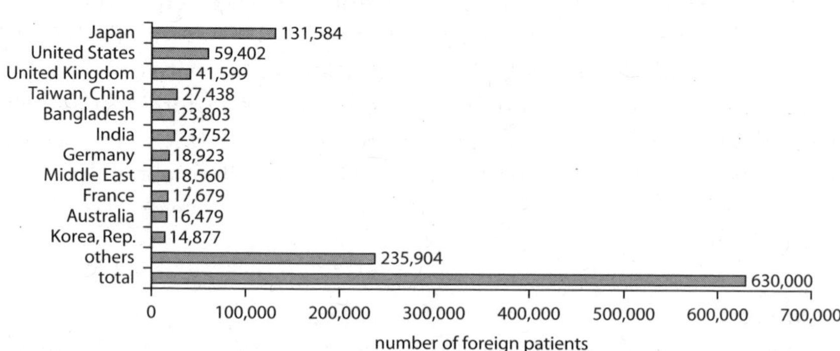

Source: Data from Mongkolporn 2005.

of the total health revenues in Thailand (figure B.2). Additionally, as figure B.3 indicates, the number of foreign patients and the revenue generated from medical tourism in Thailand have been steadily rising and are likely to continue to grow.

The impressive growth of Thailand's medical tourism industry has increased the involvement of Thailand's initially passive government, resulting in several initiatives to support and promote the growing industry. To support the increasing demand for medical tourism, the government has simplified visa procedures for traveling to Thailand and has planned a 10-year investment of US$10 billion to US$15 billion for the construction of new hospitals (Teh 2007). Moreover, in addition to heavily investing in new technologies and internationally recognized quality certifications, leading hospitals such as Bumrungrad hospital

Figure B.2 Revenues from Domestic and Foreign Patients in Thailand, 2004

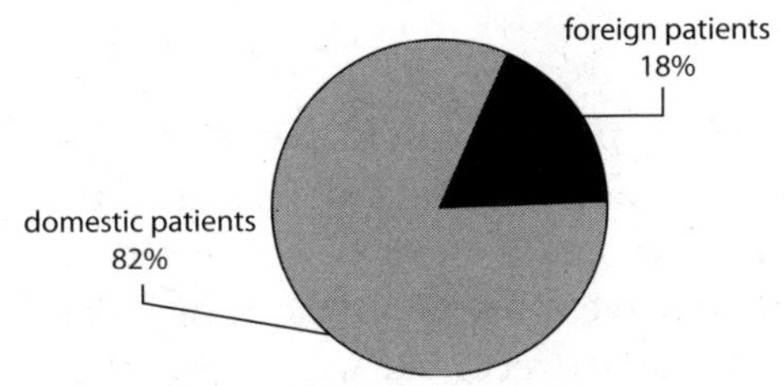

Source: Data from Mongkolporn 2005.

Figure B.3 Number of Foreign Patients Treated in Thai Hospitals and Revenue Generated, 2002–05

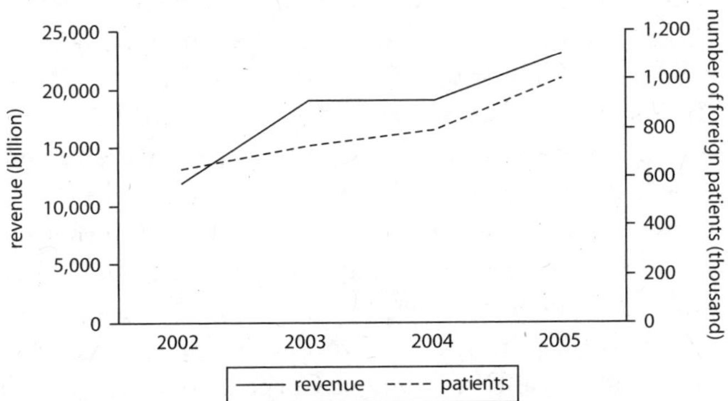

Source: Data from Danish Trade Council 2006.
Note: Figures for 2005 are estimates.

have employed a variety of marketing mechanisms. For example, relationships and affiliations with travel agents offer patients packages that combine airfare, medical treatment, and sightseeing.

Given its leading role in medical tourism, Thailand still faces strong competition in the region. India and Malaysia offer price incentives similar to those of Thailand, whereas Singapore is significantly better equipped to perform higher-value procedures, mainly because of large investments in high-technology hardware. Security in Thailand also causes concern for medical tourism and the tourism industry in general. Escalating violence in southern Thailand has thus far not affected the inflow of tourists to the capital. However, the explosions in Bangkok on New Year's Eve of 2006 might influence foreign patients to favor countries such as Singapore, despite Thailand's current price advantage. In the near future, Thailand may boost its high-technology investments and continue marketing for quality, higher-end surgical treatment.

Malaysia

Unlike Thailand, Malaysia has seen a higher level of government involvement and control in promoting the emergence of the medical tourism sector. Malaysia has become a major player in attracting medical tourism, with price advantages similar to those in India and Thailand. In 2004, Malaysian hospitals recorded a 25 percent increase in foreign patients, offering medical services to approximately 130,000 medical tourists. This considerable growth in medical tourism was estimated to have generated US$27.6 million in revenues, making medical tourism the fastest-growing sector of the tourist market and an important source of income for Malaysia (Bookman and Bookman 2007).

In an attempt to catch up with Singapore and Thailand, Malaysia has launched several marketing initiatives aimed at attracting foreign patients. In a strategic plan for 2001 to 2005, the Malaysian government identified 44 of the 224 private hospitals that were to be involved in the medical tourism market, 35 of which were to be marketed by the Ministry of Health (Henderson 2003). The Internet has been actively used as a low-cost marketing alternative; in 2006, the government of Malaysia launched a website to promote the country's medical services (Ngah 2006). In addition, recent seminars organized by the Malaysia External Trade Development Corporation, such as "Malaysian Healthcare Services," have been promoting Malaysia as a health care destination. Hotels have begun to provide packages, including medical

Figure B.4 Number of Foreign Patients in Malaysia, 2005–07

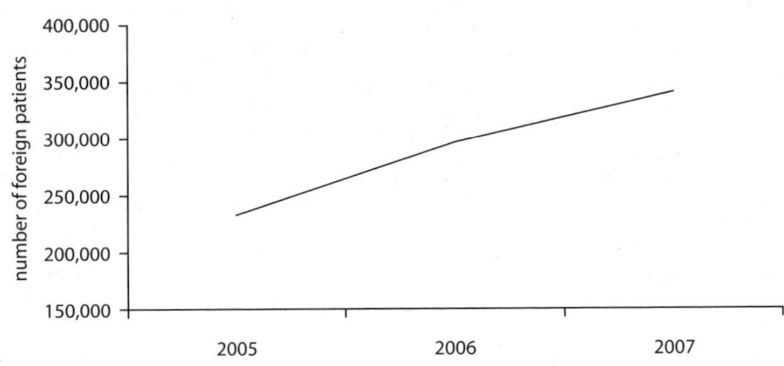

Source: Data from Cruez 2008.

checkups and recommendations of Malaysian hospitals. Moreover, leading Malaysian hospitals have introduced special services to assist foreign patients with travel arrangements, accommodations, and visa applications (William 2008a).

At present, Indonesian patients constitute nearly 70 percent of medical tourists in Malaysia. However, increased marketing to other regions has contributed to a greater diversification of patients (Ganesan 2008). By assuring patients of its religious sensitivity in such matters as prayers and *halal* food, Malaysia has attracted an increasing number of patients from Islamic countries (Henderson 2003). As figure B.4 shows, the heavy promotion of Malaysia as a destination for medical tourism has proven successful, with a steady increase in the number of foreign patients from 2005 to 2007. In addition, the Association of Private Hospitals of Malaysia has projected an annual 30 percent increase of foreign patients by 2010, amounting to approximately 849,000 medical tourists (Ganesan 2008).

Singapore

Singapore has long been acknowledged as an established medical destination in Asia. Although Malaysia and Thailand have a price advantage in attracting foreign patients, Singapore has marketed itself as the center for top-quality care and still offers a considerable price advantage compared with medical costs in the United States and probably other Western countries (table B.1). A focus on biomedical research, along with investment in the latest medical equipment, has enabled Singapore to provide the most advanced treatments and therapies and has contributed to an advantage over regional competitors in attracting medical tourists. In addition to higher-end surgeries, Singapore has established a market for organ transport, joint replacement, and reproductive and fertility issues (Healthbase 2006). Low corruption, political stability, cleanliness, and first-rate infrastructure further reinforce Singapore's reputation as a trusted center of medical excellence, resulting in additional gains compared to competitors in the region (such as India and Thailand) that struggle with urban slums and civil unrest (William 2008b). Both private and public hospitals participate in the medical tourism industry, and both entities have been collaborating with Western hospitals such as Johns Hopkins University Hospital and Kaiser to ensure their medical excellence.

According to Health Tourism in Asia, Singapore attracts more than 200,000 international patients every year.[2] This number is expected to grow by 20 percent every year, and the government of Singapore has set a target of 1 million medical tourists by 2012. The large revenue generated from medical tourism in Singapore allows for continued investment in the latest medical equipment, which will solidify Singapore's preeminent position as a destination for medical treatment (William 2008b).

The Philippines

To promote the market for medical tourism and to begin attracting foreign patients to the Philippines, President Gloria Macapagal-Arroyo issued an executive order in 2004 to form a partnership between the private and public sectors. As a result, government-led agencies, including the DoH, the Department of Tourism, and the Department of Trade and Industry, joined with the private sector to create the Philippine Medical Tourism Program (PMTP) with aims to maximize the potential benefits of the medical tourism industry (PMTP 2008).

The PMTP offers a combination of medical care from both public and private hospitals, along with various wellness services, vacations, sightseeing tours, and shopping packages. The Medical City and St. Luke's Medical Center in Manila are currently JCI-accredited, and other hospitals are undergoing periodic accreditations by DoH to monitor management of service delivery and entry to services and to ensure patient rights, safety, and proper environment (PMTP 2008). Because of advancements in its medical system in recent years, the Philippines now provides a wider variety of treatments to foreign patients (box B.1).

PMTP's strategy of offering price and accommodation incentives similar to those of Thailand has made the Philippines a more competitive player in the medical tourism market. In 2007, the Philippines attracted an estimated 200,000 foreign patients from various parts of the world

Box B.1

Selected Available Treatments for Medical Tourists in the Philippines

Medical tourists come to the Philippines for the following treatments, among others:

- Bariatric surgery
- Bone marrow transplantation
- Cancer cellular therapy
- Cardiac valvular surgery
- Cardiology
- Cataract and refractive surgery
- Clinical nutrition
- Coronary angiography
- Coronary artery bypass graft surgery
- Cosmetic and plastic surgery
- Dentistry
- Ear, nose, and throat surgery
- Endocrinology
- Gamma knife neurosurgery
- Gynecological surgery
- Hematology
- Immunology and allergology
- Infectious diseases (tropical medicine)
- Knee and hip replacement
- Laparoscopic cholecystectomy
- Lithotripsy
- Medical oncology and radiotherapy
- Nephrology
- Neurology
- Percutaneous coronary intervention
- Pulmonary and critical care medicine
- Rheumatology
- Vascular surgery

Source: PMTP 2008.

(PNA 2007). As figure B.5 shows, North America represents, by far, the largest source of foreign patients in the Philippines, followed by Northeast Asia, the Federated States of Micronesia, and Europe.

Risks and Challenges for Medical Tourism in Developing Countries

Achieving international accreditation for safe, high-quality care remains a priority for all developing countries aiming to solidify and further improve their position as leading medical tourism destinations. Although many hospitals, such as the Bumrungrad hospital in Thailand, have already gained international acceptance for medical excellence, the quality of hospitals continues to vary. Some hospitals are still reported as low quality, thus enhancing skepticism about the overall quality of medical tourism and ultimately jeopardizing a country's full potential

Figure B.5 Share of Medical Tourists in the Philippines from Selected Regions, 2007

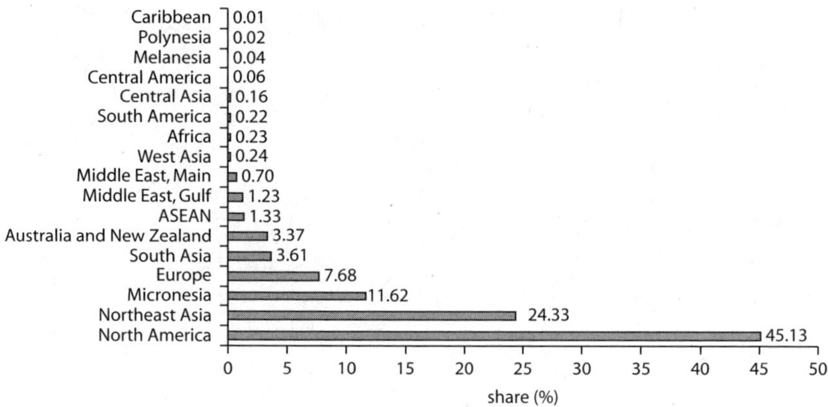

Source: Department of Health, the Philippines 2008.
Note: ASEAN = Association of Southeast Asian Nations.

for attracting foreign patients. Therefore, international accreditation from the JCI and new information websites generated by the host country will continue to play an important role in upholding quality standards and reducing concerns about credibility.

Large travel distances can also deter patients from considering treatment abroad. It has been argued that the risks of developing complications such as venous thrombosis or infections as a result of long flights are exacerbated after medical procedures (Kaiser Family Foundation 2008). By offering medical packages that include vacation and wellness treatments with sufficient recuperation time for particular procedures, hospitals could minimize postprocedure risks. If complications during or after a procedure were to occur, local laws and local authorities would have the primary responsibility of resolving the matter. The JCI does not have any initial role in malpractice cases but could potentially facilitate the conflict resolution process in the long term by actively working with hospitals and local authorities to standardize procedures and by making information on steps to take in the case of complications easily accessible to future patients.

Implications for Financing and Delivery of Care Services in the Region

Despite the apparent benefits of revenue generation from medical tourism, several concerns have been raised regarding the side effects of the emerging market in developing countries. The issue of equity (that is, access to affordable and high-quality health care for the local population) is among the primary concerns. In other words, as many developing countries struggle to provide universal quality health care to their citizens, one must question whether governments should stop marketing their medical services to foreign nations when the demands for health care of the local population have not been met (Pachanee and Wibulpolprasert 2006).

It has been argued that equitable access to quality health care for the poor will worsen because of the growing medical tourism market. With increasing government focus on meeting private hospitals' increasing number of medical tourists, the public health system has lost necessary and significant funds as well as human resources. The issue of "brain drain" of human resources from public facilities to private hospitals is exacerbated as a result of the increasing demand from medical tourists (Bookman and Bookman 2007).

According to the Ministry of Health in Thailand, most of the approximately B 200 billion generated from medical tourism has benefited private hospitals, while the public health system has experienced worsened working conditions for government-employed nurses and doctors as well as increased brain drain of public doctors to private health care. Of the 30,000 positions required to staff the public health care system in Thailand, thousands remain unfilled, partly because of the priority government gives to the private sector and medical tourism (*Nation* 2008). The large inflow of foreign patients with higher purchasing power has contributed to higher prices for private hospital services, which places additional pressure on the already underfunded universal public health care system in Thailand because middle-income Thais cannot afford private health care (Poopat 2008).

Medical tourism has become an important source of revenue for East Asian countries and may continue to grow in coming years. Concerns raised about the detrimental effect on public health care of increasing the focus on medical tourism and private hospitals might be mitigated by policies that redistribute revenues or increase the local population's access to international facilities.

Increased revenues generated by the medical tourism industry in developing countries would provide an opportunity for governments to collect taxes and reallocate sufficient resources for improving the local population's access to quality health care. Because the income from one foreign patient is estimated to cover the cost for treating approximately three local patients, permitting foreign patients into public facilities could alleviate resource deficits and reduce the brain drain from the public sector (Benavides 2002). However, this practice would have to be regulated to avoid sacrificing access to care for the country's residents. Allocating sufficient resources to uphold high-level working conditions and to make salaries competitive with the private sector will be crucial in reducing brain drain and promoting high-quality care in the public sector.

At the same time, a number of issues remain unanswered, including the following:

- Effects of medical tourism on the economy and societies of the host countries
- Cost of the investment versus the revenue earned
- Percentage of revenue that reaches the public sector versus the private sector
- Effect of international regulation on medical tourism

Notes

1. For more information on the JCI standard scoring system visit, http://www.jointcommissioninternational.org/.
2. See the Health Tourism in Asia website at http://www.healthtourisminasia.com.

References

Association of Private Hospitals of Malaysia. 2008.

Benavides, David Díaz. 2002. 'Trade Policies and Export of Health Services: A Development Perspective." In *Trade in Health Services: Global, Regional and Country Perspectives*, ed. Nick Drager and Cesar Vieira, 53–69. Washington, DC: Pan American Health Organization and World Health Organization. http://www.who.int/trade/en/THpart2chap5.pdf.

Bookman, Milica Z., and Karla R. Bookman. 2007. *Medical Tourism in Developing Countries*. New York: Palgrave Macmillan.

Cruez, Annie Freeda. 2008. "Healthy Outlook for Health Tourism: Malaysia Is Increasing in Popularity among Foreigners Seeking Medical Treatment." *New Straits Times*, July 15. http://www.malaysiahealthcare.com/15072008.htm.

Danish Trade Council. 2006.

Department of Health, Philippines. 2008. "Partial Statistics of Medical Travelers from January to December 2007." Department of Health, Manila.

Ganesan, Vasantha. 2008. "Medical Tourism Revenue Seen Growing 30pc Yearly." *New Straits Times,* March 10. http://www.malaysiahealthcare.com/medicaltourism.htm.

Global Nation. 2004.

Hansen, Fred. 2008. "A Revolution in Healthcare: Medicine Meets the Marketplace." *Institute of Public Affairs Review* 59 (4): 43–45.

Healthbase. 2006. "Medical Tourism in Singapore: Healthcare beyond Boundaries." https://www.healthbase.com/hb/pages/medical-tourism-in-singapore.jsp.

Henderson, Joan C. 2003. "Healthcare Tourism in Southeast Asia." *Tourism Review International* 7 (3–4): 111–21.

Janjaroen, Wattana S., and Siripen Supakankunti. 2002. "International Trade in Health Services in the Millennium: The Case of Thailand." In *Trade in Health Services: Global, Regional, and Country Perspectives,* 87–106, ed. Nick Drager and Cesar Vieira. Washington, DC: Pan American Health Organization and World Health Organization.

Jaw-Pyng, Hwang, and Lilian Wu. 2007." Taiwan Promoting Medical Tourism Project in New York." Ministry of the Interior, Taiwan, China.

Kaiser Family Foundation. 2008. "Medical Tourism Business Projected to Grow Eightfold by 2010, Study Finds." *Kaiser Health News Daily Report,* September 28. *http://www.kaiserhealthnews.org/daily-reports/2008/september/23/dr00054607.aspx?referrer=search.*

Mongkolporn, Veerasak. 2005. "Demand for and Supply of Medical Services for Foreign Patients: An Exploratory Study on the Impact of Human Resources in Public Health Sector in Thailand." Presentation, International Health Policy Program, Nonthaburi, Thailand, January 7. http://ihppthaigov.net/presentation/attachjournal/49/PDF/PDF1.pdf.

Nation. 2008. "Public Health Must Come First: A Balance Is Needed between the Business of Medical Tourism and the Protection of the State Health System." *The Nation,* February 6. http://www.nationmultimedia.com/2008/02/06/opinion/opinion_30064555.php.

Ngah, Zalina Maizan. 2006. "Malaysia Launches Health Tourism Website." Malaysian National News Agency, May 1. http://www.globehealthtours.com/medical_news/labels/Medical%20Tourism%20Destinations.htm.

Pachanee, Cha-aim, and Suwit Wibulpolprasert. 2006. "Incoherent Policies on Universal Coverage of Health Insurance and Promotion of International Trade in Health Services in Thailand." *Health Policy and Planning* 21 (4): 310–18.

PMTP (Philippine Medical Tourism Program). 2008.

PNA (Philippines News Agency). 2007. "Medical Tourism Earned $200M." *Asia Pulse,* November 27.

Poopat, Thana. 2008. "'Medical Hub' Push Taking a Ruinous Toll on Public Hospitals." *The Nation* June 4. http://www.nationmultimedia.com/2008/06/04/opinion/opinion_30074699.php.

Raad, Firas. 2008. "Medical Tourism in the Developing World." Doctoral dissertation, Harvard University, Cambridge, MA.

Reese, Shelly. 2007. "Care Beyond Borders: As Consumer Interest in Medical Tourism Grows, Phenomenon Remains Leap of Faith for Payers." *Managed Healthcare Executive,* May 1. http://managedhealthcareexecutive.modernmedicine.com/mhe/article/articleDetail.jsp?id=424948.

Tagpuan Tambayang Pinoy. 2007. "Philippines Joins the Medical Tourism Bandwagon." Tagpuan Tambayang Pinoy, June 27. http://tagpuan.com/philippines-joins-the-medical-tourism-bandwagon/.

Teh, Ivy. 2007. "Healthcare Tourism in Thailand: Pain Ahead?" *Asia Pacific Biotech News* 11(8): 493–97.

Teh, Ivy, and Calvin Chu. 2005. "Supplementing Growth with Medical Tourism." *Asia Pacific Biotech News* 9(8): 306–11.

Thailand Report. 2007. "The Medical Tourism Boom." *Thailand Report,* February 1.

Timmons, Karen. 2007. "The Value of Accreditation: Why Americans Needing Health Care Abroad Should Choose JCI-Accredited Facilities." *Medical Tourism Magazine,* October 17.

Travel Daily News. 2005.

William, E. 2008a. "Malaysia is Banking on Innovative Healthcare to Lure Foreign Patients." Medical Tourism: Focus Report. *Times.*

———. 2008b. "Singaporeans Claim Regional Advantage on Healthcare." Medical Tourism: Focus Report. *Times.*

Yoosuf, Abdul Sattar. 2004. "South-East Asia Regional Perspective." In *Trade and Health: Compilation of Presentations Made at the Inter-regional Workshop, New Delhi, October 2004,* 140–43. New Delhi: World Health Organization Regional Office for South-East Asia.

APPENDIX C

Health Financing in East Asia and the Pacific: Review of Project Appraisal Documents

Year	Country	Type of operation	Resource mobilization	Resource allocation	Pooling	Social health insurance	Benefits package	Contracting	Provider payment	Demand-side financing	Monitoring and evaluating health financing	Governance	Other	Health financing	Total project financing (US$ million)
2002	Cambodia	1st HSSP													31.7
2003	Indonesia	Health Workforce and Services Project													429.4
2003	Tonga	HSSP											NHAs	0.70	10.9
2003	Vietnam	2nd PRSO													100.0
2004	Vietnam	3rd PRSO													100.0
2005	Lao PDR	1st PRSO											Public expenditure management		10.0
2005	Lao PDR	Health Services Improvement Project												1.29	15.0
2005	Lao PDR	1st PRSO													10.0
2005	Philippines	Women's Health Project											PBF		38.0
2005	Vietnam	4th PRSO													100.0
2005	Vietnam	HIV/AIDS Project													35.0

2006	Indonesia	WSS											Incentive grants		275.1
2006	Lao PDR	2nd PRSO													8.0
2006	Lao PDR	Avian Flu Project													4.0
2006	Philippines	HSSP											MTEF		110.0
2006	Vietnam	5th PRSO													100.0
2006	Vietnam	Mekong Regional HSSP													70.0
2006	Vietnam	North Upland HSSP												10.00	60.0
2007	Cambodia	Avian Flu Project													11.0
2007	Lao PDR	3rd PRSO													10.0
2007	Solomon Islands	HSSP											PER and NHAs		1.5
2007	Timor-Leste	HSSP											Donor aid integration		20.3
2007	Vietnam	6th PRSO													175.0
2008	Cambodia	2nd HSSP											Aid fragmentation	14.00	204.0
2008	China	Rural Health Project											NHA in provinces	48.00	50.0
2008	Lao PDR	4th PRSO													10.0
2008	Mongolia	Avian Flu Project													4.7
2008	Samoa	Health Sector Management II											PER		3.0
													Total	**74.0**	**1,996.6**

Source: Project appraisal documents for each project, World Bank.
Note: HSSP = Health Sector Strategy Plan; MTEF = Medium-Term Expenditure Framework; NHA = national health account; PBF = performance-based financing; PER = Public Expenditure Review; PRSO = Poverty Reduction Support Operation; WSS = water supply and sanitation. Shading indicates that the project covers a topical area.

Index

Boxes, figures, notes, and tables are indicated by b, f, n, and t following page numbers.

A

absenteeism, worker, 24, 25, 225–26, 225*t*, 228
accountability in health care facilities, 202, 213, 214, 217, 218
Affiliated Network for Social Accountability for East Asia and the Pacific (ANSA-EAP), 222, 223*b*
age-dependency ratios, 11, 39, 40*t*
alcohol, taxes on, 15, 103–4
allocative efficiency, 2, 9, 243–45
Amai Pakpak Hospital, 207
American Samoa
  health spending resource-tracking activity, 268*t*
  national health accounts in, 266
ANSA-Africa, 223*f*
Argentina, debit cards in, 193
Asia-Pacific National Health Accounts Network (APNHAN), 267
Askeskin program (Indonesia), 156
Askes program (Indonesia), 88, 123–24, 156
Association of Private Hospitals of Malaysia, 297
Ateneo School of Government (Philippines), 222
Australia
  medical tourism and, 294
  national health accounts in, 267
  payment systems in, 186
  voluntary insurance in, 77
Austria, social insurance contributions in, 76
autonomy of hospitals. *See* hospital autonomy

B

Baeza, Cristian, xx
Baht Scheme. *See* 30 Baht Scheme (Thailand)
Bangladesh
  catastrophic payments in, 111
  conditional cash transfer program in, 190
  national health accounts and, 267
barangay (village) health stations, 205, 206
Basic Medical Insurance (BMI) scheme (China), 179–80*b*

bed occupancy rates, hospital, 53, 53*f*, 246, 247*f*
Belgian Development Cooperation Agency, 166
Belgium, social insurance contributions in, 76
benefits packages
  government health spending and, 161, 162*f*
  in high-income economies, 19, 152–53*t*, 157–58
  inequalities in health care and, 253, 255
  in low-income economies, 18–19, 146, 147–49*t*, 154–55, 158–59
  in middle-income economies, 19, 149–52*t*, 155–57
  resource allocation and purchasing and, 4, 12, 146–63, 147–53*t*, 253
"Big Bang" approach to decentralization, 203, 205
BlueCross BlueShield Association (U.S.), 290
BMI (Basic Medical Insurance scheme, China), 179–80*b*
BoD. *See* burden of disease
Bolivia
  informal payments in, 224
  tax revenues in, 100–101
brain drain, 226, 301
Brazil
  conditional cash transfer program in, 190
  debit cards in, 193
  private health insurance in, 89
bribes. *See* informal payments
Bumrungrad Hospital (Thailand), 288, 290, 292, 294, 295–96, 299
burden of disease (BoD), 7, 11–12, 19, 39–44, 64*n*2, 68
Burma. *See* Myanmar

C

Café Timor, 97
Calmette Hospital (Cambodia), 216
Cambodia
  benefits packages in, 146, 147*t*, 154
  conditional cash transfer program in, 21, 190
  contracting issues in, 19–20, 165–66, 169
  corruption in, 24, 224
  decentralization in, 203, 214–16, 236
  donor financing in, 7–8, 93, 94*b*, 105, 183
  health care provision in, 53
  health equity funds in, 16–17, 23, 106
  health spending in, 8, 45, 47, 50
    resource-tracking activity, 268*t*
  income level in, 34
  inequalities in, 250, 253
  infant mortality in, 35
  MDGs in, 44
  national health accounts in, 266
  as net food importer, 29
  NGOs in, 227
  out-of-pocket spending in, 93, 96, 255
  pooling of funds in, 16, 17, 125, 126–28, 129, 131
  private vs. public sector in, 25, 58, 58*t*
  provider payment system in, 172*t*
  public prepayment in, 92
  regulation of providers in, 228, 229*t*
  rural populations in, 32
  social health insurance system, source of financing in, 85*t*
  user fees and exemptions, 107*t*
Cambodia Demographic and Health Surveys, 96
Canada
  fee-for-service system in, 185
  pooling of funds in, 17, 129, 131
capacity building for payment systems, 187–88
case flow rates, 246, 247*f*
case-mix groupings, 186, 187*f*
catastrophic payments for health care
  benefits packages and, 4, 155, 158
  health shocks and, 112, 112*b*
  inequalities and, 10
  out-of-pocket payments and, 106, 111, 111*f*
Catholic Church, health organizations related to, 183
CBHI. *See* community-based health insurance
CCTs. *See* conditional cash transfers
characteristics of institutions and organizations. *See* institutional and organizational characteristics
child mortality rates. *See also* infant mortality rates

benefits packages and, 154
Country Policy and Institutional Assessment score and, 221
gender divide and, 141
per capita income and, 67
relative performance of, 35, 36*f*
trends in, 7
children, health care inequalities and, 249–50, 250*f*
Chile
pooling of funds in, 131, 132*b*
private health insurance in, 89
China, People's Republic of
age-dependency ratio for, 11, 39
bed occupancy rates in, 246
benefits packages in, 19, 149–50*t*, 155–56
burden of disease in, 7, 39
contracting issues in, 165
decentralization in, 18, 23, 27, 140, 203, 213–14, 213*t*, 236
fee-for-service systems in, 20, 173
general government revenues in, 84
health disparities in, 141–42, 142–43*f*
health insurance in, 89
health shocks in, 112–13*b*
health spending in, 7, 45, 50
resource-tracking activity, 268*t*
incentive payment systems in, 178–79, 179–80*b*
informal payments in, 24, 91, 223, 224
life expectancy in, 41
litigation in, 237
maternal mortality rates in, 37
national health accounts in, 266
natural disasters in, 29
noncommunicable diseases in, 7, 39, 45*b*
out-of-pocket payments in, 14, 90–91, 92*b*, 111, 112*b*, 214, 255
performance-based budgeting in, 145
pooling of funds in, 17, 122–23, 127–28, 128*f*, 131
private vs. public sector in, 58, 61*t*
pro-poor health services in, 10
pro-rich health services in, 9, 250
provider payment system in, 171*t*
public prepayment in, 82, 88, 99, 100
public sector in, 52
regulation of providers in, 229*t*
rural populations in, 32
size of, 5, 27, 28*f*
social health insurance in, 17, 74, 84, 95, 139
social health insurance system, source of financing in, 85*t*
strategic purchasing in, 4
tobacco taxes in, 104
traditional medicine in, 64
universal coverage in, 18, 138
urban populations in, 32, 103
user fees and exemptions, 107*t*
utilization patterns in, 54
voucher programs in, 22, 192
Chinese medicine. *See* traditional medicine
cigarettes. *See* tobacco, taxes on
Civil Servant Medical Benefit Scheme (CSMBS, Thailand), 88, 122, 157, 176
Civil Servants Scheme (Lao PDR), 126
Civil Service Health Insurance (Lao PDR), 93
CMS (Cooperative Medical Scheme, China), 95, 155–56
Colombia
conditional cash transfer programs in, 188
payroll taxes in, 103
community-based health insurance (CBHI), 126–27, 132, 154, 187
complementary health insurance, 78
conditional cash transfers (CCTs), 21, 188–90, 191–92*t*, 192–93
consumer health groups, 237–38
contracting considerations, 4, 19–20, 163–70, 215
contracting-in model, 193–94*n*2
contracting-out model, 193*n*2
in high-income economies, 164
in low-income economies, 165–69
in middle-income economies, 164–65
Cooperative Medical Scheme (CMS, China), 95, 155–56
corruption, 219–22, 220–23*f*. *See also* informal payments
Country Assistance Strategy review (World Bank), 285*b*
Country Policy and Institutional Assessment score (CPIA), 221, 221*f*

Creating a Needle Exchange Program for Intravenous Drug Users (Vietnam), 192
CSMBS. *See* Civil Servant Medical Benefit Scheme
curative care expenditures, 244, 245*t*
Czech Republic
  fee-for-service system in, 185
  payroll taxes in, 101
  pooling of funds in, 129–30, 130*b*

D

DALYs. *See* disability-adjusted life years
debit cards, 193
decentralization
  country experience and profiles, 203–19
  institutional and organizational characteristics and, 4, 22–23, 200–219, 235–36
  overview and framework for, 201–3, 202*f*
  public health services and, 163
Decentralization Act (Thailand), 217
decision rights, 202
Decree 10 on hospital autonomy (Vietnam), 208–9
Decree 43 on hospital finances (Vietnam), 209
Decree 73/PM on recentralization (Lao PDR), 210
delivery of services
  linking to health expenditures, 52–64, 53–54*f*
  medical tourism and, 300–302
  by NGOs, 227
  private providers, 58–64. *See also* private sector
demand-side financing
  conditional cash transfers and, 4, 21, 188–90, 191–92*t*, 192–93
  cost-effective considerations for, 193
  resource allocation and purchasing, 4, 21–22, 188–93
  vouchers and, 21–22, 25, 188, 190–93
demand-side governance, 222
"demographic dividend," 37–38
demographic trends, 37–44
devolution of health financing, 201, 203, 205
DHOs (district health offices), 210–11
diagnosis-related groups (DRGs), 20, 173, 174, 176, 180*b*, 182, 186
disability-adjusted life years (DALYs), 7, 39, 41*f*, 42–43*t*
Disease Control Priorities Project, 244
disease profiles, 11–12
district health offices (DHOs), 210–11
Doi Moi economic reforms (Vietnam), 207–8
"Doing Business" rankings, 29
donor financing
  decentralization and, 219
  health care spending and, 14, 105
  incentive payment systems and, 182
  increase in, 7–8
  in low-income countries, 93–95, 94*b*
  targeting of, 183
DRGs. *See* diagnosis-related groups
dual practice, 25, 226–27
duplicate health insurance, 77

E

East Asia and the Pacific (EAP). *See also* Pacific Island countries; *specific countries*
  countries in, xviii, xix*t*
  economic growth in, 5, 6*f*
  efficiency and equity of health financing in, 243–63. *See also* health financing
  institutional and organizational characteristics in, 199–242. *See also* institutional and organizational characteristics
  investing in health in, 67–72. *See also* investing in health
  macroeconomic factors and health sectors in, 27–65. *See also* macroeconomic factors
  medical tourism in, 287–304. *See also* medical tourism
  national health accounts in, 265–86. *See also* national health accounts (NHAs)
  pooling and management of funds in, 117–35. *See also* pooling and management of funds
  project appraisal documents for, 305–7
  resource allocation and purchasing in, 137–97. *See also* resource allocation and purchasing

revenues for health in, 73–116. *See also* revenues for health
East Asian financial crisis (1997), 22, 25, 201, 232, 287
economic growth, 5, 6*f*, 67–69, 68*t*
ECPS (essential and complementary package of services), 154
Ecuador, general government revenues in, 84
education rates, 7, 39
efficiency and equity of health financing, 9, 243–63
allocative efficiency, 2, 9, 243–45
curative care expenditures and, 244, 245*t*
equity issues, 246–49
gains in, 3
inequalities in health care use, 33, 249–56, 250–52*f*
public subsidies and, 243, 256–59, 257*f*
technical efficiency, 2, 9, 244, 245–46
epidemiologic trends, 39–44
"equal treatment for equal need" principle, 249
Equitap study, xviii, 111–12
equity of health financing. *See* efficiency and equity of health financing
essential and complementary package of services (ECPS), 154
Estonia
payroll taxes in, 101
pooling of funds in, 131
European Union (EU)
allocation formulas in, 142
global budget model in, 186
incentive payment systems in, 185
payroll taxes in, 139
tobacco taxes in, 15
universal coverage in, 138–39
Eurostat, 267
exemptions from user fees, 10, 106, 107–10*t*, 111, 253
Expanded Programme on Immunization (Vietnam), 163
expenditures on health. *See* health expenditures

F

Familias en Acción (Colombia), 189
family planning, 163
Farmers Insurance (Taiwan), 121
fee-for-service (FFS) reimbursements
demand-side controls and, 176
drug expenses and, 157
health equity funds and, 183
in high-income countries, 173–75
incentive payment systems and, 4, 177–78, 179–80*b*, 181, 182, 184–85
overreliance on, 20
fee schedule pricing, 178–79
fee waivers, 10, 106, 107–10*t*, 111, 253
Fernando, Tharanga, 267
fertility rates. *See* total fertility rates
FFS reimbursements. *See* fee-for-service (FFS) reimbursements
Fiji
donor support in, 219
general government revenues in, 83
national health accounts in, 266
resource-tracking activity, 268*t*
out-of-pocket payments in, 14, 47, 90
private vs. public sector in, 58*t*
public prepayment in, 82
regulation of providers in, 229*t*
social health insurance in, 84
financial crisis. *See* East Asian financial crisis (1997)
financing
demand-side. *See* demand-side financing
donors. *See* donor financing
efficiency and equity of. *See* efficiency and equity of health financing
levels and trends. *See* macroeconomic factors
fiscal space for health, 16, 97–99, 98–99*f*
Fondo Nacional de Salud (Chile), 132*b*
fragile states, 6, 33–34, 64*n*1, 95
France
complementary health insurance in, 78
dual practice in, 227
fee-for-service system in, 185
health expenditure in, 117, 118*f*
social health insurance in, 74, 76
voluntary insurance in, 255
free services
in high-income countries, 152–53*t*, 157
hospital care, 207, 209
informal payments for, 223
in low-income countries, 125, 147–49*t*, 154

free services (*continued*)
in middle-income countries, 124, 149–52*t*, 156
targeting of, 96, 106
funding mechanisms. *See* population-based formula funding mechanisms

G

gatekeeping system in contracts, 20, 164–65
general government revenues (GGRs)
public prepayment and, 13, 14, 82–84, 92–93, 100
as revenue source, 3, 73, 99–101
general practice (GP) visits, 253, 255
Germany
fee-for-service system in, 185
medical tourism from, 294
pooling of funds in, 129
social health insurance in, 74, 75
girls. *See* women and girls
Global Alliance for Vaccines and Immunisation, 97
global budget model, 186–87, 188*b*
Global Burden of Disease study, 64*n*2
Global Fund to Fight AIDS, Tuberculosis, and Malaria, 94*b*, 97
good governance. *See* governance and stewardship
Gottret, Pablo, 46, 74, 119, 131–32
governance and stewardship
absenteeism and, 24, 25, 225–26, 225*t*, 228
corruption and, 219–22, 220–23*f*
demand-side governance, 222
dual practice, 25, 226–27
informal payments and, 24, 222–24, 224*f*
institutional and organizational characteristics and, 5, 23–25, 199–200, 219–31, 236–37
patient voice and provider responsiveness, 24, 200, 227–28
pooling and management of funds, 132–34, 133*t*
regulation of providers, 24, 228–31, 229–31*t*
Government Employee Insurance (Taiwan), 121
gross domestic product (GDP)
fiscal space for health and, 97, 99
growth in, 27, 28*f*
health spending and, 44–45, 46, 49–50, 49*f*
tax revenues and, 99–100, 100*f*
Guidelines for Developing Operational Districts (Cambodia), 215

H

Harding, April, 202
Health, Nutrition, and Population Hub (World Bank), xvii
Health Authority (Hong Kong SAR), 164, 174
Health Card for the Poor program (Vietnam), 209
Health Coverage Plan (Cambodia), 214–15
health equity funds (HEFs)
benefits packages and, 154
decentralization and, 236
fee-for-service system and, 183
incentive payment systems and, 187
inequalities in health care and, 10, 253
in low-income countries, 125–26
reimbursement under, 182–83
social health insurance and, 128
health expenditures
global patterns in, 50–52, 52*f*
health outcomes and, 6–7
other regions compared to East Asia and Pacific, 49–50, 50*f*, 51*t*
patterns of, 7–8
pro-poor. *See* pro-poor health spending
pro-rich. *See* pro-rich health spending
public vs. private, 46–49, 51*t*
Health Facilities Enhancement Fund, 207
health financing. *See* financing
health insurance. *See specific type (e.g., social health insurance)*
Health Insurance program (Vietnam), 209
health maintenance organizations (HMOs), 124, 156
health outcomes, 6–7, 34–37
health savings accounts (HSAs), 78–79, 119–20, 122, 134*n*1, 158, 175
health sectors. *See* macroeconomic factors and health sectors
Health Sector Strategic Master Plan (Mongolia), 154

health shocks, 1, 112, 112–13*b*
health spending. *See* health expenditures; pro-poor health spending; pro-rich health spending
Health Systems Support project (Philippines), 145
Health Tourism in Asia, 298
health workers. *See* physicians and health workers, global comparison of
HEFs. *See* health equity funds
high-income countries (HICs)
  benefits packages in, 19, 152–53*t*, 157–58
  contracting considerations in, 164
  fee-for-service reimbursements in, 173–75
  health spending in, 7, 44, 47
  incentive payment systems in, 173–75
  inequalities in health care in, 10, 253, 255
  medical savings accounts in, 78–79
  out-of-pocket payments in, 13, 47, 79–80, 79*f*, 111
  pooling and management of funds in, 117, 119–21
  provider payment systems in, 171*t*
  public prepayment in, 74
  public vs. private sector in, 62–63*t*
  purchaser-provider split models in, 53
  regulation of providers in, 230–31*t*
  revenues for health in, 74–80, 75*f*, 76*t*
  social insurance in, 73, 75–77
  taxes in, 77
  utilization patterns in, 54
  voluntary insurance in, 13, 77–78, 78*b*, 255
HIV/AIDS, donor financing for, 183
HMOs. *See* health maintenance organizations
Honda, Chika, 251
Honduras, conditional cash transfer programs in, 188
Hong Kong SAR
  benefits packages in, 152*t*, 157–58, 159
  contracting issues in, 164
  fee-for-service system in, 174–75
  health care provision in, 161–62
  horizontal equity in, 249, 251, 253
  hospital spending in, 244
  inequalities in health care in, 255
  medical tourism in, 288
  mixed public-private health system, 259*b*
  national health accounts in, 266, 267
    resource-tracking activity, 268*t*
  out-of-pocket payments in, 13, 79–80, 249
  pooling of funds in, 119
  private vs. public sector in, 62*t*
  pro-poor health services in, 9, 10, 250, 258
  provider payment system in, 171*t*
  public sector in, 52
  public subsidies in, 256
  regulation of providers in, 230*t*
  tax payments in, 13, 74, 77
  user fees and exemptions, 107*t*
  utilization patterns in, 54
  voluntary insurance in, 77
horizontal equity, principle of, 249, 251, 253, 254*t*
hospital autonomy
  decentralization and, 23, 208–9, 215–16
  development of, 5, 236
  efficiency and, 218
  market exposure and, 211
  public facilities and, 204, 206–7, 216–17
hospital beds. *See* bed occupancy rates, hospital
HSAs. *See* health savings accounts
Hungary, payroll taxes in, 101

I

Iceland, taxes in, 77
incentive payment systems
  analysis and discussion of, 20–21, 184–88, 184*t*
  fee-for-service reimbursements and, 4, 177–78, 179–80*b*, 181, 182, 184–85
  in high-income economies, 173–75
  in low-income economies, 181–84
  in middle-income economies, 175–81
  resource allocation and purchasing and, 170–88, 171–72*t*
income elasticities, 46, 49*f*
Increasing Access to Mother and Child Care for Poor Households program (China), 192

India
- catastrophic payments in, 111
- health care quality in, 290
- medical tourism in, 233, 234, 296
- telemedicine in, 293

Indigent Program (Philippines), 156

Indonesia
- absenteeism in, 225
- accreditation processes in, 237
- allocative efficiency in, 245
- bed occupancy rates in, 246
- benefits packages in, 147*t*, 156
- burden of disease in, 7, 39
- conditional cash transfer program in, 21, 190, 191–92*t*
- corruption in, 101
- decentralization in, 18, 27, 140, 163, 201, 203–5
- general government revenues in, 84
- health cards in, 106
- health spending in, 8, 50
  - national health accounts, 266
  - resource-tracking activity, 269*t*
- hospitals in, 53
- incentive payment systems in, 181, 185
- inequalities in, 6, 33, 250, 253, 258
- literacy rates in, 32
- maternal mortality rates in, 37
- MDGs in, 44
- medical tourism and, 297
- noncommunicable diseases in, 7, 39
- out-of-pocket payments in, 14, 90, 247, 255
- payroll taxes in, 103
- pooling of funds in, 16, 123–24, 123*f*, 127
- private health insurance in, 89
- private vs. public sector in, 25, 58, 58*t*, 226
- pro-rich health services in, 9, 250
- provider payment system in, 172*t*
- public prepayment in, 88
- regulation of providers in, 229*t*
- size of, 5, 27, 28*f*
- social health insurance system, source of financing in, 85*t*
- urban populations in, 32
- user fees and exemptions, 107*t*
- utilization patterns in, 54
- voucher programs in, 22, 192

inequalities. *See* efficiency and equity of health financing

infant mortality rates. *See also* child mortality rates
- conditional cash transfer programs and, 189
- education of mother and, 189
- health disparities and, 140
- health outcomes, 7, 34–35, 34*f*
- relative performance in, 35, 35*f*

informal payments, 24, 49, 91, 222–24, 224*f*

Institute for Health Policy, xviii

institutional and organizational characteristics, 199–242
- analysis and discussion of, 235–38
- decentralization, 4, 22–23, 200–219, 235–36
  - country experience and profiles, 203–19
  - overview and framework for, 201–3, 202*f*
- governance and stewardship, 5, 23–25, 199–200, 219–31, 236–37
  - absenteeism and, 24, 25, 225–26, 225*t*, 228
  - dual practice, 25, 226–27
  - good governance and corruption, 219–22, 220–22*f*, 223*f*
  - informal payments, 24, 222–24, 224*f*
  - patient voice and provider responsiveness, 24, 200, 227–28
  - regulation of providers, 24, 228–31, 229–31*t*
- medical tourism, 24, 25–26, 231–35
  - challenges for, 235
  - costs, quality, and availability of care, 232
  - country profiles for, 233–35
  - telemedicine, 233
- overview, 199–200

International Classification of Health Account, 267

International Union of Travel Officials, 287

Internet, medical tourism promotion on, 296

investing in health, 67–72. *See also* revenues for health
- economic growth and, 67–69, 68*t*
- health care financing and, 69–71, 71*f*

Investment Priorities Plan (Philippines), 289
Iran, Islamic Republic of, payroll taxes and, 139
Ireland, voluntary insurance in, 77
Italy, dual practice in, 227

J

Jamkesmas program (Indonesia), 124
Jamsostek program (Indonesia), 88, 156
Japan
- age-dependency ratio for, 11, 39
- benefits packages in, 153*t*, 157
- contracting issues in, 20, 164
- donor financing from, 94*b*
- fee-for-service system in, 173–74, 185
- health spending in, 7, 45, 105, 244
  - resource-tracking activity, 269*t*
- horizontal equity in, 249, 253
- inequalities in health care in, 255–56
- medical tourism and, 294
- noncommunicable diseases in, 7, 39
- out-of-pocket payments in, 79
- pooling of funds in, 17, 120, 121, 128
- private vs. public sector in, 58, 62–63*t*
- provider payment system in, 171*t*
- regression line for, 50
- regulation of providers in, 230*t*
- social health insurance system, source of financing in, 85*t*
- social insurance contributions in, 74, 75–76
- supplementary health insurance in, 78
- taxes in, 77, 162
- utilization patterns in, 54
- voluntary insurance in, 77

JCI. *See* Joint Commission International
Jining Medical College Hospital (China), 180*b*
Johns Hopkins University Hospital, 298
Joint Commission International (JCI), 232, 291–92, 291*t*, 294, 300
Joint Commission Resources, 291
Jyorei system (Japan), 95

K

Kaiser, 298
Kazakhstan
- general government revenues in, 84
- payroll taxes in, 103
- pooling of funds in, 129

Kenya
- community monitoring in, 193
- conditional cash transfer program in, 190

Kiribati
- decentralization in, 219
- national health accounts in, 266
  - resource-tracking activity, 269*t*
- out-of-pocket spending in, 96
- private vs. public sector in, 58*t*
- regulation of providers in, 229*t*

Korea, Democratic People's Republic of
- national health accounts in, 266
  - resource-tracking activity, 269*t*

Korea, Republic of
- age-dependency ratio for, 11, 39
- benefits packages in, 153*t*
- complementary health insurance in, 78
- contracting issues in, 20, 164
- fee schedule in, 173–74
- health care provision in, 53
- health spending resource-tracking activity, 269*t*
- horizontal equity in, 249, 251
- inequalities in health care in, 255
- out-of-pocket payments in, 13, 79, 80, 90, 111, 255
- pharmaceuticals in, 174
- pooling of funds in, 17, 120, 120*f*, 121
- private vs. public sector in, 53, 58, 63*t*
- pro-rich health services in, 9, 253
- provider payment system in, 171*t*
- regulation of providers in, 231
- social health insurance system, source of financing in, 85*t*
- social insurance contributions in, 74, 75–76
- strategic purchasing in, 4
- taxes in, 77, 162
- user fees and exemptions, 107–8*t*
- voluntary insurance in, 77–78

Kyrgyz Republic
- benefits package in, 159–60, 160*f*
- pooling of funds in, 131

L

Labor Insurance (Taiwan), 120
Lao People's Democratic Republic
- benefits packages in, 148*t*, 154
- contracting issues in, 168

Lao People's Democratic Republic (*continued*)
  decentralization in, 23, 140–41, 203, 210–11, 236
  donor financing in, 7–8
  fee-for-service systems in, 20, 173
  health equity funds in, 16–17, 106
  health spending in, 45, 47
    national health accounts in, 266
    resource-tracking activity, 269*t*
  incentive payment systems in, 182–83, 185
  inequality in, 33, 250, 253
  maternal mortality rates in, 37
  MDGs in, 44
  out-of-pocket spending in, 96, 255
  pooling of funds in, 17, 125–26, 128, 131
  private vs. public sector in, 58, 59*t*
  provider payment system in, 172*t*
  public prepayment in, 92
  regulation of providers in, 228, 229*t*
  rural populations in, 32
  social health insurance in, 93
  social health insurance system, source of financing in, 85*t*
  user fees and exemptions, 108*t*
Lao World Health Survey (WHO), 96
Lasso, Pabón, 246, 247*f*
Law No. 22 and Law No. 25 on decentralization (Indonesia), 203
Lebanon, pooling of funds in, 131
LGUs (local government units), 205
LICs. *See* low-income countries
life expectancy
  as demographic trend, 37–38
  increase in, 11–12, 37, 38*f*, 69
  noncommunicable diseases and, 41
  per capita income and, 67
  trends in, 7
literacy rates, 7, 32, 39, 41*f*
Lithuania, general government revenues in, 84
litigation of health care issues, 237
Living Standard and Monitoring Survey (2001), 96–97
living standards, 247
LMICs. *See* low- and middle-income countries
Local Government Act 124 (Malaysia), 216
Local Government Code (Philippines), 205
local government units (LGUs), 205
low- and middle-income countries (LMICs). *See also* low-income countries; middle-income countries
  "Doing Business" rankings for, 29
  equity and efficiency goals in, 243
  health facilities in, 53
  health spending in, 44, 46
  inequalities in health care in, 10, 253
  inpatient care services in, 64
  out-of-pocket spending in, 47, 73, 249
  public sector health services in, 52
  regulation of providers, 228, 231
  revenues for health for, 73
  tax financing in, 248
  technical efficiency in, 246
low-income countries (LICs)
  benefits packages in, 18–19, 146, 147–49*t*, 154–55, 158–59
  contracting considerations in, 165–69
  donor financing in, 34, 93–95, 94*b*
  fiscal space for health and, 97
  incentive payment systems in, 181–84
  out-of-pocket payments, 91, 91*f*, 96–97, 106, 111
  pooling and management of funds in, 117, 124–27, 131
  private vs. public sector in, 58–61*t*
  provider payment system in, 172*t*
  public prepayment in, 13–14, 85–87*t*, 91, 92–95, 99–100
  regulation of providers in, 228, 229*t*
  revenues for health, 81*t*, 91–97
  voluntary health insurance, 14, 95
Low-Income Scheme (Thailand), 122
Lu, Jui-fen Rachel, 251
Luxembourg, social insurance contributions in, 76

M

Macapagal-Arroyo, Gloria, 298
Macroeconomic Commission, 1
macroeconomic factors, 27–65
  demographic and epidemiologic trends, 37–44
    age-dependency ratio, 39, 40*t*
    burden of disease and, 39–44
    demographic transition in, 37–38
    epidemiologic changes and, 39–44, 44*f*
    life expectancy, 37–38

total fertility rates and, 32, 37–38
expenditures and delivery of services, linking of, 52–64, 53–54*f*
provision of services, private, 58–63*t*, 58–64
utilization patterns and treatment-seeking behaviors, 53–57, 55–57*t*
health financing levels and trends, 44–52, 47–48*t*
global patterns, expenditures in East Asia and Pacific relative to, 50–52, 52*f*
other regions compared to East Asia and Pacific, 49–50, 50*f*, 51*t*
public vs. private expenditures, 46–49, 51*t*
health status and health outcomes, 34–37
MDGs and, 44
overview, 27–29, 30–31*t*
poor, effects on, 29–34, 32*f*
Malaysia
benefits packages in, 150*t*, 157, 159
contracting issues in, 20, 164, 165
decentralization in, 18, 27, 140, 203, 216–17
general government revenues in, 83, 84, 161
health savings accounts in, 175
health spending in, 7, 8, 45, 47, 50
national health accounts, 266
resource-tracking activity, 269*t*
medical tourism in, 25, 233–34, 288, 292, 293–94, 296–97, 297*f*
out-of-pocket payments in, 90, 111
private health insurance in, 89
private vs. public sector in, 25, 61*t*, 226
pro-poor health services in, 9, 10, 250, 258
provider payment system in, 171*t*
public health subsidies in, 256
public prepayment in, 82
regulation of providers in, 229*t*
social health insurance in, 15, 84
telemedicine in, 233, 293
user fees and exemptions, 108*t*
Malaysia External Trade Development Corporation, 296
"Malaysian Healthcare Services" seminar, 296
Malaysian Medical Association, 175
Management Board for the National Hospital (Timor-Leste), 183
Marcos, Ferdinand, 201
market exposure for health facilities, 202, 207, 211, 213–14, 217, 218
Marshall Islands
health spending resource-tracking activity, 269*t*
national health accounts in, 266
private vs. public sector in, 59*t*
regulation of providers in, 229*t*
Masseria, Cristina, 255
maternal mortality rates, 36–37, 37*f*, 154, 189
MDGs. *See* Millennium Development Goals
measles immunization rates, 141
Medical Assistance program (China), 88, 122, 128
Medical City (Philippines), 298
medical savings accounts. *See* health savings accounts
medical tourism, 287–304
challenges for, 235, 299–300
costs, quality, and availability of care, 232, 289–90, 290*t*
country profiles for, 233–35
emergence of, 287–88
enabling attributes of East Asia and Pacific, 289–93
financing and delivery of care services, implications for, 300–302
government involvement in, 288–89
institutional and organizational characteristics and, 24, 25–26, 231–35
religious sensitivity in, 297
scope of, 293–99
telemedicine and, 233, 292–93
Medical Tourism Association, 292
Medical Tourism Bureau (Philippines), 288
Medical Travel Authority, 292
Medical Welfare Scheme (Thailand), 176
Medisave program (Singapore), 78–79
Medishield program (Singapore), 79
Medium-Term Expenditure Framework exercise, 96, 285*b*
men, funding formulas for, 144

Mexico
conditional cash transfer programs in, 188, 190, 193
debit cards in, 193
out-of-pocket payments in, 90
Micronesia, Federated States of
national health accounts in, 266
resource-tracking activity, 270*t*
out-of-pocket spending in, 96
middle-income countries (MICs)
benefits packages in, 19, 149–52*t*, 155–57
contracting considerations in, 164–65
health facilities in, 53
health spending in, 46–47
incentive payment systems in, 175–81
inequality in, 33
MDGs in, 44
out-of-pocket payments in, 47, 81*t*, 90–91, 91*f*, 92*b*
pooling and management of funds in, 117, 131
private health insurance, 81*t*, 89–90
provider payment system in, 171–72*t*
public prepayment in, 13–14, 80–89, 83*f*, 100
public vs. private sector in, 61–62*t*
regulation of providers in, 228, 229–30*t*, 231
revenues for health, 80–91, 81*t*, 82*f*
universal coverage and, 73
Millennium Development Goals (MDGs), 8, 9*t*, 44, 46*t*, 154–55, 247
Mongolia
bed occupancy rates in, 246
benefits packages in, 148–49*t*, 154
contracting issues in, 20, 164, 167–68, 170
copper mining in, 29
general government revenues in, 84
government health care in, 47, 162–63
incentive payment systems in, 181–82
informal payments in, 24, 49, 91, 223
maternal mortality rates in, 37
national health accounts in, 266
resource-tracking activity, 270*t*
as net food importer, 29
out-of-pocket payments in, 14
pooling of funds in, 16, 17, 125, 127, 131
private vs. public sector in, 59*t*
provider payment system in, 172*t*
public prepayment in, 82, 88–89
regression line for, 50
regulation of providers in, 229*t*
social health insurance in, 84, 85–86*t*
user fees and exemptions, 108–9*t*
Morocco, pooling of funds in, 129, 131
mortality rates. *See* child mortality rates; infant mortality rates; maternal mortality rates
Myanmar
national health accounts in, 266
resource-tracking activity, 270*t*
natural disasters in, 29
out-of-pocket spending in, 96

N

Namibia, private health insurance in, 89
National Committee for the Promotion of Health Tourism (Malaysia), 288
National Coordinating Board for Family Planning (Indonesia), 163
National Economic and Social Development Plan (Thailand), 217
national health accounts (NHAs), 265–86
availability of, 93
constraints for, 272–86, 280–84*t*
country typology for, 265–72, 267–84*t*
institutionalization of, 285, 285*b*
National Health Accounts database, 96
National Health Fund (Chile), 132*b*
National Health Insurance (Taiwan), 158
National Health Insurance Act (Taiwan), 158
National Health Insurance Program (Philippines), 88, 124
National Health Insurance system (Korea, Republic of), 120, 120*f*
National Health Security Act (Thailand), 157
National Health Security Board (Thailand), 157
National Health Security Office (Thailand), 176–77
National Health Service (United Kingdom), 119, 144, 159, 194*n*4
National Referral System (Malaysia), 216
NCDs. *See* noncommunicable diseases
NCMS. *See* New Cooperative Medical Scheme

Netherlands, social health insurance in, 74, 76
New Cooperative Medical Scheme (NCMS, China), 88, 91, 92*b*, 143*f*
New Deal (contractual agreements in Cambodia), 166
New Economic Mechanism (Lao PDR), 210
New Organic Law of 1995 on decentralization (Papua New Guinea), 211–12
New Zealand
  medical tourism and, 290
  taxes in, 77
  voluntary insurance in, 77
NGOs. *See* nongovernmental organizations
NHAs. *See* national health accounts
Nickell, Stephen, 102
noncommunicable diseases (NCDs), 3, 6, 11–12, 19, 39, 41, 45*b*
nongovernmental organizations (NGOs)
  contracting issues and, 164, 165, 166, 167–68, 194*n*3
  incentive payment systems and, 182, 184, 187–88
  out-of-pocket spending and, 96
  pooling of funds and, 126, 127
  public health services from, 162
  service delivery by, 227
  social functions of health facilities and, 211
Northern Mariana Islands
  national health accounts in, 266
    resource-tracking activity, 270*t*
Norway, pooling of funds in, 131

O

OECD countries
  complementary health insurance in, 78
  donor financing and, 94*b*
  health care technology in, 287
  horizontal equity in, 253
  labor markets in, 102
  national health accounts in, 266, 267
  out-of-pocket payments in, 79
  pooling of funds and, 129
  pro-rich health services in, 255
  public prepayment in, 13, 74
  social insurance contributions in, 76
  technical efficiency in, 246
  universal coverage in, 139
  voucher programs and, 190
Ohkusa, Yasushi, 251
Oman, pooling of funds in, 131
ombudsman system, 238
OOP spending. *See* out-of-pocket spending
Open-Door Policy (China), 213
Oportunidades (Mexico), 188, 193
orang asli (aborigine) populations, 157
organizational characteristics. *See* institutional and organizational characteristics
outcomes for health. *See* health outcomes
out-of-pocket (OOP) spending
  benefits packages and, 146, 160
  equity considerations and, 247, 255, 256
  health care financing and, 8, 47–49, 248–49, 248*f*
  in high-income countries, 13, 47, 79–80, 79*f*, 111
  in low-income countries, 91, 91*f*, 96–97, 106, 111
  in middle-income countries, 47, 81*t*, 90–91, 91*f*, 92*b*
  pooling of funds and, 117
  private health insurance and, 89
  as revenue source, 70, 73, 99*f*, 106, 111–13
  supplementary health insurance and, 78

P

Pacific Island countries. *See also* East Asia and the Pacific (EAP); *specific countries*
  benefits packages in, 19, 154, 159
  decentralization in, 22, 203, 219
  donor financing in, 7–8
  government health care in, 47
  health care financing in, 45, 162
  incentive payment systems in, 184
Palau
  government spending in, 105
  national health accounts in, 266
    resource-tracking activity, 270*t*
  out-of-pocket spending in, 96
Papua New Guinea
  absenteeism in, 225, 226
  benefits packages in, 149*t*, 154
  brain drain in, 226

Papua New Guinea (*continued*)
communicable diseases in, 162
decentralization in, 23, 203, 211–13, 236
health care provision in, 53
hospitals in, 53
incentive payment systems in, 184
inequalities in health care in, 253
national health accounts in, 266
resource-tracking activity, 270*t*
nontax revenues in, 93
out-of-pocket spending in, 96
private vs. public sector in, 59*t*
provider payment system in, 172*t*
public prepayment in, 93
regulation of providers in, 228, 229*t*
social insurance in, 92
patient voice and provider responsiveness, 24, 200, 227–28
payment systems, incentivized. *See* incentive payment systems
payroll taxes, 101–3, 102*f*, 139, 140
People's Committees (Vietnam), 209
People's Councils (Vietnam), 208
performance-based budgeting, 145
Performance-Based Operation Fund, 207
pharmaceuticals
benefit packages for, 146, 147–53*t*, 154–58
in church health facilities, 169
fee waivers for, 106
out-of-pocket expenditures for, 160
private sector providers, 58–60*t*, 210, 231
provider payment systems for, 171–72*t*, 174, 181–82
PhilHealth (Philippines), 177–78
Philippine Medical Tourism Program (PMTP), 235, 298
Philippines
benefits packages in, 19, 151–52*t*, 156
contracting issues in, 20, 165
corruption in, 24, 101, 224
decentralization in, 18, 23, 27, 140, 201, 203, 205–7, 236
fee-for-service systems in, 20, 173
fertility rates in, 32
general government revenues in, 84
health insurance in, 89
health spending in, 8
national health accounts in, 266
resource-tracking activity, 270*t*
incentive payment systems in, 177–78
inequalities in, 250
MDGs in, 44
medical tourism in, 234–35, 288–89, 293, 298–99, 299*b*, 300*f*
noncommunicable diseases in, 7, 39
out-of-pocket payments in, 14, 90, 111, 255
performance-based budgeting in, 145
pooling of funds in, 16, 124, 127
private vs. public sector in, 58, 61*t*
provider payment system in, 171*t*
public prepayment in, 82, 88
regulation of providers in, 228, 230*t*
social health insurance in, 84, 86*t*
telemedicine in, 233, 293
urban populations in, 32
user fees and exemptions, 109*t*
PHOs (provincial health offices), 210–11
physicians and health workers, global comparisons of, 53, 54*f*
pilot programs for contracting, 169–70
PMTP (Philippine Medical Tourism Program), 235, 298
Poland, allocation formulas in, 142
"policy levers," 137–38, 138*b*, 199
pooling and management of funds, 2, 117–35
analysis and discussion of, 12, 16–17, 127–34
governance factors for, 132–34, 133*t*
health financing reform and, 70
in high-income economies, 117, 119–21
importance of, 3, 117–19, 118–19*f*, 200
in low-income countries, 117, 124–27, 131
in middle-income countries, 117, 131
the poor
health spending for. *See* pro-poor health spending
sustained economic growth, impact on, 30–34
population-based formula funding mechanisms, 142, 144–45, 145*t*
population pyramids, 37–38, 38*f*
predatory behaviors, 226
Preker, Alexander S., 202
prepayment for health care. *See* public prepayment
private health insurance, 81*t*, 89–90

private sector
contracting with, 164, 165, 167–69
dominance of, 25, 53
dual practice, 25, 226–27
duplicate health insurance systems and, 77
in low-income economies, 183
medical tourism and, 25, 231–32
in middle-income economies, 175, 178
mixed public-private health system, 259*b*
out-of-pocket payments and, 96
provision of services by, 58, 58–63*t*, 64
rationing of health services, effect on, 159, 258
rich consuming services of, 249, 258
supplementary private health insurance for, 256
in urban areas, 52
project appraisal documents, 305–7
pro-poor health spending
in health allocation, 9
inequalities in health care use and, 2, 250–51, 258–59
mixed public-private health system, 259*b*
public subsides and, 10–11, 256, 259
pro-rich health spending
in health care allocation, 9, 250–51
inequity and, 2, 259*b*
out-of-pocket payments and, 253
public subsidies and, 10, 256, 258
specialist care and, 255
provider regulation, 24, 228–31, 229–31*t*
provider responsiveness. *See* patient voice and provider responsiveness
Provincial Health Authorities Bill (Papua New Guinea), 212
provincial health offices (PHOs), 210–11
Public Finance and Management Law (Mongolia), 125, 168
public prepayment
in high-income economies, 74
in low-income countries, 13–14, 85–87*t*, 91, 92–95, 99–100
in middle-income countries, 13–14, 80–89, 83*f*, 100
as revenues for health, 16, 99–105, 100*f*
public subsidies for health care, 159, 178, 243, 256–59, 257*f*
purchaser-provider split models, 53, 186
purchasing. *See* resource allocation and purchasing

R

Rannan-Eliya, Ravi P., 267
rationing of health services, 146, 159, 258
Regional Centre for Health and Social Policy territories, 267
regression lines, 50
regulation of health care providers, 24, 228–31, 229–31*t*
Regulation 25 on decentralization (Indonesia), 203
religious sensitivity in medical tourism, 297
resource allocation and purchasing, 2, 137–97
benefits package, 4, 146–63, 147–53*t*, 253
analysis and discussion of, 12, 158–63
government health spending and, 161, 162*f*
in high-income economies, 19, 157–58
in low-income economies, 18–19, 146, 154–55, 158–59
in middle-income economies, 19, 155–57
contracting considerations, 4, 163–70, 215
analysis and discussion of, 19–20, 169–70
in high-income economies, 164
in low-income economies, 165–69
in middle-income economies, 164–65
demand-side financing, 4, 21–22, 188–93
conditional cash transfers (CCTs), 4, 21, 188–90, 191–92*t*, 192–93
cost-effective considerations, 193
vouchers, 21–22, 25, 188, 190–93
framework for, 4, 137–38
in health financing, 70
incentive payment systems, 170–88, 171–72*t*
analysis and discussion of, 20–21, 184–88, 184*t*
in high-income economies, 173–75

resource allocation and purchasing (*continued*)
in low-income economies, 181–84
in middle-income economies, 175–81
recipients of purchase services, 138–40, 139*f*
targeting and decentralization, 18, 140–45, 141*t*
Resource Allocation Working Party formula, 144
revenues for health, 2, 73–116. *See also* investing in health
analysis and discussion, 13–16, 97–113
alternative sources, 103–5, 104*t*, 140
fiscal space for health, 16, 97–99, 98–99*f*
general revenues, 99–101
government expenditures and, 105, 105*f*
out-of-pocket payments, 99*f*, 106, 111–13
payroll taxes, 101–3, 102*f*
public prepayment, 16, 99–105, 100*f*
user fees, exemptions, and targeting, 106–13, 107–10*t*
health financing and, 12, 69–70, 73–97
high-income economies, 74–80, 75*f*, 76*t*
medical savings accounts, 78–79
out-of-pocket payments, 79–80, 79*f*, 111
public prepayment in, 74
social insurance contributions, 75–77
taxes in, 77
voluntary insurance in, 13, 77–78, 78*b*, 255
low-income economies, 81*t*, 91–97
fiscal space for health and, 97
out-of-pocket payments in, 91, 91*f*, 96–97, 106, 111
public prepayment in, 13–14, 85–87*t*, 91, 92–95, 99–100
voluntary health insurance in, 14, 95
middle-income economies, 80–91, 81*t*, 82*f*
out-of-pocket payments in, 81*t*, 90–91, 91*f*, 92*b*
private health insurance in, 81*t*, 89–90
public prepayment in, 13–14, 80–89, 83*f*, 100
rich, health spending for. *See* pro-rich health spending
rural areas
absenteeism in, 225
benefits packages in, 156
incentive payment systems in, 179–80, 179–80*b*
malnutrition prevalence in, 141
noncommunicable diseases in, 45*b*
payroll taxes in, 101
poverty reduction in, 32
gaps compared to urban areas, 33
Russian Federation, fee-for-service system in, 185

S

Safe Motherhood Project (Indonesia), 192
safety net schemes, 154
St. Luke's Medical Center (Philippines), 298
Sala-i-Martin, Xavier, 68
Samoa
donor support in, 219
general government revenues in, 83
national health accounts in, 266
resource-tracking activity, 270*t*
out-of-pocket payments in, 14, 47, 90
private health insurance in, 89
private vs. public sector in, 59*t*
public prepayment in, 82
regression line for, 50
regulation of providers in, 229*t*
social health insurance in, 84
Savedoff, William D., 131–32
Schieber, George, xviii, 46, 74, 119, 132
Sector Wide Management (SWiM), 94*b*
Seila Program (Cambodia), 215
SHA (system of health accounts) tables, 267, 285*b*
SHI. *See* social health insurance
Singapore
age-dependency ratio for, 11, 39
benefits packages in, 153*t*, 158
government revenues in, 74
health savings accounts in, 175
medical costs in, 232, 289
medical savings accounts in, 78–79
medical tourism in, 233, 234, 288, 293–94, 296, 297–98
national health accounts in, 266
resource-tracking activity, 270*t*

pooling of funds in, 119–20
private vs. public sector in, 58, 63*t*
provider payment system in, 171*t*
public prepayment in, 99
regulation of providers in, 231
tobacco taxes in, 15, 104
sin taxes, 3, 104–5
Slovak Republic, payroll taxes in, 101
social functions of health care facilities, 203, 204–5, 209, 211, 218
social health insurance (SHI)
benefits packages and, 146, 154, 156, 157
contracting issues and, 164–65, 167–68
health care financing and, 248–49, 248*f*
in high-income countries, 75–77
payment systems and, 15, 176, 182
pooling of funds and, 117, 120–22, 124–25, 127–28
public prepayment and, 84, 85–87*t*, 93
as revenue for health, 74
sustainability of, 3, 15
tax financing and, 102–3
Social Health Insurance Fund (Lao PDR), 93, 126
Social Security Scheme (Thailand), 176, 177
Solomon Islands
donor financing in, 95, 105, 219
health care inequalities in, 250
national health accounts in, 266
resource-tracking activity, 270*t*
nontax revenues in, 93
out-of-pocket spending in, 47, 96
private vs. public sector in, 60*t*
public prepayment in, 93
regulation of providers in, 229*t*
social insurance in, 92
South Africa, private health insurance in, 89
Spain, taxes in, 77
Sri Lanka
country profile development in, xviii
hospital spending in, 244
national health accounts and, 267
out-of-pocket payments in, 111
pro-poor health services in, 10, 258
public health subsidies in, 256
tobacco taxes in, 104
State Social Insurance General Office (SSIGO, Mongolia), 125
stewardship. *See* governance and stewardship
subsidies. *See* public subsidies for health care
Suharto, 201
supplementary health insurance, 78, 256
Sweden
allocation formulas in, 142
pooling of funds in, 129, 131
SWiM (Sector Wide Management), 94*b*
Switzerland
general practice service use in, 255
out-of-pocket payments in, 79, 90
system of health accounts (SHA) tables, 267, 285*b*

T

Taiwan
benefits packages in, 153*t*, 158
contracting issues in, 20, 164
diagnosis-related groups in, 174
fee-for-service system in, 185
horizontal equity in, 249, 251
inequalities in health care in, 255
medical tourism in, 233, 293
national health accounts in, 266, 267
resource-tracking activity, 271*t*
National Health Insurance in, 75
out-of-pocket payments in, 79, 80
pharmaceuticals in, 174
pooling of funds in, 17, 120–21
private vs. public sector in, 58, 63*t*
pro-rich health services in, 9
provider payment system in, 171*t*
regulation of providers in, 231
social health insurance system, source of financing in, 87*t*
social insurance contributions in, 74, 75–77
taxes in, 77
traditional medicine in, 64
user fees and exemptions, 109–10*t*
voluntary insurance in, 77–78
Tangcharoensathien, Viroj, 228
targeting of health financing
decentralization and, 18, 140–45, 141*t*
user fees and, 106–13, 107–10*t*
taxes. *See also* general government revenues
on alcohol, 15, 103–4
health care financing and, 248–49, 248*f*

taxes. *See also* general government revenues (*continued*)
medical tourism and, 289
payroll, 101–3, 102*f*, 139, 140
revues for health and, 73–74
sin, 3, 104–5
on tobacco, 15, 103–4, 104*t*
technical assistance from World Bank, xvii–xviii
technical efficiency, 2, 9, 244, 245–46
Thailand
benefits packages in, 157
contracting issues in, 20, 164–65
decentralization in, 18, 140, 203, 217–18
fee-for-service systems in, 4, 20, 173
general government revenues in, 18, 84
health spending in, 7, 8, 45, 47, 50
national health accounts in, 266, 267
resource-tracking activity, 271*t*
incentive payment systems in, 176–77, 186
informal payments in, 24, 91, 223
medical costs in, 232, 289
medical tourism in, 25, 233–34, 287–88, 290, 292–96, 294–95*f*, 301
out-of-pocket payments in, 90, 111
pooling of funds in, 16, 122, 128, 131
private health insurance in, 89
private hospitals in, 226
private sector in, 25, 58, 62*t*, 64, 227–28
pro-poor health services in, 10, 250, 258
pro-rich health services in, 9
provider payment system in, 172*t*
public prepayment in, 82, 88
public subsidies in, 256
regulation of providers in, 228, 230*t*
social health insurance in, 84
social health insurance system, source of financing in, 87*t*
strategic purchasing in, 4
telemedicine in, 233, 293
tobacco taxes in, 15, 104
urban populations in, 32
user fees and exemptions, 110*t*
30 Baht Scheme (Thailand), 157, 176, 177
Timor-Leste
age-dependency ratio in, 11, 39
benefits packages in, 149*t*, 154–55
contracting issues in, 168–69
donor financing in, 105
government spending in, 105
incentive payment systems in, 183–84
MDGs in, 44
national health accounts in, 266
resource-tracking activity, 271*t*
as net food importer, 29
NGOs in, 162
out-of-pocket spending in, 96–97
pooling of funds in, 125
private vs. public sector in, 60*t*
provider payment system in, 172*t*
public prepayment in, 92
regulation of providers in, 229*t*
user fees and exemptions, 110*t*
tobacco, taxes on, 15, 103–4, 104*t*
Tonga
donor support in, 219
general government revenues in, 83
medical tourism and, 290
national health accounts in, 266
resource-tracking activity, 272*t*
out-of-pocket payments in, 14, 90
private vs. public sector in, 60*t*
public prepayment in, 82
regulation of providers in, 229*t*
social health insurance in, 84
total fertility rates, 11, 32, 33*f*, 37–38
traditional medicine, 64, 157–58, 165, 175
Tunisia, pooling of funds in, 131

U

Ukraine, general government revenues in, 84
United Kingdom
allocation formulas in, 142, 144
benefits package in, 159
donor financing from, 94*b*
fragile states, definition of, 64*n*1
incentive payment systems in, 185–86
medical tourism from, 294
pooling of funds in, 119, 129, 131
taxes in, 77
United States
donor financing from, 94*b*
fee-for-service system in, 185

health care quality in, 290, 291
litigation in, 237
medical costs in, 232, 234, 289, 290*t*, 297
medical tourism from, 289–90, 294
universal coverage
inequalities in health care and, 10, 253
insurance and, 73
pooling of funds and, 200
recipients of purchase services and, 138–40
Urban Employee Essential Medical Insurance (China), 88
urbanization and urban areas
incentive payment systems in, 179–80, 179–80*b*
noncommunicable diseases in, 45*b*
poverty reduction and, 29, 32
private sector health provision in, 52
rural areas, gaps between, 33
Uruguay, private health insurance in, 89
user fees, 106–13, 107–10*t*
utilization patterns and treatment-seeking behaviors, 53–57, 55–57*t*
inequalities in health care use, 33, 249–56, 250–52*f*

V

Van Doorslaer, Eddy, 248, 255
Vanuatu
donor support in, 219
national health accounts in, 266
resource-tracking activity, 272*t*
private vs. public sector in, 60*t*
regulation of providers in, 229*t*
Vietnam
benefits packages in, 149*t*, 155
contracting issues in, 168, 170
decentralization in, 18, 27, 140, 141*t*, 203, 207–9, 236
health spending in, 8, 46, 47, 50, 163
national health accounts in, 266, 267
resource-tracking activity, 272*t*
incentive payment systems in, 5, 20, 181
inequality in, 6, 33, 250
informal payments in, 24, 91, 223
maternal mortality rates in, 37
MDGs in, 44
out-of-pocket payments in, 8, 14, 111
pooling of funds in, 16, 125, 127, 134*n*2
postconflict recovery in, 34
private vs. public sector in, 58, 60–61*t*, 227–28
pro-rich health services in, 9, 250
provider payment system in, 172*t*
public prepayment in, 92–93
regulation of providers in, 228, 229*t*
rural populations in, 32
social health insurance in, 93, 140
urban populations in, 32
user fees and exemptions, 110*t*
voucher programs in, 22, 192
Vietnam Social Security, 134*n*2
Voluntary Health Card (Thailand), 122
voluntary insurance
in high-income countries, 13, 77–78, 78*b*, 255
in low-income countries, 14, 95
vouchers, 21–22, 25, 188, 190–93

W

Wagstaff, Adam, xviii, 69, 248
Weil, David, 68
Welfare Scheme (Thailand), 122
women and girls
education of, 189–90
funding formulas and, 144
health care access for, 141
maternal mortality rates and, 36–37, 37*f*
voucher programs and, 192
worker absenteeism. *See* absenteeism, worker
World Access (medical travel organization), 290
World Bank
accreditation processes and, 237
on health shocks, 113*b*
NHA activity survey, 265, 266
payroll taxes estimation by, 102
performance-based budgeting and, 145
pooling of funds and, 131
technical assistance from, xvii–xviii
World Development Indicators database (World Bank), 102
World Development Report 1993 (World Bank), 158, 244

World Health Organization (WHO)
burden of disease estimates, 64*n*2
DALYs estimation by, 39
on health sector financing, 70
health services quality and, 232, 291
on health systems, 69
national health accounts and, 267, 285*b*
out-of-pocket spending estimates by, 96
SHA questionnaires, 267
World Health Report 2000 (WHO), 138

ECO-AUDIT

Environmental Benefits Statement

The World Bank is committed to preserving endangered forests and natural resources. The Office of the Publisher has chosen to print ***Financing Health Care in East Asia and the Pacific*** on recycled paper with 50 percent post-consumer waste, in accordance with the recommended standards for paper usage set by the Green Press Initiative, a non-profit program supporting publishers in using fiber that is not sourced from endangered forests. For more information, visit www.greenpressinitiative.org.

Saved:

- 19 trees
- 7 million BTU's of total energy
- 1,871 lbs of CO_2 equivalent of greenhouse gases
- 8,441 gallons of waste water
- 536 pounds of solid waste